OXFORD STUDIES IN BYZANTIUM

OXFORD STUDIES IN BYZANTIUM

Oxford Studies in Byzantium consists of scholarly monographs and editions on the history, literature, thought, and material culture of the Byzantine world.

Caliphs and Merchants
Cities and Economies of Power in the Near East (700–950)
Fanny Bessard

Social Change in Town and Country in Eleventh-Century Byzantium
James Howard-Johnston

Innovation in Byzantine Medicine
The Writings of John Zacharias Aktouarios (c.1275–c.1330)
Petros Bouras-Vallianatos

Emperors and Usurpers in the Later Roman Empire
Civil War, Panegyric, and the Construction of Legitimacy
Adrastos Omissi

The *Universal History* of Step'anos Tarōnec'i
Introduction, Translation, and Commentary
Tim Greenwood

The Letters of Psellos
Cultural Networks and Historical Realities
Edited by Michael Jeffreys and Marc D. Lauxtermann

Holy Sites Encircled
The Early Byzantine Concentric Churches of Jerusalem
Vered Shalev-Hurvitz

Law, Power, and Imperial Ideology in the Iconoclast Era
c.680–850
M. T. G. Humphreys

Byzantium and the Turks in the Thirteenth Century
Dimitri Korobeinikov

Writing and Reading Byzantine Secular Poetry, 1025–1081
Floris Bernard

The Byzantine-Islamic Transition in Palestine
An Archaeological Approach
Gideon Avni

Shaping a Muslim State
The World of a Mid-Eighth-Century Egyptian Official
Petra M. Sijpesteijn

Byzantine Religious Law in Medieval Italy

JAMES MORTON

OXFORD
UNIVERSITY PRESS

OXFORD
UNIVERSITY PRESS

Great Clarendon Street, Oxford, OX2 6DP,
United Kingdom

Oxford University Press is a department of the University of Oxford.
It furthers the University's objective of excellence in research, scholarship,
and education by publishing worldwide. Oxford is a registered trade mark of
Oxford University Press in the UK and in certain other countries

First Edition published in 2021

Impression: 1

Published in the United States of America by Oxford University Press
198 Madison Avenue, New York, NY 10016, United States of America

British Library Cataloguing in Publication Data
Data available

Library of Congress Control Number: 2020947001

ISBN 978–0–19–886114–0

DOI: 10.1093/oso/9780198861140.001.0001

Printed and bound by
CPI Group (UK) Ltd, Croydon, CR0 4YY

For my mother Jane of eternal memory and my nieces Jane and Eleanor

Acknowledgements

This book started life as my Ph.D. dissertation at the University of California, Berkeley, which I began in 2013. The journey from there to here has been a long one and would not have been possible without the valuable help of many individuals and institutions. First and foremost, I would like to express my deepest gratitude to Maria Mavroudi, my Ph.D. adviser and long-time mentor in Byzantine Studies. She was the one who first alerted me to the potential of canon law as a research subject and inspired my fascination with medieval manuscript culture. Maria has been as unfailing in her support for me as she has been exacting in her expectations, for which I owe her a great debt.

I am also extremely grateful to Maureen Miller, my second-field Ph.D. adviser who shaped my education in the history and canon law of Western Christendom. She is in large part responsible for extending my intellectual horizons beyond Byzantium to the wider medieval world and remains an important mentor to me. Outside Berkeley, I would like to thank the former directors of Byzantine Studies at Dumbarton Oaks, Alice-Mary Talbot and Elena Boeck, for their invaluable advice and encouragement in recent years, and my M.A. adviser Richard Greenfield of Queen's University (Canada).

My research involved a great deal of travel and expense, and so I am deeply indebted to the organisations that have supported me along the way. The main funding for my research was provided by the History Department of U. C. Berkeley, with important support also coming from the U.C. Berkeley Graduate Division, the U.C. Berkeley Institute of International Studies, the British School at Rome, the Mary Jaharis Center for Byzantine Art and Culture, the Medieval Academy of America, and the Medieval Institute of the University of Notre Dame. I would also like to thank the Senior Fellows of Dumbarton Oaks for giving me the opportunity to spend a year in residence as a Junior Fellow in Byzantine Studies while writing my Ph.D. dissertation. Among them, I would especially like to mention the late Ruth Macrides, a kind and brilliant scholar who is sorely missed.

Several organisations also provided vital assistance in non-financial respects. I am extremely grateful to the many libraries that opened their doors to me and helped me access important materials: the Biblioteca Apostolica Vaticana, the Biblioteca Nazionale Marciana in Venice, the Biblioteca Ambrosiana in Milan, the Badia greca di Grottaferrata, the Biblioteca Vallicelliana in Rome, the Biblioteca Medicea Laurenziana in Florence, the Biblioteca Nazionale 'Vittorio Emmanuele III' in Naples, the Bodleian Library, the British Library, the Moscow State

Historical Museum, the Bibliothèque nationale de France, the Bayerische Staatsbibliothek in Munich, the Dominican House of Studies in Washington D. C., and the U.S. Library of Congress. Special thanks also go to Fr Germanos of Vatopedi on Mount Athos for allowing me to view the monastery's manuscript collection and to the monk whose quick thinking ensured that I managed to catch the boat off the mountain in time.

On a more personal note, I must thank my father Andrew, my stepmother Marjorie, my brother Peter, and all the members of my family who have helped and encouraged me through this long process. Thanks go also to my old friend Thomas Coward, who has always been ready to listen to my ideas, critique my writing, and treat me to some of his excellent cooking. I am especially grateful to my loving partner Ashley for her support, both moral and practical. She knows better than anyone how long a process this has been, not only as I worked on this book but also as I navigated the difficult transition from postgraduate student to early career academic. I could not have done this without her love and encouragement.

Last, but by no means least, I would like to thank the anonymous readers of Oxford University Press who provided insightful advice and criticism that improved this book immensely. I alone am responsible for any flaws that remain.

Contents

List of Figures

List of Tables

Abbreviations

ACO	Schwartz (ed.), *Acta conciliorum oecumenicorum*
ADM	Archivo Ducale de Medinaceli
BMFD	Thomas and Hero (eds.), *Byzantine Monastic Foundation Documents*
Fontes III	*Pontificia commissio ad redigendum Codicem Iuris Canonici orientalis. Fontes, Series III*
IP	Kehr (ed.), *Italia Pontificia*
IS	Ughelli (ed.), *Italia sacra*
Lake	Lake and Lake, *Dated Greek Minuscule Manuscripts to the Year 1200*
Mansi	Mansi (ed.), *Sacrorum conciliorum nova et amplissima collectio*
MGH SS	Monumenta Germaniae Historica. Scriptores
N14T	*Nomocanon in Fourteen Titles* [edition: RP 1.7–335]
N50T	*Nomocanon in Fifty Titles* [edition: Voell and Justel (1661): 2.603–660]
ODB	*The Oxford Dictionary of Byzantium*
PG	Migne (ed.), *Patrologiae cursus completus. Series graeca*
PL	Migne (ed.), *Patrologiae cursus completus. Series latina*
RHBR	*Repertorium der Handschriften des byzantinischen Rechts*
RP	Ralles and Potles (eds.), *Σύνταγμα τῶν θείων καὶ ἱερῶν κανόνων*
S14T	*Syntagma in Fourteen Titles*
S50T	*Syntagma in Fifty Titles* [edition: Beneševič (1937): 1–155]
X	*Liber extra* [edition: Friedberg (1881)]

Note on Translation and Transliteration

One of my main aims in this book is to make a very inaccessible body of sources more accessible, not just to specialists but also to readers from other scholarly fields or even interested members of the general public. Consequently, I try to minimise the amount of Latin and Greek in the main body of the page while still providing source texts in the original language in footnotes. For quotations from modern scholarly works in languages other than English, I have taken the liberty of providing translations without including the original text. All translations are my own unless stated otherwise.

Transliteration of Greek and Arabic proper nouns is a point of perennial contention. I am no expert in the latter language, so I have simply followed the conventions that I have seen used by scholars who are. As for Greek, my approach is to strike a balance between authenticity, clarity, and aesthetics. I follow the standard of the Oxford Handbook of Byzantine Studies, transliterating Greek names into Hellenised English spelling (e.g. 'Alexios' instead of 'Alexius'). Where a name is already widely used in an Anglicised form, however, I prefer to use that spelling so as not to unduly burden the reader (e.g. 'Constantinople' instead of 'Konstantinoupolis' or 'Basil' instead of 'Basileios').

Chronology

691/2	Council *in Trullo*
751	Lombard conquest of Ravenna
787	2nd Council of Nicaea
861	*Protodeutera* Council
878	Islamic conquest of Syracuse
883	Second ('Photian') recension of the *N14T*
c. 965	Creation of the Byzantine *katepanikion* of Italy
Late C10	Second recension of the *Synopsis of Canons* ('Symeon Metaphrastes')
c. 1000	Foundation of the Greek monastery of Grottaferrata
c. 1050	Foundation of the Greek monastery of SS Elias and Anastasios of Carbone
1054	Legation of Cardinal Humbert of Silva Candida to Constantinople
1072	End of Norman conquest of southern Italy and Sicily
c. 1090	Third recension of the *N14T* (Theodore the *Bestes* and Michael the *Sebastos*)
1098	Council of Bari
c. 1105	Visit of St Bartholomew of Simeri to Constantinople and Mount Athos
1130	Coronation of Roger II as King of Sicily
c. 1130	Alexios Aristenos' commentary on the *Synopsis of Canons*
1133	Foundation of the Greek monastery of the Holy Saviour of Messina
c. 1140	Roger II's *Constitutions* (the '*Assizes of Ariano*')
c. 1140	Gratian's *Decretum*
1144	Neilos Doxapatres' *Order of the Patriarchal Thrones*
1154	Death of Roger II
c. 1160	John Zonaras' commentary on the corpus of canons
1168	Formal establishment of the Archimandritate of Carbone
c. 1185	Theodore Balsamon's commentary on the *N14T*
c. 1190	Theodore Balsamon's commentary on the corpus of canons
1194	Holy Roman Emperor Henry VI's conquest of southern Italy
1204	Fourth Crusade
1215	Fourth Lateran Council
1220	Frederick II's coronation as Holy Roman Emperor
c. 1225	Nektarios of Otranto's *Three Chapters*
1231	Frederick II's *Constitutions of Melfi* (the '*Liber Augustalis*')
1234	*Decretals of Gregory IX* (the '*Liber extra*')
1250	Death of Frederick II
1260	Byzantine reconquest of Constantinople
1266	Angevin conquest of southern Italy
1274	Second Council of Lyon
1282	Outbreak of the War of the Sicilian Vespers
1284	Council of Melfi
1302	Peace of Caltabellotta (end of the War of the Sicilian Vespers)
1334	Raymond of Campania's failed effort to ban the Byzantine rite in southern Italy
1372	Treaty of Villeneuve (Naples and Sicily divided into separate kingdoms)
1438–1445	Council of Ferrara-Florence
1446	Creation of the Catholic monastic 'Order of St Basil'
1453	Ottoman conquest of Constantinople
1457	Athanasios Chalkeopoulos' *visitatio* to the Basilian monasteries of Calabria

1468–1474	Bessarion's donation of manuscripts to Venice
1480	Ottoman sack of Otranto
1545–1563	Council of Trent
1571	The Biblioteca Laurenziana in Florence opened to the public
1609	Opening of the Biblioteca Ambrosiana in Milan
1615	Pope Paul V's transfer of Greek manuscripts from Grottaferrata to the Vatican Library
1631	Foundation of the Greek monastery of S. Basilio *de Urbe* in Rome
1654	Arsenii Sukhanov's mission to gather manuscripts from Mount Athos
1697–1699	Pietro Menniti's consolidation of the monastic libraries of the Order of St Basil
1786	Pope Pius VI's transfer of S. Basilio *de Urbe*'s manuscript collection to the Vatican Library
1806	Suppression of the Order of St Basil
1903	Pope Leo XIII's purchase of the Barberini manuscripts for the Vatican Library

Maps

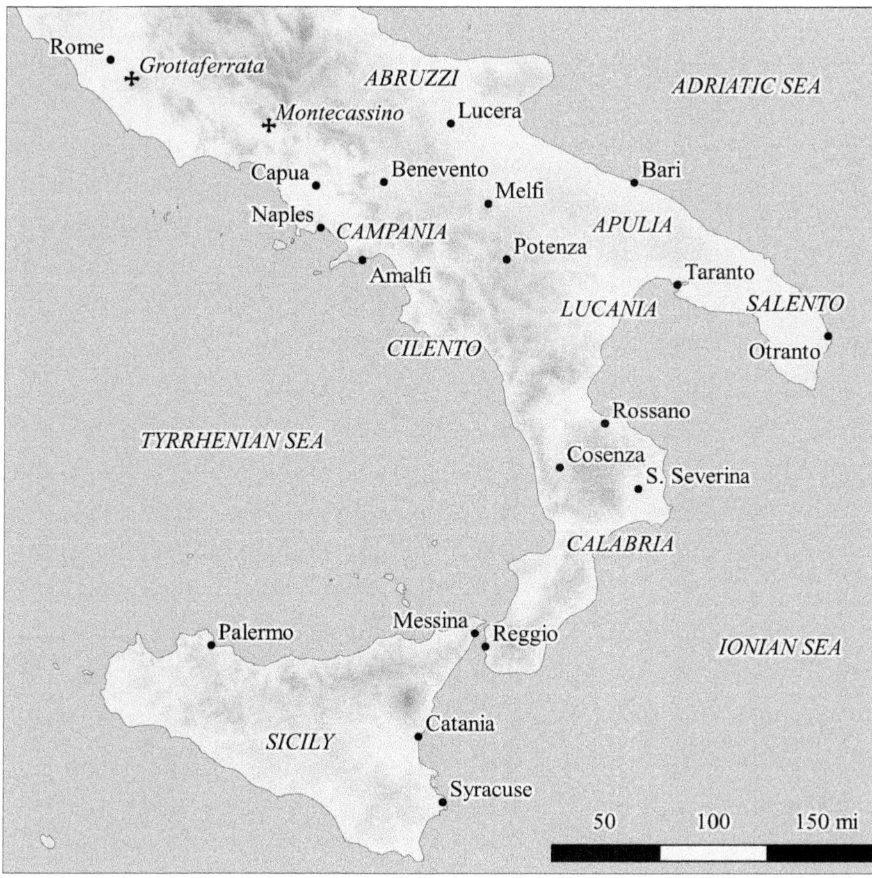

Map 1. Southern Italy: Overview

Produced using Copernicus data and information funded by the European Union—EU-DEM layers.

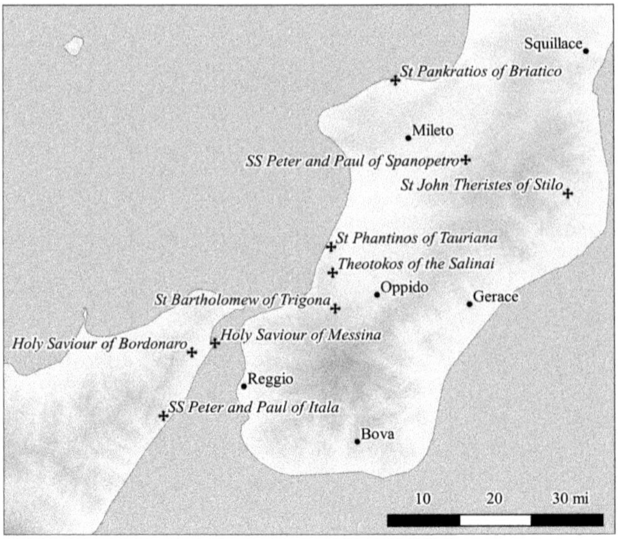

Map 2. Southern Calabria and the Straits of Messina
Produced using Copernicus data and information funded by the European Union—EU-DEM layers.

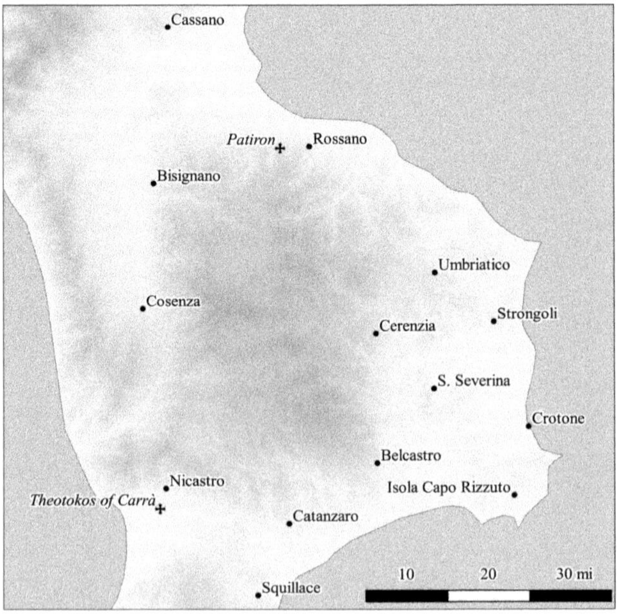

Map 3. Northern Calabria
Produced using Copernicus data and information funded by the European Union—EU-DEM layers.

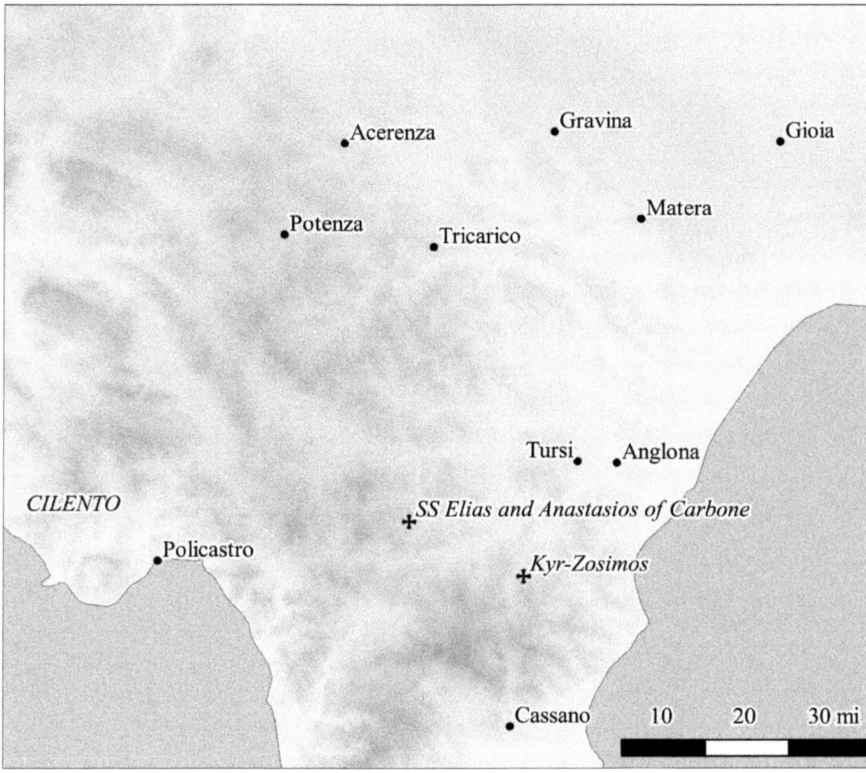

Map 4. Lucania

Produced using Copernicus data and information funded by the European Union—EU-DEM layers.

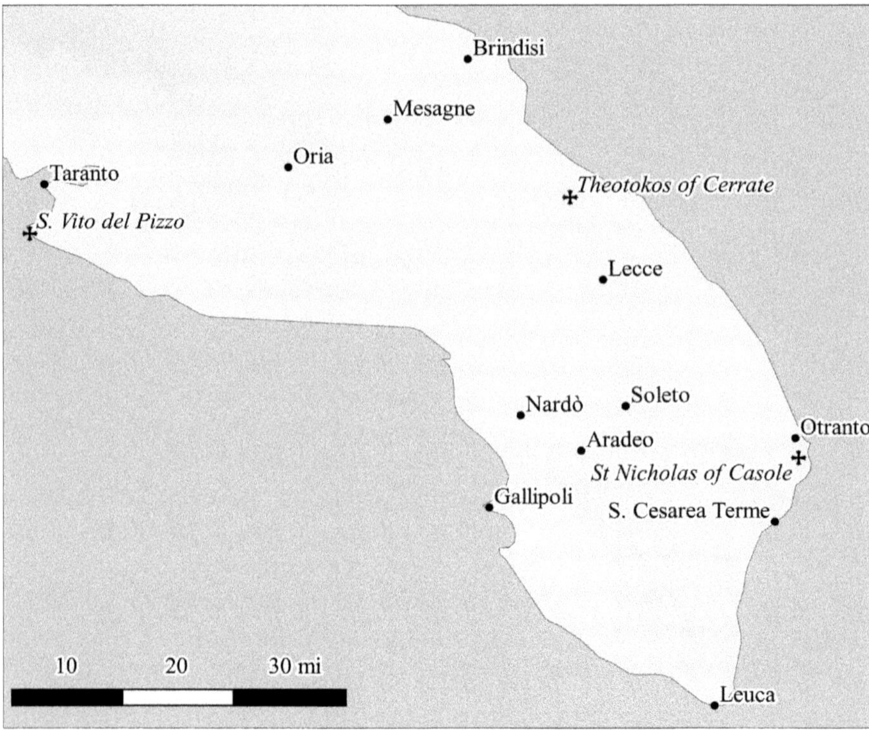

Map 5. The Salento Peninsula

Produced using Copernicus data and information funded by the European Union—EU-DEM layers.

Introduction

The last Byzantine metropolitan bishop of Reggio in Calabria passed away in the year 1079. The city had been captured by the Norman leader Robert Guiscard nearly twenty years earlier, but most of its population was Greek, a result of several centuries of continuous Byzantine rule since Late Antiquity. The then-patriarch of Constantinople, Kosmas I (1075–1081), appointed a Byzantine monk named Basil as the new metropolitan of Reggio and dispatched him to take up his see. This was a bold move, since the Norman conquest of Calabria in the 1050s–1060s meant that it was now under the effective jurisdiction of the Roman papacy. Unsurprisingly, the hostile Normans prevented Basil from ever reaching Reggio and instead installed one of their own people, Arnulf.[1]

We do not know what happened to Basil over the next decade, but he appears in the sources again in the year 1089. The Byzantine emperor Alexios I Komnenos (*r.* 1081–1118) and Pope Urban II (*r.* 1088–1099) were both seeking rapprochement between the Churches of Rome and Constantinople after several decades of hostility stemming from the Norman conquests. Basil was once again sent to Italy, this time to discuss the subject of church union with the pope. Together with the Greek archbishop Romanos of Rossano (another Greek city in Calabria), he met the pope at Melfi in November 1089 to represent the Byzantine church.

However, Basil had not yet come to terms with losing the metropolis of Reggio ten years earlier. It so happened that the see had fallen vacant again after Arnulf's death. Basil remonstrated with the pope over the injustice that the Normans had denied him his see after he was canonically consecrated by the patriarch of Constantinople. Urban replied that it was he, not the patriarch, who had the rightful jurisdiction over southern Italy, but nonetheless offered to appoint Basil as metropolitan on one condition: 'Submit yourself to me and you will receive your church.'[2] Basil could have Reggio as long as he accepted the pope, not the patriarch, as his rightful primate. He refused.

Basil's experience offers a revealing glimpse into the relations between Latin and Greek Christians in the late eleventh century. The old received wisdom on the subject, still often repeated in non-specialist publications, was that Rome and Constantinople entered into schism in 1054 when Cardinal Humbert of Silva

[1] On Basil of Reggio, see Stiernon (1964); Herde (2002): 220–3. Textual sources published in Holtzmann (1928): 59–67.

[2] 'ὑποτάγηθι μοι καὶ λήψει τὴν ἐκκλησίαν σου': Holtzmann (1928): 65 ll. 24–5.

Byzantine Religious Law in Medieval Italy. James Morton, Oxford University Press (2021). © James Morton.
DOI: 10.1093/oso/9780198861140.003.0001

Candida excommunicated Patriarch Michael Keroularios (*r.* 1043–1059) over the latter's stubborn refusal to accept the *Filioque* in the Creed and unleavened bread in the Eucharist.[3] The encounter between Basil and Urban at Melfi provides ample demonstration of the deficiencies of this narrative: not only did the pope show no awareness of a schism between Latins and Greeks, but he did not even mention theological or liturgical differences like the *Filioque*. The only issue that he stresses is authority: Basil must accept that southern Italy falls under the pope's canonical jurisdiction.

Most Greek Christians in Italy did accept papal authority as the price of continuing unharassed in their ancestral rites. Yet Basil's story points us towards an intriguing contradiction. If the Greeks of southern Italy were supposed to accept Roman jurisdiction, it surely follows that they should also have accepted Roman canon law and Roman justice. However, it is far from clear that they did. On the contrary, there is substantial evidence that Italo-Greeks continued to follow Byzantine church law for more than a century after Basil's exchange with Urban II at Melfi.

This book offers the first historical study of a significant part of that evidence: a group of thirty-six surviving manuscripts (or manuscript fragments) of Byzantine canon law, known as 'nomocanons', that were produced and used by the Italo-Greeks between the tenth and the fourteenth centuries.[4] These manuscripts were legal reference works that offered a guide to the legislation and judicial procedure of the Byzantine church; they have nothing whatsoever to say on the canon law of the Roman church in the medieval period.

How could the Greek Christians of southern Italy disregard the canon law of their Latin conquerors and persist in using nomocanons for such a long time? What does it imply about the nature of law and religion in medieval southern Italy that they were able to do so? To be more specific, what does the continued use of Byzantine canon law in the centuries after the Norman conquest say about the nature of the submission that Urban II required of Basil in return for the metropolis of Reggio in 1089?

Specialists in the fields of Byzantine legal history and codicology are aware of these manuscripts and some have been the subject of previous academic research. Nonetheless, there has to date been no attempt to conduct a broader study of the Italo-Greek nomocanons and they are not well known among non-specialists. This book has three main aims, therefore: to introduce readers to the manuscripts and their contents; to explain how and why they continued to be produced under Latin rule; and to consider what they reveal about the legal and cultural pluralism of medieval southern Italy. In pursuing these aims, it will show how these

[3] For further discussion of the 'Schism' of 1054, see Chapter 2, 'Greek Christianity in Medieval Italy', C2.P25–C2.P26.

[4] Chapter 1 provides an in-depth definition and discussion of the Byzantine nomocanon.

manuscripts should be of interest not only to medievalists and Byzantinists, but to any scholar who is interested in the intersection of law, religion, and cultural identity.

My approach to the subject has been strongly influenced by the field of legal anthropology (particularly the popular concept of legal pluralism) and by the methodological perspective of material philology. In this introductory chapter, I shall explain these foundational concepts and show how they provide a useful key to understanding the Italo-Greek nomocanons. I shall also address difficult theoretical and terminological issues surrounding the notion of culture and identity, which play a large role in this study, and finish with an overview of the contents of the book's chapters.

Byzantine Canon Law and Legal Pluralism

Legal history has long been a niche subject within Byzantine Studies; Byzantine canon law is, if anything, a niche within a niche. This is to some extent a consequence of law's reputation as a highly specialised subject, but it is also a product of the traditional interests of the field. Since the nineteenth century, Byzantine legal historians have mainly concerned themselves with *Quellenkritik*, the production of critical editions of legal source texts.[5] This is undeniably a vital and necessary task (the present book would have been impossible without it), but one effect of such a strong concentration on editing normative texts is that has created a perception of the subject as abstract and divorced from historical context. When Byzantinists have discussed canon law texts, they have often used them as supplementary texts in broader historiographical debates on topics such as Byzantine 'caesaropapism' (i.e. the role of the emperor in the administration of the church).[6] Indeed, it says a lot about the state of the field that the only overview of the history of Byzantine canon law since the 1980s (and the only one at all in English) came in a volume edited by two scholars of medieval *Western* canon law.[7]

Nonetheless, the state of Byzantine legal scholarship has begun to change gradually since the 1980s and more rapidly in the past decade.[8] In 2011, the French legal scholar Lisa Bénou published an important monograph on Byzantine legal practice during the Palaiologan era (1261–1453).[9] She examined the relationship between law 'in the books' and law as it was practised in reality, a

[5] On the role of textual criticism in the study of medieval canon law, see Rennie and Taliadoros (2014): 136–138.

[6] See e.g. Beck (1981); Macrides (1990); Angold (1995): 45–108, 121–136, 530–63; Dagron (2003): 249–310.

[7] Ohme (2012); Troianos (2012a); Troianos (2012b).

[8] See esp. Kazhdan (1989); Simon (2005).

[9] Bénou (2011).

relationship that she referred to as Byzantine '*legalité*' (a difficult term to translate into English).[10]

The years since Bénou's monograph have seen a surprising upsurge in innovative studies of how Byzantine law worked in its own historical context. Michael Humphreys has explored the role of lawgiving in shaping political ideology in the period *c.* 680–850 and Zachary Chitwood has explored the legal culture (broadly defined) of Byzantium under the Macedonian dynasty (867–1056).[11] Even Byzantine church law has received some attention with David Wagschal's excellent study of the formation of the canonical corpus in the early Middle Ages, which aims to explain 'how Byzantine canon law was *supposed* to work.'[12]

These recent works have all (to a greater or lesser extent) been influenced by important developments in twentieth-century critical legal theory and reflect a welcome trend towards interdisciplinarity in Medieval and Byzantine Studies. One of the most significant developments in legal theory, and one that is central to this study, is the idea of legal pluralism.[13] The modern concept of legal pluralism emerged in the 1970s as a reaction to the legal positivism that prevailed for much of the twentieth century.[14] Legal positivism is most famously associated with the work of H.L.A. Hart, who adopted an empirical approach to the law, viewing it as a closed intellectual system produced by an authoritative legislative body (such as the state).[15] Hart conceived the idea of a 'rule of recognition', a basic test to determine whether or not a set of normative rules can be classed as 'law'.[16] In contrast to Hart's empiricism, legal pluralists contend that law is not just the codified rules promulgated and enforced by sovereign lawgivers, but the diverse array of behavioural norms followed by different communities in different social contexts. In the pluralistic conception of law, multiple 'legal systems' can and do coexist within a society to varying degrees of formalism.[17] Take, for example, the voluntary codes of conduct often adopted by modern universities, businesses, and professional bodies. These are not backed by the coercive power of the state, yet they still set appropriate bounds for behaviour and can carry penalties of varying severity for those who violate them. They are not statute law in the technical sense,

[10] Bénou (2011): 24. [11] Humphreys (2015); Chitwood (2017).

[12] Wagschal (2015): 15.

[13] Legal pluralism has become such a popular subject of debate among legal theorists that the relevant literature is far too voluminous to adequately summarise here. The classic introduction to the subject is Merry (1988). More recently, see Tamanaha (2008); Berman (2009).

[14] This is not to be confused with the 'classic' legal pluralism, which described the coexistence in nineteenth-century colonial states of native legal traditions with the imported legal codes of European colonisers. Griffiths (1986): 5, 8 refers to this as the 'juristic' view of legal pluralism, in contrast to the modern 'social science' view.

[15] See esp. Hart (1961). [16] Hart (1961): 100–23.

[17] For a good summary of the debate between legal positivists and pluralists, see Melissaris (2009): 8–22. For criticism of legal pluralism, see esp. Tamanaha (1993); Brooks (2006): 10. I do not have the space here to explore the intricacies of the debate, but it is fair to say that legal theorists have found that the advantages of a more expansive definition of law outweigh the disadvantages. Even Tamanaha eventually came to support legal pluralism (see Tamanaha [2000]).

but they are still methods by which communities regulate and adjudicate social interaction; in that sense, they are examples of what Locchi has called 'law as a social institution'.[18]

Medieval Europe was characterised by a diverse pluralism of formal and informal legal orders. Roman civil law existed alongside canon law, mercantile law, local city laws, ethnic laws, and so forth. Historians have also observed similarly pluralistic legal cultures in other pre-modern societies such as the Roman Empire and Fatimid Egypt.[19] Southern Italy was one of the most legally plural societies of the Mediterranean world, home to Christians, Jews, and Muslims, each following their own religious laws, while Christians were subdivided again into Greeks, Normans, Lombards, and even Slavs.

That there was legal diversity in medieval southern Italy is not in itself a new insight. What is interesting, however, is the way in which these more formalistic legal orders related to the region's social, cultural, and religious orders. The relationship between law and culture was eloquently expressed by the American jurist Robert Cover, whose influential article 'Nomos and Narrative' strongly informs this book's main argument.[20] The article discusses the concept of 'jurisgenesis', the process by which a society generates legal meaning. Jurisgenesis is not simply the creation of laws but a continuous social process: 'We constantly create and maintain a world of right and wrong, of lawful and unlawful, of valid and void.'[21] The creation of legal meaning is the creation of a common legal narrative, an ongoing discourse in which a community determines the character of its normative world (the 'nomos' of Cover's title).[22]

Cover argued that jurisgenesis takes place 'through an essentially cultural medium' and identified two ideal-typical modes: the 'paideic' and the 'imperial'.[23] In the paideic mode, a community or social group develops a set of shared behavioural norms based on a common body of precept or narrative. In the imperial mode, fixed institutions (such as the state) establish and enforce a set of formal, universal laws. No legal culture is ever wholly paideic or imperial; rather, the law is a spectrum encapsulating both modes of jurisgenesis. Moreover, the process is continuous and a community's normative world can shift from one end of the spectrum to the other.

Together, legal pluralism and Cover's paideic-imperial model of jurisgenesis offer a compelling lens for the study of the Italo-Greek nomocanons. Canon law clearly embodies elements of both imperial and paideic jurisgenesis. It regulates some matters that we would traditionally associate with statute law such as divorce

[18] Locchi (2014): 74. [19] Bryen (2014): esp. 357–361; Ackerman-Liberman (2014).

[20] Cover (1983). [21] Cover (1983): 4.

[22] As Tamanaha recently put it, 'Forms of law are constituted and evolve in connection with surrounding circumstances.' (Tamanaha [2017]: 194)

[23] Cover (1983): 11. The term 'paideic' is derived from the Greek *paideia*, which refers to a combination of a person's formal education and social upbringing.

and inheritance, but it also regulates purely social customs such as the type of food a person may eat and when. Moreover, it emerged from the (paideic) practices of the Christian communities of the early centuries of the first millennium and developed into the (imperial) codification of the modern Catholic *Code of Canon Law*.

Law, Religion, and Culture

If a community's legal order is founded on a shared narrative, as Cover expressed it, then it follows that law must be inextricably bound to culture. 'Culture' is a notoriously difficult concept to define and discussions of cultural change and interactions are minefields fraught with theoretical dangers. When I refer to 'culture', I mean the common customs, social norms, and forms of expression that define a community of people. By defining a community, culture also provides the framework for a sense of identity (another fraught concept). The definitional action of culture is relational, since humans tend to base their identity on practices that make them *different* from others rather than what they have in common. People usually belong to multiple types of community (e.g. Christian, Greek, Calabrian, monastic, etc.) at the same time, giving them multiple layers of identity and cultural practice.

The southern Italian 'melting pot' has proved to be an excellent laboratory for scholars who wish to investigate historical identity and culture. Annick Peters-Custot, for example, conducted a highly detailed study of what she called the 'gentle acculturation' of the Italo-Greeks under Latin rule, while Linda Safran has examined how the art of the medieval Salento expressed the identities of its various inhabitants.[24] There is also fine work by researchers such as Jeremy Johns and Alex Metcalfe on Arabic and Islamic culture in Norman Italy.[25] Several scholars (including Peters-Custot and Safran) have made efforts to theorise cultural identity in medieval southern Italy, debating concepts such as 'acculturation', 'interculturation', 'hybridity', 'syncretism', 'transculturation', and 'third space' theory.[26] All these approaches attempt to grapple in their own way with the question of how cultural groups interact with and influence one another.

A detailed exploration of theoretical perspectives on culture and identity is beyond the scope of this book. I should emphasise, though, that I do not treat these concepts as intrinsic or immutable characteristics. Nor do I subscribe to what Peter Brown termed 'cultural hydraulics', the assumption that culture 'flows' from one reservoir (e.g. the Latin world) to another (e.g. the Greek world) through

[24] Peters-Custot (2009a); Safran (2014).

[25] Johns (2002); Metcalfe (2003); Metcalfe (2009).

[26] See Safran (2014): 230–233 for a discussion of the relative merits and demerits of these terms. On 'acculturation' and 'interculturation', see Peters-Custot (2009a): 23–231. On 'transculturation' and 'third space theory' (concepts borrowed from sociolinguistics), see esp. Houben (2013); Scirocco and Wolf (2018).

the metaphorical sluice-gates of history.[27] Cultural change does not entail abandoning one identity and replacing it with another; rather, it entails different communities adopting and adapting each other's practices in such a way that their identities may begin to seem less different.

That said, one must make terminological choices when writing about historical identities and I do not expect that every reader will agree with mine. I have attempted to achieve a compromise between authenticity and clarity, between terms that are used in the medieval sources and ones that will be easily understood by modern English-speakers. One of the most obvious compromises is my use of the word 'Byzantine', a word that Byzantine authors themselves used exceedingly rarely (they called themselves 'Romans') but has become so common in modern usage as to be indispensable.[28]

One of my more controversial choices, at least for Anglophone scholars, is my frequent use of terms like 'Latins', 'Greeks', and 'Italo-Greeks'. One could justifiably argue that these are too vague; a medieval 'Latin', for instance, could hail from almost any Christian region of Western Europe. As for the term 'Greek', this could refer to an inhabitant of the geographical region of the modern nation state of Greece or any Greek speaker from the eastern Mediterranean. The way in which Byzantine authors used the word 'Hellene' (the more authentic term for 'Greek') itself changed greatly over the centuries, as Antony Kaldellis has explained.[29] Again, the meaning changes depending on the context.

This book's primary focus is on southern Italy between the tenth and the fourteenth centuries. In this context, the terms 'Latin' and 'Greek' are not as vague or anachronistic as they might otherwise seem; they are the actual words used by medieval southern Italian authors (in both Latin and Greek texts) to distinguish between Christians of the Roman and the Byzantine rites in the region. Indeed, some southern Italian Greek writers even adopted the Latin term '*graeci*' as '*graikoi*' to describe themselves, as we shall see later in the book.[30] I have therefore chosen to use these terms as they seemed to be the most useful in the context of this book and allow me to avoid tiresome circumlocutions.[31] One anachronistic term that I have adopted is 'Italo-Greek', a commonplace of French and Italian scholarship, since it is useful for distinguishing between the Greeks of southern Italy and those of the mainland Byzantine Empire.

I have likewise chosen to use the expressions 'Latin Christian' and 'Greek Christian' to refer to the two groups' religious communities. The terms 'Catholic'

[27] Brown (1982): 171–172. [28] See recently Kaldellis (2017). [29] Kaldellis (2007).

[30] See Chapter 10, 'They Do It Like This in Romania', p. C10.S3.

[31] One must nonetheless remember that 'Greeks' and 'Latins' in southern Italy were not monolithic blocs. 'Latins' could include Normans, Lombards, Germans, or several other ethnicities who were generally perceived to be 'Western' (another term that Greek authors occasionally used) and belonged to the Roman church. 'Greeks', on the other hand, could include people of Armenian, Syrian, Slavic, or other 'Eastern' ancestry who were united by their use of the Greek language and general adherence to Byzantine cultural norms.

and 'Orthodox' to my mind carry too much anachronistic baggage, implying to modern readers the existence of separate Christian denominations (a pluralistic concept that would have been unfamiliar in the Middle Ages). Despite cultural and religious differences, most medieval Christians would not have viewed the churches of Rome and Constantinople as separate communions, at least until the Fourth Crusade of 1204.[32] Even after the Fourth Crusade, some Byzantine churchmen such as the famous canonist Demetrios Chomatenos (d. 1236) still felt that it was acceptable for Greeks and Latins to commune with one another as long as the Eucharistic bread was leavened.[33] The key distinction for medieval southern Italians lay not between denominations in the modern sense but between languages, liturgies, and associated customs; 'Latins' spoke Latin in church and 'Greeks' spoke Greek.

I began this introduction by posing the question of why the Italo-Greeks continued to produce and read nomocanons for so many years after they had been compelled to accept the authority and jurisdiction of the Roman church. The central contention of this book is that legal pluralism provides the best means of answering the question. On one level, Byzantine canon law can be seen as just another of southern Italy's many coexisting legal systems, operating alongside various other types of ethnic, religious, and institutional law. More profound, however, is the connection between Byzantine canon law and the cultural and religious identity of the Italo-Greeks. The nomocanons were not just authoritative sources for the legal system of an institutional church; they were authoritative sources for the religious practices of a distinct community in southern Italy. As such, they could remain culturally relevant even when they had lost their formal legal utility.

Sources and Methodology

Of the thirty-six manuscripts that form the basis of this study, twenty-six are either nomocanons in the strict sense of the word (mixed collections of canon and civil law) or straightforward canon law collections (see Table 0.1). The other ten manuscripts are 'nomocanonical'; while they technically comprise different types of manuscript (collections of civil law, Gospel readings, patristic texts, etc.), they have enough canon-law content to justify their inclusion in this study.

When compiling my list of primary sources, I took as my starting point the excellent three-volume *Repertorium der Handschriften des byzantinischen Rechts* published in Dieter Simon's *Forschungen zur byzantinischen Rechtsgeschichte*

[32] For highly detailed, recent discussions of the subject, see Demacopoulos (2019); Neocleous (2019).

[33] Pitra (1891): 727–30. Note that Chomatenos does not go so far as to say that Greeks may receive the Latins' unleavened communion bread (*azyma*), as stated in Angold (1995): 531.

Table 0.1. Overview of Primary Manuscript Sources

	Shelfmark	Date	Origin	Type
Florence, Biblioteca Medicea Laurenziana				
1.	plut. 5.22	12th/13th Century	Salento	Nomocanon
Grottaferrata, Badia greca				
2.	gr. 50 (Z γ VII)	14th Century	Rossano (Calabria?)	Civil law collection
3.	gr. 76 (Z γ III)	11th/12th Century	Rossano (Calabria)?	Civil law collection
4.	gr. 322 (B δ I)	Before 1135	S. Calabria	Nomocanon
London, British Library				
5.	Add. 28822	12th/13th Century	Salento	Nomocanon
Messina, Biblioteca Universitaria Regionale				
6.	S. Salv. 59	*c.* 1100–1115	Rossano (Calabria)	Nomocanon
Milan, Biblioteca Ambrosiana				
7.	B 107 sup. (gr. 128)	12th/13th Century	Salento	Nomocanon
8.	E 94 sup. (gr. 303)	13th/14th Century	Soleto (Salento)?	Nomocanon
9.	F 48 sup. (gr. 341)	Early 12th Century	Salento	Nomocanon
10.	G 57 sup. (gr. 400)	11th/12th Century	S. Calabria	Nomocanon
Moscow, Gosudarstvennij Istoričeskij Musej				
11.	Sin. gr. 397 (Vlad. 316)	13th Century	Salento	Nomocanon
12.	Sin. gr. 432 (Vlad. 317)	12th Century	Sicily/S. Calabria	Nomocanon
Naples, Biblioteca nazionale 'Vittorio Emanuele III'				
13.	II C 7	1139	Stilo (Calabria)	Nomocanon
Oxford, Bodleian Library				
14.	Barocci 86	12th Century	Salento	Nomocanon
Paris, Bibliothèque nationale de France				
15.	gr. 1370	1296/7	Salento	Nomocanon
16.	gr. 1371	Late 12th Century	Casole (Salento)	Canon law collection
Rome, Biblioteca Vallicelliana				
17.	C 11.1	*c.* 1100–1115	Rossano (Calabria)	Nomocanon
Syracuse, Biblioteca Alagoniana				
18.	gr. 3	1124	Rossano (Calabria)	Gospel lectionary

Continued

Table 0.1. *Continued*

	Shelfmark	Date	Origin	Type
Vatican City, Biblioteca Apostolica Vaticana				
19.	Barb. gr. 323	Early 12th Century	S. Calabria	Nomocanon
20.	Barb. gr. 324	Late 12th Century	Casole (Salento)	Nomocanon
21.	Barb. gr. 476	12th Century	S. Calabria	Patristic collection
22.	Ottob. gr. 186 (fols. 9–22)	12th/13th Century	Salento	Nomocanon
23.	Vat. gr. 1168	11th/12th Century	Rossano (Calabria)?	Civil law collection
24.	Vat. gr. 1287	12th Century	Lecce (Salento)?	Nomocanon
25.	Vat. gr. 1426	1213	Messina (Sicily)	Theol. compilation
26.	Vat. gr. 1506	1024	Rossano (Calabria)?	Apostolic compilation
27.	Vat. gr. 1980	Late 11th Century	Carbone (Lucania)	Nomocanon
28.	Vat. gr. 1980	Late 11th Century	Carbone (Lucania)	Nomocanon
29.	Vat. gr. 2019	Before 1234	Rossano (Calabria)	Nomocanon
30.	Vat. gr. 2060	*c.* 1100–1115	Rossano (Calabria)	Nomocanon
31.	Vat. gr. 2075	Late 10th Century	Calabria	Civil law collection
32.	Vat. gr. 2115 (fols. 78–96)	11th/12th Century	Rossano (Calabria)	Civil law collection
Venice, Biblioteca Nazionale Marciana				
33.	gr. 169 (coll. 475)	11th/12th Century	Constantinople?	Nomocanon
34.	gr. 171 (coll. 741)	*c.* 1220–1230	Grottaferrata (Lazio)	Nomocanon
35.	gr. 172 (coll. 574)	1175	Calabria	Civil law collection
36.	gr. III.2 (coll. 1131)	12th/13th Century	Salento	Nomocanon

series. In one or two cases I found with further research that some details in the *RHBR* needed to be refined or corrected (this is not intended as a criticism of the scholars who created the *RHBR*, since it is only to be expected with such a large undertaking). From this I moved on to scour relevant literature on Byzantine law and southern Italian manuscripts, particularly by codicologists such as Cavallo, Lucà, Jacob, Cataldi Palau, and others.

After studying the manuscripts themselves (or, on the rare occasions that it was necessary, microfilm reproductions), I was able to substantially refine my original list of sources. Besides correcting a small number of misattributions and cases of incorrect dating, I was able to localise several new manuscripts to southern Italy from their known history and physical characteristics. Although I have attempted to make as comprehensive a list of manuscript sources as possible, it cannot be exhaustive: new nomocanonical manuscripts could always be discovered in the future. Furthermore, there are several cases of known manuscripts of uncertain provenance that have been or could be attributed to southern Italy.[34] Nonetheless, the body of sources that I studied for this project is large enough to allow for meaningful conclusions and generalisations.

My first task in examining the manuscripts was to compile a database of important information on provenance, ownership history, contents, and physical characteristics; the results of this can be found in Appendix 1. Though many of the manuscripts' contents are already detailed in the *RHBR*, some have never been catalogued before; in other cases, it was necessary to correct or expand the descriptions in existing catalogues.

The purpose was partly to make the information more accessible to readers, but also to convey the *materiality* of the manuscripts. Manuscripts are not just sources for the edited texts that we read in print and online today; they are physical witnesses to the social and cultural contexts in which those texts were copied and read in the past. Was a manuscript created more for practical use or for show? Did it require a large investment of money or resources? Did its owners take good care of it? Was it used for a short or a long period of time?

By studying nomocanonical manuscripts as historical evidence in themselves, we gain glimpses into how medieval readers encountered their legal tradition. This is the approach advocated by proponents of 'material' (or 'new') philology, a school that originated in French post-structuralism and gained popularity among Anglophone medievalists in the 1990s.[35] Material philologists seek to historicise manuscripts by treating them as artefacts in and of themselves; in this way, they become evidence not only for texts but also for the society that read them.

As I studied the manuscripts, I attempted to corroborate (or discover for the first time) details of each one's provenance, date, and copyist/s. Very few of the codices retain their scribal colophons; these were typically inscribed in a manuscript's final quires, which are the most likely to suffer damage or be lost. As a result, one must take note of a range of factors. By cross-referencing observable patterns in production and style with evidence for how and where the manuscripts were historically preserved (e.g. through medieval and Renaissance inventories, notes of sale, etc.), it was possible in most cases to assign them to particular regions of southern Italy and to particular centuries. In some cases, most notably

[34] See Appendix 3. [35] See Nichols (1990); Westra (2014).

the monastic nomocanons of twelfth-century Calabria, it was surprising to see just how specific one could be.

I next sought to place the manuscripts in their historical context by investigating related documentary and narrative sources: papal bulls, charters of the rulers and nobles of the Kingdom of Sicily, the surviving archives of Italo-Greek monasteries, and similar materials. These texts provide extremely useful information on the manuscripts' general context and sometimes have direct bearing on specific nomocanons. There is also a large quantity of surviving letters and treatises by Byzantine and Italo-Greek authors on the subject of canon law, many of whom used nomocanonical manuscripts as direct or indirect sources. This combination of approaches—material study of the primary source manuscripts together with historical contextualisation—serves as the main basis for the analysis in this book.

Overview of Chapters

The book is divided into ten chapters grouped into three parts. Part I sets the scene by introducing the book's main source material and the context in which it was produced and preserved. Parts II and III present the two main historical phases in which the surviving Italo-Greek nomocanons were created; the former focuses on the last century of Byzantine rule and the Norman Kingdom of Sicily (the tenth to twelfth centuries), while the latter looks at important changes that occurred in the post-Norman period (the thirteenth to fourteenth centuries).

Chapter 1 introduces the reader to the Byzantine nomocanon, explaining its historical development, typical contents and layout, and principle codicological and palaeographical character. Chapter 2 then gives a narrative overview of Greek Christianity in medieval southern Italy to provide basic historical context for the rest of the book. Part I concludes with Chapter 3, on the nomocanons' history of source survival in the medieval period, showing why we have what we have and discussing what might have been lost.

Chapter 4 discusses the evidence for canon law in Byzantine southern Italy in the tenth and eleventh centuries. It shows that the main trends in manuscript production were established in the decades following the Byzantine reconquest and administrative reorganisation of the region in the late ninth century, with the result that the southern Italian nomocanons appear relatively archaic by comparison to surviving examples from the Byzantine mainland.

Chapters 5 and 6 examine monastic nomocanons from the Norman period, which form the largest surviving sample of manuscripts from the eleventh and twelfth centuries. Chapter 5 presents the evidence for the contexts in which the monastic nomocanons were copied, arguing that the Norman rulers consciously allowed independent Italo-Greek monasteries within their realm to administer their own internal legal affairs, with the nomocanons serving as practical reference aids. Chapter 6 then studies the content and codicological style of the monastic nomocanons, noting three broad categories: the practical, almost austere manuscripts of smaller independent monasteries of Calabria and Lucania; the impressive, highly decorative manuscripts of the wealthy monasteries of Rossano and Messina; and the manuscripts of St Nicholas of Casole, which seem to have a more didactic purpose and show a stronger connection with twelfth-century Constantinople. Chapter 7 completes Part II by considering nomocanons used by the Greek secular church and the laity, noting that at least some Italo-Greek bishops and even lay judges observed Byzantine canon law in their administration of justice under Norman rule.

Chapter 8 begins Part III of the book by exploring the effect on Italo-Greek religious law of the demise of the Norman dynasty in the 1190s and the Fourth Lateran Council of 1215. These events created an opportunity for the Roman papacy to become more actively involved in the administration of justice in the Kingdom of Sicily and provided the means to integrate the Italo-Greeks more closely into the Roman church's legal system.

Chapter 9 focuses on a selection of nomocanons from the Salento peninsula (produced between the late twelfth and early fourteenth centuries) that were mostly copied by and for the region's secular Greek priests. Observing the manuscripts' strong focus on subjects such as clerical marriage, liturgical practices, and the validity of the Byzantine baptismal rite, it argues that Salentine Greek priests resorted to nomocanons as sources of cultural authority that could help explain and legitimise their distinctive Greek Christian practices to critical Latin neighbours.

Finally, Chapter 10 analyses the changing role of Byzantine canon law in thirteenth-century southern Italy more broadly. It considers examples such as Nektarios of Otranto's *Three Chapters* and the baptismal controversy of 1232 to argue that canon law had become a tool to define and preserve the identity of the Italo-Greek Christian community against the pressures of demographic change and cultural assimilation. Following the conclusion, the book closes with a series of appendices that provide formal descriptions of the codices, an overview of the key statistics on the manuscript sources, and brief discussions of further manuscripts that may or may not have southern Italian provenance.

It was originally my hope to include an appendix of illustrations of the primary source manuscripts at the end of the book. Unfortunately, the image licensing practices of many libraries and archives have not kept pace with the demands of modern digital publishing, so this has proved to be impossible in many cases. Instead, I have included links where available to online photo-reproductions of manuscripts or microfilms that will allow readers to view entire manuscripts with relative ease. I have also managed to include some images in the book from the Biblioteca Ambrosiana that are not available online but are useful to help visualise certain topics.

PART I
SOURCES AND CONTEXT

1
Introducing the Byzantine Nomocanon

If you are someone for whom the Byzantine nomocanon needs no introduction, then you are one of a select few. Most scholars—including Byzantinists—are less familiar with the material. Nomocanons have traditionally been marginalised or even omitted from histories of Byzantine law, relegated to brief descriptions in more broad-ranging works or articles in highly specialised journals.[1] Exceedingly few of these are available in English. This opening chapter will therefore provide a brief overview of what nomocanons are and why we should get to know them better.

The term 'nomocanon' is used in a variety of ways that can be potentially confusing. Some historians refer to 'the Nomocanon', by which they mean a specific legal collection known to modern scholarship as the *Nomocanon in Fourteen Titles*.[2] At heart, though, 'nomocanon' is an amalgam of two Greek words: '*nomos*' (imperial law) and '*kanon*' (canon law). Unlike the medieval West, the Byzantines accepted the right of the emperor to legislate (within reason) in ecclesiastical affairs. As a result, their collections of religious law typically included both *kanones* and *nomoi* relating to the church; these became known as nomocanons.

Legal historians usually use the word 'nomocanon' to describe the textual collections themselves. The Byzantines also applied it to the manuscripts that contained the texts (in the same way that we might refer to copies of the Bible as 'Bibles', for instance). Sometimes we see it written as the variant neuter form '*nomokanonon*', which we could translate as 'nomocanon book'. By the twelfth century, the term 'nomocanon' had become so closely associated with canon law collections in general that it was occasionally employed even for manuscripts that did not technically contain any *nomoi*. When I use the word 'nomocanon' without any further qualifiers, I mean manuscript collections of Byzantine civil and canon law. There are also codices such as Gospel lectionaries and theological collections that include significant quantities of canon law without meeting the technical definition of a nomocanon; I refer to these as 'nomocanonical' manuscripts.

[1] The major exception to this trend has been the recent publication of Wagschal (2015). Wagschal's focus is more on the textual tradition of Byzantine canon law than the manuscript tradition, although he makes many valuable contributions nonetheless.

[2] This will henceforth be abbreviated to *N14T*. For more details on the *N14T*, see below, 'Origins and Development', C1.S1.

Byzantine Religious Law in Medieval Italy. James Morton, Oxford University Press (2021). © James Morton.
DOI: 10.1093/oso/9780198861140.003.0002

Nomocanons are examples of what the legal theorist Nils Jansen has termed 'non-legislative codifications': compilations of legal material created by private actors rather than by official legislative bodies.[3] Although the Byzantine church promulgated and sanctioned canon law, it never issued or endorsed any official *codification* of the law; rather, canon law collections such as the *N14T* were produced by private individuals. To use Jansen's words, nomocanons derived their authority from 'their [own] success in presenting themselves as authoritative legal institutions'.[4] People chose to read and copy them because they were seen as useful guides to the law, not because a legislative body obliged them to do so. The manuscripts' non-legislative character was responsible for a surprisingly large degree of variation in textual content, aesthetic quality, and history of use. It is in these differences that we find evidence for the range of legal, social, and cultural contexts in which the manuscripts were produced and read, which is what makes them such potentially interesting sources.

Origins and Development

The secular and religious legal systems of the Byzantine Empire developed almost in parallel in Late Antiquity.[5] Just as the Roman emperors and jurists of the first four centuries AD (the 'Classical Period' of Roman law) were the major sources of codified Byzantine civil law, so the Church Fathers and great ecumenical councils of the fourth to fifth centuries provided the foundations of Byzantine canon law. Beginning with the Council of Ancyra (314), church councils issued collections of canons to serve as disciplinary guidelines for the faithful. In addition to these, select texts by Patristic writers such as St Basil of Caesarea, St Gregory of Nyssa, and others became so influential that they were widely accepted as canons as well (see Table 1.1).[6]

By the sixth century, both the canon and civil law systems of the Byzantine Empire had begun to encounter a similar challenge: there were too many legal texts spread across too many sources to be easily understood or consulted. The emperor Justinian I (*r.* 527–565) recognised this problem and, in 529, began his famous project to codify the corpus of Roman civil law in a series of new textual collections that would meet the needs of contemporary practitioners. Justinian's efforts in the realm of civil law served as an inspiration to ecclesiastical lawyers to create new editions of their own legal texts as well.

[3] Jansen (2010): 13–49; Jansen (2012): 1–3.

[4] Jansen (2010): 140.

[5] For a more in-depth narrative and discussion of the development of the textual tradition of Byzantine canon law, see Wagschal (2015): 32–50.

[6] On early sources of Byzantine canon law, see Ohme (2012).

Table 1.1. Principle Sources of Byzantine Canon Law in Late Antiquity

Councils (*Ecumenical*, Local)		Church Fathers	
Ancyra	314	Dionysios of Alexandria	d. 264
Neocaesarea	315	Gregory of Neocaesarea	213–270
I Nicaea	325	Peter of Alexandria	d. 311
Gangra	340	Athanasios of Alexandria	*c.* 298–373
Antioch	341	Basil of Caesarea	*c.* 330–379
Sardica	343	Gregory of Nazianzus	*c.* 330–390
Laodicea	364	Gregory of Nyssa	*c.* 335–395
I Constantinople	381	Amphilochios of Iconium	*c.* 340–400
Ephesus	431	Theophilos of Alexandria	d. 412
Chalcedon	451	Cyril of Alexandria	*c.* 376–444
Carthage	419	Timothy of Alexandria	d. 477

If the canons were to serve as the basis of a functioning legal system for the church, they would have to be set out in a format that was easy to use. Early collections of canon law (of which none have survived) seem to have been arranged chronologically, but this was problematic: if a reader wanted to learn what the canons said about marriage, for example, he would first have to know *which* canons addressed the subject before he could consult them. Around 550, the Antiochene churchman John Scholastikos, a future patriarch of Constantinople (565–577), composed the *Synagoge* (collection) *in Fifty Titles* in an effort to address this problem.[7] This is the earliest extant Byzantine canon law collection, though he mentions an older *Synagoge in Sixty Titles* (thought to have been composed *c.* 535–545) that preceded his work and has not been preserved.[8] Unlike Justinian's codifications, canonical collections such as these were never officially promulgated by the church but spread by virtue of their popularity.

John Scholastikos' innovation in the *S50T* was to present the text of the canons divided into separate sections (titles) based on their subject matter, allowing the user to look up a particular topic and read all the canons that related to it. Since the Christian Roman emperors had begun to legislate on ecclesiastical matters too, there was also a need for reference guides to civil laws that affected the church. Thus, in the mid- to late sixth century, works such as John Scholastikos' *Collection in Eighty-Seven Chapters* and Athanasios of Emesa's *Epitome of Novels* were produced to meet this need.[9] The next logical step was to combine canon law and civil law collections in the same manuscript. At some point in the late sixth

[7] Text in Beneševič (1914): 1–155. This will henceforth be referred to as the *S50T*.

[8] *S50T* 5, l. 10.

[9] Texts in Pitra (1868): 385–405; Simon and Troianos (1989). The *Collection in Eighty-Seven Chapters* will henceforth be abbreviated to *C87C*. Other notable collections of church-themed civil law from this period include the *Collection in Twenty-Five Chapters* (*C25C*) and the *Tripartite Collection*: texts in Heimbach (1840): 145–201; Van der Wal and Stolte (1994).

century, an anonymous figure (or figures) combined the *S50T* with the *C87C* and other civil law texts, creating a collection known to modern scholarship as the *Nomocanon in Fifty Titles*.[10]

The *S50T* had a weakness of its own, however: if one wanted to find a specific canon (as opposed to a specific subject) then one had to know which title to consult. Moreover, most canons in the *S50T* only appear under a single title, making it inconvenient to find canons that touched on more than one subject. Another canonical compilation was composed around the end of the sixth century to address these issues: the *Syntagma* (ordered collection) *in Fourteen Titles*.[11] The *S14T* began with a systematic reference guide divided into fourteen titles dealing with different subjects in canon law; each title was itself divided into chapters. Unlike the *S50T*, this guide gave only simple textual references to canons under each subject, not the full texts. The full text of canons followed in chronological order after the guide. This was a neat solution, allowing a reader to learn which canons touched on which subjects—even if they related to more than one. At some point in the seventh century, the *S14T* was also expanded with references to civil law, creating the first recension of the *N14T*.[12]

The *N14T* is by far the best known of the Byzantine canon law collections and would go on to be hugely influential, though it went through several recensions to become the text we know today. An early sign of its influence came at the Council *in Trullo* of 691/2, one of the most important events in the formation of the medieval Byzantine canon law corpus.[13] The council's second canon established which councils and Patristic writings were to be considered authoritative sources of canon law; it is notable that the texts approved by the Trullan fathers correspond very closely to the contents of the *N14T*/*S14T*.[14] Another important collection, composed in the period between the *S14T* and the Council in *Trullo*, was the *Synopsis of Canons*. As its name suggests, this provided brief summaries of canons instead of full texts, though the original version of the work has been lost.

One irony of *Trullo*'s implicit endorsement of the *N14T* is that the council's own canons, along with those of the Second Council of Nicaea (787) and the *Protodeutera* ('First-Second') council (861), were not included in the collection.[15]

[10] Text in Voell and Justel (1661): 2.603–660. Henceforth *N50T*. As Wagschal (2015): 43–44 notes, it is not clear when or even if the Byzantines themselves began to call it by this name.

[11] Henceforth *S14T*. The original text no longer survives, but it is effectively preserved in the *N14T*.

[12] Text in RP 1.7–335. Note, though, that this represents the work in its post-eleventh-century form and is not an ideal guide to earlier recensions.

[13] The Council *in Trullo* is also known as the 'Quinisext' ('Fifth-Sixth') Council since it was thought to have completed the work of the Fifth and Sixth Ecumenical Councils (553 and 681/1 respectively) by issuing a collection of disciplinary canons. See Ohme (2012): 77–84.

[14] 'There is such a great correspondence between this list [in *Trullo* c. 2] and the content of the collection of canons belonging to the *Syntagma canonum* that it is certain that it derives from the version of this work known in 692': Van der Wal and Lokin (1985): 69.

[15] The origins of the name *Protodeutera* (which scholars sometimes refer to as *Primasecunda*) remain unclear. One possibility is that the council was held in two main sessions, as suggested by Milaš

This was rectified in the 880s with the creation of an expanded second recension that later Byzantines attributed to Patriarch Photios of Constantinople (858–867, 877–886).[16] The contents of this edition of the *N14T* effectively became the established corpus of Byzantine canon law; no new canons were added to their number after the ninth century.[17] The *Synopsis of Canons* was itself revised in the course of the tenth century in a recension that manuscripts ascribe to the famous hagiographer St Symeon Metaphrastes (also known as the Logothete or Magister).[18] Again, however, the manuscript tradition of the *Synopsis* in this early period is more complicated than such straightforward attributions would suggest, as Wagschal has discussed.[19]

The early textual history of canon law collections like the *N14T* and the *Synopsis of Canons* is unclear because very few manuscripts from before the twelfth century have been preserved. Volumes 2–3 of the *RHBR* list 198 Byzantine canon law collections from the ninth to the seventeenth centuries; only thirty-four (17 per cent) of these pre-date the twelfth and only four (2 per cent) pre-date the tenth.[20] As Bernard Stolte has noted, legal manuscripts are particularly vulnerable to being palimpsested or discarded since they would become out-of-date as new laws were passed and new codifications were published.[21] Consequently, most of our knowledge of the earlier manuscript tradition has to be extrapolated from codices of the eleventh century and later.

A third major recension of the *N14T* was produced in about 1090 by two Constantinopolitan functionaries, Theodore the *Bestes* and Michael the *Sebastos*.[22] This version incorporated references to the *Basilika*, a tenth-century codification of civil law that had become widely popular in the eleventh century.[23] The

(1905): 98. Contemporaries may also have thought of it as a 'second' First Ecumenical Council, as Stephanides (1947) proposed. Alternatively, it may have been a continuation of an earlier council of 859: Menevisoglou (1990): 448. See also Troianos (2012b): 147.

[16] It is unclear to what extent Photios was personally involved in creating this recension, if at all; he may have written the prologue. See Wagschal (2015): 47; Stolte (1997); Petrovič (1970): 31–41.

[17] The Patriarchate of Constantinople did continue to issue ecclesiastical rulings and decrees in subsequent centuries, but none of these were ever recognised as canons.

[18] See Høgel (2002): 86; Christophilopoulos (1949).

[19] On the rather complicated textual tradition of the *Synopsis of Canons*, see Wagschal (2015): 44–45.

[20] These numbers cannot be taken as perfectly accurate since the *RHBR* does not have a complete record and dating is frequently approximate. Nonetheless, they are a good general guide to what survives. The earliest surviving example of a nomocanon (not listed in the *RHBR*) is the so-called *Nomocanon Vaticanus*, a manuscript of the *N14T* copied in Palestine in the seventh or eighth century on a palimpsested manuscript of Strabo. It was later brought to Rossano in southern Italy where it was again palimpsested for a copy of the Pentateuch (see Stolte [2008]: 184–186; Broia and Faraggiana di Sarzana [1999]). The manuscript survives in the fragments Vatican City, Biblioteca Apostolica Vaticana, MSS Vat. gr. 2061A, 2306; Grottaferrata, Badia greca, MS gr. 849 (A.δ.XIII).

[21] Stolte (2008): 173–174; Stolte (2010): 522–523.

[22] Schminck (1998): 379–83; Wagschal (2015): 49, 289. For further discussion, see Chapter 6, 'Monastic Nomocanons II', C6.P31.

[23] On the *Basilika*, see Chitwood (2017): 32–35.

Synopsis of Canons also seems to have been updated around this time with the addition of several new summarised texts of the mid-eleventh century, such as Peter III of Antioch's letter to Domenicus of Grado and Leo of Ohrid's letter on *azyma*.[24] Both new recensions served as the basis for important canonical commentaries in the twelfth century: that of Alexios Aristenos on the *Synopsis* (*c.* 1130) and of Theodore Balsamon on the *N14T* (*c.* 1185).[25] Together with the legal scholar and monk John Zonaras (who produced a commentary on the corpus of canons around 1160), these became the most influential canonists in the Orthodox Christian world and their writings gained *de facto* official status in Byzantium. Their success is the main reason why so many earlier Byzantine canon law texts have been lost.

Content and Structure

Nomocanons were intended to provide readers with a practical reference guide to the corpus of Byzantine canon law. The central element of a nomocanon's textual content was, therefore, the text of the canons themselves. However, the full canonical corpus was rather long and could comprise 200–300 folia (depending on the format and *mise-en-page*), and sometimes 400 or more if the manuscript also included a commentary such as that of Zonaras or Balsamon. Because manuscripts were expensive and time-consuming to produce, abbreviated works such as the *Synopsis of Canons*, which could occupy as few as twenty to thirty manuscript folia, became popular. On occasion we find that some canons are omitted completely from nomocanons, though it can often be difficult to say whether this was done deliberately or was simply because the scribe copied from a defective prototype.

The main text of the canons was almost always preceded by some sort of index to help the reader locate desired passages more easily. In manuscripts of the *N14T*, this was provided by a rather long (usually about seventy folia) systematic section divided into fourteen titles that listed canons and civil laws by name and number under their relevant subject areas. The *S50T* began with a similar (if shorter and less detailed) index.[26] Many codices possess other introductory material such as a *pinax* (table of contents), introductory prologues such as those attributed to Photios or Balsamon, and timelines of church councils or narratives of church history.

[24] RP 4.408–409. For further discussion of the significance of the addition of these texts, see Chapter 4, 'The Byzantine Background', C4.S3.

[25] The two commentaries are published in RP 2–4, *passim*, and RP 1, *passim*, respectively.

[26] *S50T*, pp. 10–30.

The most varied section of a Byzantine nomocanon is its appendix. In addition to the corpus of canons, manuscripts frequently contain large quantities of supplementary writings ranging from treatises on canon law to collections of *erotapokriseis* (exegetical question and answer literature akin to modern 'frequently asked questions'), extracts from works of history, and even witty patristic aphorisms.[27] One common feature is the inclusion of episcopal *taktika* (known in Latin as *notitiae episcopatuum*): catalogues of bishoprics organised by hierarchical status.[28] These allowed readers to determine which suffragan bishops fell under which metropolitan's jurisdiction. Late antique *taktika* also detail patriarchal jurisdictions, which became unnecessary in manuscripts of the eighth to fifteenth centuries as the Byzantine Empire's political boundaries shrank to match the jurisdictional boundaries of the Patriarchate of Constantinople. *Taktika* are rarely present in surviving nomocanons from southern Italy, which almost all date to the period after Byzantine rule on the peninsula had ended.

The exact order of contents in a nomocanon can be quite varied, but a typical structure is as follows:

1. Front matter
2. Index of canons/civil laws
3. Collection of canons
4. Civil law appendix
5. Back matter

The eleventh-/twelfth-century manuscript Naples, Biblioteca nazionale 'Vittorio Emanuele III', MS II C 4 provides a good example of this structure (see Table 1.2).[29]

The manuscript begins with a series of useful reference texts including a glossary of Latin legal terms that remained prevalent in Byzantine civil law texts.[30] Next comes a short extract from the *Epitome of Book Eight of the Apostolic Constitutions* that purports to detail constitutions of the Apostles Peter and Paul on canon law. The front matter is completed with tables of canons from both the *S50T* and the *N14T*, an interesting example of the way that scribes could mix and match texts from different collections.

[27] On *erotapokriseis*, see Rey (2004); Papadoyannakis (2006).

[28] On episcopal *taktika*, see Darrouzès (1970a).

[29] Mioni (1992): 157 asserts that this is a thirteenth-century manuscript of southern Italy, but there are good reasons to be sceptical of this attribution. See Appendix 3, 'Uncertain and Disputed Manuscripts', CA3.S3.

[30] The corpus of Byzantine civil law was translated from Latin into Greek from the eighth to ninth centuries: see Chitwood (2017): 160–161. Nonetheless, many Latin technical terms remained untranslated (as they often do in modern legal texts), so glossaries such as the one in BN II C 4 were useful features.

Table 1.2. Sample Nomocanon Contents (BN II C 4)

1. Front Matter	**1^{r}**
1. Glossary of Latin legal terms	$1^{r/v}$
2. *Epitome of Book Eight of the Apostolic Constitutions* 22.2–28.1	1^{v}
3. *S50T*, prologue and table of canons	3^{v}
2. *N14T*	**4^{v}**
1. *N14T*, first and second prologues	4^{v}
2. Table of canons and *pinax*	7^{r}
3. Systematic index	13^{r}
4. Conciliar canons	64^{v}
5. Patristic canons	145^{r}
6. *Protodeutera* canons	220^{v}
3. Civil Law Appendix	**226^{v}**
1. *C87C*	226^{v}
2. *C25C* (excerpts)	248^{r}
3. Basil of Caesarea, c. 88–9	264^{v}
4. *Tripartite Collection*	267^{r}
4. Back Matter	**271^{v}**
1. Nikephoros the Confessor, *Brief Chronicle* (continued to 976)	271^{v}
2. List of patriarchs of Constantinople, Rome, Jerusalem, Alexandria, and Antioch (damaged)	276^{r}
3. Episcopal *taktika* of Constantinople	279^{r}
4. Hierokles, *Synekdemos*	282^{v}
5. List of the longest rivers and highest mountains in the world	288^{v}
6. List of sixteen peoples and their languages	289^{r}
7. Synod of Ephesus (431), *Deeds of the Bishops of Cyprus*	289^{v}
8. Gregory of Nazianzus, *Testament* (*des. mut.*)	292^{v}

These are then followed by the corpus of canons itself. Notice how the canons of the *Protodeutera* council of 861 appear at the end of the patristic canons, rather than where we would expect to find them at the end of the conciliar canons. This implies that BN II C 4 was based on a manuscript tradition that pre-dated the recognition of *Protodeutera*'s decrees as canonical. Once the *Protodeutera* canons became widely accepted, they were simply added onto the end of the *N14T* in one of BN II C 4's predecessor manuscripts. The scribe of BN II C 4 in turn went on to copy this unsophisticated recension into his own manuscript, even though he was by then working 200 or 300 years after *Protodeutera*.

The back matter provides the reader with further background information, not all of which was legally useful. The text of Nikephoros the Confessor's *Brief Chronicle* provides interesting historical detail on the patriarchates, while the episcopal *taktika* give an overview of jurisdiction within the Church of Constantinople. Hierokles' *Synekdemos* offers an archaic summary of the civil administrative units in the Byzantine world that serves as a parallel to the episcopal *taktika*. The utilitarian description of ecclesiastical and civil jurisdiction soon turns to geographical curiosity, however, as the manuscript compiler added lists of rivers, mountains, and ethno-linguistic groups. While it is tempting to view the inclusion of these lists as an ideological statement on the universality of the law, I suspect that he found these lists in his manuscript model and simply mistook them for a part of the *Synekdemos*.

The supplementary texts in the appendix of BN II C 4 clearly focus on ecclesiastical jurisdiction, but other nomocanons betray quite different interests. Some, for instance, contain lengthy extracts on the correct performance of the liturgy, while others concentrate on monastic discipline and spirituality. The character of a nomocanon's supplementary texts can tell us a lot about the context in which it was produced and the purpose for which it was used, as we shall see in the following chapters. Furthermore, later readers sometimes inserted new texts into old nomocanons; this can provide intriguing clues to the way in which a manuscript's use changed over the years.

These characteristics are all consequences of the non-legislative nature of Byzantine nomocanons. Since the Byzantine church did not promulgate any officially sanctioned canon law codification, copyists had some degree of freedom in choosing what to include in their manuscripts. Another important point to bear in mind is that scribes were limited by the contents of their prototypes; they could only copy from the manuscripts that they had available to them. If their prototype/s contained mistakes or strange choices of front and back matter then these usually ended up in the new manuscript as well. We therefore occasionally see Byzantine nomocanons with textual idiosyncrasies that can be traced back several centuries.

Materiality and Aesthetics

In the words of the art historian and codicologist Irmgard Hutter, 'The *raison d'être* of a Byzantine manuscript is its text, and if non-textual elements are introduced, these are subordinated to the text and to the principles governing the arrangement of the text on the page.'[31] Unlike Western medieval manuscripts, in which 'art is an autonomous partner of the text', the design and ornamentation of Byzantine manuscripts are intended to highlight their textual content.

Nomocanons conform to the typical trends of medieval Byzantine manuscript production. Most surviving examples from before the thirteenth century are made of parchment, though some are made from bombycine or 'Eastern Arabic' types of paper.[32] After the thirteenth century, Italian non-watermarked paper became more prevalent.[33] Sheets of parchment or paper were folded into quaternions—

[31] Hutter (1996): 4.

[32] On the use of paper in Byzantine manuscripts, see Kotzabassi (2017): 37; Freeman (2016); Irigoin (1977); Irigoin (1953). Paper is a much less durable material than parchment and is consequently less likely to survive, so it is possible that the Byzantines produced more paper manuscripts than we realise.

[33] On Italian non-watermarked paper, see Irigoin (1963).

booklets (quires) comprised of four sheets folded into eight folia—sewn together into a codex along the top and bottom edges of the spine. The original Byzantine binding of a nomocanon almost never survives; most were rebound by collectors in the early modern and modern periods. Scribes wrote most of the text in metal gall ink, the most widely used ink of medieval Europe.[34] This was a combination of iron sulphate and tannic acid extracted from tree galls that produced an ink with a dark brown hue (though the exact shade varies depending on the concentration of the ink).[35] When the copyist wanted to highlight a word or letter (e.g. in a title or at the start of a new paragraph) he would often use red vermillion ink made from minium, a pigment derived from lead.[36]

The overall appearance of a Byzantine manuscript is determined by its text, and the text in a nomocanon is nothing if not functional. They are 'books designed to be read and to transmit information', as Alessia Aletta has put it.[37] One important effect of the functional character of nomocanons that sets them apart from many Byzantine manuscripts is that their scripts often appear quite archaic. Byzantine handwriting became progressively more cursive—and thus harder to read—from the eleventh century on.[38] Reference books like nomocanons, however, should ideally be easy to read, so scribes tended to avoid 'modern' elements of cursive script such as ligatures and abbreviations that could be difficult to decipher. This can potentially lead scholars to make incorrect assumptions about the dating of the manuscripts.

Furthermore, nomocanons do not usually contain the sort of spectacular illuminations or elaborate miniatures that draw the attention of art historians.[39] As reference works of Byzantine canon law, they are primarily designed to help a person locate and digest technical information as efficiently as possible. Consequently, their main decorative elements consist of features to help the reader distinguish between texts and to identify where to start and stop reading: ornamental titles and coloured initial letters at the beginning of paragraphs, stylised headbands, lemmas, and so forth. We occasionally see intricate anthropomorphic and zoomorphic initial letters that resemble fish, human faces, arms outstretched in gestures of speech. Such features are not just present to look appealing but serve to make the manuscript's contents easier to read. The scribe who copied the main text was almost always also responsible for executing any

[34] For a detailed overview of metal gall ink in medieval Europe, see Zerdoun Bat-Yehouda (1983): 16–20, 143–170. See also Kotzabassi (2017): 48.

[35] Zerdoun Bat-Yehouda (1983): 305–308 provides a selection of medieval Greek recipes for metal gall inks.

[36] Thompson (1956): 100–102.

[37] Aletta (2013): 26.

[38] For an overview of Byzantine scripts and dating, see Kotzabassi (2017): 44–47; see also Easterling (2001): 54–55; Mioni (1973): 59–72.

[39] The one exception that proves the rule is Paris, Bibliothèque nationale de France, MS suppl. gr. 1085. This nomocanon (of uncertain provenance and dating) contains several decorative miniatures illustrating the great ecumenical councils. See Aletta (2009); Aletta (2013): 18–19, 25. I am not aware of any comparable manuscript.

decorative elements, as we see from the fact that the same pens and inks tended to be used for both.[40]

Nomocanons come in a range of different aesthetic qualities, but they generally fall into two broad categories: small, utilitarian books on the one hand; and large, decorative items on the other. They may have been manuscripts with a functional purpose, but that does not mean that they were always unadorned. Besides their practical use, nomocanons have a strong symbolic value as authoritative sources of law. Consequently, many wealthy institutions such as large monasteries and important episcopal sees owned visually impressive nomocanons that almost rise to the level of display items. As with most Byzantine manuscripts, there is a very strong correlation between the size of a nomocanon, the quality of parchment used, and its level of ornamentation: better parchment was obviously more expensive and could be used to make larger manuscript folia that would serve as a more appealing canvas for artistic flair. It is thus a general rule that larger nomocanons are better decorated than smaller ones.

Hutter outlined two general types of ornamental scheme in Byzantine manuscripts: the 'hierarchical' and the 'paratactic'.[41] In a hierarchical scheme, the majority (or even the entirety) of a manuscript's decoration is concentrated in the opening folia. In a paratactic scheme, by contrast, major ornamental elements such as title frames and headbands are repeated consistently throughout the manuscript. Hutter noticed that the scribe's choice of hierarchical or paratactic schemes often coincides closely with the quality of parchment used: less expensive parchment was more likely to be decorated in a hierarchical fashion, while paratactic schemes are characteristic of more expensive parchment.

Nomocanons are no exception to this rule: the smallest, least-adorned manuscripts usually follow a hierarchical scheme while the largest and most decorative ones tend to be paratactic. It is worth noting that the ornamentation at the beginning of hierarchical manuscripts can often still be quite elaborate. This shows that the manuscripts were not intended to be entirely utilitarian; the scribes clearly wanted to give them an appearance of grandeur befitting the books' status as sources of canon law. However, it was a cost-effective appearance that did not last beyond the opening folia.

There are several other interesting visual features in nomocanons besides decorative elements. Many canon law texts, especially the systematic reference guide in the *N14T*, had scholia that appear consistently across manuscripts and were evidently considered integral to the collection.[42] These are often simple finding aids in the margin to help the reader locate texts more quickly; alongside *N14T* 1.3, for instance, manuscripts usually bear a marginal note that reads,

[40] Cf. Madigan (1987). [41] Hutter (1996): 10–11.

[42] For an overview of types of Byzantine canonical scholia, see recently Wagschal (2019): 26–30.

'When custom has the force of law and when it does not.'[43] Other integral marginalia include diagrams that explain particular passages visually, such as a depiction of the minimum age of ordination to different ranks (see Figure 1.1.).

Diagrams such as this are absent from printed editions of the *N14T* but were an essential part of the experience of reading a Byzantine nomocanonical manuscript.

Nomocanons usually also contain a range of original marginalia left by the scribe/s and by later readers. These are often little more than simple notes, cross-references, and explanations, but they can reveal a lot about who used a manuscript and what subjects interested them. Some readers left asterisks or drawings of hands with fingers pointing at sections of text, while others wrote short marginal summaries of canons that they found interesting.[44] This can give us a good general idea of who used a manuscript. For example, one reader of the thirteenth-century codex London, British Library, MS Egerton 2707 systematically annotated canons relating to clerical discipline, liturgical practice, and judicial procedure in episcopal courts, which would imply that the manuscript probably belonged to a bishop. Occasionally we find marginalia that are completely unrelated to canon law, as in the case of the tenth-century nomocanon Laud gr. 39. At some point in the fourteenth century, one of the manuscript's owners left a melodramatic account of an arduous journey from the Peloponnesian town of Mystras to Corinth, during which he suffered various 'torments' at the hands of unnamed 'enemies'.[45]

All these factors played a role in a medieval reader's experience of reading a Byzantine canon law collection, yet we encounter none of them when we read modern critical editions of the texts. Who created a manuscript and how did they

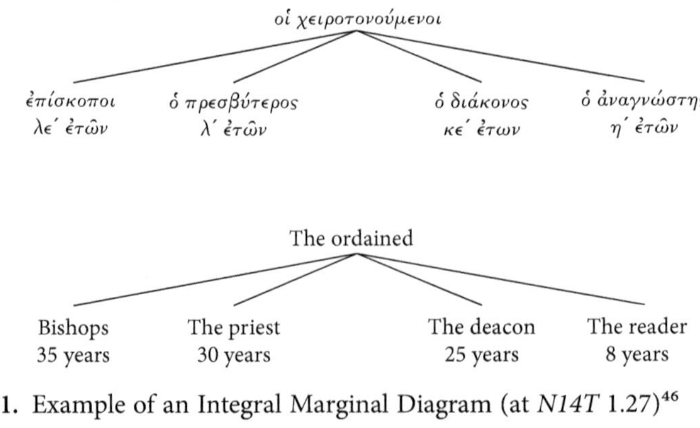

Figure 1.1. Example of an Integral Marginal Diagram (at *N14T* 1.27)[46]

[43] 'ποτε τὸ ἔθος ὡς νόμος ἰσχύει καὶ ποτε οὔ': see e.g. Oxford, Bodleian Library, MS Laud gr. 39, fol. 25r. The text of *N14T* 1.3 can be found in RP 1.38.

[44] Cf. Wagschal (2019): 39.

[45] Laud gr. 39, fol. 13r. Text partially reproduced in Zachariä von Lingenthal (1837): 323.

[46] See e.g. Laud gr. 39, fol. 28v. Main text in RP 1.65–66.

craft it? What impression did it make in the minds of people who used it (or simply saw it from a distance)? Who owned it and how well did they take care of it? By studying nomocanons as material artefacts in this way and not just as sources for textual editions, we can use them as evidence for the social, religious, and cultural contexts in which they were produced.[47]

Conclusion

The Byzantine nomocanon is much more than a printed legal text in a modern scholarly publication; it is a type of physical book that developed gradually over the centuries and was used for practical purposes in the Byzantine church. As such, we should not just study the texts of the *N14T* or the *N50T* as abstract intellectual history (although this is an important endeavour in its own right). We should also study how medieval readers encountered them in their lived experiences. How did they present and read their canon law texts, and what does this say about their legal and religious culture? What does it say about the Greek Christians of medieval Italy that they continued to use this type of Byzantine legal manuscript for several centuries after they became subjects of the Roman church? These are the questions that we shall seek to answer in the following chapters.

[47] This is an approach that has begun to be employed to great effect by art historians in the study of Byzantine illustrated manuscripts; see Kalavrezou and Tomaselli (2017): 33–34.

2

Greek Christianity in Medieval Italy

The Greek church went from being the dominant Christian religious organisation in southern Italy to one of the last cultural pillars of an ethnic minority over the course of the Middle Ages. The Greek rite in Italy developed and grew under the direction of the Byzantine Empire; once the Normans had conquered the peninsula in the eleventh century, it was through their religious institutions that the Italo-Greeks maintained their connection to Byzantine culture. That they were able to maintain their distinctive religious institutions for several centuries after the end of Byzantine rule is itself impressive and provides important background context to the study of their religious law.

Unfortunately, there is no extended historical narrative of Greek-rite Christianity in medieval Italy available in the English language, though the chapter 'Latins, Greeks and Non-Christians' in Graham Loud's *The Latin Church in Norman Italy* provides an excellent starting point.[1] Annick Peters-Custot's impressive work on *Les grecs de l'Italie méridionale post-byzantine* is by far the most comprehensive treatment of the history of the medieval Italo-Greeks. While she does not focus specifically on the church, it naturally plays a major role in her analysis and her work will be a frequent point of reference here.[2] There are many other prominent scholars such as Vera von Falkenhausen, Hubert Houben, Peter Herde, and others who have published extensively on aspects of this subject, although their work is often spread across a wide range of books and journals that can be inaccessible to Anglophone readers.

This chapter does not seek to provide a complete historical narrative of medieval southern Italian history, nor does it make any especial claims to originality. Rather, it aims to offer a brief narrative overview of the Greek church in medieval Italy and explain how its institutions could survive for as long as they did. This will give the necessary context within which the Italo-Greek nomocanons in this study can be better understood. In addition to describing the Greek church in southern Italy itself, it will also address relevant political, religious, and cultural events elsewhere in the Mediterranean world.

[1] Loud (2007): 494–524. [2] Peters-Custot (2009a).

Byzantine Religious Law in Medieval Italy. James Morton, Oxford University Press (2021). © James Morton.
DOI: 10.1093/oso/9780198861140.003.0003

Byzantine Italy in Transformation (c. 700–1000)

The reign of the emperor Justinian I saw the Byzantine Empire reconquer Italy from the Ostrogothic kingdom and place it under the provincial rule of the Exarchate of Ravenna. By the 600s, however, a wave of Lombard migration from northern and central Europe had begun the steady erosion of Byzantine authority on the peninsula. The Exarchate of Ravenna ultimately succumbed to Lombard conquest in 751, leaving only Sicily and a few mainland enclaves in the south under Constantinople's rule. In the meantime, the Byzantine Empire was largely powerless to respond as it faced major invasions from Slavic tribes in the Balkans and Islamic Arabs in the Middle East. By the end of the eighth century, Byzantium had been transformed from one of Eurasia's greatest superpowers to a mid-tier regional state based in Anatolia and Greece. Even the Mediterranean islands were threatened, as Crete and Sicily were invaded in the 820s, though the latter held out much longer than the former. Nonetheless, Syracuse eventually fell to the Muslim Aghlabids of Tunisia in 878, effectively ending Byzantine rule over the island permanently.

Severe military losses were compounded by the waves of internal political turmoil that inevitably accompanied them. The eighth and ninth centuries in Byzantine history are best known as the period of Iconoclasm (726–787, 814–842), a theological dispute over image veneration that masked an underlying struggle for political power in the diminished state.[3] The introduction of Iconoclasm in the early eighth century by Emperor Leo III the Isaurian (*r.* 717–741) also produced a rift between Byzantium and the Roman papacy that would never be fully healed. In response to papal condemnation of Iconoclasm, Leo III transferred southern Italy from the ecclesiastical jurisdiction of the church of Rome to that of Constantinople, where it remained until the Norman conquest of the eleventh century.[4] The papacy would never forgive this slight and took the opportunity presented by the Lombard conquest of Ravenna to re-align itself politically with the emerging Carolingian Empire to the north of the Alps. This culminated in Pope Leo III's (*r.* 795–816) coronation of Charlemagne (*r.* 768–814) as emperor in Rome on Christmas Day in the year 800.

The Byzantine Empire's fortunes eventually began to change for the better in the mid-ninth century. A series of military victories in the Balkans and Anatolia were accompanied by important legal and administrative reforms that allowed the empire to stabilise its affairs and turn its attention to reconquering lost territory. The seizure of power by the emperor Basil I the Macedonian (*r.* 867–886) was a significant turning point in this process. One should not accept the Macedonian dynasty's propaganda against its predecessors uncritically, of course; recent work

[3] See esp. Brubaker and Haldon (2011): 772–782.

[4] See Anastos (1957).

by scholars such as Michael Humphreys has highlighted the significance of reforms undertaken by the Isaurian emperors in the eighth century and done much to rehabilitate our image of that era.[5] That said, the reigns of Basil I and his successors were some of the most important in shaping the legal and religious culture of medieval Byzantium, and, by extension, that of the Greek church in southern Italy.

As we saw in Chapter 1, the late ninth century was the period in which Byzantine canon law effectively took on its final shape.[6] The last conciliar decrees to enter the Byzantine corpus of canons were issued at the *Protodeutera* council of Constantinople in 861.[7] In 883, the so-called 'Photian' recension of the *N14T* was published; its contents would define the Byzantine corpus of canons for the rest of the empire's history. A decade or so later (the exact date is disputed), Basil I's son Leo VI 'the Wise' (*r.* 886–912) had the Justinianic corpus of civil law re-compiled, translated into Greek, and promulgated in the collection that later came to be known as the *Basilika*.[8] Just as the Photian *N14T* became the foundational text of medieval Byzantine canon law, so the *Basilika* would be foundational for the empire's civil law.

These years were also a formative time for Byzantine southern Italy. Parts of Apulia had been under Islamic rule in the years 841–871 and subsequently fell under Lombard control. The Byzantines defeated the Aghlabids at sea in the Battle of Milazzo in 880 and, in 885/6, an army reinforced with troops from the empire's eastern frontier secured Calabria and reconquered much of Apulia. By 891, the Byzantines had largely stabilised their position in southern Italy and reorganised it into the theme (military province) of 'Longobardia', named after the Greek term for the Lombards. During the process of reconquest, Basil I is said to have settled Calabria and the Salento peninsula with Greek-speakers: Gallipoli was repopulated by Greeks from Heraclea Pontica in Asia Minor, for example, while soldiers from the Byzantine army were settled in Calabria.[9] However, these population transfers probably did not 'Hellenise' southern Italy for the first time, but likely reinforced already existing Graecophone communities there.[10] Alongside the reorganisation of civil administration, the Byzantines also redrew the region's ecclesiastical map, promoting the Calabrian archdioceses of Reggio

[5] Humphreys (2015). See also Simon (1994): 12–15.

[6] See Chapter 1, 'Introducing the Byzantine Nomocanon', C1.P11.

[7] Text in *RP* 2.647–704.

[8] Schminck (1989): 92–94 dates the collection to 888. Lokin (1994): 71 prefers to date it to *c.* 900. On the emergence of the name *Basilika* in the eleventh century, see Schminck (1986): 27–32.

[9] See Falkenhausen (1978): 25–27. On the Byzantine practice of population transfers more generally, see Charanis (1961b): 146. The emperor Nikephoros II Phokas (*r.* 963–969) would similarly settle troops on the reconquered island of Crete in 961: see Tsougarakis (1988): 59–74.

[10] Many of the Greek settlers in the Salento peninsula migrated there from Calabria in the tenth century: Martin (1985); Peters-Custot (2006): 574–575. See also Charanis (1946): 75–76.

and S. Severina to metropolitan status in 886 and placing them at the head of suffragan dioceses throughout southern Italy.[11]

Despite the Byzantines' success in reconquering Apulia and Calabria in the late ninth century, the territories were never completely safe from attack. The city of Reggio, for instance, was sacked at least eight times over the course of the tenth century by Muslim raids from Sicily and was under complete Islamic control from 952 to 956, when the cathedral was temporarily transformed into a mosque.[12] The late tenth century also saw a major threat to Byzantine Italy from a renewed alliance between the papacy and the Holy Roman Empire. Following Otto I's (*r.* 962–973) annexation of the Lombard Kingdom of Italy in 961 and imperial coronation the following year by Pope John XII (*r.* 955–964), he aimed to extend his conquests in the south. Although Otto and his son Otto II (*r.* 973–983) were initially successful, the Byzantines benefitted from an unexpected stroke of luck. In 982, Otto II's army invaded Calabria, where it was met by a Muslim invasion force led by the Sicilian Emir Abu al-Qasim at the Battle of Stilo. While the Sicilians routed the German army, Abu al-Qasim himself was killed in combat and his troops were left leaderless. The ensuing lull allowed the Byzantine governor Kalokyros Delphinas to recover lost territory and expand further into northern Apulia in 983.

This period was also important for the creation of the *katepanikion* (catepanate) of Italy, first mentioned in a document of 970.[13] This organised the Byzantine provinces in the region into a single administrative unit under a military viceroy sent from Constantinople, the *katepano* (meaning 'uppermost' in Greek). In principle, the *katepanikion* would have allowed for more efficient coordination of Byzantine military and civil government in southern Italy, as the region's thematic armies and tax revenue were coordinated under a single commander.

Around the same time, in 967/8, the Archdiocese of Otranto was raised to the rank of metropolis, providing Apulia with its first major Byzantine ecclesiastical centre.[14] The Lombard emissary Liudprand of Cremona, who visited Constantinople in 968, claims that the Byzantines attempted to outlaw the Latin liturgical rite in southern Italy at the time, though we may question whether this was seriously attempted.[15] The Byzantine elevation of Otranto did provoke a response from Pope John XIII (*r.* 965–972), however, who elevated the Latin see of Benevento to archiepiscopal status over Apulia in the following year. This sparked a contest between Constantinople and Rome to promote bishops over

[11] See Martin (2016): 12–14.
[12] See Russo (1982): 1.176–180.
[13] Trinchera (1865): 5–6 (no. 7). See Falkenhausen (1978): 86.
[14] Falkenhausen (1978): 51.
[15] As Henry Mayr-Harting has observed, Liudprand wrote this account as propaganda to win the southern Italian Lombards over to the Ottonians, so his claims deserve some scepticism: Mayr-Harting (2001): 545–546. The Byzantines evidently did not eradicate the Latin liturgy in southern Italy, so it may have just been a threat (if it happened at all).

each other's territories in an effort to win the loyalties of the Latin hierarchy in southern Italy.[16]

Although the Greek church hierarchy in Byzantine Italy was closely associated with the empire's provincial government, Greek Christianity also extended beyond the empire's borders. Sources for Christianity in Muslim Sicily are scarce, but it is evident that the Greek rite survived there throughout the period of Islamic rule. In the contemporary historian Geoffrey Malaterra's account of the Norman conquest of Palermo in 1072, he describes how the Normans entered the city and found an archbishop named Nikodemos who, 'though a timid man of the Greek race, had been celebrating the Christian religion as best he could in the poor church of St Kyriakos'.[17] Malaterra also refers to local Sicilian Christians at another point in his work simply as 'Greeks'.[18] While there seems to have been little or no formal connection between Constantinople and the Sicilian church after the fall of Syracuse in 878, Greek-rite churches and communities continued to exist on the island nonetheless.[19]

By far the best-recorded aspect of Greek Christianity in tenth-century southern Italy was its monastic life, tales of which have been handed down to us in hagiographical biographies of saintly founders written by members of their communities. The region had inherited a strong tradition of monasticism from the Near East in the early Middle Ages as Chalcedonian monks fled from the Islamic conquests, retreating first to North Africa and then to Sicily.[20] When Sicily too was lost in the ninth century, many monks were again driven to migrate to Byzantine territory on the Italian mainland where they founded new monastic communities.[21] Their historic connection to Near Eastern monasticism often shows in their monasteries' manuscript production, as we shall see in later chapters.

Not only did Italo-Greek monks maintain strong cultural links with the eastern Mediterranean, but they also built ties with the Western Christian world. The antagonism between the Latin and Greek churches in Italy largely existed at the level of high politics; relations at the local level, by contrast, were much more cordial.[22] Valerie Ramseyer has written of the presence of Greek monks and clergy in the Principality of Salerno, for instance, where several Italo-Greek monasteries were supported by the Lombard nobility.[23] Rome itself became home to a mixed

[16] Loud (2007): 32–35; Mor (1951).

[17] '*in paupere ecclesia sancti Cyriaci – quamvis timidus et natione graecus – cultum Christianae religionis pro posse exequebatur*': Malaterra, *De rebus gestis* 2.45.

[18] Malaterra, *De rebus gestis* 2.29.

[19] For further discussion of Greek Christianity in Muslim Sicily, see Metcalfe (2003): 13–21, 22–24; Metcalfe (2019): 108–112.

[20] See Ekonomou (2007): 202–203.

[21] Vitolo (1996): 101.

[22] See esp. Peters-Custot (2013).

[23] Ramseyer (2006): 84–86. For further discussion of Italo-Greeks in Salerno, see Peters-Custot (2009b).

Graeco-Latin monastery dedicated to SS Alexios and Boniface founded in 977 by Pope Benedict VII (*r.* 974–983), where communities of Byzantine- and Benedictine-rite monks lived together under the *hegoumenos* Sergios, a former archbishop of Damascus in Syria.[24]

The most famous encounter between Greek and Latin monasticism in this period, though, is that of St Neilos the Younger of Rossano (*c.* 910–1005) with the Benedictines of Montecassino. Neilos had founded the monastery of St Adrian of Rossano in 955 but, around 980, travelled to Campania to escape the invasion of the Sicilian emir Abu al-Qasim. There he was welcomed by the monks of Montecassino and established a monastery at Valleluce, where he composed a Greek hymn to St Benedict.[25] Shortly before his death in 1004, Neilos was invited by Count Gregory of Tusculum to found a monastery dedicated to the *Theotokos* (the Virgin Mary) at Grottaferrata near Rome. With monks predominantly drawn from Calabria, Grottaferrata would become a major centre of the Greek rite in Italy, which it remains to this day under the Roman Catholic Church.[26]

Italo-Greek monks also left their mark on the most famous centre of Byzantine monasticism: Mount Athos. A monastery known as '*tou Sikelou*' ('of the Sicilian') was established on the Holy Mountain in the 980s under the leadership of a certain *hegoumenos* Phantinos, who probably took his name from St Phantinos the Elder (294–336) of Tauriana in Calabria.[27] It was not just Italo-Greeks who came to Athos in this period, which was also home to a Benedictine community of monks from Amalfi.[28] Little is known about the history of these foundations, although they both survived until at least the twelfth century: the Sicilian monastery is last mentioned in a document of 1108, while S. Maria of the Amalfitans appears for the final time in a chrysobull of Alexios III in 1198.[29]

The Norman Conquest (*c.* 1000–1098)

In the meantime, the Byzantine Empire was once more entering a period of aggressive reconquest under the leadership of Basil II 'the Bulgar-Slayer' (*r.* 976–1025). The empire's armies were preoccupied with fighting in the Balkans and the Near East, leaving commanders in southern Italy to manage their affairs as best they could. The greatest threat to Byzantine rule in the region

[24] McNulty and Hamilton (1963): 188–189; Hamilton (1965). For a broader discussion of Greek monasticism in early medieval Rome, see Sansterre (1983).

[25] McNulty and Hamilton (1963): 185–186; Rousseau (1973): 1116–1128.

[26] For an overview of the history of Grottaferrata, see Parenti (2005): 165–186; Petrovič Rimljanin (2005); Falkenhausen (2014).

[27] Oikonomides et al. (1985): 151 l. 3 (a. 985). See also Pertusi (1964): 242–243. On St Phantinos the Elder, see Minuto (2003).

[28] Pertusi (1964): 227–237, 251.

[29] Millet et al. (1937): 299 l. 68; Kravari et al. (1998): 108 ll. 30, 55.

came from the Lombard population of recently conquered areas of northern Apulia. In 1009, the inhabitants of Bari rebelled under the leadership of a Lombard noble named Melus, who may have been of Armenian descent.[30] His rebellion was suppressed in 1011, but he tried again in 1016, this time with outside help. According to William of Apulia, Melus encountered a group of Norman pilgrims led by Rainulf Drengot at the shrine of the Archangel Michael on Monte Gargano and persuaded them to help in his rebellion.[31] This marks the first secure appearance of the Normans in southern Italian history.

Unfortunately for Melus, Basil II's victory over the Bulgarians at the Battle of Kleidion in 1014 freed up Byzantine forces for deployment in Italy. The *katepano* Basil Boioannes was able to draw on a large force of seasoned troops who routed Melus' army at the Battle of Cannae in 1018. Boioannes followed this victory by annexing much of northern Apulia and the Abruzzo, where he founded several new fortified settlements to secure Byzantine rule.[32] Indeed, he made such a large impact on the region's human geography that it came to be known as the 'Capitanata', a corruption of the Greek work *katepano*. Nonetheless, his success roused the opposition of the papacy and the Holy Roman Empire once again: in 1022, Henry II (*r.* 1002–1024) invaded the Capitanata at the urging of Pope Benedict VIII (*r.* 1012–1024), but his troops were unable to capture Boioannes' new fortified towns.

Byzantine Italy had withstood Henry's invasion, but it was still vulnerable to attack. Having settled affairs in Bulgaria and the Middle East for the time being, Basil II decided that it was time to prepare the reconquest of Sicily in order to secure the *katepanikion*'s western flank. In addition to Basil's military build-up, it is interesting to note a story in the chronicle of the Cluniac monk Rodulf Glaber that gives an indication of his diplomatic preparations. Rodulf reports that, in 1024, Patriarch Alexios Stoudites of Constantinople wrote to Pope John XIX (*r.* 1024–1032) with a proposal: the patriarch of Constantinople would be considered ecumenical ('universal') in his own sphere, while the pope would be considered ecumenical in the rest of the world.[33] This was presumably part of an attempt by Basil to ensure peace on the Italian mainland while his armies fought in Sicily. In Rodulf's telling, the pope almost agreed to the proposal but was dissuaded by ferocious lobbying from the monks of Cluny. Instead, John XIX

[30] His name may be derived from the Armenian 'Mleh'. See Martin (1993): 518–520; Charanis (1961a): 213, 217, 227.

[31] William of Apulia, *La Geste* 1.11–57. Amatus of Montecassino, *Ystoire de li normant* 1.17 gives an alternative account of a group of Norman pilgrims travelling to Jerusalem who helped defend Salerno from a Muslim attack in 999.

[32] Oldfield (2005): 330–333. For a recent discussion of the Byzantine presence in the area, see Falkenhausen (2016).

[33] '*Circa annum igitur Domini millesimum vicesimum quartum, Constantinopolitanus presul cum suo principe Basilio alii que nonnulli Grecorum consilium iniere quatinus cum consensu Romani pontificis liceret ecclesiam Constantinopolitanam in suo orbe, sicuti Roma in universo, universalem dici et haberi*': Rodulf Glaber, *Historiarum libri quinque* 4.1.

returned to the old strategy of meddling in the *katepanikion*'s ecclesiastical hierarchy, confirming the archiepiscopal status of the Latin see of Bari (the capital of Byzantine Italy!) and assigning it twelve suffragan dioceses in 1025.

Meanwhile, Basil II's death in the same year led to the invasion being delayed, though not forgotten. In 1038, under the emperor Michael IV the Paphlagonian (*r.* 1034–1041), a large Byzantine army under the general George Maniakes landed in Sicily. This force employed a multi-ethnic group of professional mercenaries from across Europe that notably included the Norman leader William 'Iron Arm' de Hauteville, the elder half-brother of Robert Guiscard, and the future Norwegian king Harald Hardrada.[34] Despite meeting initial success, the expedition was cut short when political intrigue led the emperor to recall Maniakes to Constantinople.

The Norman soldiers found further employment under the Lombard Argyrus, son of Melus of Bari, who began another rebellion against Byzantine rule. However, he soon defected to the Byzantines and was appointed *katepano* over their Italian provinces, leaving himself the rather absurd task of quelling the Normans that he himself had roused to war. The Normans invaded Calabria for the first time in 1044 but were defeated by Argyrus in the following year. Byzantine Italy enjoyed roughly a decade of relative peace and stability that allowed the Italo-Greek church to prosper, if not flourish. The clearest evidence for this comes from the *brebion* (inventory) of the cathedral of Reggio, a document of *c.* 1050 on a seven-metre parchment roll preserving a section of accounts on the taxation of mulberry trees (whose leaves were valuable fodder for silkworms).[35] The document's editor, André Guillou, estimated that the 8,107 mulberry trees accounted for in the *brebion* would have brought in approximately 521 gold *nomismata* or 2,085 gold *taris* per year, a considerable sum. Moreover, the roll is incomplete, and so the actual figure was probably higher.[36]

It is in this period that we have the first surviving evidence for the important Greek monastery of SS Elias and Anastasios of Carbone in Lucania. An act of donation of 1056 records a gift of land by a certain Leopardus and his daughter Helen 'to the *kathegoumenos* Luke of Carbone, to have in possession, to sell or to give away according to the power and the rights received from us'.[37] Documents from the early eleventh century mention several (probably quite small) monastic communities in the vicinity of Carbone that may have had some sort of connection with SS Elias and Anastasios. In a document of 1059, Luke of Carbone places himself in a lineage of monastic disciples going back to St Luke of Armento

[34] Ciggaar (1996): 105, 116–118. [35] Text in Guillou (1974a).

[36] Guillou (1974a): 2–16, 154.

[37] '*αφηεροσα αυ*^{τ}(*^{η}*) *σην τη εμη θυγατερα ελενη εις τω πασεπτω ναων το αγιου μρ αναστασηου* [*καὶ*] *εις των καθηγου*^{μ}(*^{ενου}*) *κ*^{θ} *λουκαν του καρβουνη. του εχην αυτα ἐξουσαν, πουλην χαρηζην εις το κυρος* [*καὶ*] *την αυθεντηαν παρ ιμον ηληφος* [*sic*]': Robinson (1929): 164–165 (no. 6).

(d. 984), a famous Italo-Greek saint of the tenth century.[38] Interestingly, it seems that the various monasteries of Lucania were effectively treated as family possessions by their founders, a practice that violated both Byzantine and Western canon law.[39] Not only did Luke of Carbone will his monastery to his kinsman Blasios, but the first two documents of Carbone's cartulary (from 1007 and 1041 respectively) record the *hegoumenoi* of two other monasteries appointing their own brothers as their successors.[40]

Ultimately, though, the wealth of such ecclesiastical foundations proved a tempting target for predatory Norman warlords, who began to raid both Latin and Greek churches alike. In a surviving manuscript colophon of 1055/6, an Italo-Greek priest of Rossano named Theodore denounced the Normans for their attacks as 'the race of atheist Franks'.[41] The threat was even great enough to bring the Byzantines, papacy, and Holy Roman Empire together in a temporary alliance, but this ended in disaster with a Norman victory at the Battle of Civitate in 1053. Pope Leo IX (*r.* 1049–1054) was captured by the Norman Hautevilles and held hostage in Benevento; it is in this context that we must view the notorious events of the following year in Byzantine-papal relations.

While the Byzantine emperor Constantine IX Monomachos (*r.* 1042–1055) and the *katepano* Argyrus had been trying to build an alliance with the papacy against the Normans, the Patriarch of Constantinople Michael Keroularios was pursuing a policy of ecclesiastical uniformity in the empire. Following Byzantine successes in Syria and Armenia in the tenth and eleventh centuries, a large body of non-Chalcedonian Christians had become imperial subjects. Not only did they reject the Chalcedonian patriarch of Constantinople, but they had differing liturgical practices including the use of unleavened bread (*azyma*) in the Eucharist. The Constantinopolitan church viewed this as a dangerous Judaising practice that challenged its authority. It was a practice that was also shared by the Latin Christians of Western Europe, and early eleventh-century Byzantine expansion in southern Italy had brought this to Constantinople's attention.[42]

In 1052, the Byzantine archbishop Leo of Ohrid wrote a letter to the Greek archbishop John of Trani in Apulia in which he condemned the Latin use of *azyma* in the Eucharist and fasting on Saturdays, both of which were seen as correct practice in the West. Leo's language is that of ecclesiastical reform; he tells John to 'send [this letter] to the archpriests of the bishops of the thrones of Italy,

[38] Robinson (1929): 50–54 (no. 7).

[39] It contravenes II Nicaea c. 12 and *Prot.* c. 1, 6.

[40] This seems to have been a widespread phenomenon throughout Byzantine Italy. For further examples, see Guillou (1970).

[41] '. . . *ἔθνως τῶν ἀθέων φράγκων* . . .': Vatican City, Biblioteca Apostolica Vaticana, MS Vat. gr. 2082, fol. 162^r. Text reproduced in Batiffol (1891): 154. See Lucà (1985): 135 n. 202; Lucà (1993): 16. The term 'Frank' denotes the Normans in particular (as was common in eleventh-century Byzantine usage) and not 'French' or 'Westerners' more generally.

[42] See Chapter 4, 'The Byzantine Background', C4.P36–C4.P38, and Kolbaba (2013): 55–56.

and make them swear that everything will be corrected . . .'[43] The Roman papacy was not pleased that a Byzantine bishop was trying to reform practices that the Western church thought were correct, especially in a territory over which the popes believed they had rightful jurisdiction. This in turn led to the infamous legation of Cardinal Humbert of Silva Candida to Constantinople in 1054 and the mutual bulls of excommunication.

There is no need to dwell at length on the 'schism' of 1054 here, which has been well-covered elsewhere.[44] It is worthwhile to say a few words about its long-term significance, however. First, it was not technically a schism: the excommunications of Michael Keroularios and Cardinal Humbert were personal in nature and did not extend to the rest of their respective churches. Second, Pope Leo died soon after Humbert arrived in Constantinople, meaning that his actions had no legal force. Third, the incident was quickly forgotten. In 1089, Pope Urban II and the emperor Alexios I entered into correspondence on relations between Rome and Constantinople and it is striking that their letters make no reference whatsoever to 1054.[45] On the contrary, Alexios claims that 'it was not by a synodal decision or judgment that the Church of Rome was cut off from our communion, but by mistake, it would seem . . .'[46] There is undoubtedly a degree of diplomatic phrasing here, but the absence of any mention of 1054 reinforces the sense that its importance was blown out of proportion by later writers.[47] Meanwhile, not a single contemporary Latin or Greek text from southern Italy even mentions the 'schism' of 1054.

Despite the crushing defeat at Civitate, the papacy soon realised that it could harness the Norman conquests as an opportunity to regain control over southern Italy.[48] At the Council of Melfi in 1059, Pope Nicholas II (*r.* 1059–1061) invested the Norman Robert 'Guiscard' de Hauteville as Duke of Apulia, Calabria, and Sicily, granting him these lands to rule as a papal vassal. First, though, he had to conquer them from the Byzantines and the Islamic emirate of Sicily. Guiscard captured Calabria rapidly, seizing Reggio by the end of 1060, and expanded into Apulia and Sicily in the decade that followed. The Byzantines were preoccupied

[43] '*καὶ ἀπόστελλε τοῖς ἀρχιερεῦσι τῶν ἐπισκόπων τῶν κατὰ τὴν Ἰταλίαν θρόνων, καὶ ὅρκιζε αὐτοὺς διορθώσασθαι ἅπαντας . . .*': *PG* 120.836–844, at 844.

[44] For a thorough study of the 'schism' of 1054, see Bayer (2004).

[45] Text in Holtzmann (1928): 60–64 (nos. 2–3).

[46] '*οὐδὲ γὰρ ἀπὸ κρίσεως συνοδικῆς καὶ διαγνώσεως τὴν ἐκκλησίαν τῆς Ῥώμης ἀπορραγῆναι τῆς πρὸς ἡμᾶς κοινωνίας, ἀλλ' ἀσυντηρήτως, ὡς ἔοικεν, τὸ τοῦ πάπα μὴ φέρεσθαι ὄνομα*': Holtzmann (1928): 60 (no. 2).

[47] In the words of Brett Whalen, 'There are no signs that contemporaries believed a lasting schism had begun in 1054,' though Whalen does note that the event left 'a considerable and lasting impression' on Western churchmen (Whalen [2007]: 17). On the (lack of) contemporary significance of the 'schism' of 1054, see also Kaplan (1995); Siecienski (2017): 240–281; Neocleous (2019): 239. On Byzantine views of 1054, see Cheynet (2007): 305–311. Later Byzantines appear to have ascribed the breakdown in relations between Rome and Constantinople to a theological dispute during the Patriarchate of Sergios II (1001–1019): see Michel (1925): 20–24.

[48] For a recent overview of relations between the Normans and the papacy, see Cantarella (2014).

fighting the Seljuk Turks in Armenia and the Sicilians were fractured by civil war. The last Byzantine stronghold in southern Italy, Bari, fell to the Normans in 1071, while Muslim Palermo was taken the following year.

As the Normans conquered Greek-speaking territories, they gradually replaced Greek bishops with Latin ones from France and Normandy.[49] This was not so much an effort to 'Latinise' Greek areas of southern Italy as much as it was to secure them politically: the Normans could count on the loyalty of bishops from France, whereas Greek bishops might be expected to act as a fifth column of the Byzantine emperor.[50] Nonetheless, they usually waited until a Greek bishop died before replacing him, as Graham Loud has noted.[51] The papacy was also more concerned with political loyalty than with doctrinal orthodoxy, as we see from the story of Basil of Reggio described in the introduction.[52] When Basil met Pope Urban II in 1089, the pope was actually willing to appoint him on condition that he submit himself to papal authority, though Basil refused.

In some instances, such as at Rossano in 1094, the local Greek population resisted strongly enough that the Normans could not install a Latin bishop.[53] In other areas they do not seem to have tried at all; sees such as Gallipoli, Bova, Oppido, and S. Severina all retained Greek incumbents at least through the twelfth century and in some cases until the fourteenth.[54] Most of the remaining Greek bishops were concentrated in Calabria and the Salento peninsula, where Greek-speakers formed a majority. Moreover, many sees retained the Greek liturgical rite even after they gained a Latin bishop. For example, the cathedral of Gerace continued in the Greek rite until 1480, Gallipoli until 1513, Rossano until around 1570, and Bova until 1573.[55] Even when a cathedral adopted the Latin rite, the language of local parish churches almost always remained Greek, as did their clergy.

The Normans enjoyed much greater freedom of action on the island of Sicily and installed an entirely new Latin hierarchy (again mostly from France).[56] Nevertheless, it is interesting to note that Muslim Sicilian converts to Christianity seem to have opted predominantly for the Greek rather than the Latin rite.[57] As we saw from Malaterra's account, the native Christians of Sicily in the Islamic era followed the Greek rite (as they had since the era of Byzantine rule), while many of the island's Muslims (or their ancestors) had originally converted to Islam from Greek Christianity. Moreover, the tenth-century Arab geographer Ibn Hawqal records that intermarriage between the Islamic and Greek

[49] Kamp (1977): 384–388.

[50] On the general subject of cultural relations between Normans and Greeks in southern Italy, see recently Loud (2016).

[51] Loud (2007): 498.

[52] See Introduction, C1.P1–C1.P5. See also Stiernon (1964); Herde (2002): 220–223.

[53] Malaterra, *De rebus gestis* 4.22.

[54] Girgensohn (1973): 33–37; Martin (2016): 13.

[55] Loud (2016): 144; Loud (2007): 497; Weiss (1951): 30–31.

[56] Kamp (1995): 64–67; Falkenhausen (2013): 65.

[57] Johns (1995): 144–149.

Christian communities of Sicily was relatively common.[58] The Greek rite would thus have been more familiar to a Sicilian convert than the Latin.

Once he had consolidated his family's rule over Sicily, Calabria, and Apulia, Robert Guiscard embarked on a far more ambitious campaign. In 1081, he launched an invasion of the Byzantine mainland to seize the throne of Constantinople, as Anna Komnene famously recounts in the *Alexiad*. Although Guiscard died and the war ended in failure, the Byzantines were in no position to try to re-invade southern Italy. Ironically, this removed a significant obstacle to good relations between Byzantium and the papacy. The stage was set for an attempt at rapprochement between the Greek and Latin churches with the accession of Pope Urban II in 1089 (a far more conciliatory pope than many of his predecessors). Unfortunately for the Byzantines, who wanted Western military aid but balked at any political interference in their sphere, Urban's grand plan for church union entailed the launch of the First Crusade in 1096.[59]

This period also saw the formalisation of the relationship between the papacy and the Italo-Greeks in the newly conquered Norman realms (southern Italy was not yet a unified state). Given the revolution in the Latin church's ecclesiastical governance that occurred in the eleventh to thirteenth centuries, it is often surprising to see how little the papacy concerned itself with its new Greek Christian flock in southern Italy. This impression is partly a consequence of poor source survival, but it is also a reflection of the Norman rulers' success in keeping the popes out of their affairs. Nevertheless, with the armies of the First Crusade approaching Jerusalem, Urban convened a church council in Bari in 1098 to prepare for the prospective future union of Eastern and Western Christendom by settling the various theological and liturgical differences between the two.

Sources for the Council of Bari are limited; no conciliar acts survive and there are only brief references to it in Latin narrative texts and correspondence. No Greek or Byzantine source mentions the council at all.[60] In practice, the only Greek hierarchs in attendance were from southern Italy, and so the council served more to settle affairs in the newly conquered Norman territories than it did to reconcile the Byzantine church. It appears to have confirmed the precedent set by Urban II's dealings with Basil of Reggio at Melfi in 1089: Italo-Greeks could continue to follow Byzantine rites and teachings as long as they subjected themselves to the papacy and did not condemn Latin customs. The only doctrinal matter that seems to have been raised was the controversy over the Western insertion of the word '*Filioque*' into the Nicene Creed. The pope instructed St Anselm of Canterbury (exiled from England by King William II) to overcome

[58] Metcalfe (2003): 15–17.

[59] Byzantine envoys representing Alexios Komnenos had travelled to the West to request mercenary forces for defence against the Seljuq Turks, which seems to have been part of the inspiration for Urban's 'great pilgrimage' to defend Eastern Christians; see Charanis (1949).

[60] On sources for the Council of Bari, see Capizzi (1999): 69–72.

the Italo-Greeks' objections to the Latin doctrine on the procession of the Holy Spirit. Anselm's biographer Eadmer gives the impression that the saint showed the Greeks the error of their ways and convinced them to recite the *Filioque* in the Creed, but this is an exaggeration to say the least: the Italo-Greeks continued to use the original formula without the *Filioque* until the sixteenth century in some cases.[61] In practice, the papacy does not seem to have made any serious effort to change the beliefs or practices of the Italo-Greeks.

A more significant event was the issuing of a papal bull in July of 1098. Following a dispute between Urban II and Count Roger I of Sicily (*r.* 1071–1101) over the pope's right to appoint legates in Sicily, Urban agreed to allow Roger to oversee the administration of the church on the island and to ask his permission when appointing legates in the future. This was a remarkable occurrence: no other Christian ruler in Western Europe was ever granted such sweeping powers to administer the church in his realm directly. As Loud put it, 'neither Roger I nor Roger II were very restrained in their interpretation of this power'.[62] In theory this was supposed to be a temporary concession, but future kings of Sicily used it to claim the right to control their church without papal interference. This had two important consequences for the Italo-Greeks: firstly, it established the Norman rulers as a barrier between them and the papacy; and secondly, it would allow the kings of Sicily to adopt a relationship to the Greek churches and monasteries of his realm that strongly resembled the one between the Byzantine emperors and their church.

The Norman Kingdom and the 'Italo-Greek Renaissance' (1098–1194)

In his influential work on the Greek monastery of the Nea Hodegetria of Rossano, Fr Pierre Batiffol stated that, 'We know now that the Norman conquest, far from suppressing the Hellenism of *Magna Graecia*, on the contrary gave it the chance for a renaissance...'[63] This 'renaissance' of the Italo-Greeks under Norman rule was not the same phenomenon as the famous 'Twelfth-Century Renaissance' of which Charles Homer Haskins wrote, although it was notionally contemporaneous.[64] Rather, it refers to a dramatic increase in the number of surviving Greek manuscripts from southern Italy in the twelfth century that Batiffol took to be a sign of an Italo-Greek cultural revival under the Normans.

[61] Eadmer, *Life of St Anselm* 414–416. As Herde has observed, the Greeks of Brindisi in Apulia were still reciting the Creed without the *Filioque* as late as the 1570s (Herde [2002]: 235). For further details, see Peri (1967): 234–235, 254.

[62] Loud (1982): 148. [63] Batiffol (1891): xxvii. [64] Haskins (1927).

The idea of an 'Italo-Greek renaissance' is highly problematic and most modern scholars treat it with caution.[65] So few manuscripts survived the disruption of the eleventh-century Norman conquest that the apparent explosion in book production in the twelfth century may be a mirage. Was it a genuine increase in activity, or does it just look like that because so much earlier material has been lost? Nonetheless, Batiffol was right in a way: the relative stability and prosperity of the Norman era (compared to the turmoil of the eleventh century) evidently created an environment that was more conducive to the *preservation* of Greek manuscripts. The Normans built a cohesive state that actively supported Greek cultural institutions. The Italo-Greeks may not have experienced a cultural renaissance in the way that the term is usually employed, but they did enjoy an economic and political renaissance of sorts in the twelfth century, which is why so much more source material survives from that period.

The most obvious beneficiaries in the Italo-Greek church of the Norman conquest were the monasteries. Several notable new monastic houses had been established in the 1090s such as St Bartholomew of Trigona in southern Calabria (*c.* 1095), the Nea Hodegetria (known colloquially as the 'Patiron') of Rossano (*c.* 1095), and St Nicholas of Casole near Otranto (1098).[66] These new foundations usually benefitted from the patronage of the Norman nobility, a trend that is clearest in the case of the Patiron monastery. The Patiron was founded in northern Calabria in the 1090s by St Bartholomew of Simeri with financial support from Count Roger I and his chamberlain, the Syrian-Greek *ammiratus* Christodoulos.[67] The foundation soon took other Italo-Greek monasteries under its protection and grew to such an extent that, in about 1105, Pope Paschal II (*r.* 1099–1118) granted it a bull of exemption from episcopal oversight.[68]

Moreover, the Norman conquest did not cut the Italo-Greeks off from the cultural and religious life of Byzantium, even if they were cut off politically. Soon after Bartholomew of Simeri established the Patiron monastery, for example, he requested (and received) permission from Roger II's mother Adelaide to travel to Constantinople to acquire liturgical books and vessels.[69] On his arrival,

[65] The French historian Léon-Robert Ménager in particular took issue with the idea of an Italo-Greek cultural renaissance, calling it merely 'a desperate effort to survive' (Ménager [1959]: 50). Lucà (1993): 88 does not reject it completely, but observes that 'this "renaissance", in any event, was failing, ephemeral, and lacking in lively and creative advances...' Lidia Perria was similarly pessimistic, remarking that 'Byzantine culture in Italy was reduced in large part to a suffocated existence, deprived of the ferment of renewal...' (Perria [1999]: 104). Peters-Custot takes a less negative view of the 'Italo-Greek renaissance', but believes that it was largely confined to monasteries (Peters-Custot [2009a]: 421–419).

[66] The term 'Patiron' appears to be a corruption of the Greek word for 'father' ('πατήρ'); it may carry the connotation of 'the father's monastery'. Other variants in common use are 'Patir' and 'Patirion'.

[67] Zaccagni (1996): 216–217 (17.1–14). See also Morton (2013): 21–23.

[68] Zaccagni (1996): 219 (21); see also Chapter 5, 'Monastic Nomocanons I', C5.P7–C5.P8.

[69] On Bartholomew's journey to Constantinople and Mount Athos, see recently Morini (2017): 197–200.

Bartholomew was fêted by Emperor Alexios I and his wife Irene, who 'were guiding the reins of the Roman [i.e. Byzantine] Empire in a most orthodox fashion at the time', in the words of Bartholomew's biographer.[70] A Byzantine nobleman named Basil Kalimeres even asked him to reform the life of a monastery dedicated to St Basil on Mount Athos; Bartholomew's *Life* claims that the monastery gained the epithet '*tou Kalabrou*' ('of the Calabrian') as a result, though an Athonite document of 1080 shows that it already had this name before his arrival.[71] Bartholomew brought back a large array of manuscripts to Italy that would serve as models for Rossanese scribes to copy.[72]

The Norman territories in southern Italy were not united until 1127, when Roger II claimed all the Hauteville lands and their dependents. Following this, he took advantage of the split papal election in 1130 between Innocent II (*r.* 1130–1143) and the antipope Anacletus II (*r.* 1130–1138). Roger recognised Anacletus and, in turn, received coronation as the first King of Sicily. After Innocent's eventual victory over Anacletus, the Second Lateran Council of 1139 excommunicated Roger for his choice of sides, but Roger went on to defeat and capture the pope in battle. The resulting Treaty of Mignano of 1139 overturned the excommunication and recognised him as king of Sicily.[73] He consolidated his new royal authority with the promulgation around 1140 of a legal code that has traditionally been known as the 'Assizes of Ariano' though, as Kenneth Pennington has argued, would be more accurately referred to by the term *Constitutions*.[74] This was the first systematic attempt in Western Europe to codify royal legislation and was significantly influenced by the Byzantine legal tradition, as Francesco Brandileone showed.[75]

Roger's ecclesiastical policy also had parallels to that of the Byzantine world. Many scholars have already highlighted his extensive use of the motifs of Byzantine rulership, a point best demonstrated perhaps by the mosaic depiction of the king in the attire and pose of a Byzantine emperor in the Palermitan church of S. Maria dell'Ammiraglio.[76] As Hubert Houben has discussed, the personnel of Roger's royal chancery and administration was mostly Greek, while Roger's only surviving golden bull (a privilege for the monastery of Cava in 1131) depicts the king in Byzantine imperial regalia.[77]

[70] '*οὗτοι γὰρ τῷ τότε τοὺς οἴακας τῆς τῶν Ῥωμαίων βασιλείας ὀρθοδοξότατα ἴθυνον*': Zaccagni (1996): 222 (25.10–11).

[71] Oikonomides (1990): 139 l. 35. An act of donation of 1108 in favour of the Great Lavra includes among its signatories the *hegoumenos* Ignatios 'of the monastery of our righteous father Basil of the Calabrians' ('*τῆς μονῆς τοῦ ὁσίου πατρὸς ἡμῶν Βασιλείου τῶν Καλαβρῶν*'): Millet et al. (1937): 299 l. 79 (a. 1108). For discussion, see Pertusi (1964): 238–241.

[72] On this subject, see the back-and-forth between Gastone Breccia and Mario Re: Breccia (1997); Re (1997); Breccia (1998).

[73] *PL* 179.478–479.

[74] Pennington (2006): 36.

[75] Brandileone (1886); cf. Kedar (1999): 321.

[76] Houben (2002): 98–135, esp. 114–16.

[77] Houben (2002): 119. On the composition of the royal chancery and the use of Greek in administrative documents, see Falkenhausen (1998): 283–286; Falkenhausen (2009); Enzensberger (2002).

The Norman royal patronage of Italo-Greek monasteries is another excellent example of this trend of emulating the Byzantine emperor. Not only did Roger II take the Patiron of Rossano under royal protection in 1130, but he also invited St Bartholomew of Simeri to establish a new monastery under royal authority in Messina in the same year.[78] This was the Holy Saviour of Messina, which was put in charge of an archimandritate (monastic federation) directly overseeing twenty-two *metochia* (subject houses) and exercising disciplinary and spiritual authority over another sixteen houses that could elect their own abbots. In the Greek terminology of the foundation documents, the Holy Saviour was a *basilike* monastery—a term that in this context translates to 'royal' but was also used in Byzantium to mean 'imperial'. Although evidence for the pre-Norman period is limited, at least two southern Italian monasteries had been granted the designation *basilike* under Byzantine rule as well: the Theotokos of the Salinai in Calabria (*c.* 904) and St Peter of Taranto (before 1033).[79] It is difficult to say whether Norman rulers like Roger II were consciously copying Byzantine practice or simply implementing policies that happened to be similar. From the perspective of Italo-Greek monasteries, the Norman king effectively played the same patronage role as the Byzantine emperor.

Having secured his kingdom in the 1130s, Roger spent most of the remainder of his reign attempting to expand overseas, particularly in North Africa. He also took the opportunity of the Second Crusade (1147–1149) to launch an attack on Byzantine Greece while the empire's forces were occupied elsewhere. Nevertheless, his foreign conquests proved ephemeral. On his death in 1154, a period of internal instability ensued as his successor William I (known to later generations as 'the Bad') assumed sole rule (*r.* 1154–1166). Both the papacy and the Byzantine Empire encouraged rebellions against William's rule and a Byzantine expeditionary force even briefly recaptured the Adriatic coast of Apulia in 1155.

William managed to recover the situation, however, and concluded a new agreement (the Treaty of Benevento) with Pope Hadrian IV (*r.* 1154–1159) in 1156: the pope recognised him and his heirs as kings of Sicily while he recognised the pope as his feudal suzerain.[80] The treaty also put the relationship between

[78] On the royal privilege for the Patiron of Rossano: Trinchera (1865): 140 (no. 106). There is no modern edition of the Greek text of Roger's royal charter for the Holy Saviour of 1133, which is preserved in a sixteenth-century manuscript copy: Vatican City, Biblioteca Apostolica Vaticana, MS Vat. lat. 8201, fols. 56^r–59^v, 130^r–132^v. A Latin translation (rife with interpolations) made in 1472 by the scholar Constantine Laskaris can be found in Pirro (1733): 2.974–276. On the history of the monastery, see Scaduto (1947): 197–219.

[79] The Theotokos of the Salinai: Rossi Taibbi (1962): 75. St Peter of Taranto (today known as San Domenico): Trinchera (1865): 31–32 (no. 27); Falkenhausen (1968): 158. On imperial monasteries in Byzantium, see Morris (1995): 138–142; Thomas (2007).

[80] See Pacaut (1981): 36–50; Loud (2007): 164–165.

church and state on a firmer footing for the rest of the Norman period, confirming the pope's right to convene councils on the southern Italian mainland and the king's authority over the church on the island of Sicily.

The ill-defined ecclesiastical authority that Roger II had exercised was thus established in terms acceptable to the Church of Rome. Nonetheless, William and his successors continued to follow an expansive interpretation of their power. In 1168, for example, William II (*r.* 1166–1189) issued a bilingual privilege in Latin and Greek that granted the title of archimandrite to the *hegoumenos* of SS Elias and Anastasios of Carbone and placed him in charge of all the 'monasteries of the Greeks' within the territory of Lucania.[81] There are a number of interesting points in this document, not least of which is that the linguistic quality of the Greek text is surprisingly poor. Furthermore, it explicitly states that the archimandritate of Carbone should be modelled on those of the Patiron of Rossano and the Holy Saviour of Messina. The explanation that it gives (which only appears in the Greek version) is fascinating: 'From the time when these archimandrites [of Rossano and Messina] were appointed, the monasteries and *metochia* of the monastic federations were reformed, and in just the fashion that [St] Basil the Great [of Caesarea] ordained, especially in those where they have the Greek rite but the Latin language.'[82]

This is an early indication of a trend that would become more noticeable in the thirteenth century and then prevalent from the fourteenth on: Greek monasteries with monks who could not understand Greek. It is hard to believe that the number of Greek-speakers had declined so rapidly in a century that monasteries were already running short of competent recruits. The reason may lie in the close patronage relationship between Greek monasteries and the Norman and Lombard nobility: perhaps lesser members of local Latin aristocratic families were entering or even taking charge of some of these houses. Peters-Custot has noted the case of the Greek monastery of Kyr-Zosimos in Lucania, for instance, which had an abbot with the distinctly Latin name of 'Falco' from 1122 onwards.[83] Loud has also drawn attention to the Latin monk St John of Matera, who lived at a Greek monastery near Taranto in the early twelfth century.[84] Evidence for monastic personnel is scarce in general, but it does seem that some Italo-Greek foundations were already being diluted with non-Greek-speaking monks in the twelfth century. Larger Greek monasteries such as Carbone, Rossano, and Messina were therefore tasked with improving their standards of education.

[81] Robinson (1930): 69–73 (no. 94).

[82] '*καὶ γἀρ ἀφ' οὖ καὶ ἐτύπωθῆσαν οἱ τοὶαὗται ἀρχϊμἀνδρίται δϊωῤθῶθησαν αἱ μοναῖ καὶ τα μέτοχ(ια) μοναχϊκοῖς πολ(ί)τήας καὶ κἀθόν τρόπ(ον) ετὔπωσεν ὁ μεγάς βασιλός πόσως μαλλόν ἐν τουτοῖς τοῖς ἔχ(ου)σιν τὴν μεν πολ(ι)ηάν γρέκον, τὴν δε δΐαλεκτον λἁτϊνον*': Robinson (1930): 70–71 (no. 94).

[83] Peters-Custot (2009a): 283. [84] Loud (2007): 471.

Greeks, Guelphs, and Ghibellines: Southern Italy between Empire and Papacy (1189–1266)

When William II died without children in 1189, his cousin Tancred of Lecce (*r*. 1189–1194) took the throne of Sicily. However, his claim was challenged by William's aunt Constance, who had married the Holy Roman Emperor Henry VI (*r*. 1190–1197) in 1185. Pope Clement III (*r*. 1187–1191) recognised Tancred as king of Sicily, but his successor Celestine III (*r*. 1191–1198) extracted a price for this: the Treaty of Gravina of 1192. This renegotiated the ecclesiastical settlement in the Treaty of Benevento in 1156 on terms that were much more favourable to the papacy. The popes could now hear legal appeals directly from churches in Sicily and the king lost his role in appointing bishops.[85]

Future popes would view the Treaty of Gravina as the settled norm for relations between the papacy and the Kingdom of Sicily, but the kingdom's future rulers did not. When Tancred died in 1194 and left his young son William III in charge, Henry VI invaded to claim his wife's inheritance. Neither he nor any of his Hohenstaufen successors would ever make any reference to the Treaty of Gravina in future laws or pronouncements. As David Abulafia has noted, the Hohenstaufen viewed the Kingdom of Sicily as 'a special source of financial and military strength' that they could draw upon in any conflict with the church or rebellious nobles north of the Alps.[86] They would view any attempt by the papacy to interfere in their kingdom's affairs as unwelcome. Nonetheless, on Henry VI's death in 1198, his son Frederick II (*r*. 1198–1250) was still an infant child. Constance placed him under the protection of Pope Innocent III (*r*. 1198–1216), though in practice he was controlled by a succession of lay nobles until he came of age in 1208. He spent much of his reign until 1220 attempting to recover and consolidate his authority in southern Italy and in Germany.

In the meantime, the turn of the thirteenth century saw a series of major upheavals in the eastern Mediterranean that had significant effects for the Italo-Greeks. The first came in 1191, when the army of Richard I of England seized control of Cyprus on its way to the Holy Land during the Third Crusade.[87] The creation of a new Kingdom of Cyprus under the rule of the French Lusignan dynasty brought a large Greek population under the Roman church's jurisdiction for the first time since the Norman conquest of southern Italy.

The Fourth Crusade of 1204 delivered an even larger shock.[88] The sudden and unexpected conquest of Constantinople by the crusader army led to the division of the Byzantine Empire into several parcels. Independent Greek successor states

[85] On the Treaty of Gravina, see Zerbi (1983): 62–64; Kamp (1985): 130–131; Loud (2007): 172–174.

[86] Abulafia (1997): 15.

[87] On the conquest of Cyprus and its impact, see Harris (2003): 140–143; Coureas (2014): 146–148; Kyriacou (2018): 1–21.

[88] On the Fourth Crusade, see Angold (2003).

were established in north-western Greece (the Despotate of Epirus) and in Asia Minor (the Empires of Nicaea and Trebizond), while the crusaders created their own Latin 'Empire of Romania' ('Romania' being the Greek word for Byzantium). Unlike in southern Italy, the Latin conquerors of Constantinople were vastly outnumbered by a subject Greek population that, under the circumstances, was much less willing to submit to the Latin church.

Pope Innocent III's efforts to persuade the Byzantine church hierarchy to submit to Roman authority proved ineffective, yet he was not deterred in his attempts to pursue church union. The papacy took the opportunity of the Fourth Lateran Council of 1215 to promulgate an official policy on Greek Christians for the very first time: the Greek rite would be tolerated, but it was to be contained and compartmentalised within the administrative structures of the Latin church.[89] This policy effectively formalised the *status quo* that had prevailed since the Council of Bari in 1098. However, there were some significant differences, foremost of which was that the Roman church began to attempt to enforce its authority over the Italo-Greeks much more proactively than it had previously. The Treaty of Gravina gave the popes a pretext to involve themselves more closely in the management of the church in the Kingdom of Sicily, while the decentralisation of the state that resulted from Frederick II's regency gave them the opportunity.

The effects are immediately clear in the documentary record. In the Pontifical Commission for the Restoration of Eastern Canon Law's edition of papal acts relating to Eastern Christians (*Fontes III*), there are eleven surviving documents relating to the Greeks of southern Italy from the entire eleventh and twelfth centuries up to Innocent III's enthronement in 1198, of which three relate to the monastery of Grottaferrata near Rome. Innocent is known to have issued at least ten documents on the Italo-Greeks while his successor Honorius III (*r.* 1216–1227) issued at least fifty-two. This development can only partly be explained by poor source survival from earlier centuries; clearly the papacy had become more interventionist in the thirteenth century. Many of these relate to monastic exemptions, but many also address disciplinary issues. Honorius' pontificate saw the first known instances of a Roman pope deposing Italo-Greek bishops (of Rossano in 1218 and Anglona in 1219) and excommunicating an Italo-Greek monastery (the Holy Saviour of Messina in 1223), for example.[90] Incidents such as these mark a noticeable departure from the papacy's more reticent attitude of the twelfth-century.

[89] For further discussion of the impact of the Fourth Lateran Council, see Chapter 8, 'The Papacy Takes Charge', C8.S1.

[90] *Fontes III* 3.59–60 (no. 35), 60–61 (no. 36), 69 (no. 44), 94–96 (no. 66), 151–152 (no. 113). For further discussion of these incidents, see Chapter 7, 'The Secular Church and the Laity', C7.P41–C7.P42; Chapter 8, 'The Papacy Takes Charge', C8.S3.

In 1225, Frederick II married Yolande, heiress to the Kingdom of Jerusalem, and promised to Honorius that he would undertake a crusade to recover the kingdom before 1228. Frederick had previously vowed to go on crusade on the occasion of his coronation as emperor in 1220 but had yet to do so. When he delayed a planned expedition in 1227 on the grounds of illness, Pope Gregory IX (*r.* 1227–1241) immediately accused him of dishonesty and excommunicated him. To make matters worse, Frederick set out anyway in 1228, succeeded in recovering Jerusalem through diplomatic negotiation with the Ayyubid sultan Al-Kamil (*r.* 1218–1238), and had himself crowned king (an honour that should technically have gone to his son by Yolande).

Gregory IX arranged for an invasion of southern Italy led by John of Brienne, Yolande's father. Nonetheless, Frederick returned in 1229 and defeated the attackers. Like Roger II nearly a century earlier, Frederick compelled Gregory to lift his excommunication in the Treaty of Ceprano of 1230. He in turn agreed to respect the papacy's rights in the Kingdom of Sicily (although he evidently had a more limited interpretation of what these rights were than Gregory did). In another parallel to Roger II, Frederick issued a legal code, the *Constitutions of Melfi*, in the following year. This famous codification centralised power in the king's hands and has led some scholars to view him as the first 'absolute monarch' of the medieval West.[91] This is certainly how Italo-Greek members of his court seem to have viewed him; the Salentine poet George of Gallipoli, for instance, called him 'the mighty and thrice-blessed king *Phryktorikos* ["blazing beacon," a play on the sound of the name Frederick in Greek], the wonder of the universe', and 'emperor of all'.[92]

It was not long before the conflict between Frederick II and the papacy (and the various towns and cities of the northern Italy that lined up on either side) was renewed in the late 1230s. Frederick was excommunicated yet again in 1239 and the war proceeded more or less continuously until his death in 1250. Reading the output of court poets such as George of Gallipoli and others, there is a temptation to see the Italo-Greeks as partisans of the imperial cause against the papacy and the Guelph cities of northern Italy. Peters-Custot has written of Italo-Greek polemics against the pope that 'manifested a Ghibelline partisanship... Paradoxically, the religious opposition of the Italo-Greeks to Rome is the mirror image of the Roman tolerance that maintained the differences and the polemics without being threatened by them.'[93]

[91] For a summary of the long-running debate on the *Constitutions of Melfi* and relevant bibliography, see Houben (1996): 177–182. For an overview of Frederick's legal and administrative reforms, see Kölzer (1996).

[92] '*Ἀλλ' ὁ κραταιὸς καὶ τρισευδαίμων ἄναξ/Φρυκτωρίκος, τὸ θαῦμα τῆς οἰκουμένης... δὸς τῷ βασιλεῖ τῶν ὅλων...*': Gigante (1979): 176 ll. 20–21, 177 l. 58. See also discussions in Wellas (1983): 89–130; Dronke (1998): 221–223.

[93] Peters-Custot (2009a): 537.

I must disagree with Peters-Custot's assessment here. Firstly, a substantial proportion of the written evidence that she cites consists of the literary output of members of Frederick's court, who would obviously take the emperor's side against the pope. Very few Italo-Greek voices from outside their circle are represented in extant sources. Secondly, the Italo-Greek 'polemics' that she mentions are in fact just two texts: the *Three Chapters* of the monk Nicholas-Nektarios of Otranto (*c.* 1222–1225) and a short, anonymous treatise on Greek baptismal rites from Calabria.[94] Neither adopts a confrontational stance to the papacy; Nicholas-Nektarios adopts an irenic and conciliatory tone towards the 'Latins' throughout his work, while the anonymous treatise makes no direct reference to them at all. Though Italo-Greeks in Frederick's court certainly supported his cause against the papacy, there is not enough evidence to say whether that sentiment was widespread among the Greeks of southern Italy more generally.

Even so, Peters-Custot is right to emphasise the papacy's tolerance of the Greek rite. Although the thirteenth century saw a dramatic increase in the level of attention that the popes paid to Italo-Greek affairs, there appears to have been no specifically 'anti-Greek' motivation in their actions. In reality, it was simply a product of an increased level of papal intervention in southern Italy more generally. Instead of opposing the Greek rite, popes from Celestine III onwards emphasised that it should be compartmentalised and separated from the Latin rite; the papal policy was not condemnation but containment.[95] What this meant in practice was that Greeks should refrain from using Latin rites and vice versa, and that the two groups should avoid attending each other's services. While this policy was not intended to harm the Greek rite, it did have a detrimental effect in combination with other contemporary social and demographic changes: as Italo-Greek elites increasingly pursued Latin educations to secure their social status in the Kingdom of Sicily, it became harder for the church to recruit clerics who were competent in the Greek rite.[96] Nevertheless, the long-term effects of these changes were slow to manifest.

The conflict between Frederick II and the papacy was still undecided on his death in 1250. His short-lived successors Conrad IV (*r.* 1250–1254), Conrad V (often known as 'Conradin'; *r.* 1254–1258), and the illegitimate king Manfred (*r.* 1258–1266) continued to resist successfully. The popes were determined to find a more loyal vassal to hold the Kingdom of Sicily (over which they were, after all, supposed to be suzerains). Eventually Urban IV (*r.* 1261–1264) and Clement IV (*r.* 1265–1268) settled upon Charles of Anjou, offering him the throne of Sicily if he would lead an army to evict the Hohenstaufen. He did this with unexpected

[94] On the *Three Chapters*, see Chapter 10, 'They Do It Like This in Romania', C10.S1. On the anonymous Calabrian polemic on the baptismal rite, see Giannelli (1944).

[95] See discussion in Brundage (1973).

[96] See Peters-Custot (2009a): 445–447, 453–458.

ease in 1266, defeating and killing Manfred in less than a month. However, events in the eastern Mediterranean had taken an unwelcome turn for the Roman church in the meantime. In 1261, the armies of the emperor Michael VIII Palaiologos (*r.* 1258–1282) had entered Constantinople and restored it to Byzantine rule, derailing the vision of Roman ecclesiastical leadership that Innocent III had promoted after the Fourth Crusade.

Union and Disunion: Italo-Greek Christianity after the Angevin Conquest (1266–1372)

Following his reconquest of Constantinople, Michael VIII recognised the real threat of another Western crusade to restore the Latin Empire. He almost immediately attempted to open negotiations with Pope Urban IV to achieve church union, though the pope rebuffed him. Michael's fears were realised when Charles I of Anjou (*r.* 1266–1285), the new ruler of Sicily, made an agreement with the exiled Latin emperor Baldwin II: he would help Baldwin recover Constantinople in return for a marriage between his daughter and Baldwin's son Philip. Should Philip die without heirs, Charles would inherit the Latin Empire himself. In 1271, Charles captured the port of Dyrrachium (modern Durrës on the Albanian coast) and began preparations for an invasion of the Byzantine Empire.

Nonetheless, Michael continued his diplomatic strategy of pursuing church union to stave off the larger threat of a crusade to restore the Latin Empire. He finally found a willing partner in Pope Gregory X (*r.* 1271–1276), who summoned the Second Council of Lyon in 1274 to discuss church reform, union with the Greeks, and a new crusade to recover the Holy Land. Despite strong public opposition in Byzantium, Michael agreed to all the Roman church's demands: like the Italo-Greeks, the Byzantines would be allowed to maintain their own customs and rites on condition that they accept papal authority. There was one significant novelty in the union agreement, though: the council insisted that the Greeks actively embrace the Latin version of the Nicene Creed including the insertion of the *Filioque*, something that the Italo-Greeks had never been compelled to do before. The council's signatories included the Greek-rite archbishops of Rossano and S. Severina, although, interestingly, the archbishop of S. Severina signed his name in Latin.[97]

The union proved short-lived: not only was it immensely unpopular within the Byzantine church, but it failed in its primary aim of preventing further Western attacks. In 1281, the French Pope Martin IV (*r.* 1281–1285) decided to simply ignore the union of Lyon and sanction an Angevin crusade against Constantinople

[97] Russo (1973): 790.

regardless of the fact that the Byzantines were supposed to be coreligionists. The union was not only divisive but clearly pointless, so Michael's successor Andronikos II (*r.* 1282–1328) put an end to it. The churches would remain divided until the Council of Ferrara-Florence (1438–1445), though the Ottoman conquest of Constantinople in 1453 put an end to the union once and for all.

Martin IV's crusade of 1281 was a failure thanks to further diplomatic moves by Michael VIII. Shortly before his death, Michael joined with Peter III of Aragon (*r.* 1276–1285) to provide funding and encouragement to rebels on the island of Sicily. At the hour of Vespers on 30th March 1282, the people of Palermo rose up against Charles of Anjou's French garrison and slaughtered them. The rebels seized the rest of Sicily with great speed, forcing Charles to cancel his crusade against Byzantium. They failed to win independence for the island, though, which fell under the control of Peter III of Aragon. Charles and his successors attempted to recover Sicily by force; the resulting War of the Sicilian Vespers lasted for twenty years and divided the Kingdom of Sicily into two separate realms (one on the mainland, one on the island) until they were reunited by Alfonso V of Aragon in 1443.[98]

An intriguing episode took place soon after the beginning of the war that provides a good insight into the state of the Italo-Greek church in the late thirteenth century. Pope Martin IV stood firmly in support of Charles of Anjou and sent Gerardo Bianchi, cardinal bishop of Sabina, to southern Italy to raise money to fight the Sicilian rebellion. Gerardo presided over a local church council at Melfi in 1284 that ended up devoting a substantial amount of time to the Greek church.[99] The council's first order of business was to proclaim that the Italo-Greeks should adopt the Latin version of the Nicene Creed in accordance with the Second Council of Lyon. Southern Italian bishops were commanded to make annual inspections of Greek churches in their dioceses to ensure that they were reading the Creed with the *Filioque*.[100] Next, it noted that some Latin priests were skirting the Roman church's ban on clerical marriage by marrying and then being ordained in Greek churches (Greek clergy were still permitted to marry as long as they did so before ordination). The council therefore decreed that a married person could only enter the priesthood if it were established that he had Greek parents.

Finally, and most strikingly, the council observed that the ninth canon of the Fourth Lateran Council (which stated that congregations should have priests who could minister to them in their own language) was being violated. However, it was not because Greeks were being forced to attend Latin masses. On the contrary,

[98] For a more detailed account of the War of the Sicilian Vespers, see Abulafia (1997): 63–80.

[99] For the conciliar acts and historical analysis, see Herde (1967): 26–29, 46–53. See also Enzensberger (1973): 1141–1142.

[100] As we saw earlier, some Italo-Greeks were still reciting the original version of the Nicene Creed without the *Filioque* as late as 1570.

'some abbots and ecclesiastical persons... [were] overcome with avarice' and employed Greek priests to serve the Byzantine liturgy to uncomprehending Latin congregations![101] Apparently it was cheaper for bishops or abbots to hire Greek clergy, probably because Greek priests typically received a simple stipend in remuneration whereas Latin priests expected to be granted a landed benefice.[102] By employing Greeks, cynical Latin hierarchs could avoid having to relinquish the revenues of church property directly to their clergy. The Council of Melfi sought to end this exploitation and instructed that Latin congregations should have Latin priests in the future.

The War of the Sicilian Vespers officially ended with the Peace of Caltabellotta in 1302, which divided the Kingdom of Sicily in two. The Angevin rulers of Naples on the mainland would launch another six invasions of Sicily in the fourteenth century, though none succeeded. By this time the Greek-speaking population of Sicily was probably very small; the majority of Italo-Greeks were concentrated on the mainland in Calabria and the Salento.

Peters-Custot has pointed to interesting evidence for demographic change among Italo-Greeks in the late thirteenth and early fourteenth centuries: a trend of translating legal documents from Greek into Latin.[103] As late as the reign of Frederick II, there had still been significant numbers of Greek-speakers in the ecclesiastical hierarchy, the royal court, and the judiciary. As the thirteenth century progressed, though, more and more Italo-Greek elites opted for education in the Latin language and Western law in order to maintain their social status, especially after the opening of the university of Naples in 1224.[104] This accelerated further after the Angevin conquest of 1266. Many of the dioceses that had managed to maintain Greek incumbents after the Norman conquest began to be taken over by Latins, a trend that was certainly linked to the creeping Latinisation of Italo-Greek elites. State and church officials could no longer be relied upon to understand Greek at the level necessary to read legal documents. In professional terms, knowledge of the Greek language was increasingly required only for the clergy who had to officiate in a liturgical capacity in Greek-rite churches and monasteries.

[101] '*nonnulli tamen abbates et persone ecclesiastice, qui sub se habent ecclesias et populum latinorum, avaritie dediti, que idolorum est servitus, non considerantes premissa quodque in diversitate huiusmodi, si grecus latinis divina officia celebret, ignorans latinus populus et greci sermonis ignarus nesciet, ut est moris, in ecclesia sacerdoti "Amen" etc. respondere, minime advertentes sacerdotes grecos latinis ipsis preficiunt, qui eisdem celebrant et ministrant ecclesiastica sacramenta, pro eo, quod eos pro minori pretio possunt obtinere conductos*': Herde (1967): 48.

[102] On clerical salaries in the Byzantine world, see Hussey (1986): 333–334. I am very grateful to Maroula Perisanidi for drawing my attention to this difference between Byzantine and Western practices; see Perisanidi (2019): 83.

[103] Peters-Custot (2009a): 499–503.

[104] Kamp (1982): 129–131. As Vera von Falkenhausen put it, 'Ultimately, Latinization was the easier option for the educated middle class, while Greek increasingly became a private language...' Falkenhausen (2013): 75.

Though some of their elites began to adopt Latin culture, most Italo-Greeks continued to speak a form of Greek for several centuries to come. Indeed, there are still communities today in the south of Calabria and the Salento peninsula where one can hear 'Griko' or 'Grikaniko' (dialects derived from medieval Greek) spoken among the older generation.[105] Furthermore, Greek liturgical and ecclesiastical customs persisted in churches and monasteries. The resilience of the Greek rite is demonstrated by an incident in 1334 when Raymond of Campania, a former monk of Cluny and papal vicar in southern Italy, made an unprecedented attempt to enforce the Latin rite throughout the region. Raymond wrote to Archbishop Peter of Reggio, commanding him that no bishop, priest, archimandrite, or abbot should be allowed to say any divine office in Greek. Instead, they were to celebrate the Eucharist with *azyma* and shave their beards.[106] Yet, even in the fourteenth century, these customs were still so deeply entrenched that the Italo-Greek bishops of Bova, Oppido, and Gerace in Calabria resisted Raymond's efforts at Latinisation and succeeded in having them overturned.

By the mid-fourteenth century, the Greek church in southern Italy had become the primary vessel for the expression of Italo-Greek cultural identity, but it no longer had a distinct jurisdictional character. While there were still many churches where bearded, married clergy officiated the divine liturgy of St John Chrysostom in Greek, they were all firmly under the management of a Latin ecclesiastical hierarchy that bore little resemblance to that of the Byzantine world. Some large Greek monasteries such as those of Rossano, Messina, and Carbone persisted, but many others had fallen under the control of Latin abbeys or had themselves converted to the Latin rite. As a long-term consequence of the Fourth Lateran Council and the Angevin conquest, the Italo-Greek church was no longer an outpost of Byzantium in the West but had become an ethnic subdivision within the Roman hierarchy.

Conclusion

Greek Christianity in medieval southern Italy was established and shaped by the Byzantine Empire in the ninth and tenth centuries as it reconquered the region and reorganised its administration. Although the Byzantines lost control of the peninsula in the late eleventh century, its Norman conquerors did not sweep away the foundations that the empire had laid. Rather, they adapted and built on them. This was as true of the church as it was of the secular administration, and the Norman rulers patronised Italo-Greek ecclesiastical institutions (especially

[105] The best introduction to the *Griko* dialect remains Rohlfs (1933): 1–81. See also Safran (2014): 215.

[106] For sources and discussion, see Garitte (1946): 31–40.

monasteries) in a fashion very similar to the Byzantine emperors. Furthermore, the Normans' success in preventing papal interference within their kingdom allowed the Italo-Greeks to enjoy a degree of autonomy from the Roman hierarchy that was rare in most other parts of Western Europe.

The thirteenth century was a significant turning point, however. The seizure of Cyprus in 1191 by the armies of the Third Crusade, followed by the unexpected conquest of Constantinople in 1204 during the Fourth Crusade, finally forced the Roman church to develop a coherent policy towards non-Latin Christians. The decrees of the Fourth Lateran Council, combined with local efforts at church reform in southern Italy, gradually brought the administration of Italo-Greek ecclesiastical institutions into line with the rest of the Western church. By the end of the thirteenth century, Greek monks and secular clergy in southern Italy had been brought firmly under Rome's jurisdictional authority. The Italo-Greeks retained their distinctive customs and liturgy for several centuries to come, but they had lost their autonomy.

3
Patterns of Source Survival

The vast majority of Italo-Greek manuscripts were still in southern Italy at the end of the Middle Ages, but today they are mostly scattered across collections in the Vatican, northern Italy, France, Germany, Britain, and elsewhere. Almost none remain in the places where they were originally produced. The Italian codicologist Santo Lucà has estimated that the surviving codices in modern libraries represent only ten percent of the Italo-Greeks' medieval output; canon law collections comprise about two percent of these.[1] Before we can look at the nomocanons in more detail, we must consider how they were preserved and the implications for how we assess them as sources.

Various factors determine the likelihood of a manuscript's survival, but the most significant is institutional longevity. To put it crudely, books fare best when kept in an organised, well-maintained library; stray books are easily lost. Most Greek monasteries and churches in southern Italy had ceased to operate or had converted to the Latin rite by the fifteenth century. The Italo-Greek nomocanons in today's collections all owe their existence to the fact that there were institutions in the early modern period that took care (to a greater or lesser extent) to keep them for posterity. Although much remains unclear, we can piece together the history of the manuscripts' ownership from documents such as inventories, records of sales and donations, and descriptions in other written sources.

There were essentially two main institutional vectors of survival for the Italo-Greek nomocanons. The first was the 'Order of St Basil', a Catholic monastic order created in the fifteenth century to administer Greek-rite monasticism under the Church of Rome. The order provided vital support to Greek monasteries in Italy in the fifteenth to seventeenth centuries and helped to limit the loss of their mobile and immobile property. The second was the development of private manuscript collections among wealthy Renaissance bibliophiles, most of which have since been absorbed into state- or university-run libraries. Many of these figures purchased books on the open market in southern Italy in the sixteenth and seventeenth centuries.

These twin historical dynamics of source survival had a strong impact on the types of manuscripts that were preserved. Some of the effects are obvious: for instance, the monastic Order of St Basil has primarily bequeathed monastic

[1] Lucà (2004b): 193; Guillou (1974b): 101–102.

Byzantine Religious Law in Medieval Italy. James Morton, Oxford University Press (2021). © James Morton.
DOI: 10.1093/oso/9780198861140.003.0004

manuscripts, as one would expect. However, others are more subtle, creating potentially misleading impressions of nomocanon production in different regions and chronological periods, as we shall see in this chapter.

Bessarion and the Formation of the 'Order of St Basil' (15th–16th Centuries)

The number of people in southern Italy who could read and write Greek had declined sharply by the fifteenth century and the endurance of the region's Greek book collections was far from assured. A number of factors contributed to their salvation, but the one that was arguably the most important was also the most ironic: the demise of the Byzantine Empire. It was increasingly clear by the 1430s that Constantinople, once the greatest city in Christendom, would soon fall victim to the Ottoman Turks, and the Byzantines were in urgent need of Western aid. In the meantime, the Roman papacy was facing a threat of its own in the Conciliarist movement at the Council of Basel (1431–1449) and was eager for the boost in authority that would come from a successful reunion with the Church of Constantinople. The resulting Council of Ferrara-Florence (1438–1445) was the venue for a meeting between churchmen and famous intellectuals from both Italy and Byzantium.

Greek professors had been teaching in Italy since the late fourteenth century and there were several competent Italian Hellenists too. Nonetheless, the presence in the Eastern delegation of famous Greek scholars such as George Gemistos Plethon (*c.* 1355–1454) and Basil-Bessarion of Trebizond (1403–1472), together with their book collections, did much to arouse Western interests in Greek manuscripts.[2] The Council of Ferrara-Florence also prompted Pope Eugenius IV (*r.* 1431–1447) to develop a vision for a united, universal church that incorporated Greek and other Eastern Christians. In Bessarion it found the man to implement that vision.

Although the union of the churches would ultimately prove unachievable, several Greeks such as Bessarion chose to stay loyal to Rome. During the Council of Ferrara-Florence, Eugenius made Bessarion a Roman cardinal and, in 1440, granted him the titulus of the Holy Twelve Apostles. Later he would become successively bishop of Sabina, Tusculum, and then Sabina again. He became commendatory abbot of Grottaferrata in 1462 and, in the following year, Pope Pius II (*r.* 1458–1464) appointed him titular Patriarch of Constantinople. Bessarion was of course unable to take up the see on account of the Ottoman conquest of 1453, so he remained in Italy to look after the interests

[2] Wilson (2017): 63–66.

of the Italo-Greeks, Grottaferrata, and the growing Greek emigré community in Venice.

At some point in the early 1440s, Eugenius named Bessarion Cardinal Protector of the 'Order of St Basil', a new monastic organisation whose general chapter was convened for the first time in November 1446.[3] Organised monastic 'orders' such as the Benedictines and Cistercians were a peculiar feature of the Western church that was not shared by Eastern Christendom. The new order was named for St Basil of Caesarea, whose writings were particularly influential among Greek monks. Though it was presented rhetorically as the restoration of an ancient monastic order, the Order of St Basil was a new creation of the fifteenth century, an attempt to refashion Byzantine monasticism after models with which the medieval Latin church was more familiar.[4]

In practice, the Order of St Basil provided a unified administrative structure to Greek monasticism in southern Italy. It is interesting to note that this structure was overwhelmingly focused on the regions of Calabria, Sicily, and – to a lesser extent – Lucania, where the historically influential archimandritates of Rossano, Messina, and Carbone were located. The Salento peninsula and Apulia are not mentioned in the relevant documentation and the Basilian Order does not appear to have had a presence there.

In the prologue to his *Rule of St Basil* (based on the writings of St Basil and modelled on the *Rule of St Benedict*), Bessarion describes the main problem facing Italo-Greek monasteries in the fifteenth century: 'The majority [of the monks] are Latins and the sons of Latins. Some cannot read Greek at all; others can, but they make mistakes most of the time and do not understand anything of what they are reading...'[5] There was a clear need to improve the monks' level of education, so, at the start of his pontificate, Pope Callixtus III (*r.* 1455–1458) asked Bessarion to arrange for a *visitatio* to the Greek-rite monasteries of southern Italy for the purpose of inspection and reform.

The *visitatio* began in September 1457 under the leadership of Athanasios Chalkeopoulos, a former Athonite monk and then-archimandrite of the Nea Hodegetria (Patiron) of Rossano. Chalkeopoulos' record of his journey is a fascinating document, describing not only the state of each monastery that he visited but also giving an inventory of its books and liturgical vessels.[6] Despite Callixtus' request, his itinerary was limited to monasteries in southern Calabria and did not include his own monastery in Rossano. Nevertheless, the text gives a

[3] For relevant documents, see Scaduto (1947): 321–352. See also Parenti (2005): 182–186. There is evidence that Pope Innocent III and his successor Honorius III had attempted to create such an order in the thirteenth century, for which see Chapter 8, 'The Papacy Takes Charge', C8.S2.

[4] For further discussion of the adaptation of the Basilian tradition, see Peters-Custot (2017).

[5] '*λατῖνοι αὐτῶν ὄντες οἱ πλείους, καὶ παῖδες λατίνων, μὴ δυνάμενοι, οἱ μὲν μηδ' ἀναγινώσκειν ἑλληνικῶς ὅλως, οἱ δ' ἀναγινώσκοντες μὲν, ἐπταισμένως δὲ γε τὰ πλείω, καὶ τῶν ἀναγινωσκομένων συνιέντες οὐδόλως*...' Text in Laurent and Guillou (1960): xliii.

[6] Laurent and Guillou (1960): 1–167.

unique insight not only into the monasteries' fifteenth-century manuscript collections, but also into the monks and nuns themselves.

Bessarion's concern about the monks' ignorance appears to have been well founded. At the monastery of St Philip *de Gruti*, for instance, one witness told Chalkeopoulos that the abbot 'rarely says the divine office because he does not know it. Also, he never celebrates mass [*sic*] in the monastery, but employs a priest to whom he pays a salary...'[7] The abbot of the monastery of St John Theristes apparently never said mass because 'he does not know what to say'; he only said it on the feast day of the monastery's saint, and then only with two priests nearby to tell him the words.[8] Not everyone comes across so badly. The abbess of St Anastasia near Reggio, for example, says the divine office every day 'and knows how to read well'.[9] Nonetheless, the linguistic competence of the monks and nuns was clearly a recurring concern to Chalkeopoulos.

Bessarion made improved access to Greek religious texts a central part of his effort to reform Italo-Greek monasticism. He sent out agents such as his secretary Niccolò Perotti to inventory monastic libraries and oversaw an extensive effort at his Roman villa to create new copies of Greek manuscripts.[10] As part of this effort, Bessarion borrowed many of the manuscript prototypes from Basilian monasteries in southern Italy, though he generally returned them to their original owners; his aim was to strengthen the monasteries, not loot them. However, there were occasional oversights and some codices remained in his personal library. Bessarion eventually donated his collection in two consignments (in 1468 and 1474) to Venice, where it became the foundation of today's Biblioteca Nazionale Marciana.[11]

Among these were three nomocanonical manuscripts that had belonged to the Order of St Basil (Marc. gr. 169, 171, and 172). Marc. gr. 169, acquired from the monastery of the Holy Saviour of Messina, bears a note of possession in Bessarion's hand ('*Leges et canones conciliorum*, [*locus*] 43, *B*[*essarionis*] *Car. Tusculani*') and appears under the pressmark 200 in his collection.[12] Marc. gr.

[7] '...*dixit quod abbas raro dicit officium, quia ignorans est et nunquam celebrat missam in monasterio, sed tenet unum presbiterum, cui dat salarium*...': Laurent and Guillou (1960): 58 ll. 16–18. The normal term for a Greek church service is not 'mass' but 'liturgy'; however, Chalkeopoulos translates this into Latin as 'mass'.

[8] '*interrogatus si dicit missam, dixit quod nunquam dicit, nisi in festo sancti Johannis, et ipse nescit aliquid dicere nisi quia stant duo sacerdotes in latere ejus, qui docent ipsum dicere missam, alias nesciret dicere unum yota*': Laurent and Guillou (1960): 87 ll. 16–19.

[9] '*soror Anastasia cum juramento interrogate si abbatissa dicit officium in ecclesia debitis horis, dixit quod semper et cotidie dicit officium in ecclesia debitis horis et scit bene legere*': Laurent and Guillou (1960): 34 ll. 9–11.

[10] See e.g. the inventory of Grottaferrata's library made in 1462 by Perotti Batiffol [1889a]: 39–41). Elpidio Mioni identified about thirty manuscripts that Bessarion copied personally (Mioni [1968]: 66).

[11] Labowsky (1979): 23–57; Zorzi (1987): 63–85.

[12] Marc. gr. 169, fol. 1^{r}. Although Bessarion acquired this manuscript from Messina, it was originally copied in the Byzantine Empire; for further discussion, see Chapter 5, 'Monastic Nomocanons I', C5. P15. On Bessarion's system of pressmarks, see Labowsky (1979): 20–21.

172 (known to scholars as the 'Epitome Marciana'), a Calabrian civil law collection of 1175 with a canon law appendix, has lost its note of possession. Despite this, we can easily identify it as number 220 in Bessarion's library.[13]

The thirteenth-century nomocanon Marc. gr. 171 is a slightly more challenging case: the manuscript was clearly acquired from Grottaferrata as a Latin note on the opening folio states, but there is no note of possession and it cannot be easily identified with any of the entries in the catalogues of Bessarion's donation to Venice (which are often quite vague). On the other hand, the codex is missing from Perotti's 1462 inventory of Grottaferrata's library and I have been unable to find any mention of the manuscript in later donations to the Biblioteca Marciana. The most likely hypothesis is that Bessarion acquired the manuscript from Grottaferrata before 1462 and that it was part of the donation that became the core of the Marciana.

Another manuscript that slipped out of Basilian ownership in this period was Vall. C 11.1, a twelfth-century nomocanon acquired from the Holy Saviour of Messina. A note in the card catalogue of the Biblioteca Vallicelliana in Rome, where the codex is currently located, states that it was previously owned by the Spanish Cardinal Juan de Torquemada (1388–1468). Torquemada must have known Bessarion well: not only did both attend the Council of Ferrara-Florence, but both were promoted to the cardinalate around the same time (in 1439 and 1440, respectively). Not only that, but Torquemada was Bessarion's predecessor as bishop of Sabina (1464–1468).[14] He developed a strong interest in canon law, writing a commentary on Gratian's *Decretum* and defences of papal authority against the Conciliarists, and so built up a sizeable library of Latin and Greek canon law manuscripts.[15] From Thomas Izbicki's work on Torquemada's library, it seems that he purchased most of his books in Rome; there is no record of him having visited southern Italy. Though one cannot be sure, it is possible that Bessarion brought Vall. C 11.1 from Messina to Rome in the 1440s/1450s. Perhaps Torquemada borrowed the manuscript from him while he was writing his commentary on Gratian and failed to return it?

With the exception of the above cases, most Italo-Greek monastic nomocanons were still in southern Italy at the end of the fifteenth century. The significance of the Order of St Basil was that it provided an institutional framework to allow for the survival of Greek monasteries and (as a consequence) their library collections, which it did for just over two centuries. It was not always successful, however. The great monastery of Grottaferrata, for example, fell under the control of the powerful Tusculan noble family of the Colonna, who held it in fief from 1494 to 1557, when it was returned to papal oversight.[16] In 1575, Cardinal Guglielmo

[13] Labowsky (1979): 166. See also Mioni (1981): 1.261.

[14] On the life of Cardinal Juan de Torquemada, see Izbicki (1981b): 1–30.

[15] Izbicki (1981a): 310.

[16] Croce (1990): 7; Rocchi (1904): 90–97.

Sirleto (1514–1585), who managed the Order of St Basil and the papal library, commissioned a new inventory of Grottaferrata's manuscript collection from Don Luca Felice de Tivoli.[17] By comparing this with Niccolò Perotti's 1462 inventory, it immediately becomes clear that Grottaferrata had lost much of its library in the meantime; most of the manuscripts recorded in the 1572 inventory had actually been brought from Calabria by Sirleto himself around 1560.[18] The Colonna family seem to have taken at least one legal manuscript, a late eleventh- or early twelfth-century civil law collection with a canon law appendix, from Grottaferrata in the early sixteenth century. It received a new binding under the Colonna family seal and was later donated to the Vatican Library by Marcantonio Colonna (Cardinal Librarian from 1591 to 1597), where it can be found today under the shelfmark Vat. gr. 1168.[19]

Sirleto was himself indirectly responsible for another Basilian nomocanon slipping into private ownership. Like Bessarion, he engaged in an effort to make copies of Italo-Greek monastic manuscripts. In 1568, he asked the Tuscan cardinal Alessandro Farnese (then archbishop of Monreale in Sicily) to look for a selection of books in Calabrian monasteries and send him a list of what he found.[20] Sirleto aimed to make copies and return the originals, but, as with Bessarion, some manuscripts never made it back to their original owners. One of these was the twelfth-century nomocanon BN II C 7 from the monastery of St John Theristes of Stilo. The manuscript bears the distinctive markings of Farnese's collection and is missing from an inventory of St John Theristes' library made in 1603; evidently Farnese acquired it at some point in the 1570s–1580s and failed to return it.[21] Charles III of Spain eventually inherited the Biblioteca Farnesiana along with the Duchy of Parma (a Farnese fief) in 1731; he later became Charles VII of Naples and III of Sicily after conquering the two kingdoms in 1734. BN II C 7 thus found its way into the Reale Biblioteca Borbonica in Naples, today known as the Biblioteca nazionale 'Vittorio Emanuele III'.

The Renaissance Book Market in Southern Italy (16th–17th Centuries)

Farnese and the Colonna were by no means the only Italian nobles to develop an interest in collecting Greek manuscripts in the sixteenth century. As Renaissance

[17] Canart (1979): 196. See also Mercati (1935): 97; Rocchi (1893): 285–289.

[18] Batiffol (1891b): 40. The scholar Leo Allatius (1586–1689) stated that Sirleto brought the manuscripts from the Patiron of Rossano and SS Elias and Anastasios of Carbone: see Mercati (1935): 85.

[19] On Marcantonio Colonna's manuscript donation, see Janz (2014): 514 n. 63; Lilla (2004): 18.

[20] Text in Benoît (1879): 171 n. 3.

[21] For the 1603 inventory, see Capialbi (1941): 143–145. On the mark of Farnese's library, see Metastasio and Calabrese (2008): 83 n. 54.

humanism developed into an increasingly powerful cultural force, libraries of learned Greek and Latin books became important status symbols for wealthy aristocrats. Although the Renaissance is best known for the promotion of profane classical literature, it must be remembered that many leading scholars were high-ranking churchmen (or their close relatives) who were also interested in acquiring ecclesiastical books. A large number of Greek canon law manuscripts entered private collections in the sixteenth to seventeenth centuries as a consequence.

Southern Italy was an obvious place for scholarly Italian churchmen to look for antique Greek manuscripts. In contrast to the codices of the Order of St Basil, Greek manuscripts purchased on the southern Italian book market mostly came from the Salento peninsula. Unlike Calabria and Sicily, where Greek culture had largely become concentrated in monasteries, the Salento peninsula had a tradition of secular literary education in parish schools run by Greek clergy dating back to at least the thirteenth century.[22] Many of the priests who oversaw these schools engaged in manuscript copying; in fact, Jacob highlighted 'dynasties' of Salentine Greek clergy in the fifteenth and sixteenth centuries such as the Rizzo of Soleto who produced books as a family enterprise.[23] Not only did they copy new books, but they evidently had collections of older manuscripts to use as prototypes.[24] The Salento also produced several educated Greek-speakers who went on to play important roles in the cultural life of Renaissance Rome such as Niccolò Maiorano (papal librarian from 1532) and Federico Mezio (1551–1626), a professor at the Roman Collegio Greco (founded in 1577).[25]

These conditions made the Salento the focus of a lively trade in antique books as the agents of Renaissance collectors descended upon it to seek out acquisitions.[26] Nine of the surviving Italo-Greek nomocanons were purchased on the open market in the Salento in the sixteenth and seventeenth centuries, while a tenth was donated by a Salentine archbishop. Only three of the nomocanons that were bought by collectors in this period came from Calabria; none were from Sicily or Lucania. It is often possible to trace the nomocanons' sources through notes of sale or other relevant documentation, though in some cases we have to rely on other factors such as a manuscript's material characteristics and contents.

The first figure known to have bought a Salentine nomocanon was Cardinal Niccolò Ridolfi (1501–1550). Ridolfi was the nephew of the de' Medici pope Leo X (*r.* 1513–1521) and (in keeping with the nepotism of the time) had an astonishingly rapid career progression, becoming a cardinal deacon at sixteen and

[22] Jacob (1986).

[23] Jacob (1980): 66. More recently, see Arnesano (2007): 91–93; Arnesano (2008b): 112.

[24] A record of one such collection survives in the manuscript Paris, Bibliothèque nationale de France, MS gr. 549, fol. 169^{v}. It contains a list of books belonging to a Greek parish school in the Salentine village of Aradeo in the early fourteenth century. See Arnesano and Sciarra (2010): 441–442; Jacob (1985a).

[25] Arnesano (2007): 86.

[26] Petta (1972b).

archbishop of Florence at twenty-three.[27] He had been taught Greek in Rome by the prominent scholar Matthew Devaris of Corfu, who went on to administer his library. When Ridolfi died, his book collection was purchased by the Florentine noble Piero Strozzi (1510–1558) and then by Catherine de' Medici (1519–1589), the Queen Consort of King Henry II of France (*r.* 1547–1559). After her death, Ridolfi's books entered the French royal library, which today forms part of the Bibliothèque nationale de France.[28]

Two of the Greek canon law collections in Ridolfi's library can be traced back to the Salento. The late twelfth-century BnF gr. 1371 contains an autograph letter and epigrams of the famous Nektarios of Otranto, *hegoumenos* of the Salentine monastery of St Nicholas of Casole (1220–1235). The second manuscript, BnF gr. 1370 (copied in 1296/7), has unfortunately lost the majority of its scribal colophon that would have identified its place of origin. Nonetheless, Jacob and Arnesano have both identified it as Salentine on palaeographical grounds.[29] To this I would add that its textual contents and highly distinctive codicological features (in particular the X-pattern ruling found in parts of the manuscript) strongly corroborate the idea of a Salentine origin.[30]

The de' Medici rulers of Florence obtained a Salentine nomocanon for their private library at around the same time as Niccolò Ridolfi. The twelfth-/thirteenth-century Laur. plut. 5.22 bears a note on the opening flyleaf that refers to 'the renowned and most honourable emperor Frederick [II of Sicily]' and contains a selection of texts and codicological features that recur frequently in Salentine canon law manuscripts (like BnF gr. 1370).[31] The Medici library in Florence was opened to scholars in 1571 (one of the first Renaissance libraries to be opened to the public) and is known today as the Biblioteca Laurenziana. The books that formed the original core of the library are known as '*plutei*' (abbreviated in shelfmarks to 'plut'.) after the wooden benches to which they were chained.

Laur. plut. 5.22 is absent from an inventory of the Medici library made by Fabio Vigili in *c.* 1510, suggesting that it was purchased after that date.[32] It had probably arrived in the collection by 1542, though, as we see from another inscription in the codex. The opening flyleaf contains a Latin description of the manuscript's contents in the hand of the great Spanish legal scholar Antonio Agustín that

[27] Muratore (2009): 1.3–51. [28] Omont (1898a): 1.xx–xxi, xxvi, xxx.

[29] Arnesano (2005): 56; Jacob (1977): 281. Astruc (1988): 42 casts doubt on Jacob's palaeographical identification, though I believe that Jacob is correct.

[30] For further discussion of X-pattern ruling, in which there are two written lines for every one ruled line, see Chapter 9, 'The Salentine Group'. As Astruc (1988): 40 notes, the ruling scheme in BnF gr. 1370 is often hard to discern.

[31] '*. . . τοῦ περιβοήτου καὶ τιμιώτατου Φρεδδερίκου βασιλέως . . .*': Laur. plut. 5.22, fol. i^{r}. Jacob has also identified Laur. plut. 5.22 as Salentine, although he does not explain why: Jacob (2008): 233. See also Arnesano (2010): 72.

[32] For Vigili's inventory, see Rao (2012).

incorrectly identifies the text as Theodore Balsamon's recension of the *N14T*.[33] Agustín received a doctorate in Roman civil and canon law from the university of Bologna in 1541 and would later go on to serve as a judge of the *rota romana* (the Roman church's highest appeals court) in 1544. However, he spent four months in Florence from 1541 to 1542 studying the famous *Codex Florentinus* of Justinian's *Pandects*, which is when he would have encountered and annotated Laur. plut. 5.22.[34] Thus, we can conclude that the manuscript entered the Medici library at some point between *c.* 1510 and 1542.

A fragmentary nomocanon very similar to Laur. plut. 5.22 was obtained in the following decades by Cardinal Antonio Carafa (1538–1591), a nephew of Pope Paul IV (*r.* 1555–1559) who graduated with a degree in law from the University of Padua in 1564. Although much of the manuscript is missing, the surviving section of Vat. gr. 1287 contains the same contents as Laur. plut. 5.22 and has the same distinctive codicological features. On his death, Vat. gr. 1287 was one of a group of his manuscripts that was donated to the Vatican Library in his will.[35] Though there is no clear evidence as to how Carafa acquired Vat. gr. 1287, he is known to have bought at least two other Salentine manuscripts (Vat. gr. 1276 and 1277) from a certain 'Master Antony of Lecce'.[36] Master Antony, or another Salentine figure like him, may have been the source of Vat. gr. 1287 as well.

The story is similar for two other Salentine nomocanons acquired in this period, Barocci 86 and the fragmentary Ottob. 186 (fols. 9–22).[37] As in previous cases, the origins of the manuscripts can only be determined by their contents and physical appearance: both contain characteristic texts found in Salentine nomocanons and Barocci 86 has the hallmark X-pattern ruling (the ruling scheme in Ottob. gr. 186 is unclear).[38] Barocci 86 was donated to the Bodleian Library along with the other 241 *codices Barocciani* in 1629 by William Herbert, 3rd Earl of Pembroke, who had in turn purchased them from the Venetian Jacopo (Giacomo) Barozzi (1562–1617). Jacopo had inherited these manuscripts from his uncle

[33] '*ex Theodoro Balsamo* (*nam id est ei nomen alio huius bibliothecae codice tribuitur*) *νομοκάνονον* ...': Laur. plut. 5.22, fol. i^{v}. The text in Laur. plut. 5.22 is actually the *N50T*. The root of Agustín's mistake lay in another nomocanon in the Medici library, Laur. plut. 9.8 (fol. i^{v}), in which a thirteenth-century Greek hand mistakenly labelled the *S50T* (which superficially resembles the *N50T*) as Balsamon's *N14T*. Agustín translated the misleading label in Laur. plut. 9.8 into Latin and then applied it also to Laur. plut. 5.22.

[34] Baldi (2010): 177.

[35] Like all the Carafa manuscripts in the Vatican's *fondo antico*, Vat. gr. 1287, fol. 1^{r} bears the Carafa coat of arms and the legend '*Antonii Card. Carafae munus ex testamento*'. In the inventory of Carafa manuscripts in the Vatican Library published by Batiffol, Vat. gr. 1287 appears as number eleven, described as '*canones sanctorum Apostolorum et diversorum conciliorum ac sanctorum Patrum, sine principio et fine*: *in folio, charta bergamena*': Batiffol (1890): 132. See also Janz (2014): 512.

[36] Batiffol (1890): 71.

[37] Fols. 9–22 are a fragment of a Salentine nomocanon. They are bound together with fragments of a civil law collection (fols. 1–8), a grammatical text (fols. 23–61), and a theological text (fols. 62–69).

[38] Hutter (1982): 104 has identified Barocci 86 as the work of a twelfth-century Calabrian scribe named Leontios; Jacob (2008): 233 instead attributes it to the twelfth-century Salentine copyist Kalos. I am not sure if we can be certain about the scribe, but it is clear from the manuscripts' various features that it is Salentine in origin. On Ottob. gr. 186, see Arnesano (2005): 32; Arnesano (2008a): 199.

Francesco (1537–1604), the notable Venetian humanist (and alleged occultist), and continued to add to their number.[39] Francesco Barozzi was a philhellene who had been born on Venetian-ruled Crete; he is known to have acquired several of his manuscripts from southern Italy, including Barocci 86.[40]

A note at the beginning of Ottob. gr. 186 refers to it as a '*Nomimon* – A book containing law – Author uncertain. From the books of Duke Giovanni Angelo d'Altemps [d. 1620]'.[41] The Altempsiana library developed in several stages, beginning in the second half of the sixteenth century with Giovanni Angelo's uncle Mark Sittich von Hohenems (1533–1595), Cardinal Priest of SS Apostoli and founder of the Palazzo Altemps in Rome. I have not been able to find Ottob. gr. 186 in the 1609 inventory of the Altempsiana library published by Alfredo Serrai, implying that Giovanni Angelo may have collected it after this date.[42] Pope Alexander VIII (*r.* 1689–1691) purchased the Biblioteca Altempsiana in 1689, although it remained in the possession of his family (the Ottoboni) for several decades more. In 1740, Pope Benedict XIV (*r.* 1740–1758) bought the collection and integrated it into the Vatican Library, where the Altempsiana manuscripts can be found today among the *codices Ottoboniani*.

The largest single collection of Italo-Greek nomocanons (outside the church) to form in this period was at the Biblioteca Ambrosiana in Milan. It is also the best documented. The library was established in 1609 by Cardinal Federico Borromeo (1564–1631), the archbishop of Milan.[43] Federico had pursued classical studies in Rome in the late 1580s and aimed to establish a public library to serve Catholic scholarship in the Counter-Reformation. He sent out agents across the Mediterranean in the early years of the seventeenth century to find Greek manuscripts for the new foundation, with large numbers coming from Corfu, Chios, Thessaly, and Venice.[44]

Borromeo's agents purchased most of their manuscripts on the open market and usually made a note of the date and place of purchase. He commissioned an inventory of the Ambrosiana's Greek manuscripts in 1608, shortly before the library opened to the public.[45] They included at least seventy-six codices in southern Italy, of which twenty-eight were from Calabria and forty-eight were from Apulia.[46] In keeping with this overall ratio, three of the four Italo-Greek nomocanons in the Ambrosiana came from the Terra d'Otranto and only one from Calabria.

The Salentine nomocanons Ambros. E 94 sup. and F 48 sup. were both acquired in 1606; a note in the former states that it was bought in Soleto while the latter gives the place of purchase as 'Messapia' (an archaic name for the Salento

[39] Philip (1983): 37–41. [40] Batiffol (1891b): 42–43.

[41] '*Nomimon – Liber ius continens – Incerti auctoris. Ex codicibus Joannis Angeli Ducis ab Altaemps*': Ottob. gr. 186, fol. ii^r.

[42] Serrai (2008): 73–341. [43] On the history of the Ambrosiana, see Paredi (1981): 1–16.

[44] Martini and Bassi (1906): 2.1281–1282. [45] Turco (2004). [46] Lucà (2004b): 207.

peninsula).[47] Soleto had become the main centre of Greek manuscript production in the Salento by the sixteenth century and was the source of at least five of the Ambrosiana's manuscripts.[48] Ambros. E 94 sup. and F 48 sup. appear in the 1608 inventory as numbers 12 and 26, respectively.

Ambros. B 107 sup. is a less clear case. The manuscript's contents and distinctive ruling system clearly mark it out as a Salentine nomocanon, but it does not bear any note of sale and does not even appear in the inventory of 1608. What it does have, however, is a sketch on fol. 44^{v} of the harbour at Genoa as it would appear to an approaching ship, labelled '*GENOVA PORTO*' (see Figure 3.1). The drawing notably includes the *Lanterna* (lighthouse), rebuilt in 1544 after an earthquake, and the *Molo Vecchio* (Old Pier) on the eastern side of the harbour. However, it does not show the *Molo Nuovo* (New Pier) that was built on the western side of the harbour in 1638. We know from surviving receipts of payment that one of Borromeo's agents, Grazio Maria Grazi, brought at least two shipments of manuscripts from southern Italy via the port of Genoa in 1607.[49] The manuscript may simply have been overlooked in the composition of the 1608 inventory, though another possibility is that it arrived in the library after it opened in 1609 but before 1638.

The Salento was not the Ambrosiana's only source of Italo-Greek nomocanons, however. The fragmentary Ambros. G 57 sup. is number 114 in the inventory and bears a note stating that it 'arrived from Calabria in 1607'.[50] As we shall see in Chapter 5, this manuscript was originally copied in Tauriana in southern Calabria, though by the seventeenth century it was in the possession of the Basilian monastery of the Theotokos of Carrà near Catanzaro.[51] The wording of the note leaves open the question of *how* the manuscript 'arrived from Calabria'; was it by purchase, donation, or some other means? We cannot say.

The last of the great Renaissance book collectors to leave us nomocanons from southern Italy were the Barberini. Like the Biblioteca Ambrosiana, the Barberini library drew its manuscripts from both Calabria and the Salento. Originally founded by Cardinal Maffeo Barberini, the future pope Urban VIII (*r.* 1623–1644), and his nephew Cardinal Francesco Barberini (1597–1679), the collection remained in private hands until Pope Leo XIII purchased it for the Vatican Library in 1903.[52]

The Barberini received manuscript donations in the 1630s–1640s from two major southern Italian sources: Archbishop Francesco Arcudio of Otranto (1590–1641), a native of Soleto in the Salento peninsula; and Paolo Emilio Santoro (1560–1635), nephew and heir to Archbishop Giulio Antonio Santoro

[47] '*Soliti in Magna Graecia emptus est. 1606*': Ambros. E 94 sup., fol. ii^{r}; '*Messapiae in Magna Graecia emptus 1606*': Ambros. F 48 sup., fol. i^{v}.

[48] Arnesano (2007); Jacob (1977): 281; Martini and Bassi (1906): 2.1282.

[49] Pasini (2005): 470–471 n. 44.

[50] '*ex Calabria adventum 1607*': Ambros. G 57 sup., fol. 1^{r}.

[51] See Chapter 5, 'Monastic Nomocanons I', C5.P25.

[52] Rietbergen (2006): 401–404.

Figure 3.1. '*GENOVA PORTO*' (Ambros. B 107 sup., fol. 44ᵛ)

of S. Severina in Calabria (1532–1602).[53] Francesco Barberini is also said to have taken manuscripts from the library of Grottaferrata, where he was commendatory abbot from 1627 onwards.[54] In addition to these, the *fondo Barberini* includes codices inherited from other families with whom they intermarried, such as the Colonna. Unfortunately, the surviving documentation for all these acquisitions is vague and incomplete.

There are two southern Italian nomocanons and one other manuscript with canon law content in the *fondo Barberini*: Barb. gr. 323, 324, and 476. Only one of these, Barb. gr. 324, is from the Salento peninsula. Its provenance can be identified from the fact that, like BnF gr. 1371, it contains both Latin and Greek marginalia in the hand of Nektarios of Otranto.[55] I have been unable to find any clear reference to this manuscript in the Barberini documents, though it seems reasonable to suppose that it was donated by Francesco Arcudio of Otranto.

The other two manuscripts originated in southern Calabria. Barb. gr. 323 is a large parchment nomocanon of the early twelfth century that lost several quires over time. These were replaced and supplemented in the sixteenth century by new quires of Italian watermarked paper.[56] Santo Lucà has convincingly identified the hand that produced these additions as that of George Basilikos, a Constantinopolitan scribe who spent the years 1539–1541 in Venice and then moved to Messina (1542–1551) and southern Calabria (1552–1573).[57] Lucà noticed that the decorative style and watermark of the paper matched other work that Basilikos executed for the monastery of St Bartholomew of Trigona near Sinopoli on the western slopes of the Calabrian Aspromonte range. The manuscript was probably among the codices given by Paolo Emilio Santoro, which included a collection of 'canons of the Holy Apostles and other things relating to Greek canon law'.[58] Santoro's inventory also mentions a 'codex… containing ascetic works' including 'the ten ascetic chapters of St Basil,' which is to be identified with Barb. gr. 476.[59]

Although the great scholars of the Renaissance did acquire some of their manuscripts in Calabria, the antique book market was far more active in the Salento peninsula. Most surviving Greek codices in Calabria in the sixteenth and seventeenth centuries belonged to monastic libraries under the management of the Order of St Basil and were not intended for sale. By contrast, the Salento

[53] For Arcudio's donation, see the letters contained in Vatican City, Biblioteca Apostolica Vaticana, MSS Barb. lat. 6526, fols. 16^{r}–19^{r}, 23^{r}–24^{v}; Barb. lat. 6455, fols. 134^{r}–141^{v}; Barb. lat. 6494, fol. 7^{r}. For Santoro's donation, see Vatican City, Biblioteca Apostolica Vaticana, MS Barb. lat. 3075, fols. 13^{v}–25^{r}.

[54] D'Aiuto and Vian (2011): 342.

[55] Some of the longer marginalia are published in Jacob (2008): 233–245. See also Arnesano (2010): 71.

[56] Barb. gr. 323, fols. 1–48, 99–102, 185–242, 307–309, 312–314, 317–374.

[57] Lucà (2001): 139–140.

[58] '*Canones SS. Apostolorum et alia de iure canonico graeco*': Barb. lat. 3075, fol. 24^{r}.

[59] '*Codex… varia continens opuscula ascetica*'; '*S. Basilij capita ascetica X*': Barb. lat. 3075, fol. 24^{r}.

peninsula had an active culture of manuscript production centred among the secular Greek clergy. As a result, the great majority of Italo-Greek nomocanons that entered private collections during the Renaissance came from the Salento and – as we shall see in later chapters – from a secular rather than monastic context.

The Consolidation of the Basilian Manuscripts (17th–18th Centuries)

With few exceptions, most of the surviving Basilian nomocanons of southern Italy were still in monastic libraries in Calabria, Sicily, and Lucania at the beginning of the 1600s. The opposite was true by the end of the century. Several factors led church authorities to consolidate the Italo-Greek monastic libraries into three key centres: Rome, Grottaferrata, and Messina. The first impulse towards consolidation came from the church's reaction to the Protestant Reformation. Like the Conciliarist movement a century earlier, Protestantism in the mid-sixteenth century posed a threat to the power and legitimacy of the papacy. Once again, the Roman church responded with a great council (of Trent, 1545–1563) and attempted to reassert its universal authority, which it did in part by emphasising its ecumenical guardianship of both Latin and Greek traditions. The papacy was also motivated by a continuing desire to bring the Orthodox churches of the East into the Roman communion, a desire that was given increased urgency by the possibility that the Orthodox might instead unite with the Lutheran or Calvinist churches.

This effort was one of the main reasons for the dramatic increase in the Vatican Library's collection of Greek manuscripts in the late sixteenth century, as Timothy Janz has described.[60] The reform of canon law scholarship played a key role in the papacy's drive to assert itself. In 1566, Pius V (*r.* 1566–1572) commissioned the *correctores romani* to develop what was to become the foundational *editio romana* of Gratian's *Decretum* of 1582.[61] Later, in 1608–1612, the very first Western edition of the Greek conciliar canons in the original language (i.e. not in Latin translation) was published as part of the *editio romana* of the general councils of the Church.[62]

One of the manuscripts that the Vatican Library acquired in these years was Vat. gr. 1426, a codex best known as the earliest surviving source for Neilos Doxapatres' theological compendium *De oeconomia Dei*.[63] Its significance for this study lies in the witness it bears to an early thirteenth-century theological and canonical compilation that I refer to as the 'Messinese Collection'. As we read in a colophon on fol. 1^{r}, the codex was produced at the Holy Saviour of Messina in

[60] Janz (2014): 505. [61] Sommar (2009). [62] Leonardi (1964).
[63] Neirynck (2010).

Sicily by a monk named Ioakeim Mboutas, a copyist who was active around 1534.[64] The original Messinese Collection must have already been damaged in the sixteenth century (all three of the later copies break off at the same point in the text) and no longer survives today. Cardinal Sirleto took Vat. gr. 1426 from Messina for his personal library in the 1570s; it was later purchased by Duke Giovanni Angelo d'Altemps, as we learn from a note in the opening flyleaf. In 1612, Pope Paul V (*r.* 1605–1621) purchased it for the Vatican Library along with 'about eighty' manuscripts from the Altempsiana collection.[65]

Three years later, in 1615, Paul V brought another fifty-two manuscripts (the *codices Cryptenses*) to the Vatican from Grottaferrata. Many of these had only just been transported to Grottaferrata from Calabria by Sirleto around 1560 to replace codices lost earlier in the sixteenth century. Among them was Vat. gr. 1506, an Apostolic compilation (with a canon law appendix) from eleventh-century Rossano; a note on fol. Ii^v marks it out as '*codex bibliothecae Cryptoferratae ΨΨ*' (the shelfmark that Luca Felice de Tivoli had assigned it in his 1575 inventory).[66] Vat. gr. 1506 may have been one of the manuscripts brought by Sirleto, but it is interesting to note that Niccolò Perotti's 1462 inventory mentions an 'unbound [collection of the] canons of the Apostles'.[67] Though this description is admittedly quite vague, it does fit Vat. gr. 1506, which was indeed unbound in the fifteenth century (the manuscript's current binding dates to the years 1878–1889).[68] Vat. gr. 1506 may thus already have been in Grottaferrata's possession by the late Middle Ages.

In 1631, the Order of St Basil established the small monastery of S. Basilio *de Urbe* near the Piazza Barberini in Rome. This soon became the venue for the Academia Basiliana, a scholarly forum established by the Barberini pope Urban VIII that was intended to help bring about the union of the Greek and Latin churches and to reform the standards of Greek clergy in southern Italy.[69] Though union once again proved elusive and the Academia Basiliana disbanded in 1640, S. Basilio *de Urbe* remained an important centre for the Basilian Order.

The key turning point for the Order's manuscript collections came in the late seventeenth century, when the Basilian Abbot General Pietro Menniti (in office 1696–1710) decided to consolidate them. His predecessor, Apollinarius Agresta (d. 1695), had been notorious for despoiling Italo-Greek monastic communities.

[64] De Groote (1995): 8 n. 12; Devreesse (1955): 12.

[65] Lilla (2004): 29–30; Mercati (1938): 109.

[66] Batiffol (1889b): 209–210 n. 3. A second note on fol. ii^v states that '*τοῦτο τὸ βιβλίον ἦν τῆς μονῆς τῆς κρυπτοφέρης* [*sic*]' ('this book was from the monastery of Grottaferrata').

[67] '*canones apostolorum non copertos*': Batiffol (1889a): 41.

[68] The binding of Vat. gr. 1506 bears the seals of Pope Leo XIII (1878–1903) and Cardinal Librarian Jean-Baptiste Pitra (1869–1889).

[69] Herklotz (2007); Herklotz (2008).

Menniti made a *visitatio* to the Basilian monasteries in southern Italy and decided to gather their documentary archives for safekeeping in two main centres: the archives from Sicilian monasteries were brought to the Holy Saviour of Messina, while those from the mainland went to S. Basilio *de Urbe*.[70] By this time there were no longer any Greek monasteries in Apulia, so he did not concern himself with that region.

Once he had dealt with the Basilians' documentary archives, Menniti turned his attention to centralising their manuscript collections.[71] The famous Benedictine monk Bernard de Montfaucon, often considered the founder of the modern discipline of Greek palaeography, met Menniti at S. Basilio *de Urbe* in 1698 and described the manuscripts there in his *Diarium Italicum*.[72] Montfaucon explains the rationale behind Menniti's consolidation: 'Since the Greek language has become obsolete and scarcely used in the various monasteries of Calabria that are subject to him, [Menniti] gathered those intact and neglected books. Now he has rescued them from imminent destruction and has seen to it that they were brought to Rome for the use of scholars.'[73]

Once again, Menniti brought manuscripts from Sicilian monasteries to the Holy Saviour of Messina. Manuscripts from Calabria and Lucania were divided by theme: 'liturgical' codices went to S. Basilio *de Urbe* while 'literary' ones went to Grottaferrata. The manuscripts collected in S. Basilio *de Urbe* henceforth became known as the *codices basiliani*. It is clear from the manuscripts in these *fondi* that Menniti considered canon law to be 'liturgical' and civil law to be 'literary', although he was not entirely consistent in this: Crypt. gr. 322, for instance, is a canon law collection that he brought to Grottaferrata rather than S. Basilio. Despite this aberration, the legal manuscripts at Grottaferrata are mostly collections of civil law while those among the *codices basiliani* are primarily canon law. Pope Pius VI (*r*. 1775–1799) acquired the *codices basiliani* for the Vatican Library in 1786 and today they form the *fondo basiliano* of the *Vaticani graeci* (Vat. gr. 1963–2123).[74]

Most of the manuscripts are indeed from Calabria, as Montfaucon stated. Both Vat. gr. 2060 and 2019 contain inscriptions that explicitly tie them to the Patiron of Rossano, while an analysis of their contents implies that Vat. gr. 2075 and 2115

[70] Batiffol (1891b): 42; Breccia (1991): 17.

[71] Batiffol (1889b): 197–198; Batiffol (1891b): 43; Lilla (2004): 76.

[72] Montfaucon (1702): 210–226.

[73] '*is enim, quia in variis sibi subjectis Calabriae Monasteriis, codices istos, obsolete pene Graecae linguae usu, jacere intactos neglectosque acceperat, imminenti jam exitio subduxit, inque Urbem advehi in usum eruditorum curavit*': Montfaucon (1702): 210.

[74] Lilla (2004): 75; Mercati (1935): 216. In addition to their current 'Vat. gr. . . . ' numbers, the codices also bear the shelfmarks 'Basil. . . . ' These are the numbers given to the manuscripts in a catalogue made by the monk Giovanni-Grisostomo Scarfò in 1697: see Scarfò (1737): 82. The codices are all bound in reddish-brown leather bearing the seals of Pope Pius IV (*r*. 1846–1876) and Cardinal Librarian Angelo Mai (1853–1854).

came from the same city.[75] Another nomocanon, Crypt. gr. 322 in Grottaferrata, appears to have been collected from the monastery of SS Peter and Paul of Spanopetro in southern Calabria.[76] Menniti also acquired several codices at the monastery of SS Elias and Anastasios of Carbone in Lucania, including Vat. gr. 1980 and 1981, two manuscript halves that originally formed a single nomocanon.[77]

Turning to Sicily, the manuscript collection of the Holy Saviour can today be found in the *fondo S. Salvatore* of the Biblioteca Universitaria Regionale in Messina. It comes as a surprise, though, that it contains only one nomocanon: the twelfth-century S. Salv. 59. This manuscript did not originally belong to the monastery of the Holy Saviour but to a monastery dedicated to St Pantaleon in nearby Bordonaro, as we read from a late medieval Latin note on fol. 1^r. Originally known (rather confusingly) as the Holy Saviour of Bordonaro, it merged with the Holy Saviour of Messina in 1490, which is when S. Salv. 59 would have entered the *fondo S. Salvatore*.[78] The codex is listed as item number four in an inventory drawn up in 1563 by the Messinese nobleman Francesco Antonio Napoli.[79] In other words, S. Salv. 59 was already in Messina long before the effort to consolidate the Basilian libraries and Menniti did not collect a single nomocanon from anywhere in Sicily.

It is difficult to account for this fact. Sicily was, after all, home to many autonomous Greek monasteries and their subject houses in the Middle Ages.[80] We know that two nomocanons had already been removed from Messina in the fifteenth century by Bessarion (Marc. gr. 169) and Torquemada (Vall. C 11.1). An inventory composed in *c.* 1465–1470 shows that the Holy Saviour of Messina possessed another nomocanon (Anon. 110) in the late fifteenth century, but this had disappeared by the time Napoli inspected the monastery's library in 1563.[81]

[75] '*Concilia et canones. Ex Biblioth. Monast. S.M. de Patiro Rossanensis*': Vat. gr. 2060, fol. ii^r. On Vat. gr. 2019, 2075, and 2115, see Chapter 4, 'Monastic Nomocanons I', C4.P19–C4.P21, and Chapter 7, 'Monastic Nomocanons II', C7.S3.

[76] See Chapter 5, 'Monastic Nomocanons I', C5.P27–C5.P28.

[77] Mercati (1935): 205–209. For further discussion, see Chapter 4, 'The Byzantine Background', C4.P25–C4.P30.

[78] Foti (1995): 332–333, 346.

[79] Mercati (1935): 233. On Napoli's mission to catalogue the library of the Holy Saviour, see Mercati (1935): 32–40.

[80] Scaduto (1947): 245–285.

[81] Mercati (1935): 279–290 (no. 110); see also 43–47. This anonymous inventory is preserved in BnF lat. 13075, fols. 290^r–296^r. Mercati dated it to the late sixteenth century on the grounds that it omits Vat. gr. 1426 (copied in *c.* 1534), which was acquired by Sirleto in the 1570s. However, the inventory also omits S. Salv. 59 (which had entered the monastery in 1490) and includes Vat. gr. 1167 (present in Messina in *c.* 1465–1587; see Appendix 3, 'Uncertain and Disputed Manuscripts', CA3.S15). Given the fact that it also omits Marc. gr. 169 and Vall. C 11.1 (removed from Messina in *c.* 1460), it makes the most sense to date the inventory to *c.* 1460–1490. This coincides with a period in which a Messinese notary named Antonio Carissimo was engaged in preparing an inventory of the Holy Saviour's library (*c.* 1465–1470) that was thought to be lost (Foti [1985]; Lucà [1986]; see also Rodriquez [2017]: 125). As far as I am aware, no scholar has yet made the connection between

A manuscript in the Moscow State Historical Museum, Sin. gr. 432, may potentially also be from Sicily.[82] However, the fate of other Sicilian canon law manuscripts is something of a mystery. One can only speculate about what may have caused their loss: the devastation of the War of the Sicilian Vespers, steady demographic Latinisation, raids by Barbary pirates, the sack of Messina by the Spanish in 1678, and the Sicilian earthquake of 1693 are all possible factors.

Miscellaneous Manuscript Acquisitions (17th–19th Centuries)

Pietro Menniti made the last major effort to gather Greek manuscripts from southern Italy, though there were still some left in the region in the eighteenth century. Francesco Russo has highlighted the observation of the Basilian abbot Gregorio Piacentini (1684–1754) in 1735 that 'many Greek books can be found in various places in the Basilian monasteries of Calabria'.[83] However, the eighteenth and nineteenth centuries were not kind to the Italo-Greek monasteries or their libraries. Natural disasters such as the Calabrian earthquake of 1783 or the burning of the Archivio Communale di Stilo in 1809 led to the loss of many codices, while others were sunk off Capo Palinuro in 1810 as they were being shipped to Naples.[84] The Order of St Basil was itself eventually suppressed when the Kingdom of Naples came under Napoleonic rule in 1806.[85]

A small number of Italo-Greek nomocanons made their way into modern collections in other ways besides the Basilian Order and the Renaissance book market. At least two can be found in the manuscript collection of the patriarchal synod in the Moscow State Historical Museum, Sin. gr. 397 and 432.[86] These were brought to Moscow from Mount Athos by the Russian monk Arsenii Sukhanov (1600–1668). Sukhanov had been sent to Athos, Constantinople, and other parts of the Orthodox world in 1654 by Patriarch Nikon of Moscow (1652–1666) as part

Mercati's anonymous inventory and Antonio Carissimo's work, but I would argue that he is likely its author.

[82] See below, C3.P52.

[83] '*In monasteriis Calabriae Ord. S. Bas. multi variis in locis codices graeci reperiuntur*': text in Capialbi (1941): 99; quoted in Russo (1969): 47.

[84] Capialbi (1941): 157; Croce (1990): 347.

[85] Davis (2006): 202–205.

[86] Fonkič and Poliakov (1993): 107–109, followed by Kurysheva (2008), identify Sin. gr. 398 and 432, not 397, as southern Italian on palaeographical grounds. On Sin. gr. 398, see Appendix 3, 'Uncertain and Disputed Manuscripts', CA3.S5. Sin. gr. 397 bears all the distinctive hallmarks of thirteenth-century Salentine nomocanons, from content to codicology. Moreover, the scribe who copied the manuscript shows a particular interest in Italian geography. In a note at the beginning of the canons of Carthage (419), he explains that Bishop Faustinus of Potentia (in the province of Piacenza), one of the participants in the council, was from Italy: '*Pikentine* is a city of Italy. It is also called *Pikenon*. Potentia is a city of Italy. It is also called *Potenton*' ('*Πικεν[τίνη] πό[λις] Ἰταλί[ας]· λέγετ[αι] κ[αὶ] Πικην[όν]· Ποτεντία πό[λις] Ἰταλί[ας]· λέγετ[αι] κ[αὶ] Ποτ[έν]το[ν]*'): Sin. gr. 397, fol. 42^{v}. He does not highlight any of the non-Italian place names mentioned in the manuscript.

of an attempt to revise the Russian church's liturgical books. Sukhanov's mission was to search for important Greek church manuscripts for the Moscow Patriarchate to serve as sources; he would return from his journey with over 500.[87]

Sukhanov left notes on the first folio of each nomocanon explaining where he acquired them: Sin. gr. 397 came from the monastery of Iviron and Sin. gr. 432 came from the Great Lavra. It is not clear how they found their way from Italy to Athos in the first place, though. There was a significant amount of contact between the two regions throughout the Middle Ages; as we saw in Chapter 2, the Holy Mountain was home to two Italo-Greek monasteries in the eleventh and twelfth centuries (and possibly later), those 'of the Sicilian' and 'of the Calabrian'.[88] It is possible that Sin. gr. 432 (which seems to have originated in southern Calabria or Sicily) was brought to one of those monasteries and later incorporated into the Great Lavra's library when they ceased to exist.

Sin. gr. 397 bears an interesting clue to its history on fol. 80^{v}. This page bears a note in a sixteenth-century Greek hand that reads, 'Of Jeremiah the Most Holy and Ecumenical Patriarch'.[89] There were two patriarchs of Constantinople named Jeremiah, who held office in the years 1522–1546 and 1572–1595 respectively, though the note gives no indication as to which one it was. As we saw earlier in the chapter, the late sixteenth century was a particularly active time for the sale of Salentine nomocanons, but most of these were bought by Italians; how did this manuscript come into the possession of a Constantinopolitan patriarch? Although one cannot be certain, one possibility is that it was part of a diplomatic gift. In 1583, Pope Gregory XIII (*r.* 1572–1585), advised by the Calabrian cardinal Guglielmo Sirleto, sent a letter to Jeremiah II along with 'certain spiritual gifts'.[90] Sirleto was of course very familiar with the Greek book trade in southern Italy, so perhaps Sin. gr. 397 was one of these gifts.

Three more Italo-Greek canon law manuscripts were acquired by collectors in the eighteenth and nineteenth centuries. The codex Alag. gr. 3, a twelfth-century Gospel Lectionary with a canon law appendix, is currently in the Biblioteca Alagoniana attached to the archiepiscopal cathedral in Syracuse in Sicily. A note on the opening folio states that it came 'from the donation of the knight Mario Landolina Nava [1760–1853]'.[91] Nava served as the Royal Custodian of Antiquities in Sicily under the Bourbon king Ferdinand though, as Lucà has noted, he was not a bibliophile himself; he probably inherited the manuscript

[87] Fonkič (1977): 68.

[88] See Chapter 2, 'Greek Christianity in Medieval Italy', C2.P16, C2.P38.

[89] '*ἰερεμου του αγιοτατοῦ καὶ οικουμένικου πατρίαρχου* [*sic*]': Sin. gr. 397, fol. 80^{v}.

[90] '*mittimus etiam per dilectos filios Michaelem Eparchum et Joannem Bonamfidem munera quaedam spiritualia*': text in Theiner (1856): 3.436.

[91] '*Ex dono equitis Marii Landolina Nava*': Alag. gr. 3, fol. 1^{r}.

from his father, Saverio (1743–1814).[92] Alag. gr. 3 was in the library of the Holy Saviour of Messina in the sixteenth century, and so Saverio probably bought it on the Sicilian book market.[93]

The last two manuscripts both originated in the Salento peninsula. Marc. gr. III.2 and Add. 28822 both contain the texts, decorative scheme, and ruling pattern that distinguish Salentine nomocanons.[94] Marc. gr. III.2 is one of the few Greek manuscripts in the Biblioteca Marciana that were not part of Bessarion's original fifteenth-century bequest. The codex belonged to the library of Jacopo Nani (1725–1797), an officer in the Venetian navy who rose to become one of the city's three *deputati straordinari al militar* in 1794.[95] Nani travelled extensively in the eastern Mediterranean during his career and built up a collection of over a thousand manuscripts, including 309 Greek codices. He left these to the Biblioteca Marciana on his death. The Bolognese abbot Giovanni Luigi Mingarelli catalogued them in 1784; Marc. gr. III.2 appears as number 226.[96]

Finally, the nomocanon fragment Add. 28822 is preserved in the British Library's Additional collection. The library purchased the manuscript in 1871 from Sir Ivor Bertie Guest (1835–1914), who became 1st Baron Wimborne in 1880 and was married to Winston Churchill's aunt Cornelia Spencer Churchill.[97] Ivor and his brother Montague were keen travellers and collectors of antiquities who would apparently return from foreign trips 'laden with china and curiosities of all sorts', in Montague's words.[98] Presumably Add. 28822 was one of these 'curiosities' that Sir Ivor had acquired abroad, though it is not clear where or when he did so.

Conclusion

The Italo-Greek nomocanons that exist in modern collections were preserved in two main institutional contexts: the monastic libraries of the Order of St Basil and the private libraries of great Renaissance book collectors (see Table 3.1). The former were concentrated in Calabria, Sicily, and Lucania, while the latter tended to acquire most of their southern Italian manuscripts from the Salento peninsula where families of clergy were still teaching the Greek language and copying Greek books in the sixteenth and seventeenth centuries.

[92] Lucà (2002): 86. On Mario Landolina Nava, see Castiglione (2011): 255–256.

[93] It is probably to be identified with the '*Evangelistarium continens evangelia distincta per menses et dies*' in Napoli's 1563 inventory: Mercati (1935): 242 (no. 87).

[94] Annaclara Cataldi Palau did not include Add. 28822 in her survey of southern Italian manuscripts in the British Library's Additional and Egerton collections, but its affinities with other Salentine nomocanons are unmistakeable (Cataldi Palau [1992]: 202–203).

[95] Negro (1971).

[96] Mingarelli (1784): 414–418 (no. 226).

[97] Add. 28822, fol. iii^{r}.

[98] Guest (1911): xxv.

Table 3.1. Acquisitions of Italo-Greek Nomocanonical Manuscripts by Modern Collections

	Modern Shelfmark	Date of Production	Region of Origin	Source of Acquisition	Date of Acquisition[a]
1.	Marc. gr. 172	1175	Calabria	Basilian Order	*c.* 1444–60
2.	Marc. gr. 169	C11/12	Sicily	Basilian Order	*c.* 1455–60
3.	Marc. gr. 171	*c.* 1220–30	Grottaferrata	Basilian Order	*c.* 1455–60
4.	Vall. C 11.1	*c.* 1100–15	Calabria	Basilian Order	*c.* 1455–60
5.	S. Salv. 59	*c.* 1100–15	Calabria	Basilian Order	1490
6.	Laur. plut. 5.22	C12/13	Salento	Purchase	*c.* 1510–42
7.	BnF gr. 1370	1296/7	Salento	Purchase	*c.* 1530–50
8.	BnF gr. 1371	Late C12	Salento	Purchase	*c.* 1530–50
9.	Vat. gr. 1426	*c.* 1534 (1213)	Sicily	Basilian Order	*c.* 1570–80
10.	BN II C 7	1139	Calabria	Basilian Order	*c.* 1570–90
11.	Vat. gr. 1287	C12	Salento	Purchase	1591
12.	Vat. gr. 1168	C11/12	Calabria	Basilian Order	*c.* 1591–7
13.	Ambros. E 94 sup.	Late C13	Salento	Purchase	1606
14.	Ambros. F 48 sup.	*c.* 1110–20	Salento	Purchase	1606
15.	Ambros. G 57 sup.	Early C12	Calabria	Basilian Order	1607
16.	Ambros. B 107 sup.	C12/13	Salento	Purchase	Early C17
17.	Ottob. gr. 186	C12/13	Salento	Purchase	Early C17
18.	Vat. gr. 1506	1024	Calabria	Basilian Order	1615
19.	Barocci 86	C12	Salento	Purchase	1629
20.	Barb. gr. 323	Early C12	Calabria	Donation	*c.* 1630–35
21.	Barb. gr. 476	C12	Calabria	Donation	*c.* 1630–35
22.	Barb. gr. 324	Late C12	Salento	Donation	*c.* 1630–40
23.	Sin. gr. 397	C13	Salento	Sukhanov	1654
24.	Sin. gr. 432	C12	Calabria/ Sicily	Sukhanov	1654
25.	Crypt. gr. 50	C14	Calabria	Basilian Order	1697
26.	Crypt. gr. 76	C12/13	Calabria	Basilian Order	1697
27.	Crypt. gr. 322	Pre-1135	Calabria	Basilian Order	1697
28.	Vat. gr. 1980	C11	Lucania	Basilian Order	1697
29.	Vat. gr. 1981	C11	Lucania	Basilian Order	1697
30.	Vat. gr. 2019	Pre-1234	Calabria	Basilian Order	1697
31.	Vat. gr. 2060	*c.* 1100–15	Calabria	Basilian Order	1697
32.	Vat. gr. 2075	Late C10	Calabria	Basilian Order	1697
33.	Vat. gr. 2115	C11/12	Calabria	Basilian Order	1697
34.	Alag. gr. 3	1124	Calabria	Purchase	Late C18
35.	Marc. gr. III.2	C12/13	Salento	Purchase	*c.* 1770–84
36.	Add. 28822	C12/13	Salento	Purchase	1871

[a] This column gives the date (exact or approximate) on which we can first trace a manuscript to an owner outside southern Italy. Some manuscripts were acquired by more than one owner before entering their current collection.

This dynamic had several effects on source survival, the most obvious of which is that extant nomocanons from Calabria and surrounding regions tend to be monastic in character and Salentine nomocanons usually seem to be geared towards the secular clergy. It also means that we have very few secular nomocanons from Calabria and very few monastic ones from the Salento. To what extent is this representative of medieval reality? As we shall see in future chapters, some exceptions such as Vat. gr. 2019 and Barb. gr. 324 have managed to slip through, implying that both regions produced a mixture of monastic and secular manuscripts.

Another effect of the historical patterns of source survival is chronological. Nomocanons from Calabria generally date to the twelfth century, as this was when most of the Italo-Greek monasteries that would constitute the Order of St Basil were originally founded. As for the Salento, the Greek clergy's literary and educational culture flourished most in the thirteenth and fourteenth centuries, and so most of the extant Salentine nomocanons were copied in that period. Not only does this create an impression of a division between monastic Calabria and secular Salento, but it also implies that the Italo-Greeks' centre of cultural gravity shifted over time from monasteries to the clergy. Is this a true reflection of what happened in the Middle Ages or a mirage created by patterns of source survival?

In truth, it is probably a mixture of fact and mirage. One could argue that the patterns of source survival reflect a reality of their own: perhaps the reason that the Order of St Basil was the main institutional vessel for the preservation of Calabrian manuscripts is that monasticism was a more powerful cultural force in the region to begin with? Perhaps the Salentine clergy were so active in literary culture because monasteries were less influential there? It is impossible to give definitive answers to these questions, but we must bear them in mind as we analyse what the manuscripts tell us about Byzantine legal and religious culture in medieval Italy.

PART II

BYZANTINE CANON LAW IN THE NORMAN KINGDOM

4
The Byzantine Background

When the Normans invaded southern Italy in the eleventh century, they brought approximately five centuries of (more or less) uninterrupted Byzantine rule in the region to an end. Greeks were established majorities in much of southern Calabria and the Salento peninsula, while the Christians of Sicily still followed the Greek rite under Islamic rule. Before we look at how Byzantine religious law in southern Italy was affected by the Norman conquest, we must first ask what sort of character it had before Robert Guiscard seized control of Reggio and Bari in the 1060s–1070s.

There has been some controversy among historians regarding the nature of Byzantine rule in medieval southern Italy. Barbara Kreutz, for instance, asserted that Byzantium only began to leave a mark on the region in the eleventh century, just before the Norman invasion: 'In the tenth century, there had been no flowering of Byzantine culture in southern Italy... Byzantium then had been mostly represented by garrisons, military governors, and the ascetic anchorite saints preaching disdain for things material... Many scholars... assume, wrongly, a continuous Byzantine flavor over the centuries.'[1] Was Byzantine culture in southern Italy simply a superficial eleventh-century veneer?

The surviving evidence indicates that it was not, at least insofar as canon law is concerned. One of the difficulties in assessing the pre-Norman period in southern Italian history is that so few contemporary sources have been preserved. The only extant Italo-Greek nomocanon that can be dated with some likelihood to the era of Byzantine rule is Vat. gr. 1980–1981, which was probably produced in the mid-eleventh century.[2] This scarcity of sources is a consequence of the Norman invasion, a chaotic and destructive process that drew a major dividing line across southern Italian history. As we saw in Chapter 3, institutional continuity was the key to the preservation of medieval manuscripts; the important Greek monasteries and parish churches that provided this continuity were almost all founded *after* the Norman conquest.

Ironically, then, we are forced to infer as much as possible about canon law (and much else besides) in Byzantine Italy from sources that post-date the Norman invasion. This can create the false impression that Byzantine culture had only a superficial presence in southern Italy in earlier centuries. Nonetheless, though

[1] Kreutz (1991): 151. [2] See section: 'Canon Law in the *Katepanikion*', C4.S2.

Byzantine Religious Law in Medieval Italy. James Morton, Oxford University Press (2021). © James Morton.
DOI: 10.1093/oso/9780198861140.003.0005

most of the surviving manuscript sources date to the Norman era, they were demonstrably based on earlier manuscripts that were already present under Byzantine rule. As we shall see in this chapter, the manuscript tradition of Byzantine canon law in southern Italy took shape alongside the formation of Greek ecclesiastical institutions in the ninth and tenth centuries. When the Normans eventually conquered the region in the eleventh century, the Italo-Greeks' system of Byzantine religious law was already deeply rooted—even antiquated.

Greek Canonical Collections in Byzantine Italy

The Church of Constantinople first gained authority over southern Italy in *c.* 733, when the emperor Leo III (*r.* 717–740) transferred the region from Roman jurisdiction during the Iconoclast crisis.[3] However, the Byzantine Empire lost most of its remaining territories in southern Italy to Lombard and Muslim powers during the ninth century, as we saw in Chapter 2. The emperor Basil I was eventually able to recover and consolidate a large swathe of Calabria and Apulia in the 880s, accompanying the military invasion with a significant reorganisation of the region's imperial and ecclesiastical administration, at least in Greek-speaking areas. The sees of Reggio and S. Severina were elevated to metropolitan status around the year 886, placing them in charge of Italo-Greek suffragan bishops throughout Calabria; Otranto was similarly elevated in *c.* 967/8 and became the chief see of Byzantine Apulia.

While the Byzantines did not have to re-create the church from scratch in all the areas they reconquered, it was nonetheless in a considerable state of disrepair. This is the impression given by a surviving canonical letter that Patriarch Photios of Constantinople sent in response to a series of legal questions that the Greek Archbishop Leo of Reggio posed in the early 880s.[4] Although we do not have Leo's original questions, Photios' five answers paint a picture of Calabria as an embattled frontier region whose local churches had been severely weakened by decades of Islamic occupation:

1. In areas where there are no Christian clergy available, laypeople may baptise new-born children.
2. If the wife of a priest or deacon has been raped by a barbarian [i.e. a Muslim], her husband may take her back if she was unwilling. If she was

[3] See Chapter 2, 'Greek Christianity in Medieval Italy', C2.P5.

[4] Text in Laourdas et al. (1985): 162–166 (ep. 297). For an in-depth discussion of the letter, see Martin (1998): 485–491.

willing, then her husband must either separate from her or renounce his ministry.

3. Christians should baptise Muslim children if their mothers promise to give them a Christian education.
4. It is permissible to give the Eucharist to worthy women to bring to Christian prisoners in Muslim captivity for communion.
5. Christian children who have been raised as Muslims may be forgiven and readmitted to communion.

The letter gives the strong impression that the Calabrian clergy had suffered losses in the course of the ninth century and that many local Christians had converted to Islam. Now that the Byzantines were back in control, they faced the challenge of rebuilding the local hierarchy and bringing apostates back into the fold after decades of Muslim rule. In other areas such as the Salento peninsula, the Byzantine church established a significant Greek ecclesiastical presence for the first time among a predominantly Latin-speaking population.

The late ninth and tenth centuries were therefore a crucial formative period for the medieval Italo-Greek church's administrative structures and, by extension, its system of religious law. This was also the time of the legal codification efforts of Basil I and his successor Leo VI; indeed, the Photian recension of the *N14T* is thought to have been composed just a few years before Reggio and S. Severina were promoted to metropolitan rank.[5] We might expect that the newly elevated sees would have received copies of this new recension, but this does not seem to have been the case. Rather ironically, the earliest surviving Italo-Greek copies of the Photian *N14T* date to the early twelfth century and were based on prototypes that were imported from Byzantium *after* the Norman conquest.[6] By contrast, the most widespread Greek canon law collection in Byzantine Italy by far was the sixth-century *N50T*, which is present in ten surviving codices; another manuscript contains the *S50T*, which predates the *N50T*.[7] Even in the eleventh-century Carbone nomocanon, which has the original recension of the *N14T*, the text is heavily interpolated with additions from the *N50T*.[8]

The surviving manuscripts thus give the impression that the Greek church in Byzantine Italy relied primarily on the sixth-century *N50T* rather than the more contemporary Photian *N14T*. Given the lack of surviving evidence from the early Middle Ages, it is hard to fully explain this archaism, but it is a phenomenon that

[5] See Chapter 1, 'Introducing the Byzantine Nomocanon', C1.P11.

[6] See Chapter 6, 'Monastic Nomocanons II', C6.S2.

[7] *N50T*: Laur. plut. 5.22, fols. 1–83; Crypt. gr. 322, fols. 70–111; Add. 28822, fols. 43–49; Ambros. E 94 sup., fols. 166–198; Sin. gr. 397, fols. 134–161; BN II C 7, fols. 1–83; Barocci 86, fols. 13–79; BnF gr. 1370, fols. 102–123; Vat. gr. 1287, fols. 45–65; Marc. gr. III.2, fols. 170–198. *S50T*: Sin. gr. 432, fols. 21–62.

[8] Vat. gr. 1981, fols. 92–181.

manuscript scholars have noted in other areas too. Commenting on the aesthetics of Italo-Greek manuscripts, for instance, Irmgard Hutter has observed that 'what distinguishes southern Italy from the centre of the [Byzantine] empire and the other eastern provinces is the tenacious survival of ancient traditions: what was a passing phenomenon in Byzantium acquired an almost immutable character in southern Italy'.[9]

The same appears to have been true with canon law codifications. However, the explanation probably does not just lie in traditionalism; it may also have been a quirk of timing. New recensions of legal texts in the Middle Ages could take a long time to spread from centre to periphery. Manuscripts were expensive and time-consuming to produce, so institutions wanted to get as much use out of a legal collection as possible before it had to be replaced. Moreover, as non-legislative codifications, Byzantine canon law collections were never officially promulgated, so it was not obligatory for users to update to the latest recension of a text. Unless there was a compelling reason to acquire the latest manuscripts from Constantinople (which did happen on occasion), it was much easier just to copy whatever was available locally. As a result of these factors, new recensions of canonical collections could potentially take decades or even centuries to spread from the imperial centre to the provincial peripheries. The textual tradition of Byzantine canon law in Calabria was probably cemented around the time of the elevation of Reggio and S. Severina in the late ninth century, before the Photian *N14T* had become popular outside Constantinople. The Byzantine church in southern Italy therefore continued using the older *N50T* and the first recension of the *N14T* right up to (and beyond) the Norman conquest.

Nonetheless, Byzantine Italy was not completely impervious to new canonical recensions from Constantinople. In a group of six nomocanons from the twelfth- to thirteenth-century Salento (which we shall examine in greater depth in Chapter 10), for instance, we find the text of the *Synopsis of Canons* in addition to the *N50T*.[10] It is not the well-known twelfth-century version of Alexios Aristenos, however, but an earlier recension that has traditionally been attributed to the tenth-century Symeon Metaphrastes.[11] Presumably this text of the *Synopsis* first crossed the Adriatic at some point between its tenth-century composition and the fall of Bari to the Normans in 1071; its arrival may be associated with the elevation of Otranto to metropolitan status in 967/8, when Apulia gained its first major Greek ecclesiastical see since Late Antiquity.

If the *Synopsis of Canons* could cross over to the Salento, then why not the Photian recension of the *N14T*? Given the paucity of manuscripts from the tenth

[9] Hutter (2006): 71.

[10] Barocci 86, fols. 156^{v}–172^{r}; Laur. plut. 5.22, fols. 119–139^{r}; Marc. gr. III.2, fols. 203–220; Sin. gr. 397, fols. 162–189; Ambros. E 94 sup., fols. 200–218^{r}; BnF gr. 1370, fols. 128^{v}–139.

[11] See Chapter 1, 'Introducing the Byzantine Nomocanon', C1.P11.

century, one can only speculate. It is notable, though, that the Salentine manuscripts containing the *Synopsis* also have the *N50T* (usually in very close proximity). As we saw earlier, the *N50T* gives the text of the canons divided into thematic categories, a format that was good for looking up a particular subject but less useful if a reader wanted to find a specific canon. The *N14T* solved this problem by joining a thematic reference guide with the full text of the canons, but this was rather long. By combining the *N50T* with the *Synopsis of Canons*, the Italo-Greek copyists of the Salento had a similar, if less elegant, solution: the *N50T* provided a thematic guide to the canons and the *Synopsis* offered a chronological one. The benefit of this grouping is that it was quite short: the *N50T* and the *Synopsis* together could perform more or less the same function as the *N14T* in about half (or even just a third) the number of folios. Despite the lack of sophistication, this combination was cheaper and easier to produce than the *N14T*.

The Italo-Greeks of the Byzantine Salento thus seem to have found their own solution to the problem addressed by the *N14T*: they simply joined the *N50T*, the most widespread canonical collection of Byzantine Italy, with the tenth-century *Synopsis of Canons*. Interestingly, though, this recension of the *Synopsis* is not attested anywhere else in southern Italy outside the Salento, and the Salentines' innovative combination did not spread beyond their small peninsula. This curious cultural division between the Salento and the Calabro-Sicilian region will be a recurring theme in later chapters.[12]

Finally, it is important to remember that some Italo-Greek civil law collections also transmitted canonical texts. Once again, the late ninth and early to mid-tenth centuries seem to have been the key formative period. The earliest surviving manuscript is the late tenth-century Vat. gr. 2075, made (unusually) by a team of seven Calabrian scribes, which combined an Italo-Greek recension of Symbatios' *Epitome of the Laws* (composed *c.* 920 and based on the late ninth-century *Procheiros Nomos*) with a canon law preface focused on matters of ecclesiastical and monastic administration.[13] This preface consists of the seventeen canons of the *Protodeutera* council, the Apostolic Canons (in the wrong order), and Justinian's Novel 5 (regulating the foundation of monasteries and the novitiate).

Two other Calabrian civil law manuscripts, the early eleventh-century Vat. gr. 1168 and the early twelfth-century Vat. gr. 2115 (fols. 78–96), contain a canonical supplement that is closely related to the one in the tenth-century Vat. gr. 2075.[14]

[12] Not only do the Salentine manuscripts have different contents from those of Calabria, but their palaeographical style seems to have undergone a separate historical development as well: see Lucà (2012): 524–525.

[13] Vat. gr. 2075, fols. 1–19. On the evidence for the manuscript's origins and composition, see Danella (1989): 113–114. On Symbatios' *Epitome of the Laws*, see Chitwood (2017): 42–43.

[14] Indeed, this canonical supplement would find its way into two later Calabrian civil law collections, the eleventh-/twelfth-century Crypt. gr. 76, fols. 129–147^{r}, and the fourteenth-century Crypt. gr. 50, fols. 141–146. Note that none of these manuscripts can be dated with precision; the dating is derived

Intriguingly, both contain a scribal error at the beginning of a selection of canons of the Council of Carthage (419), giving it the nonsensical heading: 'Title 3, Constitution 3: that it is necessary for houses in which heretics make their gatherings to be acquired by churches, of the 227 blessed fathers who gathered in Carthage.'[15] There is no such 'constitution' by the 227 fathers of Carthage; rather, an absent-minded scribe must have been looking at (or thinking about) the last text he had copied, an excerpt from the epitome of Athanasios of Emesa's *Syntagma of Novels*, while he was writing the heading for the Carthaginian canons.[16] This mistake was then faithfully copied out by later scribes for the next four or five centuries, giving an interesting insight into how much attention they paid to what they were writing![17]

The same mistake also appears in a fourteenth-century legal fragment from Byzantine Greece that can be found today in the manuscript Vall. E 55.[18] Since the error is unlikely to have spread from southern Italy to the Greek mainland, this would suggest that it was already present in the Byzantine prototype from which Vat. gr. 1168 and 2115 are ultimately derived. By analysing the various manuscripts' contents, we can surmise their approximate relationship to one another, with 'X' being their hypothetical Byzantine ancestor (see Figure 4.1).

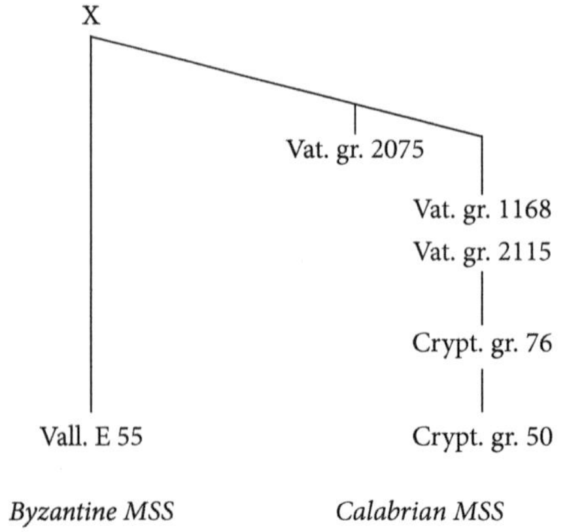

Figure 4.1. Approximate relationship of the Calabrian civil law collections and Vall. E 55 (fols. 132–164)

instead from assessments of their palaeographical and codicological features. See Lucà (1993): 60; Lucà (2012): 543; Rodriquez (2013): 631.

[15] '*τίτλος γ', διάταξις γ'. ὅτι χρή ταῖς ἐκκλησίαις προσκυροῦσθαι τοὺς οἴκους ἐν οἷς παρασυνάξεις ποιοῦσιν οἱ αἱρετικοὶ τοῖς* [sic] *ἐν Καρθαγένη συνελθόντων ,σκζ' μακαρίων πατρῶν*': Vat. gr. 1168, fol. 134v; Vat. gr. 2115, fol. 78r.

[16] For the epitome of Athanasios' *Syntagma*, see Simon and Troianos (1979): 293–315.

[17] The scribes of the two later Calabrian manuscripts made some effort to correct the problem. The copyist of Crypt. gr. 76 amended the heading to 'Title 3, Constitution 3. Of the 227 blessed fathers who gathered in Carthage' ('*τίτλος γ', διάταξις γ'. τῆς ἐν Καρθαγένη συνελθόντων ,σκζ' μακαρίων πατρῶν*'), though this still does not make sense. In Crypt. gr. 50, the heading simply became 'Six canons of the same [Council] of Carthage' ('*τῆς αὐτ[ῆs] ἐν Καρθαγένη κα[νόνες] ς'*').

[18] Rome, Biblioteca Vallicelliana, MS E 55, fol. 142r.

The *Procheiros Nomos* and Symbatios' *Epitome* provide a *terminus post quem* of *c*. 900–920 for the arrival of these civil and canon law texts in southern Italy, while the manuscript Vat. gr. 2075 gives a *terminus ante quem* of the late tenth century. Just as the appearance of the *Synopsis of Canons* in the Salento can probably be associated with the elevation of Otranto in the 960s, the texts in these civil law manuscripts were almost certainly brought to southern Italy in connection with the administrative reforms that led to the creation of the Byzantine *katepanikion* around the same time. When we look at the Italo-Greek civil and canon law manuscripts of the post-Byzantine era, therefore, we are looking at a legal tradition that was first shaped by the Eastern empire's reconquest and reorganisation of southern Italy in the late ninth and tenth centuries.

Canon Law in the Katepanikion: Evidence from the Carbone Nomocanon and a Calabrian Apostolic Collection

Very little can be said about how canon law worked in practice in Byzantine Italy, since procedural sources for the period are virtually non-existent. As far as we can tell, though, it seems safe to assume that Constantinople enforced its own legal system in Greek-speaking areas under its control, particularly after the elevation of the new metropolises of Reggio, S. Severina, and Otranto. This is the impression that we get, for instance, from Photios' canonical letter to Archbishop Leo of Reggio in the late ninth century, which suggests that it was normal for Italo-Greek bishops to request legal guidance from the patriarchate.

Italo-Greek hierarchs also travelled to Constantinople for several important councils and patriarchal decrees in the ninth to eleventh centuries. Leontios of Reggio, Nikephoros of Crotone, Demetrios of Squillace, John of Tempsa, and George of Gerace were all present at the Constantinopolitan synod of 869, while Demetrios of Squillace also attended the Photian council of 879 along with Leo of Reggio and Mark of Otranto.[19] A century later, Basil of S. Severina and one 'Leo of Catania' signed Patriarch Sisinnios II's *Tome against the Marriage of Cousins* in 997 and the signatories to Patriarch Alexios Stoudites' two *hypomnemata* (patriarchal decrees) on church administration of 1028 included Metropolitan Nicholas of Otranto.[20] It is notable, though, that none of these documents were signed by any Latin bishops from southern Italy.

The limited evidence, then, suggests that the Greek bishops of Byzantine Italy played an active role in the administration of Constantinople's canon law system.

[19] Mansi 16.189–196. See also Russo (1982): 1.213–214.

[20] RP 5.11–19, at 19; 5.20–32, at 25, 32. The reference to Catania is strange, since it was under Islamic rule at the time. It may be a mistaken reference to the bishop of Reggio, whom we would expect to have attended.

This impression is reinforced by the Carbone nomocanon (Vat. gr. 1980–1981), the only complete Italo-Greek canon law collection to survive from the pre-Norman era. This is one of the longest manuscripts in this study (at a combined total of 395 folia) and can be found today in two separate halves in the Vatican's *fondo basiliano*, having been brought to Rome by Pietro Menniti in the 1690s.[21] The great twentieth-century Vatican librarian Giovanni Mercati proved that Menniti must have acquired the manuscript at SS Elias and Anastasios of Carbone, since it bears the signature of a monk named Marcellus who made an inventory of that monastery's library in the seventeenth century and left his name in each codex.[22]

It is difficult to date the Carbone nomocanon exactly, but its contents and palaeographical style are consistent with what we would expect from the eleventh century.[23] Like the codices that we examined above, the contents of the Carbone nomocanon reflect a tradition that can be clearly traced back to the tenth century. The 'youngest' text in the codex is a list of patriarchs of Constantinople that ends with Tryphon (928–931).[24] The first half of the manuscript contains a full-text corpus of canons, but the canons of the *Protodeutera* council of 861 are noticeably absent, suggesting that the prototype on which it depends was assembled before this council became widely accepted as part of the canon law corpus. As mentioned above, the nomocanon also contains the original recension of the *N14T* with interpolations from the *N50T*, although it is interesting to note that the table of contents refers to it as the '*Syntagma* of the blessed Patriarch Photios'.[25] By the eleventh century, the *N14T* had become so closely associated in the Byzantine mind with Photios' name that the Italo-Greek scribe of the Carbone nomocanon believed that he was copying the Photian recension even though he was actually working with a much older text.

Besides the main text of the manuscript, the Carbone nomocanon is particularly interesting for the frequent interventions that the copyist left in the margins alongside the corpus of canons in Vat. gr. 1980 (see Table 4.1). I have not seen

[21] The codex seems to have already been divided in two during the Middle Ages, as we see from a note left by an anonymous reader in a fourteenth-century Greek hand: 'Look for the rest in the other book like this one, for this contains 21 titles [out of 40]' ('*ζήτει τὰ ἑξῆς ἐν τῷ ἑτέρῳ βιβλίῳ τῷ ὁμοίῳ τούτο· τούτο γὰρ περιέχει τίτλους κα*'): Vat. gr. 1980, fol. 195^{v}.

[22] Mercati (1935): 205–209, esp. 207–208. Some of the monastery's manuscripts were also brought to Grottaferrata and likewise bear Marcellus' signature: Petta (1972a): 159–163.

[23] The script is highly reminiscent of the '*scuola niliana*' or 'School of Neilos' style pioneered by St Neilos the Younger of Rossano, which flourished in northern Calabria, Lucania, and Grottaferrata in the late tenth and eleventh centuries; see Lucà (1991a); Lucà (1991b).

[24] Vat. gr. 1981, fols. 197^{v}–199^{r}.

[25] '*τοῦ μακαρίου Φωτίου πατριαρχ[οῦ] σύνταγμα ἔχων κανόνας κ[αὶ] κε[φάλαια] ἐκκλησιαστικὰ ἐκ τοῦ συντάγματος τῶν ἁγίων ἀπο[στόλων] καὶ ἑκάστης ἁγίας συνόδου καὶ τοῦ ἁγίου Βασιλ[είου] κεχωρισμέ[να] δία ιδ′ τίτλω[ν] καὶ τῶν συνᾳδόντων νομίμων*': Vat. gr. 1980, fol. 3^{v}.

Table 4.1. Vat. gr. 1980, Highlighted Canons by Subject

Subject	Canons
Limits of episcopal jurisdiction	Apost. c. 34, 35 (fol. 21^{v}); I Const. c. 2 (fol. 36^{r}); Chalc. c. 17 (fol. 50^{v}); Ant. c. 9 (fol. 147^{v}); Sard. c. 3, 4, 11 (fols. 158^{v}, 159^{v}, 163^{v})
Ecclesiastical judicial process	Apost. c. 25 (fol. 20^{v}); Chalc. c. 9 (fol. 48^{v}); Ant. c. 15 (fol. 149^{v}); Sard. c. 5 (fol. 159^{v}); Carth. c. 15, 59 (fols. 171^{v}, 187^{r})
Clerical hierarchy and discipline	I Nic. c. 16 (fol. 33^{r}); Chalc. c. 18 (fol. 50^{v}); *Trullo* c. 4, 7 (fols. 82^{v}, 84^{r}); Ant. c. 4 (fol. 146^{v}); Carth. c. 16 (fol. 172^{v})
Ordination of priests and bishops	Apost. c. 21, 68 (fol. 20^{r}, 25^{v}); I Nic. c. 9 (fol. 31^{r}); Laod. c. 12 (fol. 154^{r}); Sard. c. 6 (fol. 160^{v})
Reception of repentant heretics	I Nic. c. 8, 19 (fol. 30^{v}, 34^{r}); I Const. c. 6 (fol. 32^{r}); *Trullo* c. 95 (fol. 113$^{r/v}$)
Order of patriarchal precedence	I Nic. c. 6 (fol. 30^{r}); Chalc. c. 28 (fol. 53^{r}); *Trullo* c. 36 (fol. 95^{v})
Catechism and Baptism	Apost. c. 50 (fol. 23^{v}); *Trullo* c. 84 (fol. 110^{r}); Neocaes. c. 5 (fol. 135^{v})
Simony	Apost. c. 29 (fol. 21^{r}); II Nic. c. 5 (fol. 120^{v})
Clerical marriage	Carth. c. 4, 70 (fols. 168^{v}, 191^{v})
Diocesan administration	Chalc. c. 26 (fol. 52^{v})
Monasticism	*Trullo* c. 44 (fol. 99^{v})
Fasting	*Trullo* c. 29 (fol. 92^{r})
Miscellaneous	*Trullo* c. 28, 62, 96 (fols. 92^{r}, 104^{v}, 110^{r})

these marginalia elsewhere, suggesting that they may be of the scribe's own creation, although it is possible that they were present in his model.[26] They mostly consist of summaries of particular canons of note and occasional citations of related texts. The scribe's choice of canons betrays a strong interest in the episcopate, clerical discipline, and judicial process in ecclesiastical courts:

Although it eventually came into the possession of the monastery of SS Elias and Anastasios, the scribe's annotations imply that the Carbone nomocanon was originally intended for use by a Greek bishop with responsibility for the discipline of secular clergy. Indeed, Lucà has concluded on the basis of a palaeographical study that the scribe was probably a notary, which is what we would expect for a non-monastic nomocanon.[27] The region of Lucania (where Carbone is located) was home to several Greek bishops under the Byzantine Empire who were subsequently replaced by Latins following the Norman conquest.[28] I would

[26] Many texts such as the *N14T* have standardized annotations that frequently recur across codices, though the marginalia in the Carbone nomocanon appear to be specific to that manuscript.

[27] Lucà (2012): 508.

[28] The sees of Acerenza, Tursi, Gravina, Matera, and Tricarico were all held by Greek suffragan bishops under the Archdiocese of Otranto; see Falkenhausen (1978): 163. We do not know exactly

suggest that the manuscript was probably produced for one of these Greek bishops in the last years of Byzantine control (or the early years of Norman rule).

In addition to highlighting certain canons and citing related texts, our scribe also left a few observations of his own. Alongside canon five of the Second Council of Nicaea (787), for instance, he noted that simony is 'a deadly sin. Absolutely clear.'[29] Some of his comments give particularly revealing insights into the scribe's legal worldview. For example, canon five of the Council of Sardica (344) states that deposed bishops have the right to appeal to the bishop of Rome for a retrial. In the view of the eleventh-century Byzantine church, the twenty-eighth canon of the Council of Chalcedon (451) had granted the Patriarchate of Constantinople equal rights to the papacy and made it the default court of appeals for Eastern Christendom; indeed, that was the essence of the deal that Alexios Stoudites tried to offer Pope John XIX in 1024.[30]

The Lucanian scribe of the Carbone nomocanon not only offers the exact same interpretation of jurisdictional boundaries as that of the Constantinopolitan patriarchate, but he even adopts its rhetoric (to curious effect). Where Sardica c. 5 states that deposed bishops may appeal to Rome, the copyist left a dismissive comment stating that 'this canon is clearly about bishops in the West... Both Hosius [one of the bishops at the council of Sardica] and those who were issuing canons with him were from those parts... Until now, such a custom has not taken hold anywhere [in the East].'[31] The irony, of course, is that the council of Sardica took place to the *east* of Italy, in modern-day Bulgaria, which was under papal jurisdiction at the time. When the scribe of the Carbone nomocanon writes about 'bishops in the West', he means it not in a geographical sense but in a cultural one: bishops of the Latin rite under the Roman pope. In this way of thinking, Byzantine Italy counted as being 'in the East' on account of the fact that it fell under the Patriarchate of Constantinople. Despite having been produced in close proximity to the Latin church in southern Italy (unlike Calabria and the Salento, Lucania had a Latin majority), the Carbone nomocanon reflects a completely Constantinopolitan perspective on canonical jurisdiction.

Besides the Carbone nomocanon and the civil law collection Vat. gr. 2075, only one other surviving manuscript from the pre-Norman era has canonical content. Vat. gr. 1506 is a fragmentary codex that (unusually) preserves a colophon left by the scribe: 'This is the end of the book of the *Apostolic Constitutions* [completed]

when they were replaced by Latins, although it probably occurred in the late eleventh or early twelfth centuries, since the Normans typically waited until the Greek incumbent's death; see Loud (2007): 503.

[29] '*ἁμαρτί[α] πρὸ[ς] θάνατ[ον]. σαφῶς ὅλον*': Vat. gr. 1980, fol. 120v.

[30] See Chapter 2, 'Greek Christianity in Medieval Italy', C2.P19.

[31] '*πρόδηλ[ον] πε[ρὶ] τ[ῶν] ἐν τ[ῇ] δύσει ἐπ[ι]σκόπ[ων] ὁ καν[ῶν] οὗτο[ς]... καὶ ὁ Ὅσιο[ς] καὶ οἱ συ[ν] αὐτ[ῷ] ἐκθέμ[εν]οι κανόν[ας] τ[ῶν] μερ[ῶν] ἐκειν[ῶν]... οὐδαμ[οῦ] μέχρη τοῦ νῦν συνήθεια τοιαυτ[ή] κεκράτικεν* [*sic*]': Vat. gr. 1980, fol. 159v.

by the hand of the humble priest Abba Athanasios on 25th March, at the 4th hour, in the 6th indiction, in the year 1024. I ask everyone to pray for me in the Lord.'[32] Athanasios does not specify where he worked, but we can infer that the manuscript had a Calabrian origin from its style and from the fact that it was in the possession of the monastery of Grottaferrata in the late Middle Ages.[33] The *Apostolic Constitutions* purports to be a collection of instructions for the clergy issued by the Apostles and compiled by Pope Clement I of Rome (*r.* 88–99), though it was probably composed in Syria in the late fourth century.[34] The Council *in Trullo* was also sceptical of the work's authenticity, believing it to be a genuine work that was later altered by unscrupulous heretics. However, the council *did* accept the collection of eighty-five 'Apostolic Canons' that formed an appendix to the *Apostolic Constitutions* (the Western church only accepted the first fifty canons). The full range of these Apostolic Canons are present at the end of Vat. gr. 1506, though a small number have been omitted by mistake.[35]

The codex is large and elegant, created from high-quality parchment and decorated with a paratactic ornamental scheme; it must have been expensive to make. A reader with an eleventh- or twelfth-century Greek hand has highlighted the text of *Apost. Const.* 8.12 on fol. 59^{v}, a passage that gives the words of a liturgical prayer to be spoken by the *protopapas* (the senior priest in a Byzantine cathedral) before the Eucharist. The reader also added a quote from Gregory of Nazianzus to explain the theology behind the prayer.[36] The expensive look of the manuscript and the reader's interest in the *protopapas*' prayer lead me to suspect that Vat. gr. 1506 was most likely produced for use in a Greek cathedral of Calabria; it may even have been Rossano itself, given the city's historic connection with Grottaferrata. It is hard to infer much from the codex, but, like the Carbone nomocanon, it gives us the impression of a wealthy Italo-Greek bishopric under Byzantine rule that lived firmly within the world of Constantinopolitan canon law.

How did southern Italy's Latin-rite hierarchy fit into this picture? Considering the paucity of sources, one could be forgiven for overlooking the fact that Latin Christians outnumbered those of the Greek rite in most of Byzantine Italy.

[32] '*τέρμα εἴληφεν ἡ βίβλος τῶν Διατάξεων τῶν Ἀποστόλων· διά χειρὸς Ἀθανασίου τοῦ εὐτελοὺς ἄββα πρεσβυτέρου· μην μαρτίῳ κε′ ἡμέρ[ᾳ] δ′ ὥρ[ᾳ] ϛ′ ἰνδ[ικτιώνι] ἔτει ͵ϛφλβ′. παρακαλῶ δὲ πάντας εὔχεσθαι ὑπὲρ ἐμοῦ διὰ τὸν Κύριον*': Vat. gr. 1506, fol. 80^{v}. Such scribal colophons are extremely rare since they are typically written in the very last folia of a codex, which are usually among the first to be lost through wear and tear. In the case of Vat. gr. 1506, a large portion of the beginning of the manuscript has been lost. The text begins at *Apost. Const.* 3.7.

[33] See Chapter 3, 'Patterns of Source Survival', C3.P42. The manuscript was probably not produced at Grottaferrata itself, since Athanasios identifies himself as a priest (the copyists at Grottaferrata would have been monks). Lucà has identified the style of script in Vat. gr. 1506 with the School of Neilos style: Lucà (1991b): 349.

[34] See Metzger (1985): 13–62.

[35] Vat. gr. 1506, fols. 72^{v}–77. The text has Apost. c. 5–9, 14, 17–63, 66, 64–65, 67–84. The omission of some canons was probably not a choice made by Athanasios but rather a sign that he was working from a defective prototype.

[36] Gregory of Nazianzus, *Oration* 30.14.

Though the imperial authorities seem to have made a concerted effort to win the political loyalties of Latin bishops in southern Italy, it is difficult to say what relationship—if any—the Patriarchate of Constantinople had with them. There is almost no evidence for sustained contact between Latin bishops under Byzantine rule and the patriarchal court. There are no Latin signatories on Constantinopolitan documents in this period, while surviving writings from figures such as Leo of Ohrid, Niketas Stethatos, and Peter III of Antioch tend to imply that Constantinople lived in naïve ignorance of the Latin church.[37] In turn, Constantinople's legal system appears to have left no direct mark on surviving Latin canon law collections from southern Italy.[38] The Latin and Greek canon law systems in the region seem to have been largely isolated from one another under Byzantine rule, a trend that would continue to a surprising degree following the Norman conquest.

The Norman Conquest and Anti-Latin Polemic

The Norman invasion of Byzantine Italy was a long and traumatic affair that began in earnest in the 1040s and only concluded with the fall of Bari in 1071. Calabria in particular bore the brunt of fighting not only between Byzantine and Norman forces, but also among the Normans themselves. Although they would eventually achieve a *modus vivendi* in the twelfth century, this extended confrontation gave the Italo-Greeks a deeply negative first impression of their new rulers. It also contributed to sectarian tension between the Roman papacy and the Patriarchate of Constantinople, as Byzantine churchmen began to associate Norman aggression against the empire's territories in Italy with the perceived religious errors of the Latins.

This tension manifested itself in several Italo-Greek nomocanonical manuscripts. Medieval scribes were not always knowledgeable about the works that they were copying (especially in legal manuscripts), so they would often reproduce texts from their sources that were no longer up-to-date. As a result, the texts contained in Byzantine nomocanons are in some ways akin to the strata of an archaeological excavation, with different 'layers' dating to different historical

[37] The Byzantine Patriarch Peter III of Antioch was the author of a letter to Domenicus of Grado, the Venetian Patriarch of Aquileia, in the early 1050s (text in *PG* 120.756–781). In the letter he attempts to persuade Domenicus not to call himself 'patriarch', since there were only five patriarchs (of Rome, Constantinople, Antioch, Alexandria, and Jerusalem) in Byzantine ecclesiology. For Leo of Ohrid's letter to John of Trani, see Chapter 2, 'Greek Christianity in Medieval Italy',C2.P25; on Niketas Stethatos, see below, C4.P38–C4.P39.

[38] The Eastern patristic texts in Latin canon law collections from southern Italy such as the *Collection in Five Books* seem to have been drawn from older Latin intermediaries rather than from contemporary Byzantine sources; see Reynolds (1990): 292; Reynolds (1997): 26–27. There have been few studies of Latin canon law collections from southern Italy and further research may provide more nuance to this picture.

periods in the manuscript tradition. The Norman conquest left just such a layer in several Italo-Greek canon law codices. Although we do not have any examples from the time of the Norman invasion itself, we see a strain of Byzantine anti-Latin polemic from the 1050s appear in a crop of Calabrian nomocanons from the early twelfth century and recur in manuscripts as late as the fourteenth.

Some Byzantine criticisms of Latin religious practice were relatively old. The Latin insertion of the *Filioque* clause into the Nicene-Constantinopolitan Creed, for instance, had been a major issue in the ninth-century Photian dispute.[39] Others were older still, such as the unusually blunt denunciation of the Western practice of fasting on Saturdays during Lent in the fifty-fifth canon of the Council *in Trullo* of 691/2. However, the eleventh century saw a new anti-Latin criticism rise to prominence in Byzantine polemic: the 'Judaising' use of unleavened bread in the Eucharist. Whereas Western Christians and many non-Chalcedonian Eastern churches used unleavened wafers for communion in emulation of the Jewish Passover, it was Byzantine custom to use leavened bread (as it is in the Orthodox Church today). Eucharistic *azyma* became the target of sustained Byzantine criticism from the eleventh century on.

The Byzantine fixation with *azyma* seems to have developed as a consequence of the empire's extensive tenth- and eleventh-century reconquests in Syria and Armenia, which were home to a large population of non-Chalcedonian Christians whom orthodox Byzantines considered to be heretics.[40] These non-Chalcedonians consumed unleavened bread in the Eucharist and did not recognise the authority of the Patriarchate of Constantinople, a fact that led many Byzantine churchmen to associate the use of *azyma* with the rejection of Constantinopolitan orthodoxy. As military conflict with the Normans flared in the 1040s, the Byzantines soon noticed the fact that Westerners also engaged in the subversive, heretical practice of consuming *azyma*, a point that became a central plank of their anti-Latin polemic.

One of the most prominent examples of this polemic is the *Discourse Against the Romans* (*c.* 1054) of Niketas Stethatos (*c.* 1005–1090), a monk of the Stoudios monastery in Constantinople who played a prominent role in the confrontation with Cardinal Humbert in 1054.[41] Niketas begins the work by stating that the patriarchal synod had made enquiries of the former abbot Basil of Montecassino and the Latin archbishop of Bari regarding Western liturgical practices: 'I mean the *azyma*, fasting on Saturday, prohibition of the marriage of priests, and their daily celebration of complete Eucharists during the time of the most holy [Lenten]

[39] See in particular Photios' *Encyclical Letter to the Eastern Patriarchs* in Hergenröther (1869): 510–511.

[40] For a recent discussion of this subject, see Kolbaba (2013): 54–56.

[41] Text in Michel (1930): 320–342. On Niketas Stethatos, see Angold (1995): 28–31.

fast.'[42] He then refutes these practices using Byzantine canon law: 'I shall show you,' he says, 'all the [canonical] legislation against the *azyma*.'[43] Niketas proceeds to quote at length from the canons for seven pages of Michel's edition of the text (which is only twenty-one pages).[44]

A truncated southern Italian recension of Stethatos' work appears in two Calabrian monastic nomocanons of the early twelfth century, Barb. gr. 323 and Crypt. gr. 322.[45] It is also followed in the two manuscripts by a short, anonymous tract entitled 'On the Holy Spirit' and an extract from John of Damascus' *Exposition of the Orthodox Faith*, both of which implicitly attack the Latin addition of the *Filioque* to the Creed.[46] The same texts of Niketas Stethatos and John of Damascus can be found in BN gr. 7, a late eleventh-century theological compilation from the Calabrian town of Gerace.[47] As the German scholar Kurt Schweinburg established, the version in Crypt. gr. 322 was copied from BN gr. 7, whereas Barb. gr. 323 was based on the (now lost) manuscript that BN gr. 7 was itself copied from.[48] Niketas Stethatos' *Discourse Against the Romans* must therefore have already come to southern Italy in the second half of the eleventh century. It may even have arrived during the conflicts of the 1050s–1060s and entered the manuscript tradition of Calabrian nomocanons soon after.

A similar strain of anti-Latin polemic appears in the Gospel Lectionary Alag. gr. 3, originally copied at the Patiron monastery of Rossano in 1124.[49] Although it is not itself a nomocanon, the manuscript closes with an appendix of canon law texts on patriarchal jurisdiction, fasting, and the use of *azyma* in the Eucharist.[50] The text on patriarchal jurisdiction (entitled *Statement and Definition of the Patriarchal Thrones*) ranks the patriarchates in a surprising order: 1. Jerusalem; 2. Rome; 3. Constantinople; 4. Alexandria; 5. Antioch. Byzantine patriarchal *taktika* usually place Jerusalem last. The ultimate prototype from which Alag. gr. 3 was derived was probably brought to southern Italy by Palestinian monks

[42] '*φημὶ δὴ τῶν ἀζύμων, τῆς τοῦ σαββάτου νηστείας, τοῦ γάμου τῶν ἱερέων καὶ τῆς ἐν τῷ καιρῷ τῆς πανσέπτου νηστείας τελουμένης πρὸς αὐτῶν τελείας καθ' ἑκάστην μυσταγωγίας*': Michel (1930): 321 ll. 1–3. On the role of Montecassino as a go-between for Byzantium and the West, see Bloch (1946): 189–193. Unlike the Catholic Church, the Orthodox Church does not consecrate the Eucharist on weekdays during Lent. Instead, it consecrates it on Sunday and then celebrates a liturgy 'of the presanctified gifts' during the week.

[43] '*καὶ ἵνα δείξω ὑμῖν τὴν τούτων νομοθεσίαν κατὰ τῶν ἀζύμων . . .*': Michel (1930): 333 ll. 18–19.

[44] He quotes, in this order, *Trullo* c. 11; *Apost. Const.* 5.14, 21, 20, 19, 7.23, 3, 4; Apost. c. 64; *Trullo* c. 55; Apost. c. 66; Gangra, c. 19; Laodicea, c. 51; *Trullo* c. 51; *Apost. Const.* 6.17, 1; Apost. c. 3, 40; *Trullo* c. 13; *Apost. Const.* 6.16, 2, 3.

[45] Barb. gr. 323, fols. 85^{v}–117; Crypt. gr. 322, fols. 112–117^{r}. For further discussion of these manuscripts, see Chapter 5, 'Monastic Nomocanons I', C5.P24, C5. P27–C5.P28; Chapter 6, 'Monastic Nomocanons II', C6.P7, C6.P13.

[46] John of Damascus, *Expositio fidei* 8.189–202, 147–150.

[47] Naples, Biblioteca nazionale 'Vittorio Emanuele III', MS gr. 7, fols. 168^{r}–178^{r}. See Lucà (2004a): 147 n. 13; Lucà (2011): 167.

[48] Schweinburg (1934): 314.

[49] On the dating and localisation of Alag. gr. 3, see Lucà (2002): 72–83.

[50] Alag. gr. 3, fols. 215–219^{r}.

fleeing the Persian and Islamic invasions in the seventh century, which would explain why it puts Jerusalem in the first rank.[51]

The texts on fasting and *azyma*, however, are clearly products of the anti-Latin polemic of the 1050s. Excerpts 'from the *Apostolic Constitutions*' and 'from the 318 Fathers [of the First Council of Nicaea] on Lenten fasting' provide a series of brief, vaguely-sourced aphorisms that implicitly criticise Latin fasting practices without actually mentioning the Latins by name (the same texts appear under slightly different headings in the twelfth-century Calabrian monastic nomocanons BN II C 7 and Ambros. G 57 sup).[52] The canonical appendix of Alag. gr. 3 ends with a laconically named tract 'On Pascha and Bread'.[53] This text opens with an explanation of the symbolism of the Lord's supper: 'On that night on which he gave himself up, our Lord Jesus Christ appeared to celebrate two Paschas: one of the Law and the other of the Lord.'[54] Though Christ celebrated the Jewish Pascha with *azyma*, he celebrated his own Pascha with leavened bread. Having castigated 'certain confused people' who celebrate the Eucharist with *azyma*, the anonymous author makes a series of pointed criticisms of Western Christians: 'The Lombards do not take the knife and they do not consecrate the spiritual Lamb. And so how can they be called true priests? And they do not abstain from meat like we do, nor from cheese. And they fast on Saturdays. They thus do not honour the true Pascha of Christ with us.'[55] By 'Lombards', the author means Latin-rite Italians.

[51] See Chapter 2, 'Greek Christianity in Medieval Italy', C2.P13. The text of the '*γνῶσις καὶ ἐπίγνωσις τῶν πατριαρχικῶν θρόνων*' (Alag. gr. 3, fols. 215^{v}–216^{r}) is published in Delatte (1927): 322–323. The same text can be found in the southern Italian codices Sin. gr. 432, fols. 1–4 and Marc. gr. 172, fols. 248^{v}–249^{v} under the title 'On the Patriarchates and Their Regions' ('*περὶ τῶν πατριαρχίων καὶ τῶν τούτων κλιμάτων*'). Southern Italy received a number of texts and manuscripts from the Syro-Palestinian region in the early Middle Ages, the most famous of which are probably the Rossano Gospels (see Cavallo [1985b]). Southern Italy also preserved the earliest surviving copy of the liturgy of St James, the most widely used liturgy in Antioch and Jerusalem in Late Antiquity, in the so-called *Rotulus Messanensis* (Messina, Biblioteca Regionale Universitaria, MS S. Salv. 177); see Swainson (1884): 211–332. Radle (2012) sheds light on a number of other non-Constantinopolitan influences (mainly from Egypt) on Greek liturgical rites in southern Italy. On the relationship between the *Statement and Definition of the Patriarchal Thrones* and Neilos Doxapatres' *Order of the Patriarchal Thrones*, see Chapter 5, 'Monastic Nomocanons I', C5.P47.

[52] Ambros. G 57 sup., fols. 38^{v}–39; BN II C 7, fols. 156–157.

[53] '*περὶ τοῦ πάσχ[α] καὶ τοῦ ἄρτου*': Alag. gr. 3, fol. 220^{v}. Greek Christians use the Hebrew term 'Pascha' to refer to both Jewish Passover and Christian Easter.

[54] '*ὁ κ[ύριο]ς καὶ θ[εὸ]ς ἡμῶν Ἰ[ησοῦ]ς Χ[ριστὸ]ς· τῇ νυκτὶ ἐκείνῃ ᾗ παρεδίδετο δύο πᾶσχ' ἐπιτελῶν φαίνεται· ἓν μὲν τὸ τοῦ νόμου καὶ ἓν τὸ κύριον*': Alag. gr. 3, fol. 219^{r}. The 'law' referred to here is the Mosaic Law of the Old Testament, not to be confused with the *Mosaic Law* of the eighth century AD.

[55] '*οἱ γὰρ Λογγίβαρδοι μάχαιραν μὴ λαβῶντες· καὶ τὸν νοητὸν ἀμνὸν μὴ ἱερουργοῦντες· πῶς οὖν ἱερεῖς ἀληθεῖς ὀνομασθήσοντες; ἀλλ' ὥσπερ γὰρ μεθ' ἡμῶν οὐκ ἀποβρωματίζουσιν τὸ κρέα· οὔτε τῶν τυρῶν· ἀλλὰ καὶ τὰ σάββατα νηστεύουσιν· οὕτως οὐ δὲ τοῦ ὄντος πάσχα μεθ' ἡμῶν τοῦ Χ[ριστο]ῦ ἀξιοῦνται*': Alag. gr. 3, fol. 219^{r}. The cutting of the 'spiritual Lamb' from the bread forms a part of the Orthodox Liturgy of Preparation (*proskomide*) before the consecration of the Eucharist. This spiritual Lamb then serves as the Body of Christ during communion. 'Meatfare' and 'Cheesefare' weeks form part of the Orthodox Lenten *Triodion*, in which Orthodox Christians successively renounce meat and then dairy products before the beginning of Lent.

The same tract appears again at the end of the fourteenth-century Calabrian civil law manuscript Crypt. gr. 50, in which it is given the title *A Dispute of St John Chrysostom Against the Lombards Concerning the Legal and Christian Pascha*.[56] The attribution of the text to St John Chrysostom (d. 407) is a clumsy anachronism, since the Lombards were unknown in his time. In reality, the tract is a polemic derived from the typical anti-Latin tropes of mid-eleventh-century Byzantium: the use of *azyma*, implied 'Judaising', incorrect performance of the liturgy, and mistaken fasting practices. Indeed, we see very similar anti-Latin language used in the *Life* of St Luke (*c.* 1035–1114), a Greek bishop of Isola in Calabria.[57] The saint was apparently confronted by some unnamed Latins who attacked Greek liturgical practices; according to Luke's biographer, he retorted, 'You Latins, with your pharisaic arguments, celebrate with *azyma* like the Jews. And you practice daily baptisms and countless other heresies in your misguided thinking.'[58]

Although other criticisms of the Latin rite would creep into later Italo-Greek nomocanons, these attacks on *azyma* and other liturgical practices are qualitatively different. Their origins can be traced back quite specifically to the mid-eleventh century, when the violence of the Norman conquest created a febrile atmosphere that made the Italo-Greeks particularly receptive to anti-Latin polemic from Constantinople. Peaceful relations between Latins and Greeks in southern Italy would return in the twelfth century, but the experience of the Norman conquest left a stratum of polemical texts in some Italo-Greek nomocanons for several centuries to come.

Conclusion

The foundations of Byzantine canon law in southern Italy were primarily laid in the late ninth and the tenth centuries, when the empire's reconquest and reorganisation of the territory established the Italo-Greek church's essential institutional character. Contrary to the views of some historians, this element of Byzantine culture in southern Italy was not a thin eleventh-century veneer. Rather, the spread of Byzantine canon law in the region had its roots in the reign of Basil I.

As far as we can tell from the surviving evidence, the textual tradition of Byzantine canon law in the empire's Italian lands was quite archaic: instead of

[56] '*τοῦ ἁγίου Ἰω[άννου] τοῦ Χρυσοστόμου περὶ Πάσχα νομικοῦ καὶ χριστιανικοῦ ἀμφιβολῆ πρὸς Λόγγοιβαρδους*': Crypt. gr. 50, fol. $187^{r/v}$. Once again, the term 'legal' refers to Old Testament Mosaic Law.

[57] The modern Isola Capo Rizzuto, originally known in Greek as Asyla.

[58] '*ὑμεῖς δὲ, ὦ Λατῖνοι, φαρισαϊκῶς ὑποκρινόμενοι, ἰουδαϊκῶς ἑορτάζετε ἄζυμα, καὶ καθημερινοῦς βαπτισμοὺς, καὶ ἄλλας μυρίας αἱρέσεις οὐκ ὀρθοφρονοῦντες ἐργάζεσθε*': Schirò (1954): 106 ll. 335–337. The Byzantine church preferred to perform baptisms on Epiphany and discouraged baptism between Pascha and Pentecost.

the ninth-century Photian recension of the *N14T*, which went on to become so popular in the Byzantine mainland, the Greeks of southern Italy used the sixth-century *N50T* as their main canon law codification. With a few exceptions (such as the tenth-century recension of the *Synopsis of Canons*), they do not seem to have felt the need to keep pace with nomocanonical fashions in Constantinople. When the Italo-Greeks did incorporate new texts into their collections, such as the anti-Latin polemics of the mid-eleventh century, they did so in a piecemeal fashion.

Nonetheless, despite the archaism of their canonical texts, the Greek church of Byzantine Italy does seem to have played an active role in administering Constantinople's legal system. Just because they did not have the latest legal codifications does not mean that the Italo-Greeks were out of touch with the law itself. Indeed, the marginalia in the Carbone nomocanon imply that Italo-Greek bishops were completely attuned to Constantinople's eleventh-century perspective on jurisdictional matters. Although legal sources from before the twelfth century are unfortunately very limited, they still give the impression that Byzantine religious law was deeply rooted in the region's Greek-speaking areas. This was the state of affairs that the Normans inherited on their conquest of southern Italy in the 1040s–1070s and it would undergo surprisingly little change in the following century.

5

Monastic Nomocanons I

The Monastic Archipelago

In the decades following the Norman conquest, there was a wave of new Italo-Greek monastic foundations that enjoyed a significant level of material support from both Latin and Greek nobility, including the Norman kings themselves in some cases.[1] They received extensive grants of landed properties and smaller churches and monasteries assigned to them as subject houses (*metochia*). Not only did this patronage provide the great Italo-Greek monasteries with the resources to produce and preserve a remarkably vibrant manuscript culture, but it also allowed them to enjoy their own distinctive legal culture as well.

Any abbot has a legal role in a paideic sense, since he must direct the spiritual discipline of monks under his care. However, as monasteries acquired landed property and *metochia*, abbots also acquired a legal role in an imperial sense. They were no longer at the head of individual institutions but of larger monastic federations. In order to administer such a federation effectively, an abbot would have to become closely involved in conflict resolution between his monks, his *metochia*, and the tenants who lived and worked on the monastery's lands. This task (if carried out conscientiously) would require the use of a nomocanon as a reference guide to the relevant civil and religious law.[2]

This dynamic did not change in the aftermath of the Norman conquest. The major Italo-Greek monasteries continued to produce and read nomocanons to help them manage their territory independent of the secular church. Indeed, most of the surviving nomocanons of the twelfth century with known provenances were created for monastic, not episcopal, use. Before we look at the manuscripts in greater detail, this chapter will consider the broader jurisdictional context in which they were used. Even as the Norman conquest brought southern Italy under the notional authority of the Roman papacy, the new rulers' material and political patronage of Italo-Greek monasteries gave them the space to ignore

[1] See Chapter 2, 'Greek Christianity in Medieval Italy', C2.S3.

[2] Several examples of monastic nomocanons have survived from the Byzantine world, particularly from Mount Athos; e.g. Venice, Biblioteca Nazionale Marciana, MS gr. III.3 (Athonite monastery of All Saints, 14th cent.); Paris, Bibliothèque nationale de France, MS Coisl. 36 (Athonite monastery of the Great Lavra, 13th/14th cent.); St Petersburg, Rossijskaja Nacional'naja Biblioteka, MSS gr. 66+66a (Athonite monastery of Iviron, 10th cent.); Sofia, National Centre for Slavo-Byzantine Studies 'Ivan Dujčev, MSS gr. 21 (monastery of St John the Forerunner near Serres, 12th cent.), 158 (monastery of Kosinitze near Drama, 13th cent.), etc.

Byzantine Religious Law in Medieval Italy. James Morton, Oxford University Press (2021). © James Morton.
DOI: 10.1093/oso/9780198861140.003.0006

Western ecclesiastical legislation, becoming a virtual archipelago of islands of Byzantine canon law in the midst of Latin-ruled southern Italy.

The Royal Archimandritates of Rossano and Messina

The Byzantines did not follow any one single model of monastic governance. Nonetheless, a set of key terminology for regional monastic federations emerged at an early date. From the fifth century on, the abbot in charge of such a federation was generally known as an 'archimandrite', a word that translates as 'head of a flock' or 'shepherd', and he oversaw an archimandritate.[3] This term had originated in the fourth century as a synonym for an abbot (typically called a *hegoumenos* in Greek), but by the sixth century it had come to be seen as a sort of monastic version of a bishop. Justinian's *Novels* occasionally juxtapose the two as if they are comparable (though not exactly equivalent).[4] The institution of the archimandritate spread in Byzantine southern Italy as well. The *Life* of St Neilos the Younger of Rossano (composed at Grottaferrata in the early eleventh century), for example, quotes a self-effacing comparison that the saint made between himself and 'the bishops and archimandrites', asking, 'Who am I that I should be counted among them?'[5] Like Justinian's legislation, Neilos' remark implies a perceived similarity between the two offices.

Though an archimandrite might have been viewed as *like* a bishop, Byzantine canon law technically did not allow a monastery to exist outside the jurisdiction of the episcopal hierarchy. Canon 8 of the Council of Chalcedon states clearly that monasteries should fall under the authority of the bishop in whose diocese they were located.[6] In practice, however, medieval monasteries could be extremely

[3] See Pargoire (1907): 2743–2746. 'Archimandrite' has become an honorary title awarded to priests in the modern Orthodox Church, though it was not used as such in the Middle Ages.

[4] E.g. Just. *Nov.* 5.7: '…and so that the God-beloved bishops and those who are called archimandrites prevent this…' ('…*ὥστε καὶ τοῦτο κωλύουσιν οἱ θεοφιλέστατοι ἐπίσκοποι καὶ οἵ γε ἀρχιμανδρίται καλοῦμενοι*…'); 120.6: '…we order those who are consecrated by the most holy patriarchs, be they metropolitans or other bishops, or be they archimandrites…' ('…*κελεύομεν τοὺς μὲν ὑπὸ τῶν ἁγιωτάτων πατριαρχῶν χειροτονουμένους, εἴτε μητροπολῖται εἴτε ἄλλοι ἐπίσκοποι ὦσιν εἴτε ἀρχιμανδρῖται*…').

[5] '*ὧδε μητροπολίτης ἐστίν· – ἦν γὰρ τότε ἐκεῖ ὁ τῆς ἁγίας Σεβηρίνης μητροπολίτης· – ὧδε ἐπίσκοποι καὶ ἀρχιμανδρῖται εἰσίν· αὐτοὶ τὴν ἐπιθυμίαν σου πληρωσάτωσαν· καὶ ἐγὼ τίς εἰμι, ἵνα μεσάζωμαι;*': Giovanelli (1972): 55 ll. 28–32. Archimandrites are also mentioned in two surviving legal documents from Byzantine Italy. An act of donation of 1050 makes a passing reference to a gathering 'held in the most sacred temple of St Nicholas, the church of the archimandrite' in Lucania, while another was copied in 1061 in Taranto 'by the hand of the archimandrite Andrew': '*σύναξις γέγονεν ἐν τῷ πανσέπτῳ ναῷ τοῦ ἁγίου Νικολάου ἡ ἐκκλησία τοῦ ἀρχιμανδρίτου*' (Trinchera [1865]: 45–46 [no. 37]); '*χειρὶ Ἀνδρέου τοῦ ἀρχιμανδρίτου*' (Trinchera [1865]: 59 [no. 45]).

[6] 'The clerics of poor houses, of monasteries, and of martyrs' shrines…should remain under the authority of the bishops in each city' ('*οἱ κληρικοὶ τῶν πτωχείων, καὶ μοναστηρίων, καὶ μαρτυρίων, ὑπὸ τὴν ἐξουσίαν τῶν ἐν ἑκάστῃ πόλεθ ἐπισκόπων…διαμενέτωσαν*): RP 2.234. Theodore Balsamon's commentary on this canon criticises monks and clergy who claim 'that they are not subject to the patriarch or to their local bishop, since they belong to a "free" monastery or church…' ('*οἱ γοῦν*

effective at asserting (and gaining recognition for) their independence from the secular church's oversight.[7] The best way for a Byzantine monastery to do this was to be placed directly under the patriarch or the emperor's supervision, since they were distant figures who were much less likely than the local bishop to interfere in its internal affairs.[8] With an exemption from episcopal oversight, an archimandrite would effectively be free to exercise legal jurisdiction in his own properties. Byzantine southern Italy had been home to at least two monasteries that were exempted from episcopal jurisdiction thanks to their 'imperial' (*basilike*) status, as we saw in Chapter 2, though their nomocanons (if they owned any) have not survived.[9]

The Norman conquest of the eleventh century did not lessen the desire of the Greek monasteries to evade episcopal oversight. On the contrary, the Italo-Greeks were able to adapt their old Byzantine customs to the new circumstances of life under Latin rule with remarkable ease.[10] Instead of the emperor and patriarch, they could turn to the king or the pope for legal privileges that exempted them from episcopal supervision. The Norman monarchs, ever willing to weaken the power of the episcopal hierarchy, were more than ready to grant such privileges.

There is a strong correlation between a monastery's ownership of property, its possession of a nomocanon, and its acquisition of legal privileges. Count Roger I is known to have exempted several Greek monasteries from the episcopate on the island of Sicily as early as the 1080s.[11] The clearest example, though, is that of the Patiron monastery of Rossano, founded by St Bartholomew of Simeri in the 1090s and invested with lands and *metochia* by Roger I and his chamberlain

σήμερον λέγοντες μοναχοὶ ἢ κληρικοὶ μὴ ὑποκεῖσθαι τῷ πατριάρχῃ ἢ τῷ ἐγχωρίῳ ἐπισκόπῳ, ὡς ἀπὸ ἐλευθέρας μονῆς ἢ ἐκκλησίας ὄντες, προβαλλόμενοι δῆθεν καὶ κτητορικῶν τυπικῶν διατάγματα, τί πρὸς ταῦτα ἀπολογήσονται;'): RP 2.236.

[7] As noted by Morris (1995): 150–151.

[8] The most famous example of this in the Byzantine is the monastic federation of Mount Athos, which enjoyed imperial protection and was effectively self-governing. See *BMFD* 1.195–198.

[9] The Theotokos of the Salinai and St Peter of Taranto, respectively; see Chapter 2, 'Greek Christianity in Medieval Italy', C2.P41.

[10] There has been some debate among scholars as to the origins of the organisational structures of Italo-Greek monastic federations under the Normans. Pierre Batiffol believed that the archimandritates of Rossano and Messina were products of Benedictine influence, showing that 'the passage from Greek to Latin monastic law was complete' following the Norman conquest Batiffol [1891a]: 5–6). He was followed in this view by Lynn White and Graham Loud, though Loud admitted that there may have been other models besides the Benedictine Order (White [1938]: 69–70; Loud [2007]: 508). In fact, the surviving *typika* (foundation documents) of the archimandritates of Rossano and Messina both state that their founders 'selected [customs] from the various *typika* of the monastery of Stoudios [in Constantinople], of the Holy Mountain [Athos], of Jerusalem [i.e. the monastery of Mar Saba in Palestine], and certain others' ('*. . . συλλεξάμενοι ἐκ διαφόρων τυπικῶν τῆς Στουδίου μονῆς, τοῦ Ἁγίου Ὄρους, τῶν Ἱεροσολύμων, καὶ ἑτέρων τινῶν . . .*'): Cozza-Luzi (1905): 2.128 (c. 10). Cristina Torre is preparing an edition of the *typikon* of Rossano (Torre [2017]: 77 n. 5), which is currently only partially published in Arnesano (2014): 265–272, but the original text may be found in Jena, Thüringer Universitäts- und Landesbibliothek, MS gr. G.B. q. 6a, fols. 161–189. None of the *typika* make any reference to Western models.

[11] See Scaduto (1947): 279–285.

Christodoulos. Bartholomew's *Life* recounts that he travelled to Rome around the year 1105 to acquire a bull from Pope Paschal II that exempted the Patiron from episcopal jurisdiction.[12] The *Life* does not explain why Bartholomew did so, but we learn the reason from a fascinating colophon in a manuscript of St Basil of Caesarea's writings produced at the Patiron in 1105 by the monk Bartholomew. The underlined sections of text were written in cryptograms, perhaps because of their politically sensitive nature:

> In the same year [1105], the most holy pope Paschal granted our most holy father Bartholomew a bull of freedom for his holy monastery of the most holy *Theotokos* which is called 'of the Rossanese'. He raised and built this up for the aid of many souls and the glory of God. In the same year, Bohemond [of Taranto] returned to Calabria, fleeing from the face of Alexios [I Komnenos]. + At that time the holy monastery found respite, freed from the hands of the Maleinoi. For Archbishop Nicholas Maleinos was besieging it vigorously along with the rest of his clan.[13]

It was a classic case of a wealthy monastery trying to escape the clutches of its local hierarch. The (Greek) archbishop of Rossano, Nicholas Maleinos, was attempting ('along with the rest of his clan') to gain control of the monastery and its revenues. The Maleinoi were a noble family of Calabria with roots in the Byzantine Empire that wielded great influence in Rossano.[14] Bartholomew's solution was to appeal to the pope for a privilege of exemption. Years later, when Roger II established the Kingdom of Sicily and was excommunicated as a result, the monastery's then-abbot Luke wasted no time in having its legal independence from the episcopate confirmed in a royal privilege of 1130.[15] Roger acceded to the request, announcing

[12] See Chapter 2, 'Greek Christianity in Medieval Italy', C2.P37.

[13] '*. . . τῷ ἐνιαυτῷ ὅτε ὁ ἁγιώτατος πάπα(ς) Πασχάλιος σιγίλλιον ἐλευθερίας ἐποίησε τοῦ ἁγιωτάτου π(ατ)ρ(ὸ)ς ἡμῶν Βαρθολομαίου εἰς τὴν ἁ(γίαν) αὐτοῦ μονὴν τὴν ὑπεραγίαν Θ(εοτό)κον τὴν καλουμένην τοῦ Ῥοχονιάτη· ἣν αὐτὸς ἐκ βάθρων ἀνήγειρε καὶ ἀνῳκοδόμησεν, εἰς ὠφέλειαν πολλῶν ψυχῶν καὶ δόξαν Θεοῦ· τῷ αὐτῷ δὲ ἐνιαυτῷ ὑποστρέψας ὁ Βαϊμούνδις εἰς Καλαβρίαν, φεύγων ἐκ προσώπου Ἀλεξίου. + ἔκτοτε δὲ εὗρεν ἀνάπαυσιν ἡ ἁγία μονὴ λυτρωθεῖσα ἐκ χειρῶν Μαλαιΐνων· πάνυ γὰρ ἐπολιόρκει αὐτὴν Νικόλαος ὁ Μαλαιΐνος καὶ Ἀρχ(ι)επίσκοπ(ος) μετὰ τῆς γενεᾶς αὐτοῦ*': Vatican City, Biblioteca Apostolica Vaticana, MS Vat. gr. 2050, fol. 117^{r}. Text published in Lake 8.10 (no. 306). Note that Lake is wrong to state that Paschal's bull offered the monastery protection from the patriarch of Constantinople (why would that be necessary?). It offered protection from Archbishop Nicholas Maleinos of Rossano.

[14] The family is first mentioned in ninth-century Cappadocia, where the general Nikephoros Maleinos defeated a rebellion in 866 (Theophanes Continuatus 479.20). The Maleinoi would go on to become notable landowners and officials across the Byzantine Empire, with a strong presence in Calabria, Macedonia, and Anatolia (see *ODB*, s.v. 'Maleinos'). On the Maleinoi of Calabria, see Lucà (1985): 126 n. 164; Peters-Custot (2009a): 611. We shall encounter them again in Chapter 7, 'The Secular Church and the Laity', C7.P37–C7.P42.

[15] Trinchera (1865): 138–141 (no. 106).

in his privilege that 'the aforesaid holy monastery is royal [*basilike*] and is mine alone'.[16]

The Patiron produced no fewer than three nomocanons in the early decades of the twelfth century, which I refer to as the 'Rossanese Group': S. Salv. 59, Vall. C 11.1, and Vat. gr. 2060. As we shall see in more detail in Chapter 6, the contents and *mise-en-page* of the three manuscripts are identical, while the dimensions are extremely similar as well. The manuscripts even contain many of the same scribal errors, suggesting that they were copied from a shared prototype.[17] The Patiron's wealthy scriptorium employed several scribes in the early twelfth century, of whom we know the names of three: Bartholomew, Pachomios, and Basil (who copied the Gospel lectionary Alag. gr. 3 in 1124).[18] Maria Foti identified one of the hands in Vat. gr. 2060 as that of the monk Bartholomew, while Lucà noted that all three nomocanons of the Rossanese Group (as well as Vat. gr. 2115, fols. 78–96) show strong similarities with others by Bartholomew, who was active *c.* 1100–1115.[19]

Only Vat. gr. 2060 remained at the Patiron. The other two found their way to Messina: S. Salv. 59 belonged to the monastery of the Holy Saviour (later renamed to St Pantaleon) of Bordonaro, while Vall. C 11.1 came into the possession of the Archimandritate of Holy Saviour of Messina (founded in 1133), as we can deduce from a copy of a papal bull at the end of the manuscript.[20] It seems, then, that the Patiron copied a standardised set of nomocanons both for itself and for distribution to other monasteries, a sign of its *scriptorium*'s unusually high levels of professionalism and productivity. It is worth emphasising how unusual this phenomenon is. Considering the number of medieval manuscripts that have been lost, one wonders how many the Patiron must have originally produced for three of its nomocanons to survive.

The Archimandritate of Messina was explicitly founded by decree of Roger II as a royal monastery overseeing lands and *metochia* throughout north-eastern Sicily and southern Calabria. The king's foundation document states the archimandrite's legal powers quite explicitly (emphasis added):

> The one who is put in charge of our illustrious monastery and who has been raised to the rank of archimandrite, both this man and his successors who are put in charge of the same monastery, also archimandrites, will not be prevented...

[16] '...*διὰ τοῦ εἶναι ταύτην τὴν ῥηθεῖσαν ἁγίαν μονὴν βασιλικὴν καὶ ἰδίως ἡμετέραν*': Trinchera (1865): 140.

[17] Foti (1995): 343. At the time that she wrote the article, Foti was not yet aware of Vall. C 11.1.

[18] On Bartholomew and Pachomios, see Foti (1993): 374–375. On Basil, see Lucà (2002): 72–73. Bartholomew was the author of the colophon in Vat. gr. 2050 and the copy of the *typikon* of the Patiron in the library of the University of Jena. Santo Lucà compiled a list of sixty-one manuscripts known to have been produced at the Patiron in the early twelfth century: Lucà (1991a): 128–130.

[19] Foti (1995): 344; Lucà (1985): 117 n. 124.

[20] The bull dates to 1224 and concerns the excommunication of the archimandrite of the Holy Saviour; see Chapter 8, 'The Papacy Takes Charge', C8.P32. On the ownership of S. Salv. 59, see Chapter 3, 'Patterns of Source Survival', C3.P48.

> from examining according to the divine and holy canons the hidden and manifest cases in capital monasteries, whether criminal or financial, such as might be brought by one against another of the monks within them, or of those who are in charge of them. For it is permitted to the archimandrite to examine according to the canons or the laws as this man sees fit and to pass judgment according to what is pleasing to God and to the satisfaction of the holy canons.[21]

This passage clarifies the nature of the archimandrite's authority with regards to 'capital' (*kephalika*) and self-governing (*autodespota*) monasteries under his supervision. These were important abbeys that enjoyed a degree of legal and administrative independence, but the archimandrite had the right to intervene in cases when necessary (the document takes it for granted that the archimandrite has complete control over his dependent *metochia*).

In his *typikon* for the Holy Saviour, the first archimandrite Luke wrote that he 'brought many very fine books' to the monastery from Rossano; these presumably included the Rossanese nomocanon Vall. C 11.1, which served as the archimandrites' principle reference guide to canon law.[22] The monastery also acquired the nomocanon Marc. gr. 169 at a later date. This codex was produced in Constantinople in the eleventh or early twelfth century, but we know that it came into the possession of the Holy Saviour of Messina by the late thirteenth century as it contains a Latin legal document of 1288 recording a debt that the monastery owed to the nobleman Pandolfo Falcone.[23] Unfortunately, we cannot say how or when exactly it came to Messina.

[21] '*ἀλλ' οὐ παρὰ τούτου ὁ ἐν τῇ δηλωθείσῃ ἡμετέρᾳ μονῇ προεστώς καὶ εἰς τὴν τοῦ ἀρχιμανδρίτου τιμὴν ἀναβιβαθεὶς, οὗτος τε καὶ οἱ μετ' αὐτὸν ἐσόμενοι, ἐν τῇ αὐτῇ μονῇ προεστῶτες, καὶ ἀρχιμανδρῖται, κωλυθήσονται τοῦ ἐξετάζειν κατὰ τοὺς θείους καὶ ἁγίους κανόνας τὰ ἐν τοῖς τοιούτοις κεφαλικοῖς μοναστηρίοις ἀνακύπτοντα καὶ ἀναφαινόμενα ἐγκληματικὰ εἴτε χρηματικὰ οἷα δή τινα ζητήματα παρά τινος κατά τινος τῶν ἐν αὐτοῖς μοναχῶν, ἢ τῶν ἐν τούτοις προεστώτων. ἐφεῖται γὰρ τῷ ἀρχιμανδρίτῃ κανονικῶς ἢ δικαίως ἐξετάζειν ὡς τούτου ἐφορῶντος καὶ κατὰ τὸ ἀρέσκον Θ(ε)ῷ καὶ τὴν τῶν ἁγίων κανόνων περίληψιν διαλύειν αὐτά*': Vatican City, Biblioteca Apostolica Vaticana, MS Vat. lat. 8201, fol. 57v (cf. fol. 131r/v, which has the same text). A Latin translation made by the humanist scholar Constantine Laskaris in 1472 and rife with interpolations can be found in Pirro (1733): 2.974–976.

[22] '*καὶ βίβλους πολλὰς καὶ καλλίστας συνήγαγον τῆς τε ἡμετέρας καὶ οὐχ ἡμετέρας καὶ θείας γραφῆς καὶ τῆς πάντῃ οἰκείας ἡμῖν*': Cozza-Luzi (1905): 2.125 (c. 6). Luke had previously served as the archimandrite of Rossano and was the one who had acquired the royal privilege for that monastery in 1130. A translation of Luke's *typikon* can be found in *BMFD* 2.637–648 (no. 26).

[23] Marc. gr. 169, fol. 311b. Text in Mioni (1981): 1.253. Rodriquez and Lucà have both argued for a Constantinopolitan provenance for Marc. gr. 169 on palaeographical grounds (Rodriquez [2013]: 642–643; Lucà [2010]: 78 n. 7). Moreover, Konidaris (1982): 47 has demonstrated that the codex was made from the same prototype as the twelfth- or thirteenth-century nomocanon Munich, Bayerische Staatsbibliothek, MS gr. 380, which was itself copied in Constantinople. To these arguments I would add that Marc. gr. 169, fol. 311v contains a garbled quotation from Michael Psellos' medical poem *On the Bath* scribbled in the lower margin (text in Ideler [1842]: 2.193). This poem is otherwise only known from manuscripts from Mount Athos and Constantinople of the fourteenth and sixteenth centuries, which would make Marc. gr. 169 its earliest attestation.

The third nomocanon of the Rossanese Group, S. Salv. 59, came into possession of the Holy Saviour of Bordonaro, a monastery in the hills above Messina. This abbey was originally founded in 1099 by a wealthy Greek priest and bibliophile named Scholarios, who took the name Sabas on becoming a monk.[24] Very little is known about the institution's early history. Roger II subjected it to the new archimandritate of the Holy Saviour of Messina in 1133 but decreed that it should remain a 'capital and self-governing [monastery] *as before* [emphasis added]'.[25] This indicates that the Holy Saviour of Bordonaro had been founded as an independent monastery and retained normal jurisdiction over its own affairs when it came under the Archimandritate of Messina, though the archimandrite could intervene when necessary (as laid out in the passage quoted above).

In his testament of 1114, Sabas described the contents of his library, which contained no fewer than 'three books of canon law'.[26] One of these is very likely to have been S. Salv. 59, which would have been copied along with Vat. gr. 2060 and Vall. C 11.1 in Rossano in the first decade or so of the twelfth century (when the scribe Bartholomew was active). The lost Anon. 110 may potentially have been another one of the three.[27] One can only speculate as to why Sabas had three nomocanons; perhaps they had different contents or were used for different purposes such as teaching or copying.

Lesser Archimandritates and Autodespotic Monasteries

Rossano and Messina were by no means the only independent institutions under Norman rule. Another interesting example is the monastery of St John Theristes near Stilo on the eastern slopes of the Aspromonte mountain range in southern Calabria. This was founded by the monk Gerasimos Atoulinos around the time of the Norman conquest (perhaps *c.* 1070). It is mentioned for the first time in a document of 1098 in which a local judge of Stilo, having been referred a case by the court of Count Roger I of Sicily, confirmed its possessions in a place called Sakrai.[28] In another document of 1101/2, we learn that St John Theristes also had a *metochion* dedicated to SS Cosmas and Damian, the Holy Unmercenaries.[29]

[24] On Scholarios-Sabas and his library, see Lo Parco (1910). The surviving documentation on the Holy Saviour of Bordonaro can be found in Pirro (1733): 2.1003–1006.

[25] 'Our serenity has allowed certain monasteries to remain autocephalous and self-governing as before… [such as] the Saviour of the priest Scholarios…' ('*τινὰ δὲ κατάλειψεν ἡ γαλινότης ἡμῶν μένειν ὡς πρότερον κεφαλικὰ μοναστήρια καὶ αὐτοδέσποτα… ὁ σ[ώτ]ηρ τοῦ πρεσβυτέρου Σχολαρίου…*'): Vat. lat. 8201, fol. 57$^{r/v}$ (cf. fol. 131$^{r/v}$).

[26] '…*codices juris canonici tres*…': Pirro (1733): 2.1005.

[27] See Chapter 3, 'Patterns of Source Survival', C3.P49.

[28] Guillou (1980): 53–58 (no. 3).

[29] Guillou (1980): 62–68 (no. 5). The document is the will of the monastery's second abbot, Bartholomew, who designates his son Pankratios as his successor. Bartholomew had himself inherited the abbacy from his own father, Gerasimos Atoulinos. This contravenes Byzantine canon law but, as we have seen elsewhere, appears to have been relatively common in medieval southern Italy.

St John Theristes continued to acquire land and dependent peasants in the following years. Under the abbacy of Pachomios (1124/5–1144), it inherited a second *metochion*, a monastery of St Theodore, in the will of a monk named Bartholomew Parillas. Bartholomew had established St Theodore some years before but willed all his possessions—including his own son and future descendants!—to St John Theristes.[30] Though his original will has not survived, we know it through a copy made in 1138 by a monk of St John Theristes named Konon (presumably soon after Bartholomew's death).

A year later, in 1139, the abbot Pachomios instructed Konon to create a nomocanon, the present-day BN II C 7:

> The present *nomokanonas* [*sic*] was completed by the hand of the sinful Abba Konon of the monastery of St John Theristes in the year 6648 [A.D. 1139], in the 3rd indiction, on Saturday 16th December at the 9th hour. Remember, Lord, your servant Abba Pachomios, priest and abbot of the monastery of St John Theristes, who desired to create the present nomocanon of the Holy Apostles and the Holy Fathers, and give to him remission of his sins. Amen Lord.[31]

This nomocanon was produced at a time when the influence of St John Theristes—now in charge of at least two other monasteries and extensive agricultural lands—was increasing. Just a few years later, on 24th October 1144, Abbot Pachomios travelled to Messina to answer the royal edict *De resignandis privilegiis*.[32] Roger II had required ecclesiastical landowners in Calabria to present their documents of privilege for confirmation at his court.[33] The text of Roger's diploma for St John Theristes is unfortunately only preserved in imperfect Latin and Italian translations of the seventeenth to eighteenth centuries, though they appear to be based on a genuine Greek original. In addition to confirming a donation of lands made in 1100 by his father, Roger mandates that the monastery should 'be independent, free, and royal, and should recognise nobody but our authority preserved by God . . .'[34] It is safe to assume that the Greek original would have used the term *basilike* for 'royal'.

[30] Guillou (1980): 99–103 (no. 14).

[31] '*τέλος ἤλειφεν ὁ παρὸν νομοκάνονας χειρὶ ἁμαρτολοῦ Κόνου ἀβᾶ πρεσβυτ(έ)ρ(ου) μονῆς Ἁγίου Ἰω(άννου) τοῦ Θεριστοῦ ἔχοντα τοῦ ἔτους ͵ϛχμη΄, ινδ. γ΄, μη(ν)ὶ δεκεμβρίῳ εἰς τ(ὰς) ις΄ ἡμέραν σα(ββάτου), ὥρ(α) θ΄. μνήσθ(ητ)ι κ(ύρι)ε τοῦ δούλου Παχωμίου ἀβᾶ πρεσβυτ(έ)ρ(ου) καὶ ἡγουμένου μονῆς ἁγίου Ἰω(άννου) τοῦ Θεριστοῦ τοῦ πόθ(ου) συνδρομήσαντος τοῦ κτίσαι τὸν παρὸν νομοκάνονα τῶν ἁγίων ἀποστόλων καὶ τῶν ἁγίων π(ατέ)ρων καὶ δῶς αὐτῷ πταισμ(ά)τ(ων) λύτρον. ἀμήν κύριε*': BN II C 7, fol. 183v. Text published in Mioni (1981): 1.163–164. Image reproduced in Lake 9.667.

[32] For discussion of this decree, see Johns (2002): 115–118.

[33] Guillou (1980): 108–110 (no. 16).

[34] '*mandamus hoc monasterium esse francium et liberum et regium et neminem conoscere debere nisi nostrum a Deo conservatam potentiam et episcopi Stili . . .*': Guillou (1980): 110 ll. 20–22. The reference to 'the bishop of Stilo' must be a mistake or an interpolation by a later hand (perhaps one more

Roger's legal privilege for St John Theristes came about five years after Pachomios commissioned his monastery's nomocanon in 1139. However, there is a curious feature of the document as it has been transmitted to us. The text states that the privilege was issued in Messina on '24th October 6648 [1139], in the 3rd indiction', which Kehr (correctly) amended to 1144.[35] The transmitted text is obviously wrong, but what is interesting to note is that 1139 did indeed fall in the third indiction, as the document says, whereas 1144 fell in the eighth. Was this a deliberate mistake? Did a copyist or translator purposefully attempt to back-date the privilege to the same year that Pachomios commissioned his nomocanon? Without further evidence we can only speculate. Nonetheless, it is clearly significant that St John Theristes acquired a nomocanon and then had its exemption from episcopal jurisdiction recognised just a few years later.

The monastery of St Bartholomew of Trigona presents a similar case. Founded in *c.* 1095 near Sinopoli on the Western slopes of the Aspromonte mountain range in southern Calabria, it enjoyed lavish patronage from Norman nobles including Duke Roger Borsa and Roger II himself, as Vera von Falkenhausen has outlined.[36] It acquired at least five *metochia* and a vast array of lands and peasants. Moreover, like St John Theristes, St Bartholomew of Trigona was exempted from episcopal jurisdiction by Roger II in 1144 and designated a 'royal monastery' that answered only to the king's authority.[37] St Bartholomew of Trigona also produced a nomocanon in the first half of the twelfth century (the present-day Barb. gr. 323), though unfortunately it is heavily damaged and cannot be dated exactly.[38] As in the case of St John Theristes, we can imagine that St Bartholomew of Trigona required a nomocanon to help it govern its *metochia*; its legal authority was later recognised and given a formal character by Roger II.

There are two further twelfth-century monastic nomocanons of Calabria whose provenance has not yet been established by scholars: Ambros. G 57 sup. and Crypt. gr. 322. As it so happens, these two appear to have the same contents as BN II C 7 (from St John Theristes) and Barb. gr. 323 (from St Bartholomew of Trigona) respectively. The fragmentary nomocanon Ambros. G 57 sup. is badly damaged and has lost most of its original quires. Nonetheless, it retains a note in a

sympathetic to episcopal authority), since there was no bishop of Stilo: the town fell within the diocese of Squillace (Loud [2007]: 526).

[35] Guillou (1980): 109; Kehr (1902): 424 (no. 10). On 24th October 1139, Roger II was at the siege of Bari, not in Messina (Falco of Benevento, *Chronicum Beneventanum*, 1139.10.11–12.14). However, he was in Messina on 24th October 1144 to examine the documents presented to him in answer to his decree *De resignandis privilegiis*.

[36] Falkenhausen (1999). The text of the monastery's *typikon* has been passed down to us via a sixteenth-century recension in the Calabrian dialect of Italian written in the Greek alphabet, published in Douramani (2003): 35–320.

[37] The text of Roger's privilege, which only exists in Latin translation, can be found in Minieri-Riccio (1882): 1.14. See also Falkenhausen (1999): 96.

[38] See Chapter 3, 'Patterns of Source Survival', C3.P37.

fourteenth-century Greek hand that gives a crucial insight into its history (see Figure 5.1): 'To my spiritual brother in Christ and father Onophrios, abbot of the monastery of the Holy Theotokos of Carrà, I, your brother Hierotheos, monk and priest of the monastery of St Phantinos of Tauriana, rejoicing in the Lord and in pure love towards Him, beg for your [love] also in the Father.'[39]

Athanasios Chalkeopoulos visited the monastery of the Theotokos of Carrà in 1457 where he saw 'a book of canon law' that was evidently Ambros. G 57 sup.[40] As Hierotheos' note makes clear, though, the nomocanon was originally produced at or for the monastery of St Phantinos of Tauriana, a small town on the western coast of Calabria near modern-day Palmi. Very little is known about this foundation, since the building and its archives were destroyed in a raid by Barbary pirates in the late Middle Ages.[41] Yet it was evidently an important and wealthy foundation; when Athanasios Chalkeopoulos visited St Phantinos in 1457, he remarked that 'it was built with great architectural skill and was one of the finest monasteries of this part of Calabria . . .'[42] Like the Holy Saviour of Bordonaro, St Phantinos of Tauriana was subjected to the Archimandritate of Messina by Roger II's edict of 1133 as a 'capital and self-governing' monastery, implying that its abbot retained a limited measure of legal independence.[43]

The provenance of the nomocanon Crypt. gr. 322 is more challenging. The manuscript was one of the group that Pietro Menniti brought north from Calabria in 1697 and deposited in Grottaferrata.[44] As Santo Lucà pointed out, it has a close textual relationship with Barb. gr. 323 (from St Bartholomew of Trigona) and BN gr. 7, a late eleventh-century theological compendium from Gerace.[45] Crypt. gr. 322 has close ties to the manuscript culture of twelfth-century southern Calabria and was still present in the region in the late seventeenth century. It

[39] *'τῷ ἐν Χ(ριστ)ῷ καὶ πν(ευματ)ικῷ ἀδ(ελφ)ῷ και π(ατ)ρὶ κὺρ ἀνοφρίῳ καθηγουμ(έ)ν(ῳ) μον(ῆς) ἁγί(ας) Θεοτόκου Κάρ(ρας) ὁ ἀδελφό(ς) Ἱερόθεο(ς) μοναχὸ(ς) καὶ ὁ ἱερεὺς τῆς μονὶς ἁγίου Φαντίνου Ταβριαν(ῆς) ἐν Κ(υρί)ῳ χαὶρων καὶ καθαρίν ἀγάπιν προς αὐτ(ὸν) καὶ παρακαλῶ τιν σὺν π[ατρ]ί'*: Ambros. G 57 sup., fol. 17r. See also Lucà (2004b): 222. Lucà was aware of this note but read 'Briatico' instead of Tauriana. This is an error; though there was a monastery of St Phantinos of Tauriana, there is no evidence for one at Briatico, which instead was home to a monastery of St Pankratios.

[40] *'liber unus juris canonici'*: Laurent and Guillou (1960): 127.

[41] In a *visitatio* of 1551, Archimandrite Marcello Terrasina of SS Peter and Paul of Spanopetro stated, 'On the aforementioned day we left the monastery of St John of the Lavra and went up to the abbey of St Phantinos of Seminara [i.e. Tauriana] where we found the body of St Phantinos, but the church was destroyed by the Moors or the Turks, since the monastery was situated near the sea' (*'die predicto discessimus a monasterio Sancti Joannis de Loro et accessimus ad abbatiam Sancti Phantini de Seminara, ubi invenimus corpus sancti Phantini, sed ecclesiam destructam a Mauris vel Turcis, quia situm erat circa mare dictum monasterium'*): Laurent and Guillou (1960): 296 ll. 5–8.

[42] *'in quo monasterio fuimus et vidimus totum spinis circumdatum, licet fuisset magna fabrica constructum et fuisset de optimis monasteriis hujus Calabrie, nunc vero est deductum penitus in ruynam'*: Laurent and Guillou (1960): 112 ll. 6–9.

[43] Vat. lat. 8201, fol. 57v.

[44] See Chapter 3, 'Patterns of Source Survival', C3.P46–C3.P47.

[45] Lucà (2011): 167. In addition to Lucà's observations, I would add that Crypt. gr. 322, fols. 2v–15v contain an abbreviated version of the history of ecumenical councils found in Barb. gr. 323, fols. 49r–85v. On BN gr. 7, see Chapter 4, 'The Byzantine Background', C4.P39.

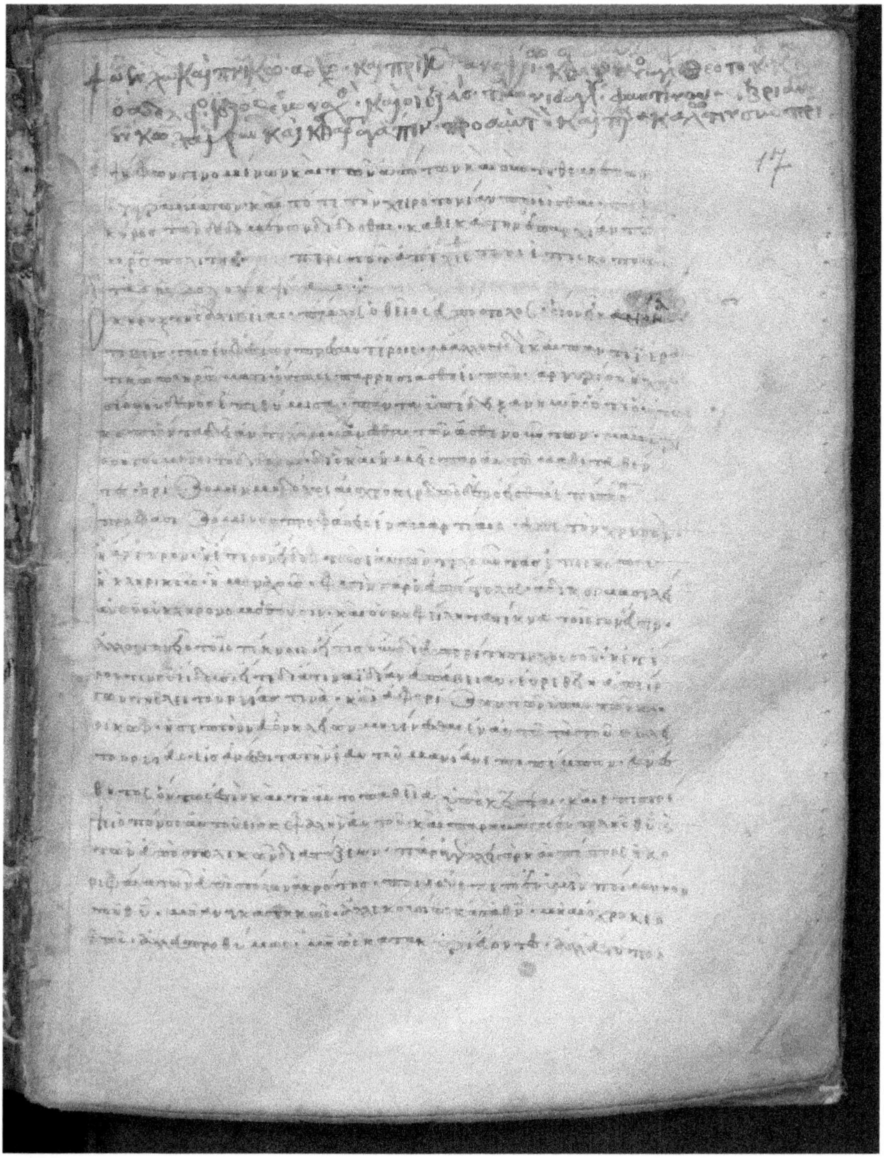

Figure 5.1. Donation note of Onophrios, abbot of the Theotokos of Carrà (Ambros. G 57 sup., fol. 17r)

follows, then, that it is almost certainly one of the manuscripts that Athanasios Chalkeopoulos recorded on his *visitatio* to southern Calabrian monasteries in 1457, since he made fastidious notes on the contents of their libraries. Besides the manuscripts at St John Theristes and the Theotokos of Carrà, Chalkeopoulos mentions another four nomocanons: a '*jus canonicum*' at a monastery of

St Phantinos near S. Lorenzo (not the same as the one at Tauriana), a '*jus canonicum*' at St Onophrios of Cao (in Vibo Valentia), a '*pars juris canonici*' at SS Peter and Paul of Spanopetro (in Ciano, near Vibo Valentia), and a '*pecium unum juris canonici*' at St Nicholas of Flagiano near Catanzaro.[46]

Archimandrite Marcellus Terracina of SS Peter and Paul of Spanopetro visited St Phantinos near S. Lorenzo in 1551 and found that it had been destroyed by pirates, so it can probably be ruled out as the source.[47] St Nicholas of Flagiano likewise no longer existed in the seventeenth century, while St Onophrios of Cao had been annexed to the Patiron of Rossano.[48] By a process of elimination, it is clear that the nomocanon Crypt. gr. 322 must have belonged to none other than Terracina's own monastery, SS Peter and Paul of Spanopetro. Not only does the damaged manuscript fit Chalkeopoulos' description of a '*pars juris canonici*,' but Menniti is known to have collected other manuscripts and documents from the monastery as well.[49]

Once again, very little is known about the early history of SS Peter and Paul. The main evidence comes from the will of its founder, a monk named Gerasimos who had been a disciple of the hermit saint Peter Chartoularios (nicknamed 'Spanopetros'). Gerasimos wrote his will in *c.* 1135 and Pietro Menniti brought a copy of it to S. Basilio *de Urbe* in 1696, where Bernard de Montfaucon transcribed it.[50] Gerasimos had been inspired to found a monastery in the late eleventh or early twelfth century and endowed it with his own property, including a substantial collection of lands, liturgical vestments, and books, among which he mentions a 'book of the nomocanon'.[51]

The will does not mention any details regarding the legal status of the monastery in the twelfth century, which would be taken under the royal protection of Frederick II in 1224 and declared an archimandritate at an unknown later date.[52] It does contain an insight into the expectations of the abbot's legal role, though. At the end of the document, Gerasimos mentions a monk named Theodoulos whom he had groomed as his successor. Theodoulos betrayed his trust, however, by stealing money from the monastery and fleeing. Gerasimos was extremely forgiving of him, ordering that he should be welcomed back as a brother if he ever chose to return: 'And let it be as I have decreed: nobody must speak of this *or put him on*

[46] Laurent and Guillou (1960): 64, 105, 115, 131.

[47] Laurent and Guillou (1960): 300.

[48] Batiffol (1891): 43, 115–116.

[49] See Batiffol (1891): 44, 94, 96, 123. On p. 123, Batiffol reproduces an inventory of the monastery's library made in 1579, although it is unfortunately far too vague to identify specific manuscripts.

[50] Montfaucon (1708): 403–407. See also Capialbi (1940): 259–260.

[51] '... *βιβλίον τοῦ νομοκανόνος* ...': Montfaucon (1708): 404. Lucà (2011): 167. has dated Crypt. gr. 322 to the 1170s–1180s on palaeographical grounds, though if it is the same manuscript that Gerasimos mentions in his will then it must date to the early twelfth century. Gerasimos also mentions that the monastery owned a 'book of the law' ('*βιβλίον νόμου*'); from the 1579 inventory we learn that this was a copy of the *Ekloge*.

[52] Montfaucon (1708): 428; Capialbi (1941): 163–164.

trial, but you must give him aid.'[53] Apparently Gerasimos suspected that his successor would prosecute Theodoulos if he returned.

The last two Italo-Greek monasteries known to have bequeathed us medieval nomocanons were SS Elias and Anastasios of Carbone in Lucania and St Nicholas of Casole in the Salento. SS Elias and Anastasios was the owner of the nomocanon Vat. gr. 1980–1981, which I have argued originally belonged to a Greek bishop of Lucania before being acquired by the monastery in the first half of the twelfth century.[54] As we saw in Chapter 2, Carbone was elevated to an archimandritate by William II in 1168.[55] However, a document issued by the Norman noble Rhanus of Rocca in 1154—over a decade earlier—shows that the abbot was already using the title 'archimandrite' during the reign of Roger II.[56] This implies that William's act provided official recognition for an archimandrital role that Carbone had been informally exercising for some time.

Finally, St Nicholas of Casole in the Salento possessed at least two nomocanons (Barb. gr. 324 and BnF gr. 1371), both of which can be identified by the presence of autograph notes made by the monk Nektarios of Otranto in the early thirteenth century.[57] Sadly, the monastery's archives were lost in the Turkish sack of Otranto in 1480, so its history must be pieced together from a selection of disparate sources. The only evidence for the twelfth century comes from a manuscript of its *typikon* that was copied in the year 1173.[58] The first five folia of contain a list of the monastery's abbots from its foundation in 1098 (continued by later hands to 1469) and brief notes on its administration and on its library.[59] The *typikon*'s dietary rule contains a tantalisingly imprecise reference to 'all the *metochia* that are under its authority', indicating that St Nicholas of Casole had a network of subject houses by the second half of the twelfth century.[60] Though we do not know what official status (if any) it had under Norman rule, an undated bull of Frederick II granted it a royal exemption from

[53] '*καῖ οὕτως ἔσεται ὅρος ὡς ἐξεθέμην, ἵνα μὴ λόγοι ὑπὲρ τοῦ τοιούτου ἔσωνται μήτε τῆς κρίσεως εἰ ἀγῶνα ὑπὲρ αὐτοῦ παραστήσειεν, ἵνα πρὸς αὐτοῦ βοηθοὶ ἔσωνται* [*sic*]': Montfaucon (1708): 406.

[54] See Chapter 4, 'The Byzantine Background', C4.P28.

[55] See Chapter 2, 'Greek Christianity in Medieval Italy', C2.P44.

[56] '...our spiritual father, the archimandrite Luke of the monastery of Carbone, came to me to make a request...' ('*...πρὸσήλθε* [*sic*] *μοι ὁ ημετερος πνικος πατὴρ καὶ ἀρχιμανδρίτης λυκᾶς, τῆς εὐαγεστάτοις μονῆς τῶν Καρβοῦνων, παρακαλῶν με...*'): Robinson (1929): 56 (no. 91).

[57] See Chapter 3, 'Patterns of Source Survival', C3.P23, C3.P36.

[58] Turin, Biblioteca Nazionale Universitaria, MS gr. 216 (C III 17). Text in Apostolidis (1983). See recently Chiriatti (2017); also Mazzotta (1989): 25–50; Omont (1890). A selection of the *typikon*'s dietary rules was published in Cozza-Luzi (1905): 2.155–166 and translated in *BMFD* 4.1319–1330 (no. 43). On the history of St Nicholas of Casole in general, see Hoeck and Loenertz (1965): 9–21; Parlangèli and Parlangèli (1951); Kölzer (1985).

[59] Summarised in Mazzotta (1989): 27–38, 41.

[60] '*...οὐ μόνον δὲ τοῦτο κρατεῖν ἐν τῇ ῥηθείσῃ μονῇ, ἀλλὰ καὶ ἐν πᾶσι τοῖς ὑπ' αὐτὴν οὖσι μετοχίοις*': Cozza-Luzi (1905): 2.155 (c. 1). We learn the names of some of these dependencies elsewhere in the manuscript: Vasto, Policastro, Trulazzo, Melendugno, Alessano, Castro, and Minervino (Torre [2017]: 66).

episcopal authority and control over an unspecified number of churches and monasteries in the Terra d'Otranto.[61]

A consistent picture emerges when we look at the Italo-Greek monasteries known to have produced and owned nomocanons under Norman rule. They were typically wealthy, well-endowed foundations that were major landowners and oversaw federations of subject *metochia*. In most cases, they also received formal recognition from the kings of Sicily of their independence from episcopal oversight: the Norman kings granted royal status to the Patiron (which also had a papal exemption from *c.* 1105), the Holy Saviour of Messina, St Bartholomew of Trigona, St John Theristes, and SS Elias and Anastasios of Carbone, while Frederick II granted it to St Nicholas of Casole and SS Peter and Paul of Spanopetro as well. The only exceptions are St Phantinos of Tauriana and the Holy Saviour of Bordonaro, both of which were subjected to the Archimandritate of Messina in 1133; nonetheless, Roger II allowed them a degree of independence as 'capital and self-governing' monasteries.

It is important to emphasise that most of these monasteries did not acquire their nomocanons as a direct result of receiving royal or papal privileges. This is only known to have happened in the case of Messina, which was established as a royal foundation from the very beginning. Instead, a monastery would usually acquire a *de facto* legal authority over its lands that would prompt it to acquire a nomocanon. This could in turn lead to a confrontation with the local bishop or nobility, as in the case of Archbishop Nicholas Maleinos of Rossano, which would prompt the monastery to seek *de jure* confirmation of its rights from a higher power. In Byzantium, that higher power would have been the emperor or the patriarch. After the creation of the Kingdom of Sicily in 1130, the Norman monarchs stepped in to fill the role.

Ecclesiastical Authority and Jurisdiction: The Monks' Perspective

Thanks to the autonomy guaranteed them by the Norman kings, the abbots and archimandrites of the realm's independent Greek monasteries were free to exercise legal jurisdiction in their territories without outside interference. How did these monasteries see themselves in the broader context of ecclesiastical law? How did they view their relation to the Latin popes under whose jurisdiction they were supposed to lie, or to the Norman kings who theoretically answered to the popes as vassals?

[61] Kölzer (1985): 425.

Extant literary sources from the period generally have little to say on the subject, but there are some interesting pieces of evidence. The nomocanons themselves contain marginalia left by readers that give small clues to their views on jurisdiction. In the Patiron's nomocanon (Vat. gr. 2060), for instance, a reader with a twelfth-century Greek hand highlighted canon 80 of the Council of Carthage. This canon states that bishops should not attempt to ordain abbots or hieromonks (monks in priestly orders) in monasteries that they do not control; next to this, the reader scrawled, 'Pay attention.'[62] Another reader highlighted the same canon in S. Salv. 59 from the Holy Saviour of Bordonaro with the note, 'What it says about monks from other monasteries.'[63] Further on in that manuscript, a different hand annotated canon 14 of the Council of Sardica, which safeguards against wrongful judgments by prejudiced bishops and ensures a defendant's right to appeal against unjust decisions. The monastic reader observed wryly that the canon is 'about the wrathful bishop'—i.e. about bishops who are so angry that they unfairly condemn a defendant.[64] Taken together, marginalia such as these imply that the Italo-Greek monks who read the nomocanons were interested in canonical texts that lessened episcopal power over monasteries.

It is no surprise that the monks were keen to evade their own bishops' jurisdiction, of course, but what of the bishop of Rome? They could not have been completely opposed to papal authority, since Bartholomew of Simeri put it to good use in his effort to evade his own Greek archbishop in Rossano. When it was not of immediate benefit to them, though, there is evidence that they preferred to think of the pope as a distant and legally irrelevant figure, when they thought of him at all.

There are two surviving Italo-Greek texts of particular interest here. The first is a set of scholia (in the form of *erotapokriseis*) that has been preserved in the manuscripts Vat. gr. 1650 (a collection of the Acts of the Apostles and New Testament epistles), Vat. gr. 1658 (containing the *Orations* of St John Chrysostom and the Gospel of Matthew), and in a mixture of Greek and Latin in Crypt. gr. 847 (a *prophetologion*) and Vat. gr. 1667 (a *menologion*).[65] These scholia are most notable for certain sections in which the author levelled pointed criticisms at the Western church for its attempts to enforce celibacy on its priests.

The philologist Ciro Giannelli argued that the text should be attributed to Nicholas, a Greek archbishop of Reggio who had originally commissioned the

[62] '*προσέχε*': Vat. gr. 2060, fol. 81^{r}. The reader left the same instruction at several other parts of the manuscript as well.

[63] '*περ[ὶ] μ[ο]ν[α]χ[ῶν] ἀπ' ἄλλ[ων] μ[ο]ν[α]στ[η]ρ[ίων] τί λέγει*': S. Salv. 59, fol. 139^{r}.

[64] '*περὶ ὀξυχόλου ἐπισκόπου*': S. Salv. 59, fol. 114^{r}.

[65] The text of these *erotapokriseis* is partially published in Giannelli (1953): 112–119; Lucà (2004a): 161–167.

manuscript Vat. gr. 1650 in the year 1037.[66] His reasoning was that Nicholas had owned the manuscript, that the hand that wrote the *erotapokriseis* seems to date to the eleventh century, and that the scholia mention 'tyrants' and 'carnal philosophers' (the Greek expression is difficult to render in English) that may be a reference to the hedonistic Pope Benedict IX (*r.* 1032–1044, 1045, 1047–1048).[67] He also suggested that one of the scholiast's comments in Crypt. gr. 847, which remarks on 'so much killing and war wrought in [the Church of Rome]', was a reference to the turbulence around Benedict's expulsion from office in 1044.[68]

More recent studies have shown that Giannelli's attribution was incorrect, even if his dating was accurate. Francesco Quaranta, Stefano Parenti, and Santo Lucà have all argued convincingly that the author of the scholia was not Nicholas of Reggio but Bartholomew the Younger (d. *c.* 1055), *hegoumenos* of the monastery of Grottaferrata in the mid-eleventh century.[69] The crucial evidence for this lies in the fact that the same hand that wrote the scholia concerning the Roman church's decrees against clerical celibacy also left marginalia in the manuscript Angel. gr. 41 that make specific reference to the end of Pope Gregory VI's pontificate in 1047; the author's perspective is clearly that of Abbot Bartholomew.[70] As Parenti has noted, the scholia on clerical celibacy were probably a reaction to the Roman synod of 1049, one of the first of many councils to denounce married priests.[71]

The monastery of Grottaferrata is geographically very close to Rome, situated in the region of Tusculum, and had close links to the papacy, yet Bartholomew still condemned the Roman decrees. The most interesting passage for our purposes comes in an *erotapokrisis* in Vat. gr. 1650 on I Corinthians 2:13 entitled, 'What does "judging spiritual matters with spiritual words" mean?'[72] Referring to Hebrews 10:1, the scholiast explains that the ancient Law (of the Old Testament) was a shadow of the truth that now exists. 'But,' he continues,

> Men want to be wiser than the God who shaped the darkness and so ordered the nature of man. For the Latins want their priests to live in celibacy and prevent them from having their lawful wives. Thus, they fall into fornication and

[66] Giannelli (1953): 108. Giannelli was followed in this view by Russo (1982): 1.214–215, 259. For the manuscript colophon in Vatican City, Biblioteca Apostolica Vaticana, MS Vat. gr. 1650, fol. 185ʳ that confirms Nicholas' ownership of the manuscript, see Batiffol (1891): 155 (no. 15).

[67] '*ἄλλην ὁδὸν βαδιζόντες, τὴν τῶν τυράννων*': Vat. gr. 1650, fol. 76ʳ; '*σαρκοφιλόσοφοι τὰς ἰδίας σάρκας φιλῶντες*': Vat. gr. 1650, fol. 76ᵛ. See Giannelli (1953): 106–107.

[68] '*quomodo . . . non reprehenditur civitas magna Roma, in qua Sion caelestis magna Ecclesia fundata est? tot homicidia et bella in ea facta et bellatores cottidie fabricant gladios*': quoted in Giannelli (1953): 100.

[69] Lucà (2004a); Parenti (2005): 136–142; Quaranta (2009). Quaranta originally presented his argument at a conference at Grottaferrata in 2004 and appears to have reached his conclusions independently of Lucà.

[70] Lucà (2004a): 162–166.

[71] Parenti (2005): 140. On the Roman synod, see *PL* 145.411B.

[72] '*τί ἐστὶ τὸ "πνευματικοῖς πνευματικὰ συγκρίνοντες";*': Vat. gr. 1650, fol. 78ʳ. Text in Giannelli (1953): 116–118.

> adultery, since the Apostle says, 'those who have wives should live as if they do not' [I Cor. 7:29] and 'judge spiritual matters with spiritual words'. But, in this respect, they do not have the wherewithal to make a spiritual judgment with spiritual words but rather an adulterous and greedy one.[73]

He goes on at some length on the subject, asking how Westerners have come to decide that marriage is evil. Bartholomew then asserts that Latin priests are falling into adultery because they have been deprived of their 'lawful wives', a subject on which he has much to say. The criticism does not seem to be a generic attack on Latin clerical celibacy but a reaction to a recent development, since the author makes repeated use of the word 'now'. For example: 'If he who preaches a Gospel contrary to that which he has received is subject to anathema, *now we see decrees* [against clerical marriage] in the Roman church contrary to the Lord's voice and Apostolic tradition, and it is clear that they are not beyond the apostolic anathema.'[74]

Bartholomew's *erotapokriseis* in Vat. gr. 1650 are a unique type of evidence for the time: a contemporary Italo-Greek monk's reaction to the Roman church's decrees against clerical marriage. He clearly opposed the decrees, even suggesting that Rome should be anathematised for them—an extraordinarily blunt assertion that indicates that he did not feel bound by the Roman church's legal pronouncements. What were the attitudes of Italo-Greek monks in the south, who were not so close to Rome as those of Grottaferrata were?

We do not receive an answer to this question until almost a century later, once the Normans had consolidated their rule over the region, when the monk Neilos Doxapatres composed his ecclesiological treatise on the *Order of the Patriarchal Thrones* in 1143/4.[75] Neilos probably belonged to the Holy Saviour of Messina or one of its dependencies and may also have been a former *nomophylax* of Constantinople, a high ranking legal official of the Byzantine Empire (though this is more difficult to prove).[76] What we can say is that Neilos was personally acquainted with King Roger II, as we learn from the work's preface:

[73] '*ἀλλὰ θέλωσιν οἱ ἄνθρωποι σοφώτεροι εἶναι Θεοῦ τοῦ τὴν σκιὰν τυπώσαντος καὶ τὴν ἀνθρωπείαν φύσιν οὕτω οἰκονομήσαντος. θέλοντες γὰρ οἱ λατῖνοι ἐν παρθενίᾳ μένειν τοὺς αὐτῶν ἱερεῖς κωλύωσιν νομίμους ἔχειν γυναῖκας, καὶ οὕτω πίπτουσιν εἰς πορνείας καὶ μοιχείας, τοῦ ἀποστόλου λέγοντος "ἔχειν γυναῖκας ὡς μὴ ἔχειν" καὶ 'πνευματικοὺς πνευματικὰ συγκρίνειν'. ἀλλ' οὗτοι ἐν τῷ μέρει τούτῳ σύγκρισιν πνευματικὴν πνευματικοῖς ὅπου ποιῆσαι οὐκ ἔχωσιν, ἀλλὰ μᾶλλον μοιχικὴν καὶ πλεονεκτικὴν*': Vat. gr. 1650, fol. 78r.

[74] '*ἐὰν ἀναθέματι ὑπεύθυνος ἐστὶν ὁ εὐαγγελιζόμενος παρ' ὃ παρέλαβεν, νῦν δὲ ὁρῶμεν ἐν τῇ ῥωμάνᾳ ἐκκλησίᾳ κηρύγματα ἐξ ἐναντίας τῆς κυριακῆς φωνῆς καὶ τῆς ἀποστολικῆς παραδόσεως, δῆλον ἐστὶν ὡς οὐκ ἔξω εἰσὶ τοῦ ἀποστολικοῦ ἀναθέματος*': Vat. gr. 1650, fol. 85r.

[75] Text in Parthey (1967): 265–308. For an in-depth discussion of this work, see Morton (2017). The chronological and political context of was obviously quite different to that of Bartholomew the Younger's scholia, but it is nonetheless instructive to see that anti-papal attitudes persisted as long as they did in the region.

[76] Morton (2017): 728–737. See also De Vos (2011): 253. There is evidence in separate manuscript colophons (including the Rossanese nomocanon Vat. gr. 2019) that there was a Byzantine *nomophylax*

> My most all-noble lord, concerning the matter about which you wrote to me, I recall that I wrote to your highness when I was in the castle of Palermo, although it was not as broad-ranging as you have now asked. Now there are many questions and they require a subtler written explanation. On account of this, and having thought out the whole work... I shall try as succinctly as possible to clearly set out in writing everything that has been commanded of me.[77]

Neilos does not say what Roger's 'many questions' were, but we can infer from the content of the treatise that he had asked for a description of the Byzantine church's episcopal hierarchy. In response to these questions, Neilos produced an essay that begins with a description of the church as a whole, outlining Byzantine views on the development of the five patriarchates (the pentarchy) and their territories, and ends with a detailed description of the episcopal hierarchy under the Patriarchate of Constantinople. For material sources he drew on lists of ecclesiastical precedence known as '*taktika*' that are frequently found as appendices to nomocanons; indeed, he even mentions 'the *taktika* of the *nomokanonon* in the throne of Constantinople' as a source.[78] Moreover, his description of the historical development of the pentarchy bears striking resemblances to texts of patriarchal *taktika* in the Calabro-Sicilian legal collections Sin. gr. 432 and Marc. gr. 172, and in the Rossanese Gospel lectionary Alag. gr. 3.[79]

The two halves of the work are each remarkable in their own way. On the subject of the pentarchy, Neilos presents the contemporary twelfth-century Byzantine orthodoxy: the five patriarchates received their privileges because of their status within the Roman Empire (which he naturally equates with the medieval Byzantine Empire), not because of any association with Apostles such as St Peter or St Andrew.[80] Indeed, he takes this argument even further than the

by the name of Nicholas Doxapatres in the first half of the twelfth century; see Chapter 7, 'The Secular Church and the Laity', C7.P26–C7.P29. If true, it is possible that he was exiled and became a monk in Sicily.

[77] '*πανευγενέστατε αὐθέντα μου, περὶ ἧς μοι ἔγραψας ὑποθέσεως, μέμνημαι ὅτι ἐν τῷ καστελλίῳ Πανόρμῳ ὢν ἔγραψα πρὸς τὴν σὴν ἀντίληψιν, πλὴν οὐχ οὕτω πλατύτερον ὡς νῦν ἠρώτησας. νῦν δὲ πολλά εἰσι τὰ ἐρωτηθέντα καὶ χρεία λεπτοτέρας γραφῆς καὶ διηγήσεως. διὰ τοῦτο καὶ παντὸς πόνου καταφρονήσας... πειράσομαι διὰ βραχέων ὅσον τὸ κατὰ δύναμιν διὰ γραφῆς σαφοῦς παραστῆσαι πάντα τὰ ἐπιτεταγμένα μοι*': Parthey (1967): 266.

[78] '*καὶ εἰσιν ἀναγεγραμμέναι καὶ αὗται ἐν τοῖς τακτικοῖς τοῦ νομοκανόνου ἐν τοῖς θρόνοις Κωνσταντινουπόλεως*': Parthey (1967): 294.

[79] Sin. gr. 432, fols. 1^r–4^v; Marc. gr. 172, fols. 248^v–249^v; Alag. gr. 3, fols. 215^v–216^r. See also Chapter 4, 'The Byzantine Background', p. C4.P40; Chapter 7, 'The Secular Church and the Laity', C7.P22; Morton (2017): 744.

[80] Neilos quotes Chalc. c. 28, commenting that, 'You thus see clearly from the above canon that those fools who say that Rome was honoured because of St Peter are refuted. For look, this canon of the holy synod clearly says that Rome has its privilege because it is an imperial city' ('*ὁρᾷς ὅπως ἀπὸ τοῦ παρόντος κάνονος προφανῶς ἐλέγχονται ληροῦντες οἱ λέγοντες προτιμηθῆναι τὴν Ῥώμην διὰ τὸν ἅγιον Πέτρον. ἰδοὺ γὰρ προφανῶς ὁ κανὼν οὗτος τῆς ἁγίας συνόδου φησὶ διὰ τὸ εἶναι τὴν Ῥώμην βασίλισσαν ἔχειν τὴν προτίμησιν*': Parthey [1967]: 289).

great twelfth-century Byzantine canonists Aristenos, Zonaras, and Balsamon. Whereas they debated whether or not Constantinople was equal or inferior to Rome (Aristenos and Balsamon felt that it was equal, Zonaras inferior), Neilos actually argued that it was *superior*: 'When [Rome] stopped being imperial because it was enslaved by foreign and barbarian tribes of Goths—and it is currently controlled by them—because of this, as it fell from that imperial rank, it also fell from the first [ecclesiastical] rank.'[81]

Neilos' claim that the Patriarchate of Constantinople outranked the Roman papacy is the best-known part of the work, but the second half is also revealing. He sets out to list all the bishoprics under Constantinople according to their rank. Unlike most *taktika*, though, Neilos begins with southern Italy, explaining that it was originally under Roman authority but was brought under Constantinople 'when barbarians captured the pope'.[82] He then outlines the region's episcopal hierarchy as it had existed under Byzantine rule over seventy years earlier. Though he does acknowledge the Norman conquest, he has nothing to say about its impact on the episcopal map.

Historians have found it difficult to reconcile the overtly pro-Constantinopolitan tone of the *Order of the Patriarchal Thrones* with the fact that it was dedicated to the Norman king Roger II, an enemy of the Byzantine Empire who was theoretically a vassal of the Roman pope. Thomas Brown saw it as an effort on Roger's part to conciliate his Greek Christian subjects in the face of 'increasing pressure from an aggressive papal monarchy', while Hubert Houben suggested that it may have been intended as an implicit threat to Pope Innocent II (*r.* 1130–1143), with whom Roger had only recently reconciled.[83] Yet neither of these is a convincing explanation: the Italo-Greeks were not facing pressure from the papacy, nor is there any evidence that Innocent would have even heard of Neilos' work, let alone been threatened by it.

We must remember that the *Order of the Patriarchal Thrones* was not Roger's idea, even if he asked the questions that prompted it. Rather, it was an expression of Neilos Doxapatres' own personal perspective on ecclesiastical jurisdiction. He was aware of the Norman conquest and of the political realities that followed from it, but he also believed that southern Italy *ought* to be part of the Byzantine church and that the patriarch of Constantinople outranked the Roman pontiff. Nor was he alone in this belief; as he says in the preface to the work, he wrote it 'at the

[81] '*ἐπεὶ δὲ ἐπαύθη τὸ εἶναι βασίλισσα διὰ τὸ ὑπὸ ἀλλοφύλων αἰχμαλωτισθῆναι καὶ βαρβάρων Γοτθικῶν, καὶ νῦν ὑπ' ἐκείνων κατέχεσθαι, δῆθεν ὡς ἐκπεσοῦσα τῆς βασιλείας ἐκείνης ἐπίπτει καὶ τῶν πρωτείων*': Parthey (1967): 289 Neilos seems to conflate the Goths who captured Rome in the fifth century with the Lombards who captured it in the eighth century and with the Holy Roman Empire of the twelfth century. For further discussion of how Neilos' arguments compare to those of other Byzantine canonists, see Morton (2017): 745–746; Siciliano (1979): 176–177.

[82] '*ὅτε βάρβαροι κατέσχον τὸν πάπαν*': Parthey (1967): 294. This is presumably a reference to the Lombard conquest of the Exarchate of Ravenna in 751.

[83] Brown (1992): 205; Houben (2002): 102.

urging of my holy father', by which he means his abbot.[84] If Neilos did indeed belong to the royal archimandritate of the Holy Saviour of Messina, then it implies that a significant swathe of Italo-Greek monasticism in the 1140s accepted the primacy of Constantinople and Byzantine canon law.

Conclusion

Neilos Doxapatres' assertion of the primacy of Constantinople would have been unacceptable anywhere else in Western Europe, yet it was apparently a palatable

Table 5.1. Monastic Nomocanons of the Norman Period with Known Provenances

	Shelfmark	Date	Owner	Location	Legal Status
1.	Vat. gr. 1980–1981	C11	SS Elias and Anastasios of Carbone	Lucania	Royal archimandritate (1168)
2.	Vat. gr. 2060	*c.* 1100–1115	Patiron of Rossano	Calabria	Papal exemption (*c.* 1105); royal archimandritate (1130)
3.	S. Salv. 59	*c.* 1100–1115	Holy Saviour of Bordonaro	Sicily	'Capital and autodespotic' subject of Holy Saviour of Messina (1133)
4.	Vall. C 11.1	*c.* 1100–1115	Holy Saviour of Messina	Sicily	Royal archimandritate (1133)
5.	Marc. gr. 169[a]	C11/12	Holy Saviour of Messina	Sicily	Royal archimandritate (1133)
6.	Ambros. G 57 sup.	Early C12	St Phantinos of Tauriana	Calabria	'Capital and autodespotic' subject of Holy Saviour of Messina (1133)
7.	Barb. gr. 323	Early C12	St Bartholomew of Trigona	Calabria	Royal exemption (1144)
8.	Crypt. gr. 322	Pre-1135	SS Peter and Paul of Spanopetro	Calabria	Royal exemption (1224); archimandritate (post-1224)
9.	BN II C 7	1139	St John Theristes	Calabria	Royal exemption (1144)
10.	Barb. gr. 324	Mid–Late C12	St Nicholas of Casole	Salento	Royal exemption (Early C13)
11.	BnF gr. 1371	Mid–Late C12	St Nicholas of Casole	Salento	Royal exemption (Early C13)

[a] This manuscript was originally produced in Constantinople; it came to Messina between 1133 and 1288.

[84] 'προτροπῆς τοῦ ἁγίου μου πατρὸς': Parthey (1967): 266. On the abbot as spiritual father, see Delouis (2009).

view for a Greek monk to hold in the Norman Kingdom of Sicily. We may presume that Roger II and his successors did not personally agree with it, but they do not appear to have made an effort to challenge it either. The Roman papacy, for its part, was at any rate largely powerless to intervene and was probably unaware of the attitudes of Italo-Greek monks.

The *Order of the Patriarchal Thrones* is indicative of two main legal dynamics in Greek monasticism under Norman rule. The first is the continuing prevalence of Byzantine canon law in independent Italo-Greek monasteries. As they accumulated lands and subject houses, they acquired nomocanons with Byzantine legal content to help them administer their territories (see Table 5.1). The second dynamic is the enabling role played by the Norman nobility and kings who supported these monasteries and eventually granted them recognition as independent judicial authorities exempt from the supervision of the episcopal hierarchy (be it Latin or Greek). This autonomy allowed them to live out a legal fiction in which they were still subject to Constantinople.

It must be said that not all Greek monasteries were in this position. Many were subjected to powerful houses such as the Patiron and the Holy Saviour, while others were subjected to Latin abbeys. It would be particularly interesting to learn what happened to the latter group, but the evidence has not survived. Those monasteries that did obtain recognition of their legal independence, however, had the freedom to continue following Byzantine canon law as they had before the Norman conquest. Some monasteries even remained in contact with contemporary Byzantine canon law scholarship well into the twelfth century, as we shall see in the following chapter.

6
Monastic Nomocanons II
Style, Content, and Influences

The appearance and content of the Norman-era Italo-Greek monastic nomocanons strongly reinforce the impression of the autonomous archipelago that we saw in the previous chapter. As manuscripts produced under Latin rule on the periphery of the Western Christian world, it would be reasonable to assume that they might show some signs of Latin influence either in terms of style or textuality. Indeed, the Italo-Greek nomocanons were produced just a short distance away from the Benedictine monastery of Montecassino, one of the most significant centres of Latin manuscript culture in Europe. Yet there are no clear traces of Latin influence in the nomocanons.

On the contrary, Italo-Greek manuscripts are generally characterised by a high degree of conservatism. It is often very difficult to tell the difference between Greek manuscripts from southern Italy and those from other parts of the Byzantine world. This is not to say that the Italo-Greek nomocanons are all identical; they do provide interesting contrasts that reward closer attention. However, the most meaningful distinctions are not between Italo-Greek and mainland Byzantine manuscripts or even between Greek and Latin, but between different groups of Italo-Greek nomocanons themselves. Although they all contain Byzantine texts and have fundamentally the same Byzantine design ethos, there are discernible variations in style and register between different chronological periods, geographical regions, and social contexts. These variations reflect the changing fortunes of the different institutions that produced and used the manuscripts.

The monastic nomocanons can be divided into three broad groups. The first are those that I refer to as 'traditional' nomocanons of the Southwest (Calabria, Sicily, and Lucania). These manuscripts contain more archaic texts inherited from the Byzantine Empire of the pre-Norman era and conform to customary Italo-Greek aesthetics. The other two categories of monastic nomocanon are the Rossanese Group from the Patiron and a pair of codices from St Nicholas of Casole. Both of these monasteries produced manuscripts under strong influence from the contemporaneous Byzantine Empire, reflecting traditions of the late eleventh and the mid-twelfth centuries respectively.

These trends echo the historical connections that each of the Italo-Greek monasteries had with the contemporary Byzantine world: most simply drew on

Byzantine Religious Law in Medieval Italy. James Morton, Oxford University Press (2021). © James Morton.
DOI: 10.1093/oso/9780198861140.003.0007

an inherited Byzantine legal tradition, whereas the Patiron and St Nicholas of Casole each had a degree of contact with Constantinople in the years after their foundation. There is a further interesting dynamic at play, however. Most of the nomocanons serve as functional reference guides to Byzantine canon law, befitting their role as practical aides in the Greek monastic legal system of southern Italy. In later manuscripts (especially those from Casole), though, we begin to see a foreshadowing of a shift in purpose that would become much more pronounced from the thirteenth century on. Over time, the interests of the people who produced and used the codices would move from their practical legal application to their potential as sources of cultural education and legitimation, or from the imperial to the paideic, in Robert Cover's terminology.[1]

Traditional Monastic Nomocanons of the Southwest

This category of manuscripts (Ambros. G 57 sup., Barb. gr. 323, BN II C 7, Crypt. gr. 322, Sin. gr. 432, Vat. gr. 1980–1981) encapsulates the utilitarian character of nomocanons as Alessia Aletta expressed it: their essential goal is the transmission of legal information.[2] Their decorative schemes are simple and hierarchical, meaning that decorative elements are heavily concentrated around the opening folia. Since many manuscripts have lost their first quire, this can sometimes give the impression that some of the nomocanons were not (or scarcely) decorated at all.[3] This may not originally have been the case, but they generally have quite austere appearances. Moreover, these manuscripts are among the best evidence for earlier canon law collections in Byzantine Italy, since their contents are strikingly archaic.[4] Hence, I refer to them as 'traditional' nomocanons.

BN II C 7 (from St John Theristes of Stilo), Ambros. G 57 sup. (from St Phantinos of Tauriana), and Crypt. gr. 322 (from SS Peter and Paul of Spanopetro) all contain the late sixth-century *N50T*. In each case, the canons of *Trullo*, II Nicaea and *Protodeutera*, all of which post-dated the composition of the *N50T*, were inserted separately (though in Crypt. gr. 322 they precede the *N50T*, unlike in the other two manuscripts in which they follow the collection).[5] Furthermore, all three manuscripts contain appendices of miscellaneous texts on canon law history and spiritual discipline, though the appendix in Crypt. gr. 322 is not identical to those in Ambros. G 57 sup. and BN II C 7 (which are

[1] See Introduction, CI.P16–CI.P17.

[2] See Chapter 1, 'Introducing the Byzantine Nomocanon', C1.P31.

[3] The nomocanons in this category that have lost their opening quires are Ambros. G 57 sup.; Barb. gr. 323, 476; and Crypt. gr. 322.

[4] See Chapter 4, 'The Byzantine Background', C4.P13–C4.P15.

[5] BN II C 7, fols. 88–130, 134–139; Ambros. G 57 sup., fols. 1–23, 25^r–26^r; Crypt. gr. 322, fols. 41–65.

identical to each other).[6] In short, these three nomocanons are clearly all descended from a manuscript tradition of the late ninth or early tenth century, after the *Protodeutera* council of 861 but before the 'Photian' recension of the *N14T* (which integrated the new canons into the collection) had become widespread.

Barb. gr. 323 (from St Bartholomew of Trigona) appears to have originally contained the full text of the canons in chronological order from the Apostolic Canons to those of *Protodeutera*. Nonetheless, it is noticeable that the *Protodeutera* canons in Barb. gr. 323 are in the wrong place, appearing before the canons of *Trullo* and II Nicaea. This would imply that Barb. gr. 323 was also descended from a manuscript tradition in which the canons of these three later councils were awkwardly inserted into an older collection. Although the canonical collection in this manuscript is different to that in the three manuscripts from St John Theristes, SS Peter and Paul of Spanopetro, and St Phantinos of Tauriana (the *N50T*), the manuscript does still have an indirect relationship to this group, as we see from the inclusion of the Italo-Greek recension of Niketas Stethatos' polemic on the *azyma*.[7]

Sin. gr. 432 (from an unidentified monastery in southern Calabria or Sicily) and Vat. gr. 1980–1981 (the Carbone nomocanon) reflect similarly archaic manuscript traditions, containing the *S50T* and the original recension of the *N14T* (with additions from the *N50T*) respectively. As we saw in Chapter 4, the appendices in the Carbone nomocanon show that it was descended from a manuscript of the mid-tenth century. Neither it nor Sin. gr. 432 include the canons of *Protodeutera* at all (the latest canons in both are those of II Nicaea), suggesting that their original prototypes may have been even older still.

Though their contents were antiquated, both Sin. gr. 432 and the Carbone nomocanon were clearly in active use in the Norman period, as we see from additions in both Latin and Greek left by readers of the twelfth to thirteenth centuries. In the opening folia of the Carbone nomocanon, one twelfth-century Greek hand inserted the text of *Trullo* c. 92 (which prohibits the kidnapping of women for marriage), while another wrote out multiple extracts from Byzantine civil and canon law texts on the role of witnesses in criminal hearings, how to handle accusations against the clergy, and the payment of interest on debts.[8] In the case of Sin. gr. 432, a Greek hand of the later twelfth or thirteenth centuries added a variation of the *Statement and Definition of the Patriarchal Thrones* (here

[6] BN II C 7, fols. 84–174; Ambros. G 57 sup., fols. 1–48; Crypt. gr. 322, fols. 1^r–70^r.

[7] See Chapter 4, 'The Byzantine Background', C4.P38–C4.P39.

[8] Vat. gr. 1980, fols. 1^v–4^v. The texts are *Trullo* c. 92; *Procheiros Nomos* 27.15, 9, 29, 20; *Ekloge* 14.10; *Basilika* 21.1.22; *Procheiros Nomos* 27.6; *Basilika* 21.1.15; and three further unidentified passages. A third hand of the later twelfth or thirteenth century also added a barely legible recipe for some sort of salad on fol. 4^r, suggesting that the manuscript may have outlived its practical purpose by that point.

entitled *On the Patriarchates and their Regions*) that we saw in Chapter 4 and the letter of Peter III of Antioch to Domenicus of Grado on the pentarchy.[9]

Despite their lack of decoration, the traditional nomocanons of the Southwest share a broadly common aesthetic rooted in local Greek codicological traditions of southwestern Italy. For example, the manuscripts all make use of knotted crosses and headbands formed from ropes (or possibly vines) to mark the start and end of different texts.[10] There are some differences between the Carbone nomocanon and the manuscripts from southern Calabria. In Vat. gr. 1980–1981, the knotted crosses and headbands are executed in combinations of red, green, and blue inks, all of which are characteristic colour choices of Italo-Greek scribes from south-western Italy.[11] The knotted crosses in Sin. gr. 432 are in red, green, and yellow, whereas in the other southern Calabrian manuscripts they are simply red.

Furthermore, while the script in the Carbone nomocanon conforms to the School of Neilos style described by Lucà, the hands in the southern Calabrian manuscripts are all much closer to the so-called 'Style of Reggio' that predominated in the region of the Straits of Messina in the twelfth century.[12] This can be explained partly by the difference in the manuscripts' geographical origins but also by their difference in age: the Carbone nomocanon was produced between fifty and one hundred years earlier than the others.

Another point of difference among the traditional nomocanons is between large and small manuscripts. They cluster into two groups, a point that becomes clear from their dimensions (see Table 6.1).

The nomocanons Crypt. gr. 322, Barb. gr. 323, and Vat. gr. 1980–1981 are among the smallest of all those that survive from southern Italy, though the latter is somewhat larger than the former two.[13] The other three manuscripts are all in the range of 230–250 mm in height and 185–195 mm in width. As we saw in Chapter 1, there is a close correlation between the size of a medieval manuscript and its aesthetic quality, and these codices are no exception to the rule.

Sin. gr. 432 and BN II C 7 are unquestionably the most appealing of the traditional nomocanons (Ambros. G 57 sup. is too badly damaged to allow for an evaluation of its aesthetic quality). Every single new text in Sin. gr. 432 is

[9] Sin. gr. 432, fols. 1–4. See Chapter 4, 'The Byzantine Background', C4.P40. Even more intriguingly, a fourteenth-century hand added a Latin translation of the Greek text of the Nicene Creed (without the *Filioque*) on fol. 12^{v}; see Chapter 10, 'They Do It Like This in Romania', C10.P25, for further discussion.

[10] The knot motif is also common in both southern Italian and Epirote manuscripts of this period: Cataldi Palau (2006): 530–531.

[11] Canart (1983): 144; Canart and Leroy (1977): 253–254; cf. Reinsch (1991): 84.

[12] On the 'Style of Reggio', see Canart and Leroy (1977). The name is misleading: most manuscripts in this style were actually produced in Messina and north-eastern Sicily, a fact that was not yet known when the term was coined by Robert Devreesse (Devreesse [1955]: 40). On the School of Neilos style, see Chapter 4, 'The Byzantine Background', C4.P26.

[13] When placed together, the approximately 400 folia of Vat. gr. 1980–1981 would have made the manuscript almost as thick (130 mm) as it is wide (145 mm).

Table 6.1. Dimensions of the Simple Monastic Nomocanons of Lucania, Calabria, and Sicily (Smallest to Largest)

	Shelfmark	Date	Origin	Dimensions (mm)	Written Space (mm)	Written Lines	Columns
1.	Crypt. gr. 322	Pre-1135	S. Calabria	155 x 120	100 x 75	21–22	1
2.	Barb. gr. 323	Early C12	S. Calabria	165 x 155	120 x 110	23	1
3.	Vat. gr. 1980–1981	C11	Lucania	190 x 145	145 x 105	22	1
4.	Sin. gr. 432	C12	Sicily/ S. Calabria	230 x 185	185 x 140	32	1
5.	Ambros. G 57 sup.	Early C12	S. Calabria	245 x 180	180 x 130	25–35	1
6.	BN II C 7	1139	S. Calabria	250 x 195	180 x 145	24–27	2

consistently marked out by a red cross in the margin, with blue and yellow ink occasionally used as well. Titles throughout the codex are written in red ink and highlighted by the application of a yellow wash over the top; this created an effect like that of a modern highlighter pen, although the colour is not so vibrant. Like the knot motif, yellow highlighting washes are quite common in Greek manuscripts from both southern Italy and Epirus (sometimes green is also used).[14]

The most impressive ornamentation in Sin. gr. 432, however, is the headpiece at the beginning of an extract from the *Apostolic Constitutions* on fol. 13ʳ that was originally the first item in the codex. This takes the shape of a rectangular band along the top of the red-ink title with inlaid roundels containing floral designs in red, blue, and yellow ink. The appearance and colours are similar to those of the Byzantine *Blütenblattstil* used in the more elaborate nomocanons of Rossano, though the quality of execution is not as high.[15] In addition to these decorative elements, a later hand drew a diagram on fol. 99ᵛ (which was originally blank) to illustrate degrees of family kinship; a similar (but not identical) diagram can be found in Marc. gr. 172.[16] Such diagrams are present in many Byzantine legal manuscripts and were intended as guides to help explain civil and canonical prohibitions on marriage between close relatives, although we do not know exactly why it was added to Sin. gr. 432.[17]

[14] See Reinsch (1991): 79–97; Cataldi Palau (2006): 32–36. Ambros. G 57 sup. and Crypt. gr. 322 also show limited traces of a yellow wash used to highlight titles and initial letters.

[15] See section: 'Deluxe Monastic Nomocanons', C6.S2.

[16] The hand is different from that of the main text and the diagram is not mentioned in the manuscript's table of contents (fol. 9ʳ). On the similar diagram in Marc. gr. 172, see Chapter 7, 'The Secular Church and the Laity', C7.P19.

[17] On Byzantine kinship diagrams, see recently Rapp (2016): 231–235. A more detailed overview of the subject (with illustrations) can be found in Patlagean (1966), esp. fig. 1.

BN II C 7 from St John Theristes of Stilo stands out the most among this group of manuscripts. Not only is it relatively large for a southern Calabrian nomocanon, but the script looks closer to the School of Neilos style than the Style of Reggio. Konon gave the manuscript a two-column *mise-en-page* that is usually characteristic of more decorative codices such as Gospel lectionaries. His execution was by no means flawless, though; on fol. 118^{r}, for example, he left a large gap in the upper left corner of the right-hand column where there should be text, perhaps because of poor spatial planning (it does not look like anything else was meant to fill the space). Moreover, the ruling in the first eighty-four folia does not align correctly with the edges of the pages.

The ruling system itself and the method of quire construction are also unusual.[18] In order to apply rule lines to the writing surface, the medieval scribe would group together a quire of (usually) eight parchment sheets folded down the centre. He would then score the rule lines into one or more surfaces so that they passed by impression throughout the whole quire. Most surviving Italo-Greek nomocanons were ruled in systems 1 (the most common ruling system in the Byzantine world) or 9 (a characteristic ruling system of Byzantine Calabria).[19] BN II C 7 is unique among the Italo-Greek nomocanons in that it is ruled in system 4 (see Figures 6.1–6.3).[20]

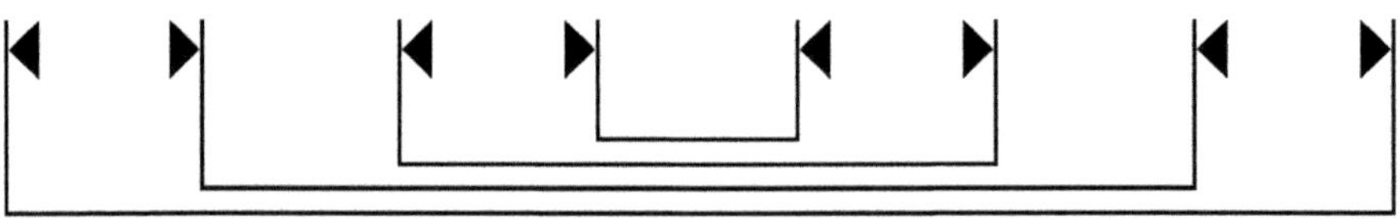

Figure 6.1. Ruling System 1. The quire is ruled on fols. 1^{v}, 2^{r}, 3^{v}, 4^{r}, 5^{v}, 6^{r}, 7^{v}, 8^{r}; rule lines travel via impression to the opposite side of each folio.

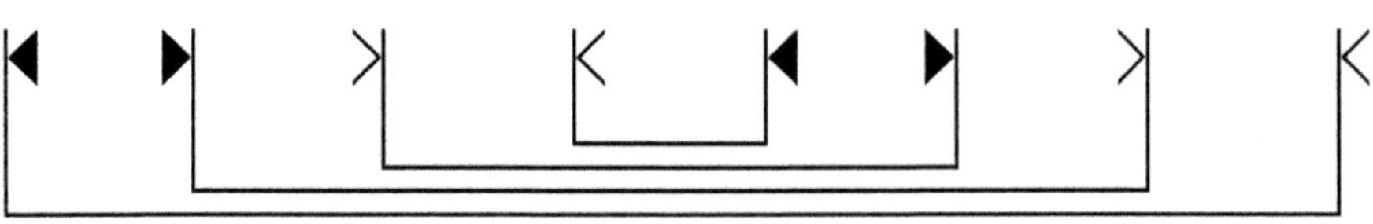

Figure 6.2. Ruling System 9. Rule lines are made on fols. 1^{v}, 2^{r}, 5^{v}, and 6^{r}, travelling via impression through the next folio.

[18] 'Ruling type' refers to the pattern of the rule lines on the manuscript page. 'Ruling system' refers to the method by which the scribe applied the rule lines. I follow here the classification scheme of Leroy (1977); the clearest overview can be found in Sautel and Leroy (1995): 16–28.

[19] On the use of ruling system 9 in Calabria, see Leroy (1983): 60–61; Canart and Leroy (1977): 251.

[20] It should be noted, though, that Leroy has observed system 4 in other Greek manuscripts from southern Italy: Leroy (1978): 60–61.

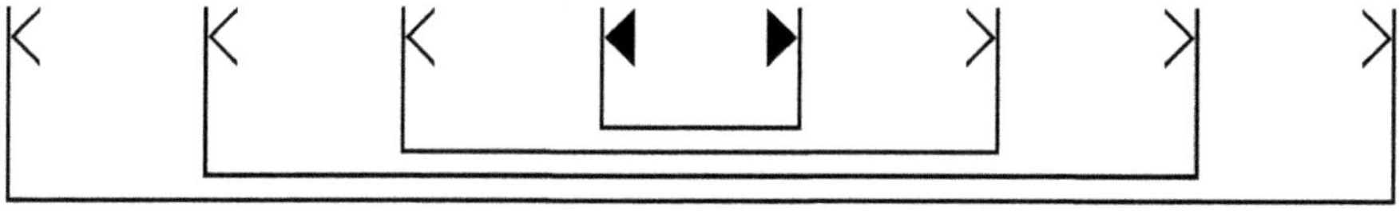

Figure 6.3. Ruling System 4. Quires are ruled on fols. 4^v and 5^r, travelling by impression from the centre of the quire to the outer folia.

BN II C 7 has several other idiosyncrasies. The quires present the hair side of the folia on their exterior, unlike most Byzantine manuscripts which present the flesh side of the folia.[21] Whereas several other manuscripts make use of a yellow (or occasionally green) wash to highlight titles, BN II C 7 uses an orange-red wash that does not appear in the other nomocanons. None of these features are unique to BN II C 7, as they can be found in other Byzantine manuscripts, but they are highly uncommon. Even the knotted headband surmounting the title of the *S50T* on fol. 2^v looks different from the other southern Calabrian nomocanons: a loose, expansive, sprawling jumble of knots instead of the tight displays that usually feature. Stylistic choices such as these imply a degree of creativity on Konon's part that we do not often see in the nomocanons.

The overall simplicity of this group of nomocanons undoubtedly reflects both their functional nature and the relatively small size and wealth of the monasteries that produced them. Although they were influential enough to require nomocanons in their administration, they did not have the capacity of archimandritates such as the Patiron of Rossano or the Holy Saviour of Messina to produce large, decorative codices. Nor did they enjoy those institutions' ongoing cultural connections to Constantinople. Rather than importing up-to-date legal collections from the Byzantine world, these smaller monasteries were obliged to copy locally available texts such as the *S50T* and *N50T* that dated back to the sixth and seventh centuries. Even so, the lack of any clear Latin influence on their contents or codicology is also striking. The monasteries that produced these nomocanons drew on a conservative, isolated regional book culture based on codicological traditions inherited from the era of Byzantine rule in southern Italy.

Deluxe Monastic Nomocanons: The Rossanese Group

The three surviving nomocanons copied in the early twelfth century at the Patiron of Rossano (S. Salv. 59, Vall. C 11.1, Vat. gr. 2060) provide a marked contrast to

[21] Following 'Gregory's Law', medieval manuscript quires were typically arranged so that the flesh side of one folio would face the flesh side of the next folio (and the hair side would face another hair side). This trend is named for Caspar René Gregory (1846–1917), the scholar credited with its discovery; see Avrin (1991): 213, 221.

the traditional manuscripts discussed above. With a standardised set of contents and luxurious finishing, they seem to have been the products of a relatively professional operation on the monastery's part to supply legal manuscripts both for its own needs and for those of other Greek monasteries in the Calabro-Sicilian area. The other monastic nomocanons in this study all appear to have been created by and for individual institutions.

The Rossanese Group manuscripts are among the largest in this study, copied on high-quality parchment, decorated with a paratactic scheme of varying head-bands and initial letters (see Table 6.2).

Furthermore, the Rossanese Group all contain an identical combination of texts in the same order:

1. Epitome of Book Eight of the Apostolic Constitutions 22.2–28.1
2. S50T, preface and table of canons
3. N14T ('Photian' recension)
4. Corpus of conciliar and patristic canons
5. Civil law appendix: Just. *Nov.* 77; *C87C*; *C25C*; the *Tripartite Collection*; Heraclius, *Novels* 4, 1, 3, 2
6. John Moschos, *Spiritual Meadow* 149.

No other surviving Italo-Greek nomocanon has this pattern of textual content; indeed, none even have the 'Photian' recension of the *N14T*.[22] However, the combination of items 1–5 (without the extract from Moschos' *Spiritual Meadow*) in the above list is well attested elsewhere in the Byzantine world. The earliest manuscript to contain them seems to be RNB gr. 66+66a, which the editors of the *RHBR* date to the tenth century.[23] The eleventh-century manuscripts Laur. plut. 10.10 and *Παν. Τάφ.* 635 contain the texts in the same order, while another eleventh-century codex, Barocci 185, has them together with other scholia

Table 6.2. Dimensions of the Rossanese Group

	Shelfmark	Date	Origin	Dimensions (mm)	Written Space (mm)	Written Lines	Columns
1.	Vat. gr. 2060	*c.* 1100–1115	Rossano	305 x 240	235 x 160	37	2
2.	Vall. C 11.1	*c.* 1100– 1115	Rossano	325 x 240	205 x 175	29	2
3.	S. Salv. 59	*c.* 1100–1115	Rossano	325 x 255	200 x 165	29–32	2

[22] The manuscript Paris, Bibliothèque nationale de France, MS gr. 1324 contains items 1–5 on the list and may be related to the Rossanese Group, though its provenance is unclear; see Appendix 3, 'Uncertain and Disputed Manuscripts', CA3.S3.

[23] RNB gr. 66+66a, fols. 2–362; see *RHBR* 2.146–149 (no. 386/7).

and texts not present in the Rossanese Group.[24] The eleventh/twelfth-century BnF gr. 1320, BN II C 4, and Sin. 1111 are similar cases.[25] Items 1–5 appear yet again in the pair of related manuscripts Marc. gr. 169 (eleventh century) and Staatsbibl. gr. 380 (twelfth century); the former of these coincidentally later came to the Holy Saviour of Messina, as noted in Chapter 5.[26]

The combination of texts in the Rossanese Group evidently emerged in the tenth century and became widespread in Byzantine nomocanons in the eleventh century. Bartholomew of Simeri visited Constantinople in *c.* 1105 to acquire books and vestments for his new foundation of the Patiron; he must have brought back a Byzantine nomocanon with these contents to serve as the model for the Rossanese Group. The scribes of the Patiron added their own touch by inserting a short excerpt from John Moschos' *Spiritual Meadow*, a seventh-century collection of tales and aphorisms recounted by the monks of Syria and Palestine, as a coda.[27]

Alert readers may point out that the Photian recension of the *N14T* was hardly a 'modern' Byzantine canon law text in the early twelfth century: after all, it was over two centuries old by then and had been superseded in *c.* 1090 by a third recension composed by Theodore the *Bestes* and Michael the *Sebastos*.[28] As we have seen already, though, it could take decades or even centuries for new legal codifications to enter widespread circulation. Even in 1105, most Byzantine ecclesiastical institutions were probably still using older nomocanons. Indeed, Bartholomew might have been given the manuscript precisely *because* it was being replaced by a newer version and was thus no longer needed by its previous owner.

As the Patiron imported a new Byzantine legal collection to southern Italy, it also imported new Constantinopolitan styles of writing and manuscript ornamentation. They did not completely discard local Calabrian book culture, but they were noticeably influenced by trends from eleventh-century Byzantium. This is most noticeable in changes to the script, as the School of Neilos style of northern

[24] Florence, Biblioteca Medicea Laurenziana, MS plut. 10.10; Athens, *Μετόχιον Παναγίου Τάφου*, MS 635, fols. 1^r–276^r; Oxford, Bodleian Library, MS Barocci 185, fols. 9^r–288^r.

[25] Paris, Bibliothèque nationale de France, MS gr. 1320, fols. 1–246; Naples, Biblioteca nazionale 'Vittorio Emanuele III,' MS II C 4, fols. 1^v–271^v; Sinai, *Μονὴ τῆς Ἁγίας Αἰκατερίνης*, MS 1111, fols. 1–342.

[26] Marc. gr. 169, fols. 1^r–302^r; Munich, Bayerische Staatsbibliothek, MS gr. 380, fols. 62–520. On Marc. gr. 169, see Chapter 5, 'Monastic Nomocanons I', C5.P15.

[27] The excerpt is an anecdote told by Patriarch Amos of Jerusalem (*r.* 594–601) about Pope Leo the Great of Rome (*r.* 440–460) praying to St Peter at the beginning of Lent. The pope asks the saint to intercede with God for the forgiveness of his sins. Later, Peter reveals to him that 'I have prayed for you and all your sins are forgiven, except for [sins of] ordination. This alone will be demanded [of you]: whether you have ordained bad [clergy] or good' ('*ἐδεήθην ὑπὲρ σοῦ, καὶ συνεχωρήθη σοι πάντα τὰ ἁμαρτήματα, πλὴν τῶν χειροτονιῶν. τοῦτο οὖν μόνον ἀπαιτηθήσῃ, εἴτε κακῶς εἴτε καλῶς ἐχειροτόνησας*'): *PG* 87.3013. The addition of this brief excerpt on the importance of ordaining good clergy may reflect twelfth-century enthusiasm for church reform, though the fact that the scribes chose a passage from a Greek text of the seventh century rather than anything from contemporary Italy says a lot about their cultural priorities.

[28] See Chapter 1, 'Introducing the Byzantine Nomocanon', C1.P13.

Calabria merged with Constantinopolitan *Perlschrift* ('Pearl Script') to produce what Lucà has dubbed the 'Style of Rossano'.[29] The ornamental headbands and frames that decorate the text are likewise executed in the Byzantine *Blütenblattstil* ('Flower-Petal Style').[30] Neat titles in red ink are enclosed within *pylai* (decorative frames in the shape of rectangular gateways) made of flower petals with leafy tendrils emerging from the corners. Even the style of uncial script used in the titles would not be out of place in an eleventh-century manuscript from Constantinople or Mount Athos. It is one of the great ironies of Italo-Greek book culture that it does not appear to have adopted these Byzantine styles until *after* Italy had ceased to be part of the empire.

As with its textual content, the Rossanese Group's ornamental and palaeographical characteristics were already going out of fashion in mainland Byzantium when they came to Calabria and Sicily.[31] One must bear a couple of important caveats in mind when discussing this. The first is that there are relatively few surviving Italo-Greek manuscripts from the eleventh century in general; while the *Blütenblattstil* and *Perlschrift* seem to appear suddenly in twelfth-century Calabria, it is possible that there were examples from before that time that have not been preserved. The second caveat is that palaeographical styles in Byzantine Italy typically lagged behind those of Constantinople by about fifty to eighty years even in the tenth and eleventh centuries, as Jean Irigoin has pointed out.[32] The delay in the adoption of *Blütenblattstil* and *Perlschrift* is consistent with this trend.

Nonetheless, it is hard not to associate the appearance of these Byzantine styles in Rossano with the visit of Bartholomew of Simeri to Constantinople in *c.* 1105. This is just one recorded visit and there were other occasions on which manuscripts were brought from Byzantium to southern Italy in the twelfth century.[33] Even so, the emperor's gift was memorable enough to be included in Bartholomew's *Life*, so it clearly made an impression on the monks of the Patiron. It is very likely that the ornamentation in the Rossanese Group nomocanons was significantly influenced by the books that Bartholomew brought from Constantinople.

It should be said that the Rossanese nomocanons are not completely identical among themselves and retain (to varying degrees) many traditional Calabrian decorative elements, in particular the use of colour combinations of red, green, blue, and yellow. They are also all ruled in system 9, a popular choice in Calabria (though not unheard of in Constantinople either). In addition, not all of the manuscripts are of equal quality. The most accomplished of the

[29] Lucà (1985): 99–100; cf. Lucà (2002): 75. The *Perlschrift* derives its name from the neat, pearl-like appearance of the minuscule letters; see Hunger (1954).

[30] The classic description of the *Blütenblattstil* can be found in Weitzmann (1935): 22–32.

[31] See Canart and Perria (1991): 83–86.

[32] Irigoin (1966): 263.

[33] Perhaps the most famous example is the 'Madrid Skylitzes', copied in twelfth-century Sicily from a Byzantine prototype: see Boeck (2015): 32–42.

three is S. Salv. 59, which has exceedingly neat 'Rossano-style' *Perlschrift* and *Blütenblattstil*; the parchment is also very fine.[34] Vat. gr. 2060 is damaged and has lost its opening and closing quires, but what does survive contains elegant paratactic ornamentation.[35]

Vall. C 11.1 is the plainest of the three, though it is still an impressive piece in its own right. The *pyle* over the opening text on fol. 2^{r} is an impressive example of the *Blütenblattstil*, though the arrangement of the colours (red, yellow, and dark blue) is much simpler and starker than in S. Salv. 59. The initial letter of the text, an omicron, takes the unusual form of a human head with rosy cheeks, whereas in S. Salv. 59 the equivalent letter is made up of red flower petals. Unlike the other two nomocanons, the titles and initial letters in Vall. C 11.1 are not written in red but in ordinary brown ink highlighted by yellow wash (which the other two manuscripts do not use at all). In addition, the uncial script used in the titles of Vall. C 11.1 is far more archaic than in the other two and more closely resembles forms used in the School of Neilos script. In short, Vall. C 11.1 has the most 'traditional' Calabrian appearance of the three.

Maria Foti (who was unaware of Vall. C 11.1 when she was writing) previously observed that the ornamentation in S. Salv. 59 is more elaborate than that in Vat. gr. 2060.[36] Both manuscripts, in turn, are better decorated than Vall. C 11.1. It is conceivable that the scribe changed his style over time, though another possible explanation may lie in the fact that the three nomocanons were all produced for different monasteries: perhaps the quality and style of ornamentation depended (at least in part) on the patrons' varying tastes and ability to pay.

Whatever the case may be, the Patiron monastery of Rossano produced a set of standardised nomocanons with text and stylistic choices drawn from a Byzantine prototype of the eleventh century. Unlike the simpler nomocanons produced by smaller abbeys in southern Calabria and Sicily, these were relatively impressive display items that were clearly meant to be seen as well as read. Again, though, they bear no clear traces of Latin influence. With the wealth and ability to look beyond the traditional Greek book culture of Calabria, the monks of the Patiron chose to turn to Constantinople for inspiration rather than Rome or Montecassino.

[34] The manuscript is not without its flaws. For example, on fol. 15^{r} (the *pinax* of the *N14T*), the scribe left a space for a decorative headband that was never inserted and confused two of the chapter titles. On fol. 96^{r} (the beginning of the canons of Laodicea), he inexplicably omitted to add colour to another decorative headband.

[35] Esp. Vat. gr. 2060, fols. 40^{r}, 42^{v}, 50^{r}, 52^{r}, 119^{r}, 137^{r}.

[36] 'The only verifiable difference between them is the ornamentation: [it is] extremely simple, and almost completely absent, in the Vatican codex, in which there are few *pylai* reddened with the "réserve" technique...': Foti (1995): 343–344. Foti's description of the simplicity of Vat. gr. 2060 is slightly exaggerated, since it is still well decorated by comparison to most nomocanons.

A Komnenian Conduit: The Casulan Manuscripts

Positioned near the eastern coast of the Salento peninsula, the monastery of St Nicholas of Casole faced the Byzantine world both geographically and intellectually. This fact is strongly reflected in the two mid- to late twelfth-century Casulan canon law manuscripts, Barb. gr. 324 and BnF gr. 1371. Though their spartan appearance brings to mind the simple, archaic codices of southern Calabria, they contain the most 'modern' Byzantine canon law texts of any of the southern Italian nomocanons.

In addition to this, they also signal a subtle shift in the purpose of Byzantine canon law collections that was beginning to take place in late twelfth-century southern Italy. While the simple and deluxe monastic nomocanons discussed above contain some texts that could be viewed as commentary on contemporary culture (such as Stethatos' polemic on the *azyma* or the excerpt from Moschos' *Spiritual Meadow*), the main aim of those manuscripts was to provide a practical legal guide. In the case of the Casulan manuscripts, however, we begin to see the canons used for non-legal, educational ends.

The manuscript Barb. gr. 324 is damaged at the end, but from the table of contents at the beginning we can tell that it originally contained Alexios Aristenos' commentary on the *Synopsis of Canons* without any other supplementary texts.[37] Curiously enough, the title of the work in the manuscript mentions Aristenos' positions of 'most learned deacon of the Great Church of God [i.e. Hagia Sophia] and *nomophylax*', though it does not actually give his name.[38] Aristenos composed his commentary around the year 1130, about sixty years after the Norman conquest of southern Italy; though we do not know how St Nicholas of Casole acquired the text, the fact that it did implies that the monastery remained in contact with the mainland Byzantine church. As André Jacob remarked, 'Regarding cultural relations between Constantinople and the Terra d'Otranto, one cannot help but underline the rapidity with which the nomocanon of Aristenos arrived [at Casole] and was recopied.'[39]

Aristenos' commentary is not arranged thematically but chronologically. This means that Barb. gr. 324 would not be very useful as a legal reference guide on its own; the reader would have to combine it with a thematic collection such as the *N50T* or the *N14T* to locate canons on particular subjects. It is useful, however, for explaining (briefly) what each canon does and why. The didactic potential of

[37] The manuscript breaks off on fol. 165 in the middle of St Basil of Caesarea's *First Canonical Letter*. Nektarios of Otranto would insert some new texts at the beginning of the manuscript in the early thirteenth century, which we shall discuss further in Chapter 9, 'The Salentine Group', C10.P14.

[38] '*τοῦ λογιωτάτου διακόνου τῆς τοῦ Θ[εο]ῦ μ[ε]γ[ά]λ[ης] ἐκκλησί[ας] καὶ νομοφύλακο[ς]*': Barb. gr. 324, fol. 16^{r}. Cf. Vat. gr. 2019 (the 'Nomocanon of Doxapatres'), which completely substitutes Aristenos' name and titles for those of Nicholas Doxapatres; see Chapter 7, 'The Secular Church and the Laity', C7.P29.

[39] Jacob (2008): 233. Jacob uses the term 'nomocanon' to refer to the text of Aristenos' *Synopsis*.

canon law is clearer still in BnF gr. 1371, a canonical compilation that seems to have been meant primarily for educational purposes. The manuscript opens with a short compilation of essays 'On the Lenten Fast' and 'On the Presanctified Gifts', as well as two letters of the seventh-century Patriarch Sophronios of Jerusalem on the two natures of Christ.[40] These are followed by a short history of the ecumenical councils and a garbled version of Patriarch Nicholas III Grammatikos' (1084–1111) canonical *erotapokriseis* to monks that the manuscript simply calls 'Canonical Questions and Answers of the Holy Synod'.[41] Next come a selection of canon and civil laws relating to monastic discipline.[42]

The centrepiece of the manuscript is the Athonite monk Arsenios of Philotheou's *Synopsis of Canons*, thought to have been composed around the year 1140.[43] This is not the same as the *Synopsis of Canons* that served as the basis for Alexios Aristenos' commentary. Unlike that collection, Arsenios did not give summaries of the conciliar and patristic canons in chronological order. Instead, he composed a thematic series of 140 dogmatic assertions accompanied by brief references to canons that supported them. Here, for example, is how Arsenios presents the subject of fasting on the Sabbath (a key point of difference between Latin and Greek religious practice):

111. That one should not fast on Saturday or Sunday, with the sole exception of Great Saturday [of Holy Week] (but do not eat cheese or eggs on Saturdays or Sundays during Lent), for this is heretical and anyone who does this should be deposed if he is ordained or anathematised if he is a layperson. And every Christian should fast on Wednesday, Friday, in holy Lent, and during Holy Week. On Great Friday and Great Saturday [of Holy Week], one should not eat at all until midnight on those days. One should fast faithfully for all the other fasts, which we have received from ecclesiastical tradition, unless one is prevented by physical weakness. Whoever does not do this should be deposed if he is ordained or anathematised if he is a layperson.

[40] BnF gr. 1371, fols. 1–24^{r}. The manuscript does not give an attribution for the texts on the Lenten fast and the presanctified gifts, though they appear to be a composite of canonical *erotapokriseis* issued by Patriarch Photios of Constantinople in the ninth century (cf. Photios, *Amphilochia* 130). The same composite text appears in the Salentine theological compilation Cambridge, Corpus Christi College, MS gr. 486, fols. 168–173^{r}; see Delle Donne (2014): 383–385.

[41] '*ἐρώτησεις κανονικαὶ καὶ ἀποκρίσεις τῆς ἁγίας συνόδου*': BnF gr. 1371, fols. 34^{v}–43. Cf. RP 4.417–426.

[42] BnF gr. 1371, fols. 44–71. The texts are, in order: Chalc. c. 4, 24; II Nic. c. 13; *Trullo* c. 49; *Prot.* c. 1, 6; II Nic. c. 17; Just. *Nov.* 131.7, 120.7, 123.35–40; Carth. c. 14; II Nic. c. 21; *Apost. Const.* 8.32 (in part); Gangra c. 3; Just. *Nov.* 123.34; Chalc. c. 3, 8, 23; *Trullo* c. 31–34, 45–6; *Prot.* c. 2–5; Just. *Nov.* 123.42; Chalc. c. 7, 18; Gangra c. 15–16; Just. *Nov.* 133.6; *Basilika* 4.1.25; II Nic. c. 14.

[43] BnF gr. 1371, fols. 72–114. Text in Voell and Justel (1661): 2.749–784. This manuscript is the only surviving witness to Arsenios' canonical collection. Voell and Justel identified Arsenios of Philotheou with Patriarch Arsenios Autoreianos (in office 1255–1259 and 1261–1265), but this cannot be correct, since BnF gr. 1371 clearly dates to the twelfth century and Autoreianos was not associated with the Philotheou monastery. For further discussion, see Troianos (2011): 406; Allison (1996): 139.

Apostolic Canons 64 and 69. Synod of Gangra, canons 18 and 19. 6th Synod [*in Trullo*], canon 55. Synod of Laodicea, canon 50. 6th Synod [*sic*], canons 29 and 89. And of St Dionysios, canon 1. Of St Peter of Alexandria, canon 15. Of St Timothy, canons 7 and 10. And of Theophilos, canon 1.[44]

Arsenios thus distils the content of various sets of canons into succinct didactic statements on religious belief and practice. It is less a legal reference guide than it is a teaching text, listing the canonical authorities behind the dogmatic positions of the twelfth-century Byzantine church.

Arsenios' *Synopsis* is followed in the manuscript by several more didactic texts: Michael Psellos' late eleventh-century *Synopsis of the Nomocanon* in fifteen-syllabus verse, the same author's verse explanation of the Nicene Creed, and an anonymous 'Clear and Brief Synopsis of Our Faith in the Holy Trinity'.[45] The two works of Psellos were originally companion pieces to a (slightly) better known verse explanation of Roman civil law that he produced in the 1050s or 1060s for the education of the future emperor Michael VII Doukas (*r.* 1071–1078).[46] The *Synopsis of the Nomocanon* is quite literally a description of the contents of the Photian recension of the *N14T*; the use of verse was intended to help the reader memorise it.

The final item of the original manuscript was Alexios I's *Edict on the Reform of the Clergy*, one of just two surviving copies of this text.[47] This decree was issued by the Byzantine emperor in either 1092 or 1105 (the date is disputed) and set out a range of proposals to improve religious education, one of which was that the *N14T* should be read out before the patriarchal synod and 'renewed'.[48] The edict is not didactic in itself, but it provides a thorough programme for the religious education of the clergy and the laity.

[44] '*ρια΄. ὅτι οὐ δεῖ νηστεύειν ἐν σαββάτῳ ἢ ἐν κυριακῇ, δίχα τοῦ μεγάλου καὶ μόνου σαββάτου· ἀλλ' οὔτε ἐν τοῖς σάββασι, καὶ ταῖς κυριακαῖς τῆς τεσσαρακοστῆς τυρὸν, ἢ ὠὸν ἐσθίειν· αἱρετικῶν γὰρ τοῦτο· καὶ ὁ τοῦτο ποιῶν καθαιρεῖται, ἐὰν ἱερωμένος ἐστίν· ἐὰν καὶ λαϊκὸς, ἀναθεματίζεται· καὶ ὅτι δεῖ νηστεύειν πάντα Χριστιανὸν τετράδα καὶ παρασκευὴν καὶ τὴν ἁγίαν τεσσαρακοστὴν καὶ τὴν μεγάλην ἑβδομάδα· τὴν μέντοι μεγάλην παρασκευὴν, καὶ τὸ μέγα σάββατον, μηδ' ὅλως ἐσθιειν ἄχρι τοῦ μεσονυκτίου ἀυτῶν· καὶ τὰς λοιπὰς καὶ νηστείας πάσας πιστῶς νηστεύειν, ἃς ἐκ παραδόσεως ἐκκλησιαστικῆς ἔχομεν, εἰ μὴ δι' ἀσθένειαν σωματικὴν ἐμποδίζονται. οἱ γὰρ μὴ οὕτω ποιοῦντες, εἰ μὲν ἱερωμένοι εἰσὶ, καθαιροῦνται· εἰ δὲ λαϊκοὶ, ἀναθεματίζονται. τῶν ἁγίων Ἀποστόλων κανών ξδ΄ καὶ ξθ΄. συνόδου Γάγγρας κανών ιη΄ καὶ ιθ΄. συνόδου ς΄ κανών νε΄. συνόδου Λαοδικείας κανών ν΄. συνόδου ς΄* [sic] *κανών κθ΄ και πθ΄. καὶ τοῦ ἁγίου Διονυσίου κανών α΄. τοῦ ἁγίου Πέτρου Ἀλεξανδρείας κανών ιε΄. τοῦ ἁγίου Τιμοθέου κανών η΄ καὶ ι΄. καὶ Θεοφίλου κανών α΄*': BnF gr. 1371, fols. 104^{v}–105^{r}; Voell and Justel (1661): 2.776.

[45] Text in Westerink (1992): 77–80 (no. 5).

[46] See Troianos (2011): 284–286; Bernard (2014): 69–70.

[47] BnF gr. 1371, fols. 125^{v}–150^{v}. Text in Gautier (1973): 178–201. The only other surviving witness to this edict is Venice, Biblioteca Nazionale Marciana, MS gr. 49, fols. 343–346. For further discussion of the edict, see Magdalino (1996).

[48] Gautier (1973): 197 ll. 282–289. The decree has traditionally been dated to *c.* 1107, although Peter Wirth has proposed the year 1092: Dölger and Wirth (1995): 132–133. Theodore the *Bestes* and Michael the *Sebastos* created the third recension of the *N14T* around the year 1090, which would fit well with Wirth's dating: it would make sense for Alexios to ask the patriarchal synod to check the text of the nomocanon if a new recension had just been produced.

BnF gr. 1371 was evidently made for teaching purposes rather than legal reference. The didactic turn in canon law that it represents was not unique to southern Italy, though, since its Byzantine prototype must have been (directly or indirectly) a product of Alexios Komnenos' efforts to reform the professional standards of the Church of Constantinople.[49] Nonetheless, as an outpost of Greek religious culture in an increasingly Latinised landscape, one can see why St Nicholas of Casole would have been interested in such an educational collection.[50]

The two manuscripts Barb. gr. 324 and BnF gr. 1371 clearly highlight St Nicholas of Casole's ongoing contact with the Byzantine Empire in the twelfth century, a point that naturally invites comparison with the Patiron of Rossano. However, the material character of these two canon law manuscripts could scarcely contrast more with that of the Rossanese nomocanons. Whereas the Rossanese Group are among the largest manuscripts in this study, the Casulan manuscripts are among the smallest.[51]

Their writing surfaces are far cheaper and less impressive too. Barb. gr. 324 was copied on brownish paper of the 'Western Arabic' style, a material that was used by the Italo-Greeks but rarely survives.[52] BnF gr. 1371, for its part, was a palimpsest—reused parchment with older texts erased to make a new writing surface. However, to make the new text legible against the underlying palimpsest, the scribe was forced to write in unusually large script, so that there are only between eighteen and twenty-one lines per page. For comparison, the smaller Barb. gr. 324 has twenty-two to twenty-four lines per page. Thanks to the choices of writing surface, it is impossible to discern the ruling pattern in either manuscript.

In terms of decoration, they follow a hierarchical pattern broadly similar to the simple monastic nomocanons of southern Calabria, with moderately elaborate headbands over the titles of the first item in each manuscript (Aristenos' *Synopsis of Canons* in Barb. gr. 324, fol. 16^{r} and the extract from a synodal encyclical of Sophronios of Jerusalem in BnF gr. 1371, fol. 9^{r}). Subsequent texts are marked out by much smaller headbands and far smaller titles. Unlike the knotted ropes of southern Calabria, though, the dominant motif in the Casulan manuscripts is of leafy, twisting vines coloured in red ink. This was a characteristically Salentine aesthetic that would be employed more extensively in the thirteenth century.[53]

49 On professionalisation among the patriarchal clergy in the twelfth century, see Tiftixoglu (1969): 35–40. More recently, see Gaul (2014): 253–256.

50 For further discussion of this subject, see Chapter 10, 'They Do It Like This in Romania', C10.S3.

51 See Appendix 1, 'Manuscript Descriptions'.

52 Jacob (2008): 232 n. 6. 'Western Arabic' paper is attested in southern Italy and Sicily from the eleventh century on: Irigoin (1977): 47. It is difficult to know how widespread its use was, since the fragile nature of paper meant that it was less likely to survive than parchment. On the characteristics of 'Western Arabic' paper in comparison to other types of paper, see Canart et al. (1993): 327.

53 See Chapter 9, 'The Salentine Group', C9.P21–C9.P23.

Similarly, the scribal hands in the two manuscripts take on a cursive form that reflects the early stages of the development of what Daniele Arnesano has dubbed the 'baroque minuscule' style of Otranto.[54] This was likely under the influence of the script in twelfth-century manuscripts brought from Constantinople such as the ones that must have served as the prototypes for Barb. gr. 324 and BnF gr. 1371.[55]

Beyond the potential influence of twelfth-century Constantinopolitan cursive hands, the Casulan canon law manuscripts are unremarkable for their appearance and ornamentation. However, they are remarkable for the fact that they contain Byzantine canon law texts from the 1130s and 1140s. St Nicholas of Casole in the mid- to late twelfth century seems to have enjoyed a degree of legal autonomy akin to that of the Patiron and the other Greek monasteries of Calabria and Sicily in earlier decades. Like the Patiron, it used this autonomy to import the products of Komnenian canon law scholarship, apparently paying no heed to developments in the contemporary Roman church.

Perhaps even more interestingly, there are few if any clear signs of influence between the Casulan nomocanons and those of the Calabro-Sicilian area. The latter region had easily discernible shared manuscript traditions based on either the archaic legal texts of Byzantine Italy or the eleventh-century prototype brought to Rossano by Bartholomew of Simeri. None of the Calabro-Sicilian canon law texts or aesthetic motifs appear in the Casulan manuscripts. This reflects the cultural division between the Salento and the Southwest that we previously encountered in Chapter 4 and will see in more detail in Chapter 9.[56] It often appears that the intellectual culture of the twelfth-century Salento was closer to that of Constantinople than it was to other Greek areas of southern Italy.

Conclusion

In Chapter 5, I argued that the Norman rulers of southern Italy permitted the independent Italo-Greek monasteries and archimandritates of their realm the freedom to establish and govern their own legal jurisdictions. In Chapter 6, our examination of surviving twelfth-century monastic nomocanons has demonstrated how they did so: they took the opportunity [*etc.*]. The exact way in which they did so depended on the situation of the monastery. Less wealthy institutions in Lucania and the Calabro-Sicilian region copied manuscript traditions that had first arrived in southern Italy under Byzantine rule, producing nomocanons with archaic contents and traditional Italo-Greek aesthetics.

[54] Arnesano (2008a): 19–58. [55] Arnesano (2008a): 23–9.

[56] See Chapter 4, 'The Byzantine Background', C4.P16–C4.P18, Chapter 9, 'The Salentine Group', C9.S3.

By contrast, the Patiron of Rossano was much richer and was allowed direct access to books from Constantinople, so it was able to produce a 'standardised' set of nomocanons based on an eleventh-century model. Even more impressively, it seems to have sold or distributed some of these manuscripts to other new Italo-Greek monastic foundations such as the Holy Saviour of Messina. St Nicholas of Casole also seems to have had direct access to Constantinople (how is unclear), though the later date of its canon law manuscripts meant that it was able to import more recent Komnenian texts such as the *Synopsis of Canons* of Alexios Aristenos and that of Arsenios of Philotheou. In both monasteries, the aesthetics of the new canon law manuscripts were influenced by Constantinopolitan styles, though the Patiron was seemingly able to devote far more resources to visual presentation.

The availability (or lack thereof) of newer Byzantine canon law texts was likely the main limiting factor in determining the contents of Italo-Greek nomocanons. Yet there is also the question of purpose. The monastic nomocanons of Calabria, Sicily, and Lucania appear primarily intended to serve as guides to what Byzantine canon law said about particular subjects, a factor that made them more useful as practical reference works in a judicial setting. The two manuscripts from Casole, on the other hand (especially BnF gr. 1371), seem more geared towards a didactic goal of explaining the canons and using them as sources of religious education. This reflected a contemporary trend in the Byzantine world, it is true, but it also presaged a marked shift in the use of Byzantine canon law among the Italo-Greeks that would take place in the thirteenth century.

7
The Secular Church and the Laity

The Greek church in southern Italy may be most famous for its monasteries, but it naturally also encompassed secular (i.e. non-monastic) clergy and lay believers who attended services and provided it with material support. The Calabrian sees of Rossano, S. Severina, Bova, Oppido, Gerace, Crotone, Squillace, Cerenzia, Belcastro, Umbriatico, Isola, and Strongoli were all held by Italo-Greek hierarchs in the twelfth century, as was the Salentine see of Gallipoli.[1] What became of their system of religious law once they had been conquered by the Normans and placed under the Roman church?

Sources for the Italo-Greek secular church and laity are sadly much scarcer than those for monasteries for the reasons outlined in Chapter 3. We do not know of any nomocanons that can be specifically tied to any Italo-Greek bishop, partly because many must have been lost and partly because the ones that remain do not contain scribal colophons or notes of possession. There are several nomocanons from the Salento peninsula that may date to the late twelfth century and may have belonged to bishops, though we shall deal with these as a group in Chapter 10. Furthermore, documentary evidence for judicial activity by Italo-Greek bishops in the twelfth century is essentially non-existent.

Nonetheless, one cannot discuss Greek canon law in southern Italy without discussing the secular church. Italo-Greek bishops must have continued to oversee canonical proceedings in their dioceses and there are a number of clues that they did so using Byzantine legal texts. Even more intriguingly, we have concrete evidence that Italo-Greek civil judges—that is to say, laypeople—owned and used canon law manuscripts as well. Despite the paucity of sources, we get the impression that the Greek church in southern Italy enjoyed a considerable degree of judicial autonomy from the Roman papacy, which allowed it to maintain the system of canon law that it had inherited from the Byzantine Empire largely intact.

The Italo-Greek Episcopate after the Norman Conquest

Bishops in both East and West had adjudicated disputes within Christian communities even before the 313 Edict of Milan permitted the free practice of the

[1] The sees of Squillace, Umbriatico, Cerenzia, and Belcastro were placed under Latin bishops in the twelfth century; see Girgensohn (1973): 34–38.

Byzantine Religious Law in Medieval Italy. James Morton, Oxford University Press (2021). © James Morton.
DOI: 10.1093/oso/9780198861140.003.0008

religion and their legal authority was recognised soon after in a law of Constantine the Great in 318.[2] There is very little evidence for the functioning of Greek episcopal courts in medieval southern Italy, unfortunately; unlike documents concerning land ownership and inheritance, which were of long-term financial importance and which have survived in relatively large numbers, there was little incentive for church institutions to maintain records of canonical judgments.[3]

Clearer evidence survives from the Byzantine mainland. Substantial bodies of legal opinions issued by the early thirteenth-century Epirote hierarchs Demetrios Chomatenos (d. 1236) and John Apokaukos (*c.* 1155–1233) were preserved for posterity, perhaps because succeeding generations of Byzantine churchmen felt that they were good examples to emulate.[4] We also have many decisions of the patriarchal court of Constantinople (mostly from the fourteenth century).[5] The writings of Chomatenos and Apokaukos show that they were heavily involved in issuing legal judgments, both civil and canonical. Indeed, the German legal historian Dieter Simon has commented that, by the thirteenth century, 'the episcopate no longer stands beside the judicial system as in the beginning, but rather within it; [the bishop] has become [the system's] integral part, without which the whole complex would collapse'.[6]

To carry out his legal duties properly, a bishop would need to use a nomocanon as a legal reference guide. In a letter to Metropolitan Basil Pediadites of Corfu concerning marriage contracts, for instance, Demetrios Chomatenos writes, 'Look, I have set out here [the synodal decision] for your holiness, taken from my nomocanon.'[7] Moreover, we know of several surviving nomocanons that belonged to and were used by Byzantine bishops; indeed, it was considered bad practice for a bishop *not* to use a nomocanon.[8] John Apokaukos chastises an unnamed bishop of Leukas (on Greece's western coast) in one of his surviving

[2] For a brief overview of the judicial role of the Byzantine bishop, see Moulet (2011): 383–386. On the late antique origins of episcopal legal authority, see Rapp (2005): 242–252.

[3] That Italo-Greek bishops continued to have a judicial role is not in doubt, however. See for instance the twelfth-century additions at the opening folia of the Carbone nomocanon (Chapter 6, 'Monastic Nomocanons II', C6.P9) and the case of the archdiocese of Rossano below (section: 'Aristocratic Authority in Rossano', C7.S3).

[4] A large number of Chomatenos' writings have recently been edited and published in Prinzing (2002). There is no single edition of Apokaukos' writings, which are dispersed among a number of (often inaccessible) journals; see Troianos (2012a): 193.

[5] Hunger et al. (1981). [6] Simon (1986): 339.

[7] '*ἡ συνοδικὴ δὲ διάγνωσις ἡ περί τοῦ συναλλάγματος προβᾶσα τοῦ ἀγαγομένου τὴν δισεξαδέλφην τῆς γυναικὸς αὐτοῦ εἰς γυναῖκα μετὰ θάνατον ἐκείνης, ἰδοὺ ἐστάλη τῇ σῇ ἁγιότητι, παρεκβληθεῖσα ἀπὸ τοῦ ἡμετέρου νομοκανόνου*': Prinzing (2002): 52 (*PD* 8.8 l. 172–175).

[8] E.g. *Παν. Τάφ.* 635 (Bishop John of Archangelos, *c.* 1255); Genf, Bibliothèque publique et universitaire, MS 23 (Metropolitan Isaac of Chalcedon, *c.* 1380); Istanbul, Topkapı Sarayı, MS 115 (multiple successive Metropolitans of Trebizond from 1311 on); Milan, Biblioteca Ambrosiana, MS L 49 sup. (Bishop Gabriel of Kastoria, 13th cent.); Oxford, Bodleian Library, MS Laud gr. 39 (Metropolitan Thomas of Corinth, 14th cent.); Paris, Bibliothèque nationale de France, MSS gr. 1263 (Bishop Makarios of Servia, 14th cent.), Coisl. 209 (Bishop Matthew of Amathous, *c.* 1260–1295); Vatican City, Biblioteca Apostolica Vaticana, MS Pal. gr. 376 (an official of the Metropolis of Adrianople named Nikephoros, 14th cent.).

letters because 'I hear from some of your clergy that you apparently never touch your *nomokanonon*, nor do you do what you do with proper discernment.'[9] Even if these professional standards were an innovation of the twelfth or thirteenth century, the bishop's judicial role and need for a nomocanon was not.

What happened to the Italo-Greek nomocanons and episcopal courts after the Norman conquest brought them under papal jurisdiction? In areas such as Lucania and Sicily where Greek bishops were replaced by Latins (or where entirely new Latin dioceses were established), Western canon law would have supplanted Byzantine. In those areas of Calabria and Apulia that retained a Greek hierarchy, bishops were obliged to swear obedience to the Roman papacy, as we saw in Chapter 2.[10] We have evidence that some Italo-Greek bishops even participated in Roman church councils such as the Synod of Guastalla in 1105, the Lateran Council of 1112, and the Third Lateran Council of 1179.[11] It would be natural to wonder, under these circumstances, whether they might also have begun to adopt (or at least adapt) Latin canon law in their own dioceses.

The answer seems to be that they did not. There is no evidence that Italo-Greek bishops possessed or used Latin canon law collections in the eleventh or twelfth centuries (indeed, we would not expect them to, since all their other legal texts and documents remained in the Greek language until the thirteenth century in most cases). Nor did any Latin canon law texts find their way into Greek books: not a single surviving Italo-Greek nomocanon shows any trace of contemporary Latin legal influence. Even the contemporary Roman synods of the twelfth century failed to leave a mark. All our manuscripts' contents remained steadfastly Byzantine right up until the sixteenth century. Instead, we get the impression that the remaining Greek hierarchs in Norman Italy continued to follow traditional Byzantine canon law texts; dioceses probably only changed over to Latin canon law when they received a Latin bishop.

There are several other signs that Italo-Greek bishops and secular clergy under Norman rule continued to view themselves as being dependent on Constantinople in spirit even if they were formally dependent on Rome. St Luke of Isola, the bishop who castigated the Latins of his diocese for celebrating the Eucharist with *azyma*, offers an interesting example.[12] Luke was probably enthroned as bishop in the 1070s–1080s, not long after the Normans conquered Byzantine Italy. He soon travelled to Sicily to evangelise and ordain clergy in the newly reconquered island. Following his return to the mainland, Luke's biographer tells us that 'he wanted to travel also to the Queen of Cities [i.e. Constantinople]. But when he arrived at

[9] '*ἐξ ὧν δὲ ἀκούω παρά τινων κληρικῶν σου, φαίνεται, ὅτι οὔτε νομοκάνονον λαμβάνεις εἰς χεῖράς ποτε, οὔτε μετὰ συντηρήσεως ποιεῖς, ἃ ποιεῖς*': John Apokaukos, *Letter* 81 ll. 6–8; text in Bees-Seferli (1971): 139–140.

[10] See Chapter 2, 'Greek Christianity in Medieval Italy', C2.P33.

[11] Mansi 19.610, 21.51, 70; Russo (1973): 789–790.

[12] See Chapter 4, 'The Byzantine Background', C4.P42.

Taranto, he did not have consent for his wish from Him [i.e. God] who knew everything before his [i.e. Luke's] birth.'[13] The *Life* does not clarify exactly why Luke could not travel to Constantinople, but it is possible that his attempt coincided with one of the efforts of Robert Guiscard or Bohemond of Taranto to invade the Byzantine Empire (in 1080–1085 and 1104–1108 respectively). The brief anecdote implies that Luke still viewed Constantinople as his mother church, even though he must have sworn allegiance to the papacy to take up his see. There is a strong parallel to the case of Bartholomew of Simeri, who was permitted to travel to Constantinople in *c.* 1105 to obtain liturgical books and vessels for his new monastery of the Patiron.[14]

Other sources corroborate this impression. A good example is the correspondence between Bishop-Elect Paul of Gallipoli in the Salento peninsula and an unnamed patriarch of Constantinople, in which Paul asked how to correctly perform the *proskomide* (the liturgy of preparation) and the presanctified liturgy. Paul's original letter has not survived, but the patriarch's response has been preserved in an array of manuscripts from the Salento peninsula including the *typikon* of St Nicholas of Casole copied in 1173.[15] The dating of the correspondence has been disputed: Giuseppe Cozza-Luzi originally placed it in the 1080s, but André Jacob argued that it should be dated to 1174, a year after the Casulan *typikon*.[16] More recently, Valerio Polidori has argued (I believe convincingly) for the traditional dating of *c.* 1081, which would mean that the patriarch was either Kosmas I Attikos (1075–1081) or Eustratios Garidas (1081–1085).[17] Whether it was ten years after the Norman conquest or 110 years, Paul would have sworn an oath of loyalty to the papacy, yet he still turned to Constantinople for liturgical guidance. The patriarch's reply was then dutifully copied and read by Greek monks and clergy in the Salento peninsula down into the fourteenth century.[18]

The general lack of evidence for the Italo-Greek episcopate in the twelfth century makes it difficult to draw a detailed picture of their canonical life, but this lack of evidence itself has some interesting implications. As mentioned in Chapter 2, the *Fontes* collection of papal documents relating to Eastern canon law has only eleven entries pertaining to the Greek church of southern Italy between 1000 and 1198; of these, only one has any relevance to the Italo-Greek episcopate (a bull of Alexander III in 1165 permitting the Latin archbishop of Reggio to

[13] '*οὕτω διατελῶν καὶ τὸν ἴδιον θρόνον καταλάβων, ἀπάρας ἐκεῖθεν, ἠβούλετο διαπερᾶσαι καὶ ἐπὶ τὴν βασιλεύσουσαν. φθάσαντος δὲ αὐτοῦ ἄχρι τῆς Τερέντου* [*sic*], *οὐκ ἔσχε συνευδοκοῦντα τῷ βουλήματι τὸν τὰ πάντα πρὶν γενέσεως ἐπιστάμενον*': Schirò (1954): 90 ll. 129–132.

[14] See Chapter 2, 'Greek Christianity in Medieval Italy', C7.P38.

[15] Text in Polidori (2012): 212–215.

[16] Cozza-Luzi (1905): 2.153–154; Jacob (1987): 158–159.

[17] Polidori (2012): 192–199. Delle Donne (2015) argues against Polidori in defence of Jacob's dating of *c.* 1174.

[18] On the manuscript tradition of Paul's letter, see Polidori (2012): 199–203.

consecrate Greek bishops under his jurisdiction).[19] There are also two papal letters of the 1180s–1190s that deal in general terms with the children of Italo-Greek clergy and prohibit the mixture of Latin and Greek liturgical rites.[20] One has to wait until the pontificates of Innocent III (*r.* 1198–1216) and especially Honorius III (*r.* 1216–1227) to see papal letters on the Italo-Greek episcopate in significant numbers. This contrasts sharply with the approximately 150 documents addressed to the Latin episcopate in the Norman Kingdom of Sicily (a number that is itself admittedly far below that for other Western kingdoms such as England and France).[21] It appears that Italo-Greek bishops had relatively little contact with the papacy in the twelfth century.

What explains this? In the first instance, the notorious hostility of Roger II to papal intervention in his kingdom undoubtedly insulated both Latin and Greek bishops from contact with the papacy. Yet, as Graham Loud observes, 'after the Treaty of Benevento [in 1156] appeals to the Curia and the operation of papal justice [in southern Italy] appear to have developed unhindered. While legations . . . were rare, there was no suggestion from the Curia that this was because the king prevented them.'[22] If the king did not prevent contact between Rome and the Italo-Greeks, then what did? It was most likely a combination of ignorance and cultural habit. The Italo-Greek bishops had continued to follow Byzantine canon law under Roger II and saw no need to make legal appeals to the papal Curia (indeed, they probably had an incentive not to do so). For its part, the papacy had limited awareness of the Italo-Greeks and felt little inclination to learn about them until the thirteenth century, as we shall see in Part III.

The legal situation of Greek bishops under Norman rule was probably analogous to that of the independent monasteries and archimandrites examined in the previous chapters. Norman rulers from Roger I onwards had been so effective in keeping the papacy out of their internal affairs that it was unable to effectively influence or even learn about the Italo-Greek hierarchy. As far as the Normans were concerned, it was no bad thing if their Greek bishops continued to observe Byzantine canon law and feel a sense of loyalty to the patriarch in Constantinople. The patriarch was distant and unthreatening, whereas the Roman pope posed a much more immediate danger to the political authority of the Sicilian king, as Roger II and several of his successors would discover. From the perspective of the Norman rulers, the cultural and legal autonomy of the Italo-Greek bishops was preferable to them falling under the sway of Rome.

[19] *Fontes III* 1.802–803 (no. 389). See also Chapter 2, 'Greek Christianity in Medieval Italy', C2.P51.

[20] *Fontes III* 1.814 (no. 397, a. 1185–1191), 817 (no. 400, a. 1191–1199).

[21] Pacaut (1981): 51.

[22] Loud (2007): 256.

Canon Law in a Civil Law Collection: The *Epitome Marciana*

Further evidence for the legal autonomy of the Italo-Greek church comes, surprisingly, from manuscripts of civil law, which the Byzantines referred to as '*nomima*' ('civil law books', sing. '*nomimon*'). As we have seen, Byzantine canon law manuscripts often mixed legal genres by incorporating texts of civil law (hence the name 'nomocanon'). However, the genre mixing could run in the other direction too, with *nomima* incorporating texts of canon law. This blurring of legal spheres ran counter to the prevailing ideology of the twelfth-century Roman papacy, which strongly insisted on the church's legal independence from the state. It is often difficult to prove who owned a civil law manuscript (notes of possession are few and far between), so the presence of ecclesiastical canons in a Byzantine *nomimon* can sometimes be explained by the possibility that it belonged to a bishop. However, there is one Italo-Greek *nomimon* that we know for a fact was produced by and for lay officials: the so-called *Epitome Marciana* (Marc. gr. 172).

The law of the Norman Kingdom of Sicily was pluralistic not just in a vertical sense (with separate legal systems of state, church, guilds, etc.), but also in a horizontal sense: different ethnic groups had their own legal officials who enforced their own ancestral legal systems (Lombard, Byzantine, Islamic, etc.). Peters-Custot has noted that surviving legal acts from Messina in Sicily attest to separate 'judges of the Latins' and 'judges of the Greeks'.[23] This parallelism was reproduced on a larger scale in Calabria, which had two 'great judges', one Latin and one Greek.[24] Unlike Messina, most towns and cities in Calabria would probably have been either mostly Greek or mostly Latin, so officials at the local level usually did not need to declare their ethnicity. Instead, we can deduce it from the Greek titles that they use: '*krites*' ('judge'), '*nomikos*' ('legal official'), and in one case even the grandiose '*nomophylax*' ('guardian of the laws').[25]

The surviving manuscript evidence indicates that Italo-Greek judges continued to follow Byzantine civil law in the Norman period, though how strictly (or accurately) they applied it is unclear.[26] The *Epitome Marciana* (named for the fact that it contains a copy of Symbatios' tenth-century *Epitome of the Laws* and is currently kept in the Biblioteca Marciana in Venice) is one of the most impressive surviving examples. Unusually for a legal manuscript of its time, the *Epitome*

[23] Peters-Custot (2009a): 387. See Guillou (1963): 1.89 (no. 8, a. 1152), 117 (no. 13, a. 1187/8).

[24] Rognoni (2004): 250 (ad. 8, a. 1176). The judges were the Latin Matthew of Salerno and the Greek Nicholas of Gerace.

[25] Rognoni (2011): 71 (no. 3, a. 1153), 80 (no. 5, a. 1154/5); Trinchera (1865): 372 (no. 271, a. 1219).

[26] See e.g. Ménager (1958); Peters-Custot (2011). Ménager in particular argued that Italo-Greek judges mostly ignored the stipulations of legal texts when making decisions. Note, though, that this phenomenon was not unique to southern Italy. Bénou (2011): 318 found that civil judges in the fourteenth-century Byzantine Empire were similarly lax in applying the letter of the law.

Marciana retains the scribe's original colophon in which he tells us his name and the date on which he completed his work:

> The present *nomimon* was completed in the month of July, in the eighth indiction, in the year 6683 [1175], by the hand of the humble notary John. You who come upon it, pray for its maker that the Lord God grant him a long life for many years. Amen. [And also] that the one who has written these things be not at all cursed but that he be strengthened, for the one who writes is the one who signs.[27]

The presence of a law of Roger II on inheritance (promulgated in 1150) proves that the manuscript is southern Italian, though John unfortunately does not mention exactly where he produced it.[28] Lucà has argued on palaeographical grounds that it was copied in southern Calabria, which may be correct.[29] Two notes in the upper and lower margins of fol. 179^r in a late twelfth- or thirteenth-century hand bear the name of another notary named Philip Malegras who owned the manuscript at some point in its history.[30] The term 'notary' does not necessarily imply that John and Philip were low-level legal officials. As Peters-Custot has observed, Italo-Greek legal documents often show 'notaries' acting in the role of judges, which she suggests 'leads one to think that the term "notary" might designate in some cases less a function than an educational requirement for taking on judicial charges'.[31] It seems likely, then, that Philip Malegras (and perhaps also John) was a civil judge.

This idea is certainly corroborated by the size and expensive appearance of the manuscript. At 365 x 260 mm, it is the largest codex in this study. It is also one of the most visually impressive. The paratactic decorative scheme is consistently elaborate throughout, while the design is varied and non-repetitive. The large *Blütenblattstil* headbands and *pylai* in red, blue, green, and yellow are more accomplished even than those in S. Salv. 59, the most polished of the Rossanese Group of nomocanons. Yet the most striking and unusual images in the manuscript come on fol. 27^v. At the top of the page is a miniature depiction of the Byzantine emperors Justinian I (*r.* 527–565), Leo III (*r.* 717–741), and Constantine V (*r.* 741–775) in their roles as famous lawgivers.[32] Beneath these is a detailed

[27] '*ἐτελείωθη τὸ παρὸν νόμιμον βιβλίον μνηὶ ἰουλίῳ ἰνδ. ὀγδ.* [*sic*] *ἐν ἔτει ,ςχπγ' διὰ χειρὸς Ἰωάννου εὐτελοῦς νοταρίου. οἱ ἐντυγχάνοντες εὔχεσθε τῷ κτήσαντι ταῦτα, ὅπως κύριος ὁ θεὸς δώῃ αὐτῷ μακροβίωσιν ἐν πολλοῖς ἔτεσιν. ἀμήν. τῷ δὲ ταῦτα γράψαντι μὴ ὅλως καταρᾶσθαι, ὁ γὰρ γράφων παραγράφει, καὶ ἔρρωσθαι*': Marc. gr. 172, fol. 256^v. Text in Mioni (1981): 1.261.

[28] Marc. gr. 172, fols. 257–258.

[29] Lucà (1993): 35. The style of script was also be characteristic of Messina, though southern Calabria would have had a larger Greek population in 1175.

[30] '*Φιλίππ(ου) Μαλεγρᾶ*'; '*νοτ(άριος) φίλιπ(πος) δοῦλος Κ(υρίο)υ*': Marc. gr. 172, fol. 179^r. The name 'Malegras' may be related to the Greek word for fishing bait (*μαλάγρα*).

[31] Peters-Custot (2009a): 375.

[32] See Prinzing (1986): 96–97.

diagram of degrees of kinship surrounded by an elaborate *Blütenblattstil* frame; the content of the diagram is similar—but not identical—to that inserted into a blank folio of the Calabro-Sicilian nomocanon Sin. gr. 432.[33] Unlike that example, the diagram in Marc. gr. 172 was clearly part of the scribe's original plan for the manuscript and would have been intended to serve as an interpretative guide to Byzantine civil and canonical legislation on marriage prohibitions between family members.

The script is a pristine example of the Style of Reggio, a calligraphic form that developed from the *Perlschrift*-inflected Style of Rossano pioneered by the monks of the Patiron monastery and is most visible in twelfth- to thirteenth-century manuscripts of Sicily and southern Calabria.[34] That this manuscript was copied by a lay official—a notary—proves that the production of fine Greek manuscripts was not a monopoly of monasteries in southern Italy, even in Calabria. One can only wonder at the number of other high-quality codices that have been lost simply because they were copied by laypeople and were not preserved in a monastic library.[35]

The bulk of the *Epitome Marciana* consists of a Byzantine civil law collection. Besides the *Epitome of the Laws*, we also find two lexicons of Latin legal terms (translated into Greek for Byzantine readers), the so-called *leges speciales* (the *Sailor's*, *Farmer's*, and *Soldier's Laws*), and brief excerpts of legislation passed by Leo VI (*r.* 886–912), Irene (*r.* 797–802), and Justinian I.[36] This is followed by an appendix of texts on canon law and related themes (fols. 243^{v}–250^{r}), excerpts from the eighth-century *Mosaic Law* (fols. 250^{v}–255; not to be confused with the Mosaic Law of the Old Testament), an oath for Jews to swear to Christians and various aphorisms on fair judgment (fol. 256$^{r/v}$), and finally the novel of Roger II on inheritance translated into Greek (fols. 257–258).[37]

The appendix of canon laws on fols. 243^{v}–250^{r} is primarily concerned with the discipline of the clergy and to a lesser extent with family law. A complete set of the Apostolic Canons is followed by a ranked list of the five patriarchates of the pentarchy and a selection of canons excerpted from the councils of Laodicea,

[33] See Chapter 6, 'Monastic Nomocanons II', C6.P15. The diagram in Marc. gr. 172 is reproduced in Rapp (2016): 233 fig. 5.1 and Lake 2.91.

[34] On the palaeographic style of Marc. gr. 172, see Lucà (1993): 35. Mario Re offers a good summary of the style: 'The style of Reggio, an evolution from the Rossanese minuscule, of which it represents a sort of final stage, reached maturity at the end of the 1120s in the environs of the Patiron thanks to the work of a few copyists. A few years later, some of these copyists followed the first archimandrite Luke and transferred to the Holy Saviour. There and in other Calabrian writing centres [the style] continued to be used for the whole twelfth century and beyond.' (Re [2001]: 104).

[35] Cf. scholars' views on the supposedly monastic nature of the 'Italo-Greek Renaissance': Chapter 2, 'Greek Christianity in Medieval Italy', C2.P36 n.65.

[36] On the *leges speciales*, see recently Humphreys (2015): 131–135, 152–232; Burgmann (2009).

[37] On Roger's inheritance law, see Brandileone (1886): 223–225. This is the only known instance of a post-Byzantine law being adopted into an Italo-Greek legal collection.

Neocaesarea, Gangra, and the Apostolic Canons (again).[38] The excerpted canons deal with topics such as whether a priest needs his bishop's permission to travel (he does), how old a person must be to be ordained a priest (thirty years), and whether a priest may be a guest at a second wedding (he may not). They also touch upon some familiar subjects of polemic between Greeks and Latins: clerical marriage, fasting on the Lord's Day, and what sort of services may be performed during Lent (and when). None of the texts relates in any way to monasticism.

Why would the lay notary John include a canon law appendix on the theme of clerical discipline? Perhaps notaries like John and Philip might sometimes have been called upon to advise or even adjudicate in cases regarding church affairs. As educated lay professionals, they would certainly have been familiar with (and likely related to) figures in church administration. The canon law appendix of the *Epitome Marciana* hints at a relatively close relationship between Greek secular and ecclesiastical legal circles in twelfth-century Norman Italy. The same may also be true for the *nomima* Crypt. gr. 76 and 50 discussed in Chapter 4 though there is no evidence regarding their ownership.[39]

This relationship ran completely counter to the prevailing legal ideology of the Roman papacy, which insisted strongly on *libertas ecclesiae*, the 'freedom of the church' from any interference by civil authorities.[40] Twelfth-century Byzantine views on the relationship between imperial and ecclesiastical officials were much more flexible than Rome's. The emperor Manuel I Komnenos, for instance, famously exercised a vaguely defined 'disciplinary role' (*epistemonarchia*) over the church's legal affairs that saw him frequently intervene in the proceedings of the patriarchal synod.[41] Theoretical questions about the role of the emperor in canon law would probably not have been of much concern to Italo-Greek notaries such as John and Philip, of course. Nonetheless, they likely did not share the West's growing aversion to secular intervention in ecclesiastical affairs. I would argue that the combination of civil and canon law in the *Epitome Marciana* is thus a sign of the autonomy from Roman influence that the Italo-Greeks enjoyed under Norman rule even in the late twelfth century.

[38] The list of patriarchal thrones is the same pro-Jerusalem version as the one in the Alag. gr. 3 (copied in Rossano in 1124 and later brought to Messina), though under a slightly different title; see Chapter 4, 'The Byzantine Background', C4.P40. Presumably the two manuscripts derived the text from a common ancestor that had been brought from Palestine in the seventh century.

[39] See Chapter 4, 'The Byzantine Background', C4.P20 n.14.

[40] For further discussion of the idea of *libertas ecclesiae* in the twelfth century, see Szabó-Bechstein (1991): 151–152.

[41] A good example of this came in 1147, when the emperor personally interrogated a monk named Niphon who was accused before the patriarchal court of heresy: RP 5.307–311. On the idea of Byzantine imperial *epistemonarchia*, see Macrides (1990): 61–65; Magdalino (1993): 277–295.

Aristocratic Authority in Rossano: The 'Nomocanon of Doxapatres'

Nowhere was the confluence of secular and religious legal authority more obvious than in the northern Calabrian city of Rossano, which had managed to resist Roger Borsa's efforts in 1094 to impose a Latin bishop. Like the city's famous monastery of the Patiron, the twelfth-century archdiocese of Rossano maintained a cultural connection with the Byzantine Empire under Norman rule, as we see from a nomocanon in the Vatican Library that today bears the shelfmark Vat. gr. 2019. This codex seems to have been copied in the late twelfth or early thirteenth century on palimpsested parchment, but it attests to a local manuscript tradition dating back to the mid-twelfth century.[42]

Vat. gr. 2019 has been dubbed the 'Nomocanon of Doxapatres' on account of its infamously misleading opening title:

> A *nomokanonon* [*sic*] with God's help containing a synopsis of all the canons of the holy and ecumenical seven synods and of the holy Apostles and of [St] Basil the Great and the other God-bearing Fathers, interpreted at the command of the most of august emperor the lord John Komnenos [*r.* 1118–1143] by the most learned deacon of the Great Church of God [i.e. Hagia Sophia in Constantinople] and *nomophylax* of the Roman [i.e. Byzantine] Empire, the patriarchal notary and *protoproedros* of the *protosynkelloi* Doxapatres.[43]

Vat. gr. 2019 would appear to be the only surviving example of this 'Nomocanon of Doxapatres'. However, while it is a commentary on the *Synopsis of Canons*, its author was not Doxapatres. The great nineteenth-century Prussian legal historian Karl-Eduard Zachariä von Lingenthal studied this manuscript and quickly realised that it was none other than Alexios Aristenos' commentary of *c.* 1130.[44]

Jean Darrouzès suggested that the name 'Nomocanon of Doxapatres' might refer to the whole manuscript (which contains a large number of appendices in addition to Aristenos' work), but this is not the case.[45] In fact, the title in Vat. gr. 2019 is an exact copy of the standard title that we find in manuscripts of Aristenos'

[42] See C7.P35. The parchment used in Vat. gr. 2019 was palimpsested from a Greek Old Testament manuscript; this is surprising, since legal manuscripts were more often palimpsested for copying Biblical texts (which had more popular appeal); see Stolte (2008): 173–174.

[43] '*νομοκάνονον σὺν Θεῷ περιέχον συνοπτικῶς ὅλους τοὺς κανόνας τῶν ἁγίων καὶ οἰκουμενικῶν ἑπτὰ συνόδων καὶ τῶν ἁγίων ἀποστόλων καὶ τοῦ μεγάλου Βασιλείου καὶ ἑτέρων θεοφόρων πατέρων ἑρμηνευθεὶς προτροπῇ τοῦ εὐσεβεστάτου βασιλέως κυροῦ Ἰωάννου τοῦ Κομνηνοῦ παρὰ τοῦ λογιωτάτου διακόνου τῆς τοῦ Θεοῦ μεγάλης ἐκκλησίας καὶ νομοφύλακος τῆς τῶν Ῥωμαίων βασιλείας, πατριαρχικοῦ νοταρίου [καὶ] πρωτοπρόεδρου τῶν πρωτοσυγκέλων τοῦ Δοξαπατρῆ*': Vat. gr. 2019, fol. 9^{v}. The grandiose title '*protoproedros* of the *protosynkelloi*' (literally 'first president of the first companions [of the patriarch]') is purely honorific.

[44] Zachariä von Lingenthal (1887): 1159–1161.

[45] Darrouzès (1967): 293.

commentary with one exception: it substitutes Doxapatres' name and titles for those of Aristenos.[46] As I have discussed elsewhere, this may be the same person as the monk Neilos Doxapatres whom we encountered in Chapter 5, though this enticing conjecture is impossible to definitively prove.[47]

The manuscript belonged to a thirteenth-century nobleman of Rossano named Sinator of Kritene, as we read in two notes that he left in his own hand on a blank folio:

> + On the 15th April, at the 9th hour [3:00pm] of Great and Holy Thursday [in Lent], in the 7th indiction, in the year 6742 [1234], a daughter was born to me, Sinator of Kritene, and was given the name Alpharana in holy baptism, during the reign of our God-crowned great emperor and *autokrator* of the Romans and ever-Augustus Frederick [II Hohenstaufen]; in the fourteenth year of his emperorship; the thirty-seventh of his reign over Sicily; the ninth of his reign over Jerusalem. +++
>
> + On the 18th September, towards the evening, in the 9th indiction, in the year 6744 [1235], the lady Guarrera (wife of me, Sinator of Kritene) gave birth to a second child, a boy whom we called Michael. His birth brought us great joy. But in this way, as the depth of the evening took hold, my aforementioned wife gave up her spirit to the Lord. And on Wednesday 19th of the same month, she was buried honourably in the most sacred church of the *Theotokos Acheiropoietos* [the cathedral of Rossano]. My two dearest aforementioned children, Alpharana and Michael, were left to me. May God grant them prosperity and success. May he give [my wife] forgiveness of her sins and respite in the lands of the just. +++[48]

[46] Cf. the thirteenth-century BN II C 8, which carries the exact same title but correctly attributes the work to 'the most learned deacon of the Great Church of God and *nomophylax* the lord Alexios Aristenos' ('*τοῦ λογιωτάτου διακόνου τῆς τοῦ Θεοῦ μεγάλης ἐκκλησίας καὶ νομοφύλακος κυροῦ Ἀλεξίου τοῦ Ἀριστηνοῦ*'): Naples, Biblioteca Nazionale, MS II C 8, fol. 25r.

[47] Morton (2017): 732–735.

[48] '*+ κ(α)τ(ὰ) τὸν ἀπρίλλ(ιον) μῆνα εἰς τ(ὰς) ιη΄ τῇ ἁγ(ίᾳ) καὶ μεγ(ά)λ(ῃ) τρίτ(ῃ) ὥρα θ΄, ἰνδικ(τιῶνος) ζ΄, ἔτ(ους) ,sψμβ΄, ἐγεννήθ(η) ἡ θυγάτηρ ἐμοῦ, Σινάτορος τῆς Κριτν ἡ ἐν τῷ ἁγ(ίῳ) βαπτίσμ(α)τ(ι) ὀνομασθεῖσα Ἀλφαρ(ά)ν(α), βασιλεύοντος ἡμῶν τοῦ θεοστέπτου μ(ε)γ(ά)λ(ου) βασιλέως καὶ αὐτοκρ(ά)τ(ο)ρο(s) Ῥωμ(ά)νων [sic] καὶ ἀεὶ αὐγούστ(ου) Φρεδδερίκου. δεκάτῳ τετάρτῳ χρόνῳ τῆς αὐτοῦ βασιλείας. βασιλεύοντο(s) δὲ Σικελίας τριακοστῷ ἑβδόμῳ. Ἱερουσαλὴμ δὲ ἐννάτῳ +++ / + κ(α)τ(ὰ) τὸν σεπτ(έμβ)ρ(ιον) μῆνα, εἰς τ(ὰς) ιη΄ ἡμέρ(ᾳ) τρίτ(ῃ) πρὸ(s) ἑσπέρ(αν), ἰδικ(τιῶνος) θ΄, ἔτ(ους) ,sψμδ΄, ἡ σύζυγο(s) ἐμοῦ Σιν(ά)τορο(s) τῆς Κριτν, κυρ(ὰ) Γουαρρέρ(α), ἐγέννησε παιδίον δεύτερον ἄρσεν, ὅπερ ὠνομάσαμεν Μιχα(ὴ)λ. ὑπὲρ οὗ μεγάλη χαρὰ παρ᾽ ἡμῖν ἐγεγόνει. οὕτω δὲ, βαθείας ἑσπέρας καταλαβούσης, καὶ ἡ προρηθεῖσα μοι σύζυγος, τὸ πν(εῦμ)α τῷ κ(υρί)ῳ παρέδωκε. καὶ ἡμέρ(ᾳ) τετρ(ά)δ(ι) τοῦ ῥηθ(έν)τ(ος) μηνὸ(s) εἰς τ(ὰς) ιθ΄, ἐντίμως ἐτάφη ἐν τῷ πανσέπτ(ῳ) ναῷ τῆς ὑπεραγίας Θ(εοτό)κου τῆς Ἀχειροποιήτ(ου). καταλείψασά μοι τὰ ῥηθ(έν)τ(α) δύο παμφίλτ(α)τ(ά) μοι τέκνα, τὴν Ἀλφαρ(ά)ναν, καὶ τὸν Μιχα(ήλ). οἷς ὁ θ(εὸ)ς δῴη [sic] προκοπὴν καὶ αὔξησιν. ἐκείνῃ δὲ ἄφεσιν ἁμαρτιῶν καὶ ἀνάπαυσιν ἐν τοῖς τῶν δικαίων χοροῖς +++*': Vat. gr. 2019, fol. 115v. The text has also been published in Turyn (1964): 29. Though it may strike some readers as odd, 'Sinator' was a relatively common name in medieval Calabria; see e.g. Trinchera (1865): 56 (no. 13, a. 1058), 57 (no. 14, a. 1059), 141 (no. 106, a. 1130), 387 (no. 281, a. 1228), 512 (ad. 1, a. 1102). It is probably a Hellenised form of the Latin word *senator*. It is intriguing to note that his wife and daughter have Lombard names (Guarrera and

As Lucà pointed out, the name 'of Kritene' is not Sinator's place of origin (nor is it a botched attempt to write the Greek word for 'judge', *krites*), but rather an actual surname that was passed down through his family (equivalent to *de Critena*).[49] Indeed, the Criteni remained a distinguished family of Rossano for quite some time: in 1331, one Stefano Critenio was appointed *capitano* of the city by King Robert I 'the Wise' of Naples (*r.* 1309–1343), while several members of the family are known to have served as local judges and lawyers in the seventeenth and eighteenth centuries.[50]

There is one further interesting note. Vat. gr. 2019 contains a group of miscellaneous manuscript fragments inserted at the back of the codex after it was first compiled.[51] At the end of this miscellany a thirteenth- or fourteenth-century Greek hand wrote, 'A book called the *Chronicle* that also has the nomocanon. Donation of Raudas'.[52] The note gives no evidence as to who this 'Raudas' was nor to whom he donated the manuscript; perhaps he gave it to the Patiron, since that is where it ended up before being brought to Rome by Pietro Menniti. 'Raudas' may have been a surname: we know of a Nicholas Raudas who owned land near Crotone (a Calabrian city not far from Rossano) in the mid-twelfth century, for instance, while a certain Antonius Segerentinus de Rauda served as archbishop of Rossano in the years 1434–1442.[53] The Raudas who left the note in Vat. gr. 2019 was possibly a member of the same family.

In short, a thirteenth-century Rossanese nobleman of the Criteni family owned a copy of Alexios Aristenos' commentary of *c.* 1130 on the *Synopsis of Canons*. At some point in the thirteenth or fourteenth century it was also in the possession of a certain Raudas, who may have later donated it to the Patiron. However, this is not the only attestation of Aristenos' work in Rossano. Zachariä von Lingenthal discovered another mention of a 'nomocanon interpreted by Nicholas

Alpharana), whereas he and his son have Greek names; on gendered naming patterns in southern Italy, see Heygate (2013): 179–185, who notes a comparable phenomenon in mixed Norman-Lombard families.

[49] Lucà (1985): 125–126 n. 163. Turyn (1964): 33 incorrectly surmised that Kritene was Sinator's place of birth.

[50] Rosis (1838): 374–375, 550. Interestingly, at least two known female members of the family in the early modern period bore the name 'Achiropita' (the colloquial term for the cathedral of Rossano where Sinator's wife was buried). Sinator was undoubtedly one of their distant ancestors. For the 'Malena' (Maleinos) family of Rossano in the late Middle Ages and early modern period, see Rosis (1838): 488–496.

[51] Vat. gr. 2019, fols. 156–166.

[52] '+ *βιβλίον λεγόμενον χρονικὸν ἔχων καὶ τὸν νομοκάνοναν* [*sic*]. *ἀφιέροσις τοῦ Ῥαυδ*[*ᾶ*]': Vat. gr. 2019, fol. 165^{v}. 'The *Chronicle*' is a reference to an excerpt from the seventh- or eighth-century *Chronicle* of Hippolytos of Thebes that immediately preceded the note (fols. 161–164). Such careless descriptions of manuscript contents are quite common in the late Middle Ages and early modern period.

[53] Trinchera (1865): 207 (no. 157, a. 1159); *IS* 9.407 (no. 25). 'Raudas' could also be a first name, as in the case of the Greek cleric and notary Raudas of Nardò in the Salento who wrote a legal document of 1134: Trinchera (1865): 513 (ad. 2, a. 1134).

Doxapatres' at the beginning of Marc. gr. 179, a twelfth-century collection of the Novels of Justinian and Leo VI. A note in the opening flyleaves of Marc. gr. 179 tells us that it formed part of a donation made to the Patiron:

> Various books were donated by the great judge, the lord Synator Malenos [*sic*], to the holy and great monastery of the father [i.e. the Patiron of Rossano], among the first of which were the daily *Apostolos* with musical notation, the Book of Psalms, the nomocanon interpreted by Nicholas Doxapatres, and the great *nomimon* book [i.e. Marc. gr. 179] containing the legal novels of the emperor Leo and the blessed Justinian that are called authentic, and in addition to these [Justinian's] edicts.[54]

The person mentioned here is *not* Sinator of Kritene but Sinator Maleinos, a prominent judge of Rossano who lived about a generation or so earlier.[55] He is probably to be identified with the 'Synator Malenos' who, in the late twelfth century, authenticated a copy of a legal act of 1130 issued by Roger II in favour of the Patiron (which was also coincidentally authenticated by a judge named Basil of Kritene).[56] Though the 'nomocanon interpreted by Nicholas Doxapatres' mentioned in Marc. gr. 179 was donated to the Patiron, it has unfortunately not survived (perhaps Raudas donated Vat. gr. 2019 as a replacement?). Nonetheless, it was undoubtedly a misattributed copy of Alexios Aristenos' canonical commentary like the one in Vat. gr. 2019.

We have encountered the Maleinoi in Chapter 5 when Archbishop Nicholas Maleinos of Rossano ('along with his clan') attempted to gain control over the newly founded Patiron monastery in *c.* 1105.[57] Together with the Criteni, they were evidently one of the most powerful families in the city and appear in several documents of the period (see Table 7.1).

[54] '*ἀφιερώθη παρὰ τοῦ μεγάλου κριτοῦ κυροῦ Συνατῶρος τοῦ Μαλένου ἐν ῇ ἁγίᾳ καὶ μεγάλῃ μονῇ τοῦ πατρὸς βιβλία διάφορα, ἐν πρώτοις ὁ ἀπόστολος ὁ καθημερινὸς καὶ τονιμένος, καὶ ἡ βίβλος τῶν ψαλμῶν, καὶ ὁ νομοκάνων ὁ ἑρμηνευθεὶς παρὰ Νικολάου Δοξαπατρίου, καὶ τὸ μέγα βιβλίον τὸ νόμιμον αἵ νεαραὶ αἵ τῶν νόμων ἐπανορθώσεις παρὰ Λέοντος τοῦ μεγάλου βασιλέως καὶ τοῦ μακαρίου Ἰουστινιανοῦ οἵ ἐπονομαζόμενοι αὐθεντικοὶ, σύν τούτοις καὶ τὰ ἴδικτα τούτου*': Venice, Biblioteca Marciana, MS gr. 179, fol. 2v. Text in Zachariä von Lingenthal (1881): viii.

[55] The variant spelling in Marc. gr. 179 is not unusual for medieval Greek documents from southern Italy, which often demonstrate flexible attitudes to orthography. We also see the name spelled as 'Sinator' within the very same manuscript: the top half of the first page of Marc. gr. 179 is taken up by a large decorative motif of a cross in red ink; at the top and slightly offset to the right, the letters '*σ ι ν α τ ω ρ*' ('*s i n a t o r*') are inset using a *réserve* technique.

[56] Trinchera (1865): 141 (no. 106). Zachariä von Lingenthal (1881): ix states that the copy of the document (and hence Sinator Maleinos' donation) was made *c.* 1190, following Montfaucon (1702): 384–385, 397–401. However, Montfaucon offers no clear reason for this date. The most that one can say is that it was made at some point in the late twelfth century, as argued by Lucà (1985): 123 n. 156. Note that Trinchera's translation of Basil's surname as 'of Crotone' is incorrect.

[57] See Chapter 5, 'Monastic Nomocanons I', C5.P8.

Table 7.1. Four Generations of the Maleinoi and Criteni in Rossano (11th–13th Centuries)

	Maleinoi	Criteni	Source
1086	–	Peter of Kritene	Trinchera (1865): 65 (no. 49)
c. 1105	Nicholas Maleinos (archbishop)	–	Vat. gr. 2050, fol. 117^r
Late C12	Sinator Maleinos (judge)	Basil of Kritene (judge)	Trinchera (1865): 141 (no. 106)
	Sinator Maleinos (judge)	–	Marc. gr. 179, fol. ii^v
1234/5	–	Sinator of Kritene	Vat. gr. 2019, fol. 155^v

The Criteni and Maleinoi both counted judges among their family members. Given his ownership of Vat. gr. 2019, it is likely that Sinator of Kritene was a legal official as well. The Maleinoi also provided Rossano with at least one (and probably more than one) archbishop. Perhaps the Criteni did too, though no evidence of this has survived. Like many other medieval noble families, the Maleinoi and the Criteni attempted to maintain a grip on both the civil and ecclesiastical administration of Rossano.

Vat. gr. 2019 and the missing codex mentioned in Marc. gr. 179 provide the only two known attestations of the 'Nomocanon of Doxapatres'; clearly one was copied from the other or both shared a common source.[58] Even the scribal hands of Marc. gr. 179 and Vat. gr. 2019 are similar (though not identical), showing 'evident graphical relations' as Lucà has noted.[59] How exactly Aristenos' work came to be attributed to Nicholas Doxapatres is unclear and need not detain us here.[60] What is important to emphasise is that these two Rossanese noble families (and, perhaps, the Rauda family as well) possessed related copies of a Byzantine canonical commentary that was composed in Constantinople a full seventy years after the Norman conquest of Calabria.

It is easy to see why a noble house such as the Maleinoi or the Criteni would own a nomocanon as well as a *nomimon*: different members of the same family could and did serve as lay judges and as archbishops. Indeed, sometimes the same individual might do *both* jobs, as we learn from a letter of Pope Honorius III of 1218. The letter itself comes from a thirteenth-century context in which the papacy was able to intervene more directly in southern Italian ecclesiastical affairs, but it serves as important evidence of a *status quo* that had prevailed under

[58] Lucà (1985): 125 has pointed out that the *réserve* technique used to inscribe Sinator's name in the title of Marc. gr. 179 was also used by a different scribe for the title of the canons of Trullo in Vat. gr. 2019, fol. 55^v.

[59] Lucà (1985): 125.

[60] For further discussion of the question, see Morton (2017): 737.

Norman rule in Rossano up until that point. Honorius instructs the Latin archbishop of Cosenza to investigate the Greek archbishop of Rossano, Basil, who had been accused of acquiring his office through simony. Basil, we learn, was a 'judge of Rossano' who was married, had held no previous ecclesiastical office, and 'had often pronounced death sentences'.[61] Basil's consecration was ultimately allowed to stand, but the accusation must have seemed plausible enough for Honorius to take it seriously.[62]

We are not told what Basil's surname was, but he undoubtedly belonged to one of Rossano's noble houses such as the Maleinoi or the Criteni. The rapid elevation of laypeople to high ecclesiastical office had some precedent in the Byzantine Empire; the most famous example is that of the ninth-century patriarch Photios, who was tonsured and promoted through the ranks of the clergy within just one week (as his uncle Tarasios had been in 784).[63] However, the Rossanese nobility's efforts to control the archiepiscopal office cannot simply be explained by the fact that they were Greek or that they were influenced by Byzantine precedent. The nobility of the Latin West also strived to control local ecclesiastical offices where possible, sometimes in creative ways.[64]

The key difference in the case of Rossano (and, presumably, the other remaining Greek sees of southern Italy) was that the Roman church made no serious attempt to interfere in its affairs until the thirteenth century. This seems to have been partly a product of the papacy's genuine ignorance of Italo-Greek Christians in the twelfth century, but it was also a consequence of the Norman rulers' success in maintaining control over the church in the Kingdom of Sicily. Roger II and his Norman successors evidently did not mind if the nobles of Rossano controlled their local cathedral and continued to follow the canon law of the contemporary Byzantine Empire if it meant that papal influence was weakened as a result.

Conclusion

The Italo-Greek secular church and laity reveal fascinating aspects of the legal pluralism of the Norman Kingdom of Sicily. The cultural pluralism that we see in the realm of civil law, in which the kingdom had parallel Latin and Greek judges, was replicated to some extent in the canon law of the church. Following their annexation to the jurisdiction of the Roman papacy in the 1060s–1070s, the Greek

[61] '... *B[asilium] iudicem Rossanensem, qui pluries sententias dictaverat sanguinis, uxoratum et ordinem ecclesiasticum aliquem non habentem ...*': *Fontes III* 3.60 (no. 36). IV Lateran c. 18 specifically prohibits churchmen from pronouncing 'blood sentences': C.9, X, Ne cler. vel. monach., III, 50. See also Herde (2002): 228.

[62] *Fontes III* 3.69 (no. 44).

[63] See Hussey (1986): 72.

[64] To give just one example, Count Theobald the Great of Champagne (*r.* 1125–1152) tried in 1151 to have his young son William made a bishop; see Brittain Bouchard (1987): 73.

bishops of southern Italy continued to read their inherited texts of Byzantine religious law and look to Constantinople for spiritual leadership. As in the case of the monasteries, it was not in the interests of the Norman kings for the Italo-Greeks to be integrated more closely into Rome's legal and administrative system, since this would give the papacy greater influence over their kingdom.

This picture admittedly lacks nuance, since so few sources on the twelfth-century Italo-Greek episcopate have survived. It would be particularly interesting to learn more about the legal fate of the Greek clergy and laity in areas where Latin bishops were installed. Nonetheless, the paucity of source material is revealing in its own way. Most of the surviving documentary evidence on Latin bishops in Norman southern Italy comes from papal correspondence; the fact that there is almost no preserved papal correspondence relating to Greek bishops suggests that they had little official contact with Rome. As far as their own canon law was concerned, all the extant source material indicates that they ignored even contemporary Latin legislation. This was a form of legal pluralism within the southern Italian church itself, as Greek and Latin Christians followed their own legal traditions in their own ecclesiastical spaces.

The picture becomes more complex when we take the laity into account. Medieval society had many types of legal pluralism, with various legal systems for church and state, for cities, guilds, and feudal nobility, as well as for different ethnic groups. As we have seen above, the Italo-Greeks effectively had their own ethnic legal system within the legal system of the church. In addition to this, we also see that the Italo-Greeks' secular and religious legal spheres could overlap strongly in places like Rossano, where local noble families attempted to monopolise control over both, consolidating Byzantine civil and canon law into the foundation of their local authority. Indeed, it is quite telling that we have more direct evidence for nomocanons belonging to the secular aristocracy than we do for episcopal nomocanons.

What makes this so striking is that it occurred against the backdrop of sweeping legal reforms in the Western church. Numerous councils were held in Rome and elsewhere in the eleventh to twelfth centuries that sought to reform ecclesiastical governance and the discipline of the clergy, yet they appear not to have touched the Italo-Greek hierarchy. The nature of Norman rule in the twelfth century afforded it a degree of autonomy that allowed them to enact a similar sort of legal fiction to the monasteries, following the law in Byzantine nomocanons as if they were still a part of the Byzantine church. The situation would not last, however.

PART III
FROM LEGAL TO CULTURAL AUTHORITY

8
The Papacy Takes Charge

The turn of the thirteenth century brought two major political developments that would upend the Italo-Greeks' legal *status quo*.[1] The first was the demise of the Norman Hauteville dynasty and the turmoil of the early years of the young Frederick II's reign (1198–1208), which gave his guardian Pope Innocent III an incentive and an opportunity to assert greater papal authority over the Kingdom of Sicily and its church.[2] The second was the Fourth Crusade of 1204, which resulted in the break-up of the Byzantine Empire and the creation of a new Latin Empire in its place. Though remnants of the Byzantine state survived in Nicaea, Epirus, and Trebizond, the majority of Greece and Thrace fell under the control of the crusaders.[3]

This was not the first time that Latin crusaders came to rule over large numbers of indigenous Greek Christians in the eastern Mediterranean; the conquest of Cyprus during the Third Crusade (1189–1192) and the creation of the Lusignan kingdom had provided an important recent precedent.[4] Nonetheless, the broader relationship between the Latin and Greek churches had been a primarily diplomatic one until the Fourth Crusade. The Patriarchate of Constantinople was, first and foremost, the state church of the Byzantine Empire. Whatever its claims to universal primacy, the Roman papacy had never been able to exert its will over Greek Christians without the Byzantine emperor's consent (it was almost always the emperor who took the lead in church union negotiations, not the patriarch).[5]

The Fourth Crusade did not eliminate the diplomatic dimension of the relationship between Latin and Greek Christianity, since independent Byzantine emperors continued to rule in Nicaea and would eventually recapture Constantinople in 1260. What it did do, however, was introduce a significant legal dimension to the relationship for the first time.[6] The new Patriarch of Constantinople, the Venetian Thomas Morosini (*r.* 1204–1211), was a Latin,

[1] See Chapter 2, 'Greek Christianity in Medieval Italy', C2.S4.

[2] Peters-Custot (2009a): 505 notes that papal clergy were inserted into ten dioceses (including three metropolitan sees) in the Kingdom of Sicily in the decade between 1198 and 1208.

[3] For an overview of the relationship between Latin and Greek Christians in the conquered lands, see Coureas (2014).

[4] See Chapter 2, 'Greek Christianity in Medieval Italy', C2.P48.

[5] See Geanakoplos (1966): 84–86. Dagron (2003): 310 observed that 'it was not the role of the emperor that was ill-defined in Byzantine ecclesiology, it was that of the patriarch'.

[6] The Norman conquest of southern Italy in the eleventh century had brought numerous Greek Christians under Latin jurisdiction in the eleventh century, as we have seen, but not on the same scale as the Fourth Crusade.

Byzantine Religious Law in Medieval Italy. James Morton, Oxford University Press (2021). © James Morton.
DOI: 10.1093/oso/9780198861140.003.0009

and Pope Innocent III was determined to integrate the Byzantine church directly into the Roman hierarchy.[7] Combined with its increased influence in southern Italy, this effort had the long-term effect of severely curtailing the legal autonomy that the more powerful Italo-Greek institutions had enjoyed in the twelfth century.

The Fourth Lateran Council (1215) and Greek Christianity

Innocent's initial attempts to persuade the Greek clergy of the Latin Empire to submit voluntarily to the Latin hierarchy met with mixed success. A legation in 1205–1207 led by Benedict Caetani, cardinal priest of S. Susanna, took a relatively benign approach, but only won over a small number of Byzantine bishops. A few years later, in 1213–1214, the papal legate Pelagius, cardinal bishop of Albano, adopted harsher tactics, imprisoning recalcitrant Greek clergy and closing churches and monasteries that refused to pledge obedience. Pelagius' methods backfired, causing such an outcry that the Latin emperor Henry of Flanders (*r.* 1206–1216) ordered the prisoners released and the churches reopened.[8] Meanwhile, the troublesome Latin lords of Frankish Greece often harassed even those clergy who did submit. The crusaders may have captured Constantinople, but the churches remained disunited.

The integration of the Byzantine church into the Roman hierarchy was, from the papacy's perspective, as much a legal challenge as it was diplomatic or theological. As Nicholas Coureas has remarked, the Greek church in the former Byzantine lands 'presented a jurisdictional obstacle . . . in that its clergy refused to recognise papal supremacy and the jurisdiction of the Roman Catholic Church'.[9] This is reminiscent of the Norman conquest of southern Italy in the eleventh century, when the Roman church cared more about obtaining the Italo-Greeks' fealty than liturgical or theological change. Since Rome viewed church union as a legal problem, it sought a corresponding legal solution.

Innocent III began preparations for the Fourth Lateran Council in 1213 and it convened on 11th November 1215. The council set out a sweeping programme of reform, which John Watt has called 'the most comprehensive expression of the classical policies of the medieval papacy in its heyday, at once typifying its major aspirations and identifying its goals'.[10] Amongst the various issues that it addressed, one of the council's key aims was to reorganise the ecclesiastical settlement of Latin territories in the eastern Mediterranean, as Schabel and

[7] See Van Tricht (2011): 307–349. On Thomas Morosini and the Latin Patriarchate of Constantinople, see Madden (2018).

[8] Van Tricht (2011): 314–315; Hoeck and Loenertz (1965): 30–61.

[9] Coureas (2014): 145.

[10] Watt (1999): 119.

Tsougarakis have described.[11] In so doing, the Fourth Lateran Council set out a clear, formal policy on non-Latin Christians under Latin rule for the first time.

The council issued three canons of especial relevance to Greek Christians in the eastern Mediterranean and, by extension, southern Italy: canons 4, 5, and 9.[12] Perhaps the least consequential of these for the Italo-Greeks was canon 5. It endorses the ancient Byzantine concept of the pentarchy, the body of five patriarchs (of Rome, Constantinople, Alexandria, Antioch, and Jerusalem, in that order) that collectively govern the church.[13] Though the canon affirms the patriarchs' various rights and privileges, it adds the peculiarly Western stipulation that the Roman pontiff should have absolute ultimate authority over the other four patriarchs. The patriarchs have the right to hear legal appeals from within their own territories, for instance, but must respect any appeals directed to the pope. This canon represents an interesting attempt by Innocent to reconcile the ancient collegial model of ecclesiastical governance with the authoritarian impulses of the thirteenth-century Roman church.[14] It remained moot for the Italo-Greeks, at any rate, who were already under direct Roman jurisdiction.

The other two canons had much more important consequences for the Greeks of southern Italy. Canon 4 expresses outrage over the alleged Byzantine custom of re-baptising Latins according to the Greek rite and washing altars that had been used by Latins.[15] In addition to prohibiting these practices, the text neatly encapsulates the papacy's view on the integration of the Greek church and so is worth quoting at length (emphasis added):

> Though we wish to favour and honour the Greeks who in our days are returning to the obedience of the Apostolic See by *permitting them to retain their customs and rites* as much as we can in the Lord, yet, in those things that cause danger to souls and diminish ecclesiastical propriety, we neither wish nor ought to defer to them... We strictly command... that [the Greeks] conform themselves *as*

[11] Schabel and Tsougarakis (2016): 752–755.

[12] Mansi 22.990–992, 997–998. See also discussion in Herde (2002); Schabel and Tsougarakis (2016): 755–758. For a more general overview of thirteenth-century Latin canon law on the Greek rite, see Brieskorn (2010).

[13] Interestingly, the concept of the Pentarchy of patriarchs was first established not in canon law but in Justinianic civil law (Just. *Nov.* 109). On Byzantine views of the Pentarchy in the twelfth century, see Siciliano (1979). Roman popes continued to use the title 'Patriarch of the West' until it was formally renounced by Pope Benedict XVI in 2006.

[14] See also Siecienski (2017): 291–292.

[15] The accusation that Greek clergy would wash altars after Latins had celebrated the Eucharist on them dates to at least the Second Crusade (1147–1149): Odo of Deuil, *De profectione Ludovici VII* 3 (pp. 54–55). It is difficult to know to what extent this was a common occurrence or simply a figment of anti-Greek polemic; it was certainly never the official policy of the Byzantine church, as noted by Kolbaba (2005). See also Neocleous (2019): 58–65; Jotischky (2003): 15; Angold (1995): 511.

> *obedient children to the Holy Roman church*, their mother, that there may be 'one fold and one shepherd' [John 10:16].[16]

The Roman church did not object (in principle) to the Greeks' distinctive rites and practices, though it was understood that they might potentially need to be curtailed.[17] What it insisted upon was legal submission.

Canon 9 does not mention the Greeks explicitly, but its stipulations applied nonetheless. It notes that there are many dioceses in which Latin-rite bishops oversee congregations who follow non-Latin rites and speak other languages. In such cases, the bishop is to provide clergy who can suitably minister to those congregations; if necessary, he should appoint an episcopal vicar who can act as an administrator on his behalf. In Greek areas of southern Italy and the former Byzantine Empire, this vicar would take the Byzantine title of *protopapas* or 'first priest'.[18]

While this canon aimed to spiritually benefit minority groups such as the Italo-Greeks, it also had an important administrative consequence. As James Brundage observed, 'In effect this [canon] resulted in a *de facto* separation of the Greek and Latin clergy, each being treated as a separate community with distinct corporate status, within the over-all [*sic*] framework of the Latin diocesan organization.'[19] On one hand, this created a decentralised administration that helped to ensure the continued survival of the Greek rite under Latin bishops. On the other hand, it gave Latin bishops the means to control their Greek clergy more effectively. Moreover, these conditions would come to apply to an increasing number of Italo-Greeks as sees such as S. Severina (1254) and Crotone (1276) passed from Greek to Latin hands over the course of the thirteenth century.[20]

In their substance, the decrees of the Fourth Lateran Council were not a complete novelty. They essentially reiterate Pope Urban II's ultimatum to the Byzantine archbishop Basil of Reggio in 1089: Greeks could continue as they were on condition that they swore loyalty to the Roman pontiff, a position that was probably affirmed at the Council of Bari in 1098.[21] Some details were new, such as the arrangement that Latin bishops should appoint Greek vicars to act on their

[16] '*Licet Graecos in diebus nostris ad obedientiam Sedis Apostolicae revertentes fovere at honorare velimus mores ac ritus eorum quantu cum Domino possumus sustinendo, in his tamen illis deferre nec volumus nec debemus quae periculum generant animarum et ecclesiasticae derogant honestati… Destricte praecipimus ut talia de caetero non praesumant conformantes se tamquam obedientiae filii sacrosanctae Romanae Ecclesiae matri suae ut sit "unum ovile et unus pastor"*': Mansi 22.998.

[17] See Andrea (2005).

[18] The *protopapas* was traditionally the head priest in a Byzantine cathedral. On the use of the title in southern Italy, see Peters-Custot (2009a): 435–436; Martin (1993): 641–647.

[19] Brundage (1973): 1077.

[20] See Herde (2002): 231. The last bishop of Crotone was Nicholas of Durazzo, a bilingual figure who also served as an emissary in church union negotiations leading up to the Second Council of Lyon (1274); see Sambin (1954).

[21] See Chapter 2, 'Greek Christianity in Medieval Italy', C2.P32–C2.P33.

behalf where necessary. However, the real novelty lay in the act of promulgation: the Fourth Lateran Council was the first to formally enshrine these principles into Latin canon law. As Herde put it, 'Whereas canon law sources of the late twelfth century depict a peaceful symbiosis between the Latin and Greek Churches [*sic*] in southern Italy, a hardening of the papal stance can be observed from the time of Innocent III.'[22] Future popes would no longer allow the Italo-Greeks to be left to their own devices as they had been under the Norman kings of Sicily.

The Papacy and the 'Order of St Basil': The Grottaferrata Nomocanon

It did not take long for the Italo-Greeks to feel the effects of the papal interventionism. We have already seen the example of Basil, the Greek judge of Rossano whose questionable elevation to archiepiscopal rank in 1218 prompted Honorius III to open an investigation into accusations of simony.[23] In the same year, Honorius also investigated the Greek archbishop of S. Severina for various alleged infractions 'against the statutes of the General Council [i.e. Lateran IV]'.[24] He intervened in Calabria yet again in 1220, this time in an effort to stop the Greeks of Rossano from conducting child marriage.[25]

The papacy did not limit itself to simple corrective or punitive actions, however. Lateran IV also marks the beginning of an effort on the part of the Roman church to comprehend and rationalise Italo-Greek Christianity, something that is clearest in the realm of monasticism. As we saw in Chapter 3, the medieval Latin church had become accustomed to categorising types of monastic discipline by rule or order.[26] One of the Lateran council's aims was to improve the regulation of these orders; canon 13, for instance, commanded that no new monastic orders could be established and that anyone who wished to become a monk was required to enter an existing approved order.[27] Although the canon does not mention it by name, it evidently considered the Greek 'Basilian' order of monasticism to be one of these.

As we saw in Chapter 3, the 'Order of St Basil' was not a formal institution until the fifteenth century. However, the terms 'Rule of St Basil' and 'Basilian' had been used in an offhand way by Latin writers to describe Greek monasticism since at least the tenth century; papal documentation began to use them more and more frequently from the thirteenth century on.[28] Even though no 'rule' or 'order' of

[22] Herde (2002): 250. [23] See Chapter 7, 'The Secular Church and the Laity', C7.P41.

[24] '. . . *contra Generalis Concilii statuta* . . .': *Fontes III* 3.59 (no. 33).

[25] *Fontes III* 3.99 (no. 70). This was not a case of cultural difference between Latins and Greeks: Byzantine civil law set the marriageable age at 14 for males and 12 for females (Just. *Cod.* 5.23.24), the same standard as in Western canon law (Donahue [2008]: 20–21). The Greeks of Rossano were in violation of *both* legal traditions.

[26] See Chapter 3, 'Patterns of Source Survival', C3.P8. [27] Mansi 22.1002–1003.

[28] Peters-Custot (2009a): 458–461; Enzensberger (1973): 1141–1142; see also Peters-Custot (2017).

St Basil existed in the sense that the Western church would have understood it, it was an easy way for the Latins to conceptualise Greek monasticism.

From the popes' perspective, the Italo-Greek monastery of Grottaferrata near Rome was the most familiar 'Basilian' institution. Founded by St Neilos the Younger of Rossano in 1004 on land granted by the counts of Tusculum, it enjoyed close ties to the papacy from its early years. It was formally dedicated by Pope John XIX in 1024 and steadily acquired lands and dependent churches through the patronage of the local nobility. In 1116, Pope Paschal II issued it a bull of papal protection (as he had done for the Patiron of Rossano a few years earlier), which was subsequently reaffirmed by Callixtus II in 1119, Eugenius III in 1150, and Adrian IV in 1158.[29]

Soon after the Fourth Lateran Council, in 1216, Innocent III wrote to Abbot John of Grottaferrata to confirm the monastery's status as a papal protectorate yet again, affirming 'that the monastic order, which we know to be established following God and the Rule of the Blessed Basil in the same monastery [of Grottaferrata], should be observed inviolate there in perpetuity'.[30] His successor Honorius III soon put the abbot of Grottaferrata to work on the papacy's behalf. In a letter of 24th November 1220, he instructed the abbot to join the Latin archbishop of Cosenza for a *visitatio* to inspect and reform the Greek monasteries of Sicily. He wrote to him again on 10th May 1221, telling him to do the same for Greek monasteries in Calabria, Apulia, and Campania (this time in the company of the Greek bishop of Crotone).[31]

Unfortunately, nothing is known about the outcome of these visits. Nevertheless, the letters suggest that the pope may have viewed Grottaferrata as sort of motherhouse for the reform of 'Basilian' monasticism in Italy, which Eugenius IV would turn into reality in the fifteenth century.[32] We do not have an explicit statement that this was Honorius' intent, but it would not have been far-fetched. Not only did the Norman kings create such federations (admittedly on a smaller scale) in the twelfth century, but Innocent III had explored the possibility of creating a similar federation of Greek monasteries in Hungary under direct papal protection in 1204, as Neocleous has recently pointed out.[33]

[29] Breccia (2002): 9 (no. 8), 10 (no. 9); *Fontes III* 1.798 (no. 386), 818–820 (ad. 1), 820–821 (ad. 2). Roger II is also purported to have granted legal privileges to Grottaferrata in 1131, including the right to criminal jurisdiction over its land holdings in the Kingdom of Sicily. However, Follieri (1988) has shown that there are several reasons to doubt this document's authenticity.

[30] '*in primis siquidem statuentes, ut ordo monasticus, qui secundum Deum et Beati Basilii Regulam in eodem monasterio institutus esse dignoscitur, perpetuis ibidem temporibus inviolabiliter observetur*': *Fontes III* 2.470 (no. 222) = Breccia (2002): 13 (no. 19). The letter is not preserved in Innocent III's register, but it was copied into that of Eugenius IV in the year 1435. See also Parenti (2005): 180–181.

[31] Breccia (2002): 14 (nos. 22–23).

[32] If Honorius had any concrete plans to this end, they were undoubtedly frustrated by the decades-long conflict with the Hohenstaufen in the 1220s–1260s. On Eugenius IV, see Chapter 3, 'Patterns of Source Survival', C3.P6–C3.P8.

[33] Neocleous (2019): 190.

It was in this context that the Grottaferrata Nomocanon Marc. gr. 171 was produced. This manuscript is unique in that it is the only surviving Italo-Greek nomocanon made of Italian non-watermarked paper, a material that emerged in the northern cities of Fabriano and Treviso around the year 1220.[34] The paper's chain lines are more or less equidistant at approximate intervals of 60 mm, which Paul Canart found to be characteristic of manuscripts produced around the year 1240, though one must bear in mind that this is not a precise method of dating paper.[35] A heavily damaged note in a thirteenth-century Greek hand at the beginning of the manuscript helps to narrow the date range further: 'In the name of the Father and of the Son and of the Holy Spirit. In the [?] indiction there was an agreement between the lords Jacob and John Frangipane and me, Pankratios the *praepositus*... of the castellan. And... before the refectory... of Grottaferrata... first harvest and fruits... worker... the monastery... bread... and one... and the worker... just as...'[36]

The text describes an agreement between Pankratios, the *praepositus* of Grottaferrata from 1222 to 1230, and the Roman nobles Jacob and John Frangipane, though the exact details are unclear.[37] The note in Marc. gr. 171 may have been a rough draft of the final text. Von Falkenhausen has suggested that it relates to a Latin document of 1230 that records a land exchange between Pankratios and the Frangipane family, though I am not convinced of this; the Greek text does not obviously discuss land and omits the names of several participants mentioned in the Latin document.[38] Nonetheless, it is clearly the same Pankratios in both.[39]

Pankratios' note gives a *terminus ante quem* for Marc. gr. 171 of 1230, meaning that the manuscript can most plausibly be dated to the years 1220–1230 (perhaps at the earlier end of that period). In other words, it was produced soon after the Fourth Lateran Council and around the time that Honorius III instructed Grottaferrata's abbot to undertake inspections of Italo-Greek monasticism in

[34] Irigoin (1963); Bresc and Heullant-Donat (2007). This 'Italian' paper was not an entirely new commodity but developed out of techniques imported from the Muslim world.

[35] Canart et al. (1993): 327.

[36] '*ἐν ὁματι* [*sic*] *τοῦ π(ατ)ρ(ὸ)ς καὶ τοῦ ὑιοῦ καὶ τοῦ ἁγ(ίου) πν(εῦματο)ς : ινδ... ἐγένετο συμφονήα ἀναμεταξὶ κυρῶν Ἰακώβου καὶ Ἰω(άννου) Φραγαπάναι καὶ ἐγῶ τοῦ Πανκρατ(ίου)... πρε(πό)σιτο(υ)... ἴτοι... τί... κάλδ καστελάνου καὶ... μεσχὸν τε ἐνόπιον τῆς τραπ(έ)ζου... Κρυπτωφέρρης... τοῦτω προκοπ... καὶ καρπῶν... του... τον ἐκάλ... την... τὸ ὅπερ ἐστὶν... ἐργάτην... κατάχ... τὸ μοναστήριον... σιτάρη... καὶ μίαν... καὶ τὸν ἐργάτην... καθὸς...*': Marc. gr. 171, fol. 1^r^. Mioni (1981): 1.256 published an imperfect transcription of the text. Besides omitting several legible lines, Mioni misread the name 'Pankratios' as '*πανκρυπ... ης*'.

[37] Malatesta Zilembo (1965): 148; see also Rocchi (1893): 39, 84. The Latin term '*praepositus*' is equivalent to the Greek '*oikonomos*', the administrator of a monastery's estate and finances. The fact that Pankratios uses the Latin word transliterated into Greek shows the linguistic influence exerted on Grottaferrata by its surroundings.

[38] Falkenhausen (2015): 69. For the Latin text, see Fedele (1905): 216–217.

[39] The lords Jacob and John Frangipane are also mentioned in an inscription of 1267, which records that Grottaferrata inherited some of their estate after their death (Rocchi[1893]: 46).

mainland southern Italy. As we saw in earlier chapters, the production and survival of monastic nomocanons tend to correlate closely with a monastery's acquisition of legal privileges. In the case of the Grottaferrata Nomocanon Marc. gr. 171, we should associate it with the monastery's increased prominence as a papal centre for 'Basilian' monasticism in the aftermath of Lateran IV.

Despite the fact that the manuscript's use of paper and Pankratios' note indicate a thirteenth-century central Italian context, its contents and appearance are much more reminiscent of tenth-century Byzantium. The nomocanon opens with a table of contents followed by the first and second prologues of the *N14T* (i.e. up to the Photian prologue of the ninth century, but not including Balsamon's twelfth-century prologue). Next come a pair of simple narrative histories of local and ecumenical church councils; these texts, which end with the Second Council of Nicaea in 787, are recognisable from numerous other Byzantine nomocanons and do not mention any medieval Western councils.[40]

Though it begins with the first and second prologues of the *N14T*, the manuscript does not contain the *N14T* itself. Instead, the main section consists simply of the text of the Byzantine canon law corpus, albeit with some interesting omissions.[41] The conciliar canons stop at II Nicaea; *Protodeutera* is absent, as are Constantinople (394) and the letter of Patriarch Tarasios to Pope Hadrian, all of which are standard contents of the Photian *N14T*. The conciliar canons are followed by Gregory of Nyssa's canonical letter to Letoius, Athanasios of Alexandria's fifth canon (prohibiting the taking of communion on the same day as sexual intercourse with one's spouse), Theophilos of Alexandria's first canon (that Sunday should be honoured as the day of resurrection), and the canons of Basil of Caesarea. No other patristic canons are included.

Marc. gr. 171 was probably a copy of an earlier (now lost) nomocanon that the monastery would have acquired on or after its foundation in the early eleventh century. Presumably this prototype had lost some of its final quires by the thirteenth century, which would explain Marc. gr. 171's omission of the patristic canons after those of Basil: they would have been missing from the scribe's model. The contents of the Grottaferrata Nomocanon are evidently based on a tradition dating back to the ninth or early tenth centuries, before the canons of *Protodeutera* became widely established in Byzantine manuscripts. As we saw in previous chapters, this is quite common for Italo-Greek nomocanons created before the Norman period such as Marc. gr. 171's prototype.

At 265 x 170 mm (with 195 x 120 mm of written space), the Grottaferrata Nomocanon is among the larger codices in this study but does not approach the dimensions of the most impressive Calabrian and Sicilian codices. The scribal

[40] Text in Beneševič (1905): 73–79.

[41] The one addition is the presence of *Epitome of Book Eight of the Apostolic Constitutions* 19–21, 18.2–3, 22.2–14, 16, 15, 17–24.7, 25–26 on fols. 22^{v}–26^{v} between the Apostolic Canons and I Nicaea.

hand is clearly based on the School of Neilos style brought to Grottaferrata by its founders in the eleventh century, showing few signs of development.[42] There is almost no decoration to speak of save for the use of red ink in titles and initials and the presence of wavy lines to denote text breaks, both simple utilitarian features for ease of reference. The most remarkable visual characteristic of the manuscript, besides its use of paper, is the fact that it is ruled in system 13 (see Figure 8.1).

This is a rare system of ruling and unique among the Italo-Greek nomocanons, though it has been observed in other Byzantine manuscripts.[43]

One could argue that the archaic Byzantine character of the Grottaferrata Nomocanon is unsurprising: medieval scribes often copied their prototypes without critically engaging with them, especially in the case of technical literature such as law. On the other hand, the glaring absence of any Latin canon law (or even basic acknowledgement thereof) from the manuscript is telling in its own way. The monks of Grottaferrata were certainly aware of the important legislative developments taking place just a few miles away in the Lateran palace, yet they made no effort to include them in their nomocanon. Ironically, it was the monastery's close relationship with the papacy that made this possible: the repeated guarantees of Grottaferrata's independence from the episcopal hierarchy meant that its continued use of Byzantine canon law could only be challenged by the popes themselves, and they apparently did not (yet) pay close enough attention to do so.

The Archimandrite and the Archbishop: Italo-Greek Resistance to Papal Authority in Messina

While Grottaferrata enjoyed an amicable relationship with the papacy, the same cannot be said for the Holy Saviour of Messina, the most prominent Greek monastery in Sicily. Founded under the royal protection of Roger II, its extensive possessions attracted the envy of the archbishops of Messina from an early date. In

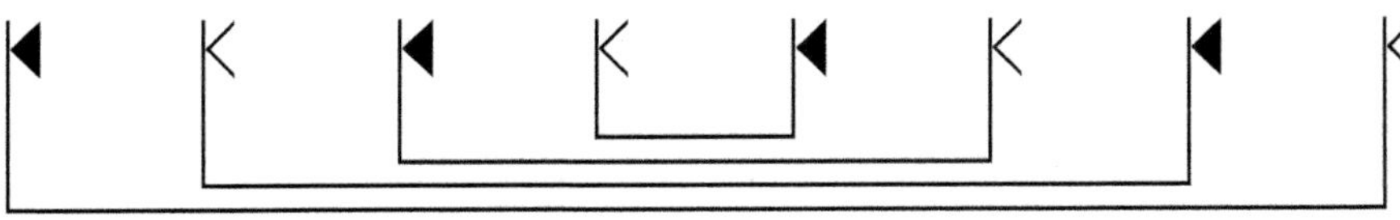

Figure 8.1. Ruling System 13. Rule lines are made on fols. 1^{v}, 3^{v}, 5^{v}, 7^{v}, travelling via impression to the opposite side of each folio.

[42] On the 'School of Neilos' script in the manuscripts of Grottaferrata, see Lucà (2004a): 152.
[43] Leroy (1977): 33.

c. 1160, Archbishop Robert of Messina (*c.* 1150–1160) attempted to compel Archimandrite Onouphrios I of the Holy Saviour to swear a loyalty oath.[44] Following further efforts by the archbishop to extract money from the monastery, Onouphrios II persuaded Pope Alexander III to take it under direct papal protection in 1175.[45] In the tumultuous political circumstances of the early thirteenth century, Archimandrite Luke III (1202–1223) asked Honorius III to confirm the Holy Saviour's exemption, which he did in 1216.[46]

All might have been well for the archimandritate had it not been for the renewed efforts of the archbishop of Messina, Berardus (1196–1226), to gain influence over it in the early years of Honorius III's pontificate.[47] The problem seems to have begun in 1218, when Berardus claimed the right to confirm the election of the archimandrite and the heads of the Holy Saviour's subject houses (*metochia*). The monks appealed to Honorius in the same year, but, after a lengthy investigation, he ruled in the archbishop's favour in 1222, declaring that the monks should accept the archbishop's right to confirm their archimandrite or face excommunication.[48]

The monks chose excommunication rather than acknowledge the archbishop's authority. In 1223, the monastery sought the royal protection of Frederick II, who had by then managed to consolidate his rule over Sicily. This appeal to the secular power resulted in a swift excommunication from the pope, though it was lifted the following year after Luke's death to allow for his successor's election. Nonetheless, the monks refused to consult the archbishop in electing their new archimandrite, Makarios. Honorius excommunicated the monastery again and tried to hold a new election, but his legates were unable to reach Messina (perhaps because they were prevented by Frederick II). Pope Gregory IX would attempt to remove Makarios a second time in 1231, but his efforts were likewise frustrated.

The story has so far been known primarily from papal correspondence and a small number of documents from Messina that are currently in the Archivo Ducal

[44] The text of Onouphrios' oath to Robert survives in Madrid, Biblioteca Nacional de España, MS 4552, fol. 134^{r}, published in Buchthal (1955): 338; Falkenhausen (2017): 252 n. 73.

[45] *Fontes III* 1.818–821 (ad. 3). See Falkenhausen (2017): 260–262.

[46] *Fontes III* 3.18–22 (no. 3). The *Fontes* collection also contains two purported bulls of Innocent III in favour of the Holy Saviour in 1210 and 1216 (*Fontes III* 2.398–399 [no. 168], 469 [no. 221]), but Enzensberger (2000): 216–218 has shown that these were fourteenth-century forgeries. There is also some uncertainty about the date of Archimandrite Luke's death. Scaduto and Kamp state that an archimandrite named Nymphos died in 1223, but I am unsure what their source is (Scaduto [1947]: 239; Kamp [1973]: 1023). As Enzensberger (2000): 219 n. 48 notes, no archimandrite named Nymphos is attested in surviving documentation, so it was probably Luke who died in 1223.

[47] For the classic (albeit dated) overview of this episode, see Scaduto (1947): 235–240. More recently, see Enzensberger (2000); Loud (2016): 143–144. On Archbishop Berardus, see Kamp (1973): 1018–1024.

[48] Honorius did not always rule against Italo-Greek monasteries in such circumstances. In 1219, for instance, he granted an episcopal exemption to the monastery of the Theotokos of Carrà, which he then upheld in the face of a legal challenge from the Latin bishop of Nicastro: *Fontes III* 3.80–81 (nos. 54–55).

de Medinaceli in Madrid.[49] However, we can gain a different perspective on it from studying the Holy Saviour's own nomocanon, Vall. C 11.1. The last folia of the codex contain a damaged copy in a thirteenth-century Latin hand of an otherwise unknown document of Honorius III from the year 1224.[50] In the letter, the pope writes to the abbot of the Cistercian monastery of S. Maria de Novara in the diocese of Messina to announce that he has reinstated the excommunication of the Holy Saviour following the improper election of the new archimandrite (Makarios).

The nomocanon also contains an interesting set of marginalia left by a single, distinctive Greek hand of the thirteenth century. This reader made a series of asterisk-like crosses next to sections of the text that he wished to highlight and occasionally wrote notes for extra emphasis. Alongside II Nicaea c. 12, which forbids bishops or abbots from alienating church property, he left a cross and the words 'look well'.[51] There is also a Latin translation of the canon in the left margin of the page, though it is difficult to be certain if it was left by the same person. Our reader further annotated several texts on simony and monastic obedience.[52] His interest in the misuse of church property by bishops resurfaces alongside the *C25C* and the *Tripartite Collection*. In the margin of a section that forbids bishops from despoiling churches for the benefit of their families, the reader left a large cross with the word 'look'.[53] We find another large cross at the beginning of *Tripartite Collection* 3.2.1, which also prohibits the alienation of ecclesiastical property.[54]

The alleged misuse of the Holy Saviour's property was one of its complaints against Archbishop Berardus; were these marginalia related to that dispute? In the margin between the texts of canons 4 and 5 of Sardica, which grant deposed bishops the right to take their cases to the bishop of Rome for appeal, our reader left one of his typical crosses with the words 'look well'.[55] Sardica c. 5 is quoted in a section of the canons of Carthage, at which the reader inserted yet another cross and the words 'here again, pay attention'.[56] The Holy Saviour did indeed appeal its case to the papal court in 1218, albeit unsuccessfully. That one could appeal to the Roman pontiff was well-established in the Western church by the thirteenth century, but the concept would have been unfamiliar to many Byzantines,

[49] *Fontes III* 3.18–22 (no. 3), 32–33 (no. 14), 33–34 (no. 15), 46 (no. 27), 52–53 (no. 29), 78 (no. 52), 79 (no. 52a), 84–87 (no. 60), 98 (no. 68), 98–99 (no. 69), 140 (no. 103), 141–142 (no. 104), 143 (no. 107), 151–152 (no. 113), 160–161 (no. 116), 163–164 (no. 120), 165 (no. 129), 184–185 (no. 138). On the ADM documents, see Enzensberger (2000): 225.

[50] Vall. C 11.1, fol. 347v–348r. Martini (1902): 57 (no. 33) and; Kehr (1903): 125 both mention the existence of this document, but neither provide any specific details on it. I am indebted to my former colleague Joel Pattison for his invaluable help in reading the Latin text.

[51] '*ὅρα καλῶς*': Vall. C 11.1, fol. 177v.

[52] Particularly II Nicaea c. 19–21 (fols. 178v–179v), *Prot.* c. 2–5 (fols. 184v–185v).

[53] '*ὅρα*': Vall. C 11.1, fol. 279r, alongside the *C25C* version of Just. *Nov.* 120; text in Heimbach (1840): 145–201, at 199.

[54] Vall. C 11.1, fol. 331v; text in Van der Wal and Stolte (1994): 139.

[55] Vall. C 11.1, fol. 101r.

[56] '*ἐνταύθα πάλιν πρόσεχε σεαυτὸν*': Vall. C 11.1, fol. 106v.

which is presumably why the reader felt the need to highlight these texts. He also annotated *Protodeutera* c. 9, which states that priests who physically strike sinners (whether by their own hand or by ordering someone else to do so) should be deposed; it further states that the secular authorities should enforce the law if the cleric does not agree to reform.[57] Again, this elaborates a legal principle that seems to relate to the Holy Saviour's dispute: after the failure of its appeal before the papal curia, the monastery turned to the secular authority, Frederick II, for protection.

It is impossible to fathom exactly how the manuscript was used from the marginalia alone. Nevertheless, one cannot help but notice how they were all made by the same hand and seem to respond to aspects of the Holy Saviour's dispute with Berardus and Honorius. Faced with an archbishop whose authority he was unwilling to recognise, the archimandrite seems to have consulted his nomocanon to plan his legal strategy: he made an appeal to the papal curia (Sard. c. 4, 5) on the grounds that the archbishop was alienating the monastery's property (II Nicaea c. 12 et al.). When this failed, he turned instead to the secular power, Frederick II (*Prot.* c. 9). That the Holy Saviour of Messina would use an early twelfth-century Byzantine nomocanon to help shape its legal strategy seems naïve in hindsight, yet it makes sense when viewed against the background of legal autonomy that the monastery had enjoyed in the twelfth century. The archimandrites of Messina had followed the Byzantine canons ever since the 1130s and may have been unfamiliar with the legal procedure of the Roman church.

Ultimately, the Holy Saviour's independence from papal and episcopal authority only lasted as long as the Hohenstaufen dynasty; it was brought to an end with Charles of Anjou's conquest in 1266. Yet it was not the only Italo-Greek monastery to resist the papacy during the Hohenstaufen years. As we saw in Chapter 5, St Nicholas of Casole in the Salento peninsula also received a royal exemption from Frederick II at some point during his reign.[58] The documentation for this monastery is worse than for the Holy Saviour, but there is a clue in the opening folia of the manuscript of its *typikon*.[59] A marginal note records that a cardinal named Randulf visited on 14th November 1266 to reconsecrate the monastery church and replace its abbot Basil with a certain Jacob.[60] Another note in the same manuscript states that, on 2nd April 1267, the new abbot Jacob paid the customary tithe (*decima*) to the church of Rome, 'and we settled our debt for the previous 25 [!] years'.[61] The monastery had not paid tithes since 1241/2. Like the Holy Saviour of Messina, St Nicholas of Casole had evidently decided to cast its lot in

[57] Vall. C 11.1, fol. 186^{v}. [58] See Chapter 5, 'Monastic Nomocanons I', C5.P32.

[59] Taur. gr. 216, fol. 4^{r}. Text in Hoeck and Loenertz (1965): 12–13 (n. 23). See also Mazzotta (1989): 30.

[60] Hoeck and Loenertz (1965): 13 suggest that this was Rudolf of Chevrières, who had been papal legate to the Terra d'Otranto the previous year.

[61] '...καὶ ἐπληρώσαμεν αὐτὸν διὰ κε΄ παρεληλυθότα ἔτη...': Taur. gr. 216, fol. 1^{v}.

with the Hohenstaufen rather than submit to the authority of the pope or the archbishop of Otranto. The effort was to prove futile in both cases, however, thanks to the Angevin conquest.

Conclusion

The thirteenth century marks a turning point for the religious law of the Italo-Greek church. From the pontificate of Innocent III onwards, Roman popes made a concerted effort to reorder the whole church—including the Greeks and other non-Latins—according to the vision set out by the Fourth Lateran Council and later codified in Gregory IX's *Decretals* (*Liber extra*) of 1234. This vision did not have room for Italo-Greek archimandrites and bishops who followed their own legal regime and rejected the primacy of the popes.

Enforcing papal policy was easier said than done, of course. The thirteenth-century conflict between pro-papal Guelphs and pro-imperial Ghibellines in the 1220s–1260s gave cover to influential monasteries like the Holy Saviour of Messina and St Nicholas of Casole, frustrating any Roman plans to reorganise 'Basilian' monasticism under Grottaferrata's leadership. Nevertheless, the demise of the Norman Hauteville dynasty created an opening for papal control over the Sicilian church; the Angevin conquest made it a reality.

The Fourth Lateran Council was the beginning of the end of Byzantine canon law as a juridical system in medieval southern Italy. Henceforth, with the exception of internal monastic discipline, the Italo-Greek nomocanons lost their practical purpose as sources of legal authority; all judicial matters would be settled in Latin church courts according to Latin canon law. Yet, for the time being, it did not mark the end of the nomocanon in southern Italy, as Italo-Greeks continued to copy and read the manuscripts until at least the early fourteenth century. We shall explore how and why they did so in the final two chapters.

9
The Salentine Group

At least six known surviving Greek nomocanonical codices were produced in southern Italy in the years after the Fourth Lateran Council. Considering the uncertainties surrounding the dating of other manuscripts, the real number is undoubtedly higher. Although a small number of these were of Calabrian or possibly Sicilian origin, the majority belonged to a set of eleven manuscripts that I refer to as the 'Salentine Group'. Before we turn to a more broad-ranging discussion of their purpose in Chapter 10, this chapter will first introduce the codicological, palaeographical, and textual features of the Salentine Group.

As we saw in Chapter 3, the group is a collection of nomocanons characterised by recurring, idiosyncratic codicological features and textual content that sets them apart from the other manuscripts in this study.[1] Even the two nomocanons of St Nicholas of Casole, Barb. gr. 324 and BnF gr. 1371, have little in common with the Salentine Group, as a result of which I have discussed them separately in Chapters 5 and 6.[2] That the group has survived at all, let alone in such numbers, is a testament to the unique nature of the Salentine book market during the Renaissance.

The manuscripts are interesting not only for their codicology and content. Unlike the nomocanons that we have seen in previous chapters, which were produced for abbots, bishops, and judges, the Salentine Group manuscripts appear to have primarily been read by priests. Whereas abbots and bishops played an active role in the judicial process, priests and other lower orders traditionally did not. The fact that priests, who did not normally require canon law collections, were so interested in acquiring the manuscripts indicates a broader shift in the role of nomocanons among the Italo-Greeks from that of legal to cultural authorities.

Salentine Priests as Copyists and Readers of Nomocanons

The Salento peninsula seems to have become a major centre of manuscript production in the second half of the twelfth century, a status it maintained all the way into the sixteenth.[3] What makes the region unique is the abundant

[1] See Chapter 3, 'Patterns of Source Survival', C3.P24.
[2] See Chapter 5, 'Monastic Nomocanons I', C5.P32; Chapter 6, 'Monastic Nomocanons II', C6.S3.
[3] See Chapter 3, 'Patterns of Source Survival', C3.S2; Appendix 2, 'Statistical Overview', CA2.F2*f*.

Byzantine Religious Law in Medieval Italy. James Morton, Oxford University Press (2021). © James Morton.
DOI: 10.1093/oso/9780198861140.003.0010

evidence for the role of non-monastic Greek clergy in copying books. Of the extant Salentine manuscripts with colophons, five were produced by monks, two by laypeople, and *twenty-seven* by secular priests.[4] Perhaps surprisingly, only six Salentine manuscripts (of any kind) have ties to the monastery of St Nicholas of Casole.[5] This stands in stark contrast to Calabria and Sicily, where monks of important centres like Rossano and Messina are far more prominent in surviving colophons.

As we have seen previously, this is partly a consequence of patterns of source survival: most Salentine manuscripts were acquired not from monasteries but from towns such as Soleto where there were still literate Greek clergy during the Renaissance. However, it is also a result of the region's strong tradition of Greek parish schools that dated back to at least the thirteenth century.[6] A good example of this is the fascinating manuscript BnF gr. 549, a mid-thirteenth-century copy of Niketas of Herakleia's commentary on the *Discourses* of Gregory of Nazianzus.[7] It was owned by a parish school in Aradeo (a village about 16km from Gallipoli) and contains Greek annotations left by teachers and students from the years 1280 to 1320 as well as a list of books in the school's library. From notes left in the manuscript it appears that the school was run by a priest named Philip de Strudà; he had a son, Nicholas, who served as a deacon.[8]

Priests were also some of the most avid readers of Greek manuscripts in the Salento. The earliest manuscript of the *typikon* of St Nicholas of Casole contains a fascinating list of sixty-eight books that were loaned out externally by the monastery's library in the fourteenth century.[9] Not only does it give the names of the borrowers, but it also states their professions. An astonishing thirty-nine were priests and only two were monks; a further five were deacons and three were laypeople (two notaries and a judge).[10] Intriguingly, one of the loans was a nomocanon borrowed by a priest named Andrew from Vignacastrisi (a small town near S. Cesarea Terme).[11] The list indicates that the Salento's Greek priests were active readers and some of the region's most frequent library users.

This is the context in which the Salentine Group was produced. Unfortunately, only a few of the manuscripts contain clues that would allow us to identify their scribes or places of origin. Ambros. F 48 sup. bears a heavily faded note of possession stating that it was one of a collection of books belonging to '[the

[4] Jacob (1980): 62, 70–77.

[5] In addition to Barb. gr. 324 and BnF gr. 1371, these are: Taur. gr. 216 (the monastery's *typikon*); Vatican City, Biblioteca Apostolica Vaticana, MS Barb. gr. 350; Paris, Bibliothèque nationale de France, MS gr. 1685; Milan, Biblioteca Ambrosiana, MS B 39 sup.

[6] Jacob (1986).

[7] Paris, Bibliothèque nationale de France, MS gr. 549. See Jacob (1985b); Arnesano and Sciarra (2010).

[8] Jacob (1985b): 291.

[9] Taur. gr. 216, fols. 181^r, 182^v.

[10] Chiriatti (2017): 434.

[11] 'The priest Andrew of Vignacastrisi has borrowed a nomocanon' ('*ὁ ἱερεὺς Ἀνδρέας τοῦ Βινιακαστρίσι ἔχει δανεικόν νομο[κάνονον]*': Chiriatti (2017): 436. This may have been Barb. gr. 324, which belonged to Casole and has the word 'nomocanon' in its title.

church?] of our righteous father St Lawrence'.[12] This is most likely S. Lorenzo *fuori le mura* in Mesagne (approximately 10km south of Brindisi), a Greek church that predates the Norman conquest and still retains traces of its medieval iconography.[13] Ambros. E 94 sup. may have been copied in Soleto since that is where the agents of the Biblioteca Ambrosiana purchased it.[14] Only one of the manuscripts can be dated with precision: BnF gr. 1370 retains just enough of its colophon to reveal that it was copied in 1297/6.[15] Besides this instance, the other codices can only be dated by their script; most are consistent with Salentine styles of the late twelfth and thirteenth centuries.[16]

The majority of the group were likely copied by members of the clergy. Not only is this a statistical probability given what we know about Salentine scribes, but their textual content is heavily biased towards subjects that would concern Greek priests such as clerical marriage.[17] Moreover, three of the manuscripts contain a fascinating *opusculum* entitled *The Ecclesiastical Ranks* (*οἱ ἐκκλησιαστικοὶ βαθμοί*).[18] It provides a list of the ranks in a parish church alongside the equivalent Latin terminology written in Greek letters:

First the gatekeeper [*pyloros*], whom the Latins call *hostiarius*, who is a *deputatus* [lay attendant].

Second the reader [*anagnostes*], whom they call *lector*, who is one of the clergy.

Third the exorcist [*eporkistes*], whom they call *exorcista*.

Fourth the server [*hyperetes*], whom they call *acoluthus*.

Fifth the subdeacon [*hypodiakonos*], whom they call the same thing.

Sixth the deacon [*diakonos*], whom they call the same thing.

Seventh the priest [*presbyteros*], whom they call the same thing.[19]

[12] '+ *ταῦ[τα] εἰσίν [τῆς ἐκκλησίας?] ἁγίου ὁσίου π(ατ)ρ(ὸ)ς ἡμων Λαυρεντίου* . . .': Ambros. F 48 sup., fol. i^r. The rest of the note is virtually illegible. Jacob (2001): 38 proposed on palaeographical grounds that the copyist of Ambros. F 48 sup. was the monk Joacheim (active *c.* 1110–1120). If true, it is still possible that he copied it for the church of S. Lorenzo. He also attributes Barocci 86 to the priest Kalos (first half of the twelfth century): Jacob (2001): 41.

[13] See Andreano (2000); Brunella (2004).

[14] See Chapter 3, 'Patterns of Source Survival', C3.P31.

[15] The manuscript's colophon reads, '[This book] was written . . . [approximately ten lines missing] in the year 6805 [= 1296/7]' ('*ἐγ[ράφη]* . . . *καου* [?] + *ἐν ἔτει ͵ϛωε´*'): BnF gr. 1371, fol. 143^r. Astruc (1988): 42 cast doubt on the dating of the manuscript, suggesting that the colophon was written by a different hand from the main text. I find this unconvincing; the text is located in the exact place we would expect a colophon and reads like a colophon. Moreover, it was not unusual for a scribe to write the colophon in a different style from the main text.

[16] See section: 'Salentine Style', C9.S2.

[17] See section: 'Textual Content and Relationship', p. C9.S3.

[18] Ambros. B 107 sup., fol. 4^v; Marc. gr. III.2, fol. 6^v; Sin. gr. 397, fol. 11^r. The text may also have been present in other members of the Salentine Group, but four of the manuscripts have lost the opening folia in which we would expect to find it.

[19] '*πρώτος πυλωρός. ὁ παρὰ λατίνων ὁστιάριος λεγόμενος, ἤτοι δεπὸτατος. δεύτερος ἀναγνώστης. ὁ παρ᾽ αὐτοῖς λέκτωρ λεγόμενος, ἤτοι κληρικὸς. τρίτος ἐπορκιστὴς. ὁ παρ᾽ αὐτοῖς ἐξορκιστὴς λεγόμενος.*

The same text also occurs in Milan, Biblioteca Ambrosiana, MS F 10 sup., a fourteenth-century compilation on fasting practices that was acquired by the Ambrosiana in 1606 from Cutrofiano in the Salento. I have not encountered the list in any non-Salentine manuscripts, though it does bear a passing resemblance to a Latin aetiological text entitled *De septem gradibus aecclesiae* in a twelfth-century Beneventan canon law collection studied by Roger Reynolds.[20] The Greek tract lacks the Beneventan manuscript's Biblical explanations and lists altar servers among the ranks rather than bishops, but there are enough similarities to suggest that an indirect relationship is possible. If so, it may be the only instance of Latin textual influence on the Italo-Greek nomocanons in the twelfth to thirteenth centuries.

In two of the manuscripts that contain this list of ecclesiastical ranks, Marc. gr. III.2 and Sin. gr. 397, the scribes' marginalia reveal a great interest in canons 6–10 of the Council of Antioch. These canons focus on the relationship between bishops and the different ranks of clergy beneath them.[21] The scribe of Sin. gr. 397 also highlighted Chalc. c. 18 (which forbids clergy from conspiring against each other or their bishops), remarking that 'this agrees very much with canon 35 [actually 34] of the [council] *in Trullo*', which he also highlighted.[22] One can only speculate as to what aroused his interest in this canon.

It is not difficult to imagine who would be interested in texts on the hierarchy of roles within parish churches (with their Latin equivalents) or canons on the relationship between priests and bishops. Many or even most of the Salentine Group were evidently copied by and for the region's secular Greek priests like the Fr Andrew of Vignacastrisi mentioned in Taur. gr. 216 who borrowed a nomocanon from St Nicholas of Casole. This is curious: nomocanons in the Byzantine world were normally the tools of bishops and abbots, figures who played an important role in the judicial process. Why would priests want to consult them?

τέταρτος ὑπηρέτης. ὁ παρ' αὐτοῖς ἀκολούθος λεγόμενος. πέμπτος ὑποδιάκονος. ὁμοίως καὶ παρ' αὐτοῖς. ἕκτος διάκονος. ὁμοίως καὶ παρ'αὐτοῖς. ἕβδομος πρεσβύτερος. ὁμοίως καὶ παρ' αὐτοῖς.'

[20] 'This is how Christ instituted the seven ranks. The reader was when the prophet Isaiah produced his book and said, "The Spirit of the Lord is upon me." [Isaiah 61:1] The exorcist was when he [Christ] cast out six demons from Mary Magdalen. The subdeacon was when he made wine from water in Cana of Galilee. The deacon was when he washed the feet of his disciples. The priest was when he took bread, blessed it, broke it, and gave it to his disciples. He instituted those five ranks before his passion. The gatekeeper was when he said, "Lift up your heads, o ye gates." [Psalm 24:7, 9] The bishop was when he raised his hand over his disciples and blessed them' ('*quomodo implevit Christus septem gradus. lector fuit quando apparuit librum Esayae propheta et dixit Spiritus Domini super me. exorcista fuit quando eiecit sex demones de Maria Magdalena. subdiaconus fuit quando fecit de acqua vinum in Cana Galileae. diaconus fuit quando lavit pedes discipulorum suorum. sacerdos fuit quando accepit panem, benedixit ac fregit deditque discipulis suis. istos quinque gradus ante passionem suam implevit. hostiarius fuit quando dixit "Tollite portas, principes vestras." episcopus fuit quando levavit manu* [*sic*] *super discipulos suos et benedixit eos*': New York, Hispanic Society of America, MS HC 380/819, fol. 109^{v}). Text in Reynolds (1987): 493–494.

[21] Marc. gr. III.2, fols. 24^{v}–25^{r}; Sin. gr. 397, fol. 23^{v}.

[22] '*πάνυ τοῦτο ὁμοφωνεῖ ὁ λε´ κανῶν τῆς ἐν τῷ Τρούλλῳ*': Sin. gr. 397, fol. 38^{r}.

As we shall see later in this chapter, C9.S4, the answer to this question reveals a great deal about the role of Byzantine canon law in southern Italy from the thirteenth century on.

Salentine Style: Codicological and Palaeographical Characteristics

In terms of their appearance, the manuscripts are similar in some ways to the traditional monastic nomocanons discussed in Chapter 6.[23] Most are relatively small: folio dimensions are in the range of roughly 180 × 120 to 220 × 170 mm. Decorative elements are sparse and hierarchical (i.e. they are most impressive at the beginning of the manuscript), while texts are arranged in a single-column *mise-en-page*. The materials are of a relatively low quality and the scribes evidently tried to make the most cost-efficient use of the writing space available to them. This accords with previous studies' observations on the apparent unavailability of high-quality parchment and paper in the Salento that resulted in a prevalence of palimpsests among the region's manuscripts.[24] Surprisingly enough, only one of the Salentine Group, the fragment Ottob. gr. 186 (fols. 9–22), is a palimpsest, though it may simply be the case that other such manuscripts have been lost.

However, the manuscripts of the Salentine Group also possess a remarkable body of shared codicological features and idiosyncratic aesthetics that distinguish them from the other Italo-Greek nomocanons. One of the most striking characteristics is their unusual ruling types. Of the eleven codices in the group, the ruling type is visible in ten (Ottob. gr. 186, a fragmentary palimpsest, is the exception). Of these ten, nine are ruled in the X index, which is to say that there are two written lines for every rule line, giving the page an unusual 'laddered' appearance (see Figure 9.1).[25]

To put this in context, Sautel and Leroy's reference work on Greek manuscript ruling lists the types of approximately 3,780 codices from throughout the medieval world; among these, I have only counted 167—a mere 4.4 per cent—that have X-pattern ruling. The frequent recurrence of this type of ruling in the Salentine Group is obviously not a coincidence and suggests that they were the products of a coherent local tradition of book production (a point that will be corroborated by the study of their textual contents below).

Jacob's work has found that this remarkable codicological feature appears to have been characteristic of Greek manuscripts from the Salento more broadly.[26]

[23] See ch.Chapter 6, 'Monastic Nomocanons II', C6.S1.

[24] 'Palimpsests are innumerable in the Terra d'Otranto. One can affirm without exaggeration that copyists or their assistants carved up everything they could put their hands on': Jacob (1980): 55. See also Canart (1978): 114–115.

[25] See Sautel and Leroy (1995): 27.

[26] Jacob (1977): 273.

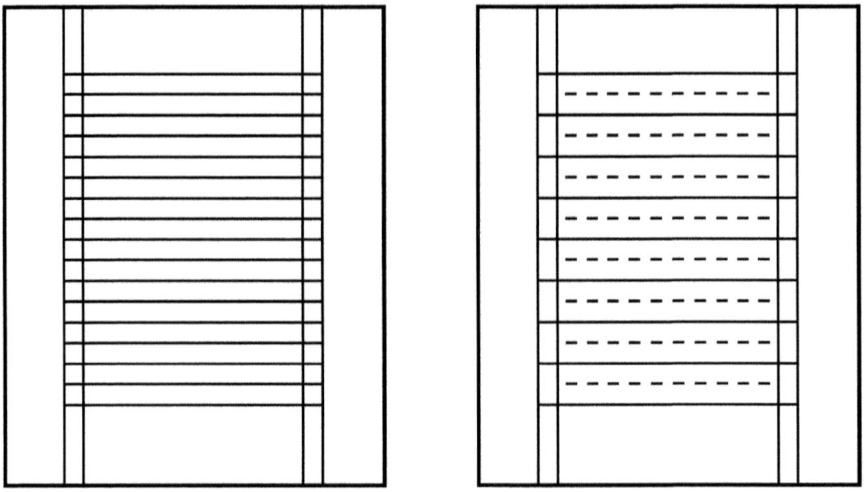

Figure 9.1. Ruling Types 20D1 (Left) and X20D1 (Right). Solid lines represent text written on rule lines; dashed lines represent text with no rule lines.

There does not seem to be a practical purpose for ruling a quire in this fashion; if anything, one would think that it would make the scribe's task slightly harder. It seems instead to be a regional custom. It is notable, though, that the two Casulan nomocanons, Barb. gr. 324 and BnF gr. 1371, are not ruled in the X index. This is one of many indications that the nomocanons of the Salentine Group were not the products of monastic *scriptoria.*

X-pattern ruling is not entirely unique to Salentine manuscripts: it is also present in Vat. gr. 2115 (fols. 78–96) and Crypt. gr. 76, both civil law collections from northern Calabria. The former is a heavily damaged fragment that unfortunately does not permit further analysis, while the latter dates to the late twelfth or early thirteenth century. This was a time when the Salento was becoming a more prominent centre of book production and when Salentine copyists seem to have become increasingly active in Calabria and Sicily, as Mario Re has argued.[27] The presence of X-pattern ruling in Crypt. gr. 76 may thus be a sign of the region's growing prominence in Italo-Greek manuscript production in this later period.

[27] 'It is probable . . . that there were other Greek copyists from the Salento who plied their trade on Calabrian or Sicilian soil, even before the end of the 13th century; in any case, in effect, it is possible to hypothesise such a presence on the basis of elements of a codicological and/or palaeographical nature discovered in surviving codices': Re (2004): 95. See also Jacob (1985a); Jacob (1993): 134. Besides Re's examples, we might also mention the monk Nikodemos who inscribed his name with a thirteenth-century hand in the Calabrian manuscript Barb. gr. 476: 'Remember, Lord, Brother Nikodemos of St Caesarea ('*μνηστητι* [*sic*] *κ*(*ύρι*)*ε του αδελφου νικοδιμου αγιας καισαρειας*': Barb. gr. 476, fol. 136v). As Mazzotta (1989): 66 has suggested, Nikodemos was probably a native of the modern S. Cesarea Terme on the southern coast of the Salento.

The scribal hands in the Salentine Group likewise conform to local traditions. The earliest of the manuscripts, Ambros. F 48 sup. and Vat. gr. 1287, offer textbook examples of the script that Jacob has called the 'classic style of Otranto'. This has a flat, narrow, rectangular form that gives the viewer 'a strong impression of archaism.'[28] Over time, the Salentine script evolved into a less hieratic form, a progression that can be traced in the Salentine Group nomocanons. By the early thirteenth century, we see the emergence of what Arnesano terms the 'baroque minuscule of Otranto', probably under the influence of twelfth-century Constantinopolitan fashion.[29] This appears in several of the later manuscripts under consideration, though one most strike a note of caution: there is a circularity to dating manuscripts on the basis of their calligraphic style and then explaining their calligraphic style by reference to their date. As we noted in chapter one, nomocanons often utilise scripts that appear older than they really are, so it is always possible that our reliance on palaeography (as necessary as it unfortunately is) leads us to misdate the manuscripts.[30]

BnF gr. 1370 provides an excellent example of this problem, as it can be dated precisely to 1296/1297. We can compare it to BnF gr. 2572, a schedographic manuscript copied in Aradeo in 1295/6.[31] Despite being produced within a year of one another in the same region of southern Italy, their scripts are remarkably different. BnF gr. 2572 closely resembles Arnesano's 'baroque minuscule', but the nomocanon BnF gr. 1370 looks much more like the older 'classic style'. Were it not for the damaged colophon at the end, it would be tempting to date the manuscript to earlier in the thirteenth century.

The most 'baroque' of all the scripts in the Salentine Group belongs to Ambros. E 94 sup., which sadly cannot be dated with certainty. It bears a certain resemblance to the *Fettaugenstil* ('fat-eye style') common in the late Byzantine Empire (so-called because the rounded, expansive letterforms reminded the Austrian scholar Herbert Hunger of the globules of fat in a hearty Alpine soup).[32] This style became increasingly widespread in the Salento from the late thirteenth century on; given the conservatism of nomocanonical hands, Ambros. E 94 may have been copied as late as the fourteenth century.

Another aspect of the Salentine Group's appearance that sets the manuscripts apart is their decorative aesthetic. With the exception of the fragmentary Ottob. gr. 186 and Ambros. E 94 sup., the codices contain a remarkably consistent set of ornamental motifs based on the stylised form of twisted, leafy vines. Unlike the calligraphy in the manuscripts, these motifs remain surprisingly stable over time. Foremost among them is an impressive *pyle* that frames the manuscript's opening

[28] Jacob (1977): 270. [29] Arnesano (2008a): 23–29.

[30] See ch.Chapter 1, 'Introducing the Byzantine Nomocanon', C1.P31. If scholars have erred in dating the manuscripts, it is probably in favour of assuming that they are older than they really are.

[31] Paris, Bibliothèque nationale de France, MS gr. 2572. See Hoffmann (1984).

[32] Hunger (1972).

title, which is usually written in bold red uncials.[33] The *pyle* takes the shape of a rectangular arch filled with trailing and twisting vine tendrils; more vines, forming curved 'U' shapes, surmount the top and outer corners of the *pyle*. The exact layout varies from one manuscript to another, but the general idea is clearly the same in each case. I suspect that this patterning is based loosely on antecedents in Byzantine manuscripts of the tenth and eleventh centuries.[34]

The twisted-vine motif became the basis of a coherent stylistic repertoire in the Salentine Group that can be sub-divided into two groups: those that have a *pyle* drawn entirely in red ink (which, for want of a better term, I call the 'red-leaf' manuscripts) and those that have a combination of red and black ink (which I call the 'black-leaf' manuscripts). Another difference is that the design of the vine motifs seems to be stiffer and more geometric in the red-leaf manuscripts, whereas the black-leaf manuscripts have looser, more natural-seeming vines. Not all the manuscripts have retained their decorated opening folia, but the six that do are divided evenly between red- and black-leaf styles (see Table 9.1).

The red-leaf manuscripts seem to belong to an earlier period than the black-leaf, though the sample size is admittedly small and the chronology uncertain. Nevertheless, the chronological progression from stiff, geometric red-leaf designs to more naturalistic black-leaf ones seems to parallel the development in scribal hands from the rigid 'classic style of Otranto' to the more rounded 'baroque style'. It is also possible, of course, that the different styles denote different places of origin; we know of a wide range of Salentine towns where Greek copyists were active in the period, and it may be that some areas preferred one style over the other.[35]

In sum, these nomocanons were the product of a highly localised book culture among the Greeks of the Salento. Their copyists developed a recognisable visual style for the manuscripts that was rooted in Byzantine and Italo-Greek motifs yet still quite distinctive. The small scale of the codices suggests that the scribes did

Table 9.1. Red- and Black-Leaf Nomocanons

Red Leaf	Black Leaf
Ambros. F 48 sup. (*c.* 1110–1120)	Marc. gr. III.2 (C12/13)
Barocci 86 (C12)	Sin. gr. 397 (C13)
Laur. plut. 5.22 (C12/13)	BnF gr. 1370 (1296/7)

[33] Barocci 86, fol. 93^{v} (at the beginning of a summary of the canons of the Council *in Trullo*) also has a large, knotted rope-style headband in red and yellow ink that is reminiscent of some of the Calabrian nomocanons, but this is unique in the Salentine Group.

[34] Cf. e.g. Weitzmann (1935) nos. 41, 42, 103, 121, 143, 260, 457, 458, 470, 487, 489, 493, 498.

[35] Jacob (1977): 65 lists Galatina, Soleto, Gallipoli, Otranto, Maglie, Nardò, Aradeo, Sanarica, Melpignano, and Casole as towns with active Greek copyists in the thirteenth to fifteenth centuries.

not have access to the same quality of materials as the monasteries of twelfth-century Calabria or Sicily, but they made the most of what was available. There are strikingly few points similarities with the nomocanons of St Nicholas of Casole, a monastery that was long thought to be the main cultural centre of the Greek Salento. Rather, the Salentine Group nomocanons seem to have belonged to a different cultural or institutional world, which I have suggested was that of the secular clergy.

Textual Content and Relationship

The coherence of the Salentine Group as a related family of manuscripts becomes even clearer from their textual content. We touched on the subject briefly in chapter four, when we saw that six of the manuscripts are structured around an interesting combination of the *N50T* (supplemented by the full text of those canons promulgated after the *N50T* was composed) and the tenth-century *Synopsis of Canons*.[36] This forms one of two main stems within the group; the other had the full-text corpus of canons as its central feature. The two stems seem to have begun as separate manuscript traditions that, over time, gradually merged and cross-fertilised.

The Salentine Group's versions of the *N50T* and the corpus of canons are characteristically idiosyncratic, a point that helps us to trace the two stems' histories more easily. In the one that contains the corpus of canons, not only is the text of each council preceded by a brief historical introduction excerpted from a range of different sources, but the canons of II Nicaea and *Protodeutera* are inter-mixed in the wrong order, a quirk that I have not seen in other manuscripts. As for the stem containing the *N50T*, it is subdivided into two further groups: those that do not attribute the *N50T* to any author and those that (wrongly) attribute it to the late antique bishop Theodoret of Cyrrhus (c. 390–460).[37] As the late twelfth and thirteenth centuries progressed, a series of supplemental texts gradually accrued in the manuscripts until they came to form substantial appendices (see Table 9.2).

We shall discuss this daunting array of texts in more detail below. For the time being, we can use the textual comparisons to extrapolate an approximate stemma between the manuscripts (see Figure 9.2). The letters X, Y, and Z represent the earlier generations of the *N50T* that lie behind the Salentine Group.

[36] See ch.Chapter 4, 'The Byzantine Background', C4.P16. A further two manuscripts, Add. 28822 and Vat. gr. 1287, have the *N50T* alone; however, they are fragmentary, so it is possible that the *Synopsis of Canons* has simply been lost from both.

[37] The origin of the misattribution is unknown.

Table 9.2. The Salentine Group: Comparison of Textual Content

	A	B	C	D	E	F	G	H	I	J	K
Conciliar Canons (complete)	✓				✓			✓	[✓]	✓	✓
Conciliar Canons (partial)		✓	✓			✓	✓				
N50T (Unattributed)		✓	✓			✓				✓	✓
N50T (Theodoret)				✓				✓	✓		
Synopsis of Canons		✓				✓		✓	✓	✓	✓
The Ecclesiastical Ranks					✓			✓		✓	
Tome of Union (920)	✓			✓	✓		✓	✓	✓	✓	
Sisinnios II	✓	✓	✓	✓	✓	✓	✓	✓	✓	✓	✓
Alexios Stoudites				✓	✓		✓	✓	✓	✓	✓
Leo of Calabria				✓	✓		✓	✓	✓	✓	✓
Civil laws on marriage				✓	✓	✓	✓		✓	✓	✓
Apost. Const. (excerpts)				✓	✓			✓	✓	✓	✓
Rule of the Holy Apostles				✓	✓			✓	✓	✓	✓
I Nicaea, *Decree on Pascha*				✓	✓	✓		✓	✓	✓	✓
John Moschos 149				✓	✓			✓	✓		
Nikon of the Black Mountain				✓	✓			✓	✓		
Carthage (excerpts)				✓				✓	✓		
Photios, *Encyclical Letter*				✓				✓	✓		
Photios, *Five Can. Letters*						✓		✓	✓	✓	✓
II Const., *Actio* 8						✓				✓	✓
Proklos of Constantinople						✓				✓	✓
Victor of Carthage						✓				✓	✓
History of the Councils						✓				✓	✓
Theodoret, *Eccl. History*						✓				✓	✓
From the Life of Chrysostom										✓	✓
Nikephoros the Confessor										✓	✓
Leontios of Constantinople										✓	✓

Key:

A	Ambros. F 48 sup.	E	Ambros. B 107 sup.	I	BnF gr. 1370
B	Barocci 86	F	Laur. plut. 5.22	J	Sin. gr. 397
C	Vat. gr. 1287 (frag.)	G	Ottob. gr. 186 (frag.)	K	Ambros. E 94 sup.
D	Add. 28822 (frag.)	H	Marc. gr. III.2		

Note that this is only a general and incomplete illustration; we are ignorant of many or most of the nomocanons that were originally produced so it is not possible to give a strictly accurate account of how the surviving examples relate to one another. What does seem apparent is that the two stems based on the *N50T* and the corpus of canons ('X' and Ambros. F 48 sup. in the above figure) merged and then re-divided into two later groups. For simplicity's sake, I refer to the two later groups as 'Branch A' (Laur. plut. 5.22, Sin. gr. 397, Ambros. E 94 sup.) and 'Branch B' (Ambros. B 107 sup., Add. 28822, Marc. gr. III.2, BnF gr. 1370).

The earliest codices, Ambros. F 48 sup. and Barocci 86, were originally quite straightforward canon law collections. The former manuscript is fragmentary today, but its *pinax* survives (fol. 1^r–3^r) and confirms that it only contained the

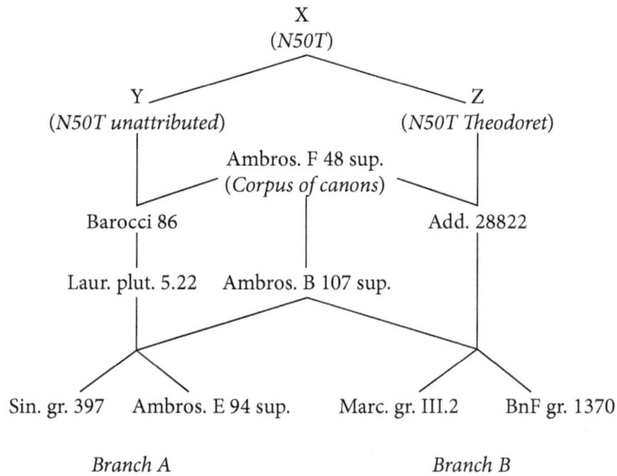

Figure 9.2. Approximate Relationship of the Salentine Group MSS (not including the fragmentary Vat. gr. 1287 or Ottob. gr. 186).

corpus of canons, Gennadios of Constantinople's *Encyclical Letter*, the *Tome of Union*, and the *Tome* of Sisinnios II.[38] Barocci 86 began life as an *N50T-Synopsis of Canons* combination, though at some point in its history (presumably the thirteenth century) two quires with texts on Latin-Greek controversies were inserted at the beginning of the codex and a reader added a set of miscellaneous notes on confession, the creed, and the illegality of marriages between godparents and godchildren at the end.

Around the end of the twelfth and beginning of the thirteenth century, however, scribes began to intentionally add a range of supplementary writings to the nomocanons.[39] In Laur. plut. 5.22 (descended from Barocci 86 or a related manuscript), the collection of canons is immediately followed by a text entitled On the Rights of the Most Holy Throne of Constantinople, an assemblage of quotations from Byzantine civil and canon law that is clearly meant to establish the Patriarchate of Constantinople as a legal and spiritual rival to the Roman papacy (the copyist's loyalties are difficult to miss).[40] This is followed by a short

[38] Texts in RP 4.368–374, 5.3–19.

[39] For a more comprehensive overview of these texts, many of which are short fragments, see Beneševič (1914): 33–69.

[40] Laur. plut. 5.22, fols. 165ᵛ–166ᵛ. Text in Beneševič (1906): 2.56–63. Schiano (2017): 212–213 has recently highlighted a marginal comment left by Nektarios of Otranto in the nomocanon Barb. gr. 324 alongside Chalc. c. 28 (fol. 67ᵛ), in which he quoted Just. *Cod.* 11.21 ('The City of Constantinople shall not only enjoy the privileges enjoyed by Italy, but also those of ancient Rome'). Schiano notes that the Justinianic law refers to the city's juridical and administrative status, not the rank of its patriarchate, and so postulates that Nektarios was making a legal argument based on the intrinsic correlation between Constantinople's administrative and ecclesiastical rank. This may be correct, but it is worth noting that the same law is cited in Laur. plut. 5.22, where it is quoted without context alongside other

selection of excerpts from Byzantine canon and civil law on marriage; later manuscripts would dramatically expand on it and we shall return to the topic below.

The scribe next assembled a group of theological texts from Late Antiquity that, when read together, convey an implicit but unmistakeable message. They begin with an extract from the eighth act of the Second Council of Constantinople (553) entitled: 'That one must not remain silent or retreat from those who speak against the truth or piety.'[41] Next comes an extract from a letter of Patriarch Proklos of Constantinople to Patriarch John of Antioch (c. 438) in which the writer warns the recipient to be on guard against heretics; this is followed in turn by an excerpt from a letter of Bishop Victor of Carthage to the Greek pope Theodore I of Rome (c. 647) asking him to quell the Monothelite heresy. The message of this group of texts is clear: orthodox Christians have a duty to speak up against heresy.

The Branch A nomocanons are mostly laconic on question of who the heretics are, leaving the reader to infer it from the various excerpts on fasting and marriage. The thirteenth-/fourteenth-century Ambros. E 94 sup. does contain one text that makes it clear, though: near the end of the manuscript is a tract headed: 'A *synodikon* [conciliar proclamation] promulgated in the city of Constantine by John the renowned Patriarch of Jerusalem.'[42] Louis Petit showed that this was John VIII (early twelfth century), a Greek patriarch who was forced into exile in Constantinople as a result of the First Crusade.[43] The *synodikon* begins by explaining that the papacy was formerly commemorated in the diptychs of Constantinople until the patriarchate of Sergios II (1001–1019), after which it 'was cut off [from Constantinople] because of the errors committed by the Romans.'[44] It enumerates a list of Latin theological errors, chief among which was the Filioque. The *synodikon* stops short of accusing the Latins of heresy outright, yet, by including it in the nomocanon, it appears that the scribe of Ambros. E 94 sup. endorsed the Byzantine view that Rome was in theological error.

legal writings that promote the authority of the patriarch of Constantinople. Nektarios may have seen a similar textual compilation and simply assumed that Just. *Cod.* 11.21 referred to the patriarchate.

41 '*ὅτι οὐ δεῖ σιωπᾶν καὶ ὑποστέλλεσθαι τοῖς ἀντιλέγουσι τῇ ἀληθείᾳ ἤγουν τῇ εὐσεβείᾳ*': Laur. plut. 5.22, fol. 172^{r}; also Sin. gr. 397, fol. 125^{r}; Ambros. E 94 sup., fol. 219^{r}. Text in *ACO* 4.1.239.1–14.

42 '*συνοδικὸν ἐκτεθὲν ἐν Κωνσταντίνου πό[λει] παρὰ Ἰωάννου τοῦ ἀοιδίμου πατριάρ[χου] Ἱεροσολύμων*': Ambros. E 94 sup., fols. 230^{r}–235^{r}. The same text can also be found in Milan, Biblioteca Ambrosiana, MS A 45 sup., fols. 131^{v}–139^{v} and, under a different title, in Paris, Bibliothèque nationale de France, MS gr. 1295, fols. 26^{r}–29^{r}. It remains unedited at the time of writing.

43 Petit (1924).

44 '*μετὰ τούτον δὲ ἐξεκόπη δια τὰ ὑποτεταγμένα ῥωμαῖων σφάλματα*': Ambros. E 94 sup., fol. 230^{r}. This is a reference to Pope Sergius IV (*r.* 1009–1012), who, on his accession to the papacy, sent the customary declaration of faith to the Eastern patriarchs but included the *Filioque* in the Creed for the first time. In response, Sergios II of Constantinople refused to commemorate the pope's name in the diptychs, a traditional recognition of orthodoxy. The papacy was later restored to the Constantinopolitan diptychs in the reign of Alexios I Komnenos; see Bayer (2004): 36–45.

If the Branch A manuscripts are reticent about openly criticising the Roman church, the Branch B manuscripts (Add. 28822, Marc. gr. III.2, and BnF gr. 1370) show no such hesitation. Each one includes a copy of Photios' *Encyclical Letter to the Eastern Patriarchs* (c. 867).[45] This is a composite letter made by a later redactor of excerpts from Photian writings against perceived errors in the Western church, most notably the addition of the *Filioque* to the Creed, fasting incorrectly and on the wrong days, and the prohibition of clerical marriage.[46] Looking at the appendices to the Salentine Group nomocanons, it becomes clear that the manuscripts were copied for a readership that was increasingly critical of the Roman church and its practices as the thirteenth century progressed. The Branch B manuscripts are certainly more overt in this, but it is also implicit in Branch A.

'Against the Latins': Critical Concerns of the Salentine Greek Clergy

The Salentine Group were not the first Italo-Greek nomocanons to contain texts that criticised Latin-rite Christians; this was true also of those manuscripts produced in Calabria during and immediately after the Norman conquest, as we saw in Chapter 4.[47] What is interesting, however, is the character of the criticism. The Calabrian manuscripts focused on issues that had arisen during the mid-eleventh century, above all the *azyma*. By contrast, the *azyma* are barely mentioned in the Salentine Group and eleventh-century polemicists like Niketas Stethatos are nowhere to be seen.

Instead, the Salentine manuscripts have two principle interests: marriage and fasting. The two earliest manuscripts of the group, Ambros. F 48 sup. and Barocci 86, touched on marriage to a limited extent by including the texts of the *Tome of Union* (920) and Patriarch Sisinnios II's *Tome against the Marriage of Cousins* (997).[48] As Tia Kolbaba noted, the Byzantines had a stereotype in the eleventh and twelfth centuries that Westerners liked to marry their cousins, which may be implicit in the inclusion of Sisinnios' decree.[49] Nevertheless, the texts' presence is not unusual in a nomocanon and may simply reflect a natural interest in marriage law.

Later Salentine nomocanons added a further fixed collection of legal texts on marriage: Alexios Stoudites' *Synodal Act on Marriage* (1038), *Ekloge* 2.2, and a canonical *erotapokrisis* by a certain 'Leo of Calabria'.[50] Like the *Tome of Union*

[45] Add. 28822, fols. 37ᵛ–43ʳ; BnF gr. 1370, fols. 196ᵛ–201ᵛ; Marc. gr. III.2, fols. 163ᵛ–169ᵛ. Text in *PG* 101.721–742.

[46] For a recent discussion of the text's history, see Turner (2016): 480.

[47] See Chapter 4, 'The Byzantine Background', C4.S3.

[48] Barocci 86 only seems to have included Sisinnios' *Tome* (fols. 144ᵛ–145ʳ).

[49] Kolbaba (2000): 44–46.

[50] The *Tome of Union*, *Tome* of Sisinnios II, and the *Synodal Act* of Alexios Stoudites are also all present in Vat. gr. 2019, fols. 114ᵛ–117ᵛ.

and *Tome* of Sisinnios, Alexios Stoudites' *Act* and the excerpt from the *Ekloge* both outline prohibited degrees of marriage. Leo of Calabria's canonical *erotapokrisis* has the distinction of being the only surviving Greek canon law text to have been composed in southern Italy itself.[51] It begins with a question submitted by a priest named John to 'the teacher of teachers and my spiritual father, Leo Grammatikos, archbishop of Calabria'.[52] Jean-Marie Martin has demonstrated that this Leo was archbishop of Reggio from *c.* 878 and may still have held the see when it was elevated to metropolitan status in 886.[53] John has a very specific question to ask: 'There is a certain cleric, teacher, who married a woman, and he wants to be ordained a priest before cohabiting with her, expecting to take her virginity after his ordination. Tell me if this is possible.'[54] Leo answers that it is not possible: a person is not truly married until he has consummated the union with his wife. If the cleric tried to consummate the union after his ordination, it would be a kind of fornication since Byzantine clergy could only marry *before* their ordination (a rule that is still in force in the modern Orthodox Church).[55] The cleric must take his wife's virginity 'legally', i.e. before becoming a priest.

As useful as it is to know this, it seems unlikely that the Greek clergy of the thirteenth-century Salento were especially concerned with exactly when a priest could consummate his marriage. The main interest for readers, I suspect, lay in the fact that a priest could marry or cohabit with a wife *at all*, something that the ninth-century *erotapokrisis* takes for granted. By the thirteenth-century, Latin-rite priests were strictly forbidden from marrying or cohabiting with women. Although Greek priests were still permitted to do so, Western popes and canonists often worried that this could set a bad example for their own clergy.[56] Greek- and Latin-rite communities lived in close proximity to one another in the Salento, so it is not difficult to see how the marriage issue could have been a source of controversy.[57] Indeed, we have a surviving example of this in the mid-thirteenth century manuscript Laur. plut. 5.36, which contains a polemical defence of the use of crowns in the Byzantine marriage rite by a priest of Taranto named Nicholas.[58]

The Salentine nomocanons are the only surviving manuscripts to contain Leo's *erotapokrisis*. If clerical marriage had not been a controversial topic in the Salento,

[51] The text of Leo's *erotapokrisis* can be found in *PG* 120.177–180.

[52] '*τῷ καθηγητῇ τῶν καθηγητῶν καὶ πνευματικῷ μοῦ πατρὶ κυρῷ Λέοντι τῷ Γραμματικῷ καὶ ἀρχιεπισκόπῳ Καλαβρίας Ἰωάννης πρεσβύτερος δοῦλος Ἰησοῦ Χρίστου ἀνάξιος*': *PG* 120.177.

[53] Martin (1998): 481–485.

[54] '*κληρικός τις ἔγημε γυναῖκα, διδάσκαλε, καὶ πρὶν ἢ συνοικῆσαι αὐτὸν τῇ γαμετῇ, βούλεται χειροτονηθῆναι πρεσβύτερος, ἐκδεχόμενος μετὰ τὴν χειροτονίαν ἐκπαρθενεῦσαι αὐτὴν. εἰ οὖν ἔξεστι τοῦτο, δήλωσόν μοι*': *PG* 120.177.

[55] The view that sexual consummation was necessary for a valid marriage was shared by several Western canonists such as Gratian and Rolandus; see Brundage (1987): 260–278.

[56] Brundage (1973): 1080; more recently, see Perisanidi (2017).

[57] Safran (2014): 128–132.

[58] Florence, Biblioteca Medicea Laurenziana, MS plut. 5.36, fols. 1r–3v. See Quaranta (2001).

the text would not have survived at all.[59] Other texts on clerical marriage feature too. Both Ambros. B 107 sup. and Marc. gr. III.2, for example, have a short anecdote on 'Paphnoutios the bishop, who was from a city in the Upper Thebaid'.[60] The story tells of how the Fathers of the First Council of Nicaea were planning to prohibit priests from having conjugal relations with their wives, prompting the Egyptian bishop Paphnoutios to speak out and argue that celibacy was not necessary or helpful for married clergy (see Figure 9.3).[61] Since he was such a renowned ascetic, Paphnoutios' word carried the day. The anecdote was adapted from Socrates, *Ecclesiastical History* 1.11.1–17, as Saulo Delle Donne has observed, and appears alongside other texts on Latin-Greek controversies in another Salentine manuscript as well.[62] The text was also once present in the nomocanon Sin. gr. 397 (the manuscript has lost some leaves from the end), as we can see from a note left by the copyist in the margins of the introduction of I Nicaea instructing the reader to 'see the statement of Paphnoutios'.[63]

The Branch A manuscripts Sin. gr. 397 and Ambros. E 94 also contain short texts on Lenten fasting, which was a significant topic of controversy between Greeks and Latins in the Middle Ages, as we saw in Chapter 4.[64] Both have three canons of Patriarch Nikephoros the Confessor of Constantinople (806–815) on the subject: the first permits fish and wine on the Annunciation Feast if it should fall on Great Thursday or Friday of Holy Week, the second states that a sick monk may consume fish, wine, and oil during Lent, and the third mandates that monks should fast strictly on the Wednesday and Friday of Cheesefare Week.[65] Both manuscripts also include a lengthy extract from Leontios of Constantinople's (485–543) *Homily* 6, which was originally delivered on Great Thursday of Holy Week and criticises those who do not keep the Lenten fast properly. Sin. gr. 397 also has an excerpt from Patriarch John the Faster's (582–595) *Kanonarion*, which states that one should not consume meat, cheese, or eggs during Lent.[66] As Tia Kolbaba has discussed, medieval Western Christians did not have a Cheesefare Week, continued to eat fish during Lent, and sometimes gave permission to individuals to consume eggs and dairy products on Sundays.[67] The excerpts in the nomocanons appear to be targeted at these Western practices.

[59] Martin (1998): 482 was aware of BnF gr. 1370 and Ottob. gr. 186. It is present in every single Salentine Group manuscript except for Ambros. F 48 sup., Barocci 86, and Laur. plut. 5.22.

[60] '*Παφνούτιος ἐπίσκοπος, ὅστις ἦν ἐκ μίας πόλεως τῆς ἀνῶ Θηβαΐδος*': Ambros. B 107 sup., fol. 158^{v}; Marc. gr. III.2, fols. 128^{v}–129^{r}.

[61] See also Parrish (2010): 65–71, which includes an English translation of the anecdote.

[62] CCC gr. 486; Delle Donne (2014): 383.

[63] '*ζήτει τῆς ὑποθέσεως τοῦ Παφνουτίου*': Sin. gr. 397, fol. 8^{r}.

[64] Ambros. E 94 sup., fols. 221^{r}–222^{r}; Sin. gr. 397, fols. 126^{v}–127^{v}, 183$^{r/v}$. See Chapter 4, 'The Byzantine Background', C4.P36–C4.P42; see also Kolbaba (2000): 41–43.

[65] RP 4.427 (no. 5); Pitra (1868): 328, 331. They are numbered 3, 39, and 40 in Pitra's text. Cheesefare Week (*τυρόφαγος*) is the last week before the beginning of Lent, during which cheese and dairy products may be consumed but meat is forbidden.

[66] Text in Allen and Datema (1987): 211–219.

[67] Kolbaba (2000): 41–42.

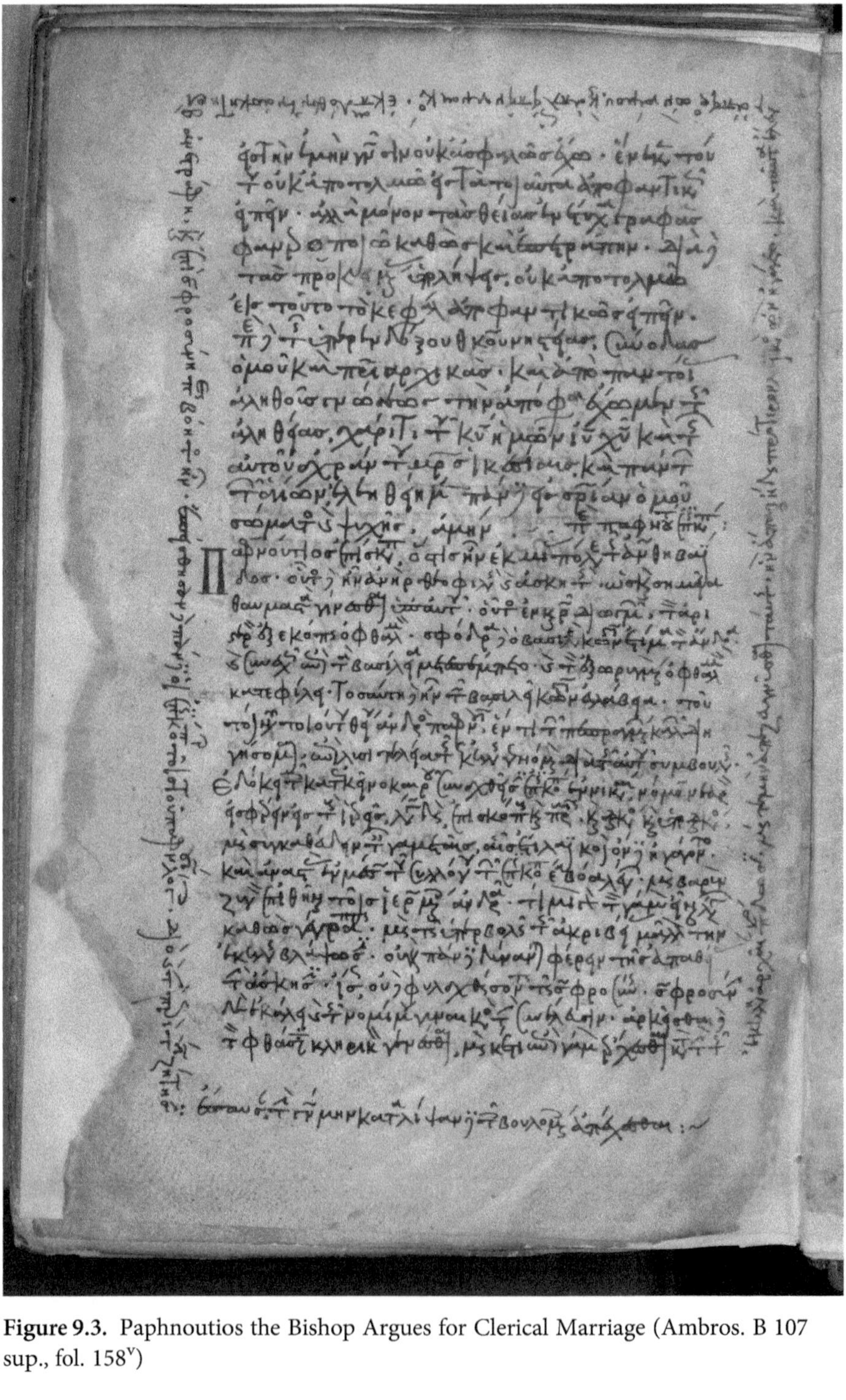

Figure 9.3. Paphnoutios the Bishop Argues for Clerical Marriage (Ambros. B 107 sup., fol. 158^{v})

As fascinating as the choice of texts are the marginalia that both the copyists and their readers added to the manuscripts. In particular, the more overtly anti-Latin Branch B manuscripts (Add. 28822, Marc. gr. III.2, and BnF gr. 1370) all contain a scribal annotation that I have not seen in any other nomocanons: '*κτ`λατ´*', an abbreviation of *κατὰ λατίνων* ('against the Latins'). This appears in the margins next to canons or canonical authorities that address controversial issues that separated the Latin and Greek rites (see Figure 9.4 and Table 9.3). Although it was not originally present in Ambros. F 48 sup. or B 107 sup., later hands of the thirteenth or fourteenth century added it to those manuscripts as well.

From an analysis of the hands, it appears that the annotations in BnF gr. 1370 and Marc. gr. III.2, in addition to at least two of those in Add. 28822, were made by the scribe who copied the manuscript. The annotations in Ambros. B 107 sup. and F 48 sup., which are older than the three aforementioned codices, seem to have been inserted by later hands (three different hands in the case of Ambros. F 48 sup.). Since the two Ambrosian manuscripts are older than the other three, this implies that the practice of tagging canons as 'against the Latins' began in later manuscripts—probably in the thirteenth century—and was then retroactively applied to earlier ones.

As the expression suggests, the annotation was used as a reference guide to help readers find canonical texts that were thought to contradict the religious practices of 'the Latins'. In most of the manuscripts, they are concentrated on the canons of the Council of Carthage (419), with some further additions in BnF gr. 1370. Ambros. B 107 sup. does not contain any of the Carthaginian canons, but the person who added the annotation allowed their hand to roam more widely through the canonical corpus.

The canons highlighted in Ambros. B 107 sup. are probably some of the most famous 'anti-Roman' ones.[68] Chalcedon c. 28 grants the see of Constantinople 'equal privileges' to those of Rome, while *Trullo* c. 13 and 55 explicitly criticise the Roman church for compelling clergy to live in celibacy and for fasting on the Sabbath during Lent (contrary to the practice of the Church of Constantinople).[69] *Trullo* c. 12 also relates to clerical marriage, stating that bishops should separate from their wives after ordination; the reader probably wanted to underline that the council required *bishops* to do this, not priests. On a related note, I Nicaea c. 3 affirms that bishops, priests, and deacons should not live with an unmarried woman (*subintroducta*) and Basil of Caesarea c. 89 underlines this point; presumably the annotator took this as a sign that clergy should only live with married women (i.e. their own wives).

Meanwhile, *Trullo* c. 52 decrees that the presanctified liturgy should be said instead of the regular liturgy on weekdays in Lent and canon 55 criticises the

[68] On the 'anti-Roman' canons of *Trullo*, see Ohme (1995).

[69] Cf. Chapter 4, 'The Byzantine Background', C4.S3.

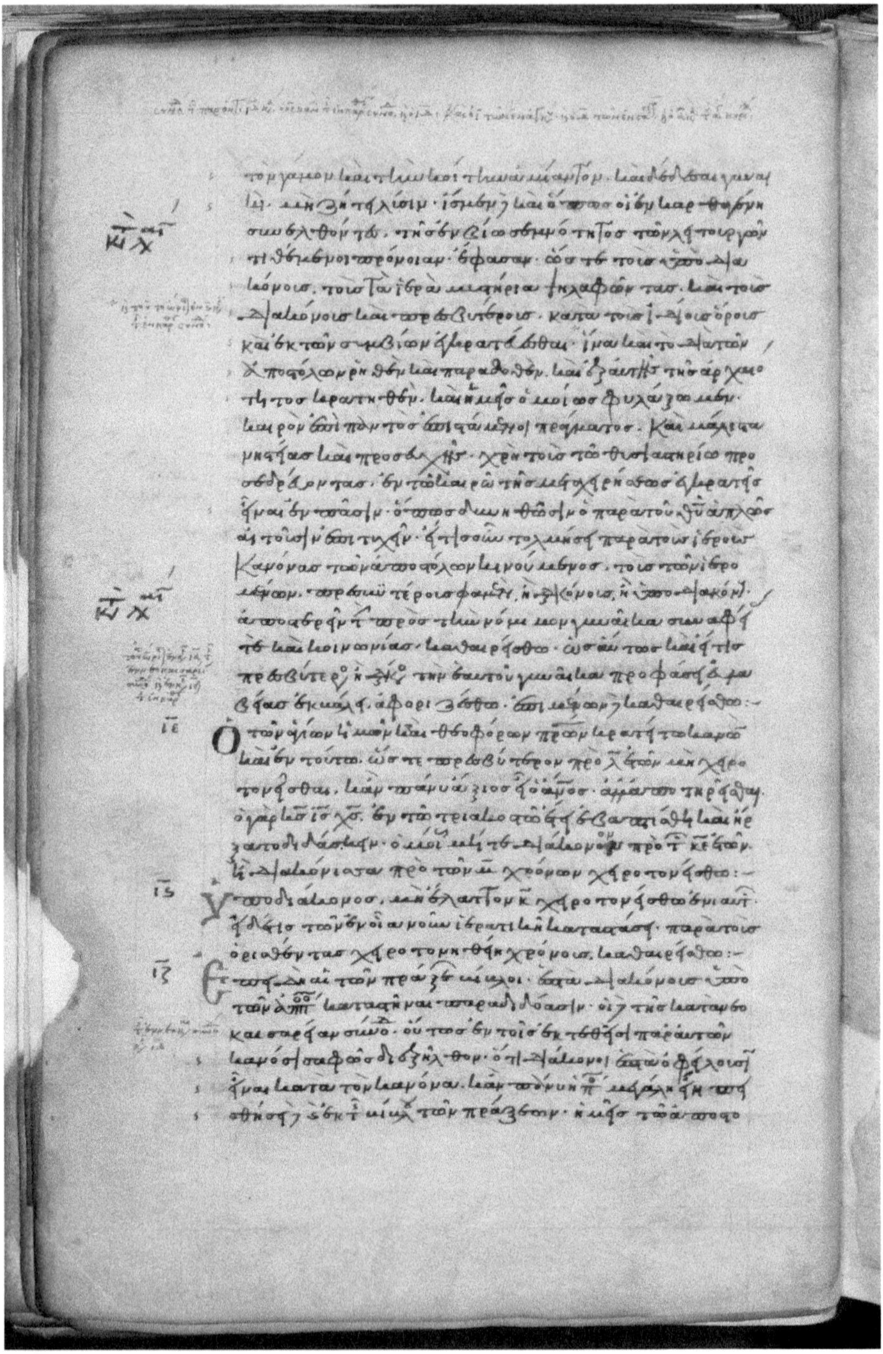

Figure 9.4. 'Against the Latins' (Ambros. B 107 sup., fol. 55[v])

Table 9.3. Occurrences of the 'Against the Latins' Annotation

Ambros. B 107 sup.		**Ambros. F 48 sup.**		**Add. 28822**	
2^{r}	Apostolic c. 53*	96^{r}	Carthage c. 15*	16^{r}	Carthage c. 25
6^{r}	I Nicaea c. 3*	96^{v}	Carthage c. 16*	16^{v}	Carthage c. 27*
41^{v}	Chalcedon c. 28*	97^{r}	Carthage c. 21*	25^{r}	Carthage c. 70
55^{r}	*Trullo* c. 12*				
55^{v}	*Trullo* c. 13*				
62^{v}	*Trullo* c. 52*, 55*				
63^{r}	*Trullo* c. 56*				
72^{r}	II Nicaea c. 4*				
107^{v}	Basil c. 89*				
148^{r}	*Apost. Const.* 1.3*				
BnF gr. 1370		**Marc. gr. III.2**			
72^{v}	Carthage c. 3, 4	135^{r}	Carthage c. 3, 4		
73^{r}	Carthage c. 6	135^{v}	Carthage c. 6		
74^{r}	Carthage c. 16	136^{v}	Carthage c. 16		
75^{r}	Carthage c. 21	137^{r}	Carthage c. 21		
75^{v}	Carthage c. 25, 27	137^{v}	Carthage c. 25, 27		
84^{r}	Carthage c. 70				
111^{v}	*N50T* 26, 27, 27, 29				
125^{v}	Basil, *Lesser Asketikon* 310				
128^{v}	*Synopsis*, proem 1.5				
135^{r}	*Synopsis*, Carthage c. 25				

* Asterisks denote annotations made by later hands (not the scribe's).

Armenians for eating cheese and eggs during the Lenten fast. Apost. c. 53 asserts that all bishops, priests, and deacons should partake of flesh and wine on feast days. These all relate to a rich vein of Byzantine criticism of the Western church's practices surrounding fasting and the Lenten period (as we saw in the supplementary texts above). Finally, II Nicaea c. 4 forbids bishops from extorting money from their priests in return for ordination and *Apost. Const.* 1.3 states that men should not shave their beards, since God gave men beards to distinguish them from women. The prohibition on shaving remains a notable difference between Eastern and Western clergy to this very day; as for extortion, this is not an anti-Latin issue per se (the Byzantines were just as prone to simony), but it may have been an area of conflict between Greek priests and Latin bishops in the Salento.

The 'Against the Latins' annotations alongside the Carthaginian canons in the other manuscripts mostly relate to the issue of clerical marriage. Canons 3, 4, 16, 21, 25, and 70 all state that bishops, priests, and deacons should abstain from their wives. These might seem to be strange canons for Salentine Greek clergy to emphasise, since the Byzantine tradition was for priests *not* to abstain from their wives. However, the fact that the Carthaginian canons acknowledge clerical marriage at all contradicted the thirteenth-century Roman church's blanket ban on priests having wives.[70] Besides the marriage question, two other canons (6 and 27) discuss chrismation and baptism respectively; they were highlighted because of their relevance to a specific controversy of 1231 that we shall discuss in the following chapter.[71]

Why should the annotators have focused on the somewhat equivocal canons of Carthage rather than the much more strongly pro-Byzantine canons of *Trullo* or the Apostles? It is impossible to know for certain, but one possibility is that they were more useful in debates with Latin-rite Christians. The Apostolic Canons and the Council *in Trullo* were still largely unknown (and still less accepted) in the medieval West at the time, whereas the Carthaginian canons were themselves Western in origin. The annotators probably wanted to highlight canons whose validity the Latins could not deny.

Clerical marriage clearly emerges as the manuscripts' biggest concern 'against the Latins', with fasting in second place. The scribe of BnF gr. 1370 also annotated several lines from the *N50T* and the tenth-century *Synopsis of Canons* supporting the idea that clerical marriage is not only acceptable, but that priests who give up their wives should be deposed and excommunicated. We do not know of any explicit effort on the part of the papacy to prevent Italo-Greek priests from having wives, but it is quite possible that Rome's disapproval of clerical marriage in general could have contributed to tensions and criticism at a local level.

It is telling that none of the scribes or readers chose to highlight texts on traditional subjects of Latin-Greek polemic such as the *azyma* (even though the Council *in Trullo* issued canons on the subject); as for the *Filioque*, it is only mentioned in Photios' *Encyclical Letter* and John VIII's *Synodikon*. Instead of abstract theological polemic, the Greek clergy who read these nomocanons were more interested in canon law that explained and justified why they lived a different life from the Latin clergy who shared their communities. The manuscripts indicate that this interest intensified as the thirteenth century progressed.

Conclusion

The manuscripts that we have examined in this chapter are a coherent, related group of Italo-Greek nomocanons produced in the Salento peninsula in the twelfth to fourteenth centuries (see Table 9.4). Their codicological features indicate that they were all produced in a similar cultural and institutional context,

[70] A Salentine Greek polemic of the thirteenth century (which appears in the nomocanon Barocci 86, fols. 1^{v}–2^{r}) gives this exact interpretation: Darrouzès (1970b): 229 ll. 20–30. For further discussion of this text, see Chapter 10, 'They Do It Like This in Romania', C10.P29–C10.P32.

[71] See Chapter 10, 'They Do It Like This in Romania', C10.P16–C10.P17.

Table 9.4. The Salentine Group

	Shelfmark	Date	Scribe	Ruling	Style
1.	Ambros. F 48 sup.	Early C12	Joacheim (monk)?	X20D1	Red-Leaf
2.	Barocci 86	C12	Kalos (priest)?	X20D1	Red-Leaf
3.	Vat. gr. 1287	C12	Unknown	X11D1bm et al.	Unclear
4.	Add. 28822	C12/13	Unknown	X31D1b	Unclear
5.	Ambros. B 107 sup.	C12/13	Unknown	X32D1 et al.	Unclear
6.	Laur. plut. 5.22	C12/13	Unknown	X20C1	Red-Leaf
7.	Marc. gr. III.2	C12/13	Unknown	X21D1b	Black-Leaf
8.	Ottob. gr. 186	C12/13	Unknown	Unclear	Unclear
9.	Sin. gr. 397	C13	Unknown	X20A1	Black-Leaf
10.	BnF gr. 1370	1296/7	Unknown	22C1, 32C1	Black-Leaf
11.	Ambros. E 94 sup.	C13/14	Unknown	P2 X20D1 et al.	Unclear

while their textual content and marginalia indicate that they were aimed at a specific readership: the Salentine Greek clergy. This is counter-intuitive in two ways: not only was this group subject to the legal system of the Roman papacy by the mid-thirteenth century, but it had never been involved in the administration of ecclesiastical justice even under Byzantine rule.

However, they did not read manuscripts as legal sources in the positivistic sense. Instead, the Salentine Group nomocanons demonstrate how Byzantine canon law remained relevant for Italo-Greeks even when it no longer applied as a formal legal system. The Byzantine canons may not have served as imperial law for these manuscripts' scribes and readers, but they remained sources of paideic law, to use Robert Cover's terminology. They were instructive texts with the authority of antiquity and (almost) universal acceptance among Christians that could be invoked to explain and justify why Greeks practised their religion differently to Latins. Indeed, they could even be turned against the Latins to show that it was Rome that had deviated from ancient tradition, not Constantinople; after all, the best defence is a good offence.

The specific practices that the manuscripts sought to defend were ones that were undoubtedly the most prominent points of contention for Greek priests in medieval southern Italy: their right to marry and cohabit with wives, their Lenten discipline, and the validity of their baptism. Other topics such as the *Filioque* and beard shaving feature, but less prominently. These were defining attributes of medieval Greek Christians' religious (and thus also cultural) identity, the outwardly noticeable practices that marked them out as different from their Latin-rite neighbours. Byzantine canon law proved that the Italo-Greeks were right to be different, or at least not wrong.

This chapter may have created the impression that Greek- and Latin-rite Christians in the late-medieval Salento were riven with sectarian tension. There is probably a grain of truth to this, but it is by no means the full story. The nexus between canon law and identity was rather more nuanced: as we shall see in the following chapter, legal texts directed 'against the Latins' were not necessarily directed at a Latin audience.

10
'They Do It Like This in Romania'

In the opening decades of the thirteenth century, the Greek clergy of the small Apulian town of Gioia del Colle had a dispute about how to correctly perform the *proskomide*, the service of preparation for the Eucharistic gifts that would be offered in the liturgy. They specifically wanted to know how many pieces of *prosphora* (bread offered for the liturgy by the congregation) they should bless.[1] To resolve this dilemma, they wrote to Nektarios, abbot of St Nicholas of Casole, whose response has been preserved in the nomocanon BnF gr. 1371 and provides the only surviving evidence of the episode.[2]

The most interesting aspect of Nektarios' letter (in my view) is not its discussion of ritual but what it reveals about his correspondents' perspectives and assumptions. One group of the priests, we read, argued that all the *prosphora* should be blessed, while an opposing group said that it should only be three or five pieces. 'And,' writes Nektarios, '[the opposing group] heard that they do it like this in Romania and in the monasteries.'[3] This is a revealing line: one faction of the Greek clergy in Gioia felt that their practice was more authentic because they thought that it more closely reflected the ritual of the Byzantine Empire and of monasteries like St Nicholas of Casole. In other words, even after the Fourth Crusade and the Fourth Lateran Council, Byzantine practice was still viewed by some Italo-Greeks as the ideal standard.

There is another important point here: the priests who thought that they did the *proskomide* like the Byzantines did were wrong. Nektarios tells them that it is the first group (who said that all the *prosphora* should be blessed) who are correct.[4] While many Italo-Greeks sought to emulate the Constantinopolitan rite, they did not always understand what it was. As a cultural minority with a complex history living amidst a Latin majority, it was inevitable that some members of the community would (consciously or otherwise) diverge from Byzantine orthodoxy.

[1] On the Byzantine *proskomide* or *prothesis* rite, see Pott (2010): 196–228. Hawkes-Teeples (2014) provides a good overview of the state of scholarship on the subject.

[2] BnF gr. 1371, fols. 151^r–157^r; text in Hoeck and Loenertz (1965): 130–135. How to perform the *proskomide* seems to have been a matter of perennial concern to the Italo-Greeks; Bishop-Elect Paul of Gallipoli had asked about another aspect of the ritual in his letter to the patriarch of Constantinople, for example (see Safran [2014]: 143; Hoffmann [1989]: 80–83).

[3] '*ἤκουσαν δὲ κἀκεῖνοι ὡς καὶ ἐν τῇ Ῥωμανίᾳ καὶ ἐν τοῖς μοναστηρίοις οὕτω ποιοῦσι*': Hoeck and Loenertz (1965): 131 ll. 48–49.

[4] '*οἱ λέγοντες πάσας τὰς εὐλογίας ἤτοι τὰς προσφορὰς ἁγιᾶσαι καὶ θῦσαι καλῶς φασι*': Hoeck and Loenertz (1965): ll. 63–64.

Byzantine Religious Law in Medieval Italy. James Morton, Oxford University Press (2021). © James Morton.
DOI: 10.1093/oso/9780198861140.003.0011

The previous chapter highlighted some of the ways in which some Salentine Greek priests turned to nomocanons to explain and justify why they followed Byzantine religious practice. In this chapter, we shall look at the broader context of cultural change in which they read their canon law collections and see that their arguments were often directed as much at fellow Greeks as they were at Latins.

Canon Law as Cultural Authority: Nektarios of Otranto's *Three Chapters*

There is a tendency among modern scholars to treat Byzantine canon law in isolation from other forms of medieval literature, a consequence no doubt of its technical character and reputation as a niche subject. Nonetheless, the nomocanons that we have examined in this study did not exist in a vacuum; rather, their contents informed a great deal of medieval Italo-Greek writing that sought to defend the orthodoxy of the Byzantine rite.

The clearest example of this can be found in a work known today as the *Three Chapters*, a fascinating bilingual treatise in Greek and Latin by Nektarios of Otranto.[5] He composed the work around 1220–1225 but framed it as a rebuttal of arguments made by Cardinal Benedict Caetani during his mission to Constantinople in the immediate aftermath of the Fourth Crusade.[6] Nektarios was the interpreter for Benedict's delegation, yet he leaves the reader in no doubt that his sympathies lay with the Byzantine clergy. This comes across clearly in a closing verse dedication that he wrote in his own hand in one of the surviving manuscripts:

> [This is] the end with God's help of the book of dialogue between Greeks and Latins. You have what I enjoined myself to write for you, my beloved in Christ, most wise Andrew, this little writing here, which I composed and arranged in Hellenic [i.e. Greek] from [the words of] many great philosophical men and

[5] The text survives in two autograph manuscripts: Paris, Bibliothèque nationale de France, MS suppl. gr. 1232, fols. 15r–164r; Vatican City, Biblioteca Apostolica Vaticana, MS Pal. gr. 232, fols. 3r–131r. There are also several later copies of the work, detailed in Muci (2008): 455. The prologue of the first chapter and the entirety of the second and third chapters were published in Švecov (1896). The third chapter has recently been re-edited and published in Muci (2008): 477–500. See also Muci (2005); Hoeck and Loenertz (1965): 88–109. Nektarios' own name for the work was the *Synopsis*.

[6] '[The work was] composed and put together by Nicholas [Nektarios] of Otranto, translated at the time from Greek into the Latin language in Constantinople at the command of the Lord Cardinal Benedict, who was the representative of Innocent III, then reigning pope of Rome' ('*συλλεγεῖσα καὶ συνταχθεῖσα παρὰ Νικολάου Ἱδρούσης, ἔπειτα δὲ καὶ ἐξ ἑλληνικῆς εἰς ῥωμαικὴν διάλεκτον ἑρμηνευθεῖσα ἐν Κωνσταντινουπόλει, προτροπῇ τοῦ κυροῦ Βενεδίκτου τοῦ καρδηναρίου* [*sic*] *καὶ τοποτηρητοῦ τότε ὑπάρχοντος Ἰννοκεντίου τοῦ τρίτου πάπα Ῥώμης*'): text in Muci (2005): 29. On the dating of the work, see Muci (2008): 453; on Cardinal Benedict's legation to Constantinople, see Chapter 8, 'The Papacy Takes Charge', C8.P4.

> translated into Roman [i.e. Latin]. Let it be for you and for every orthodox [believer] an armament against certain arrogant Latins. May you always be healthy in the Lord.[7]

The addressee was Andrew of Brindisi, a Salentine Greek notary with refined literary tastes to whom Nektarios also addressed a short epigram.[8] Despite the conceit that the work was a synopsis of the Constantinopolitan clergy's response to Benedict, the *Three Chapters* was in reality intended to be of practical apologetic use to Italo-Greeks such as Andrew who would have to defend their distinctive rites 'against certain arrogant Latins'. Not surprisingly, this was one part of the text that Nektarios chose not to translate into Latin.

Although it is important to emphasise that Nektarios' tone is generally irenic and conciliatory, he creates a consistent binary opposition between 'we Greeks' and 'you Latins', identifying himself unambiguously with 'the church of the Greeks'.[9] This is a striking turn of phrase, as it uses a translated Latin vocabulary word—'Greek'—instead of the actual Greek term, which was 'Hellene'. The Byzantines of the early thirteenth century would almost certainly not have used the word 'Greek' and were still reticent about calling themselves 'Hellenes' (they preferred to think of themselves as 'Romans').[10] Nektarios' use of language here neatly encapsulates the Italo-Greeks' liminal situation in the early thirteenth century, continuing to identify with Byzantine Christianity even as they lived under Rome's jurisdiction and absorbed Latin terminology.

The *Three Chapters* begins with a lengthy preface in which Nektarios explains the history of the seven ecumenical councils (omitting the regional councils and *Protodeutera*).[11] The aim of the passage is to establish the validity and authority of the Byzantine church councils to a Latin audience so that he can use them as the basis for his arguments in the rest of the treatise. While the Western church theoretically accepted all the Byzantine conciliar canons except those of *Trullo* and Chalcedon c. 28, many Westerners were only familiar with the more famous councils of antiquity such as I Nicaea that had been translated into Latin. Historical summaries of church councils are quite common in the Italo-Greek

[7] '*τέλος σὺν Θεῷ τῆς βίβλου τῆς ἀναμεταξὺ Γραικῶν καὶ Λατίνων διαλέξεως. Ἔχεις ὅπερ μοι ἐντείλω γράψαι σοι, ἐν Χριστῷ ἀγαπητέ, Ἀνδρέα σοφώτατε, ταυτηνὶ τὴν μικρὰν δέλτον, ἥτις ἐκ πολλῶν καὶ μεγάλων ἀνδρῶν φιλοσόφων, συλλεγεῖσα καὶ παρ᾽ἐμοῦ συνταχθεῖσα, ἑλληνιστὶ, καὶ ῥωμαϊστὶ μεταφρασθεῖσα, ἔστω σοι καὶ παντὶ ὀρθοδόξῳ πανοπλία κατὰ τῶν τινῶν ὑψαυχενούντων Λατίνων, ὑγίαινε ἐν Κυρίῳ πάντοτε*': BnF suppl. gr. 1232, fol. 164[r]. Text in Muci (2008): 500. On the dating of the work, see Muci (2008): 453.

[8] Gigante (1979): 78 (no. 12).

[9] E.g. 'The church of the Greeks holds to many [traditions] that are pleasing to God, as I have already mentioned, and which are also written in your holy books, O Latin men…' ('*πολλὰ μὲν θεαρέστως ἡ τῶν γραικῶν ἐκκλησία κρατοῦσα, ὡς ἤδη καὶ εἴρηται, ἃ καὶ ἐν ταῖς ἱεραῖς ὑμῶν βίβλοις γέγραπται, ὦ ἄνδρες λατῖνοι…*'): Muci (2008): 478 ll. 7–9.

[10] See Page (2008): 46–52, 63–67. See also Introduction, CI.S2.

[11] BnF suppl. gr. 1232, fols. 28[v]–39[r]; Pal. gr. 232, fols. 7[r]–19[r].

nomocanons and Nektarios may have used one as his source here, though he reworked the material in his own words.[12]

As its name suggests, the treatise is divided into three main sections. The first and longest of the three concerns the procession of the Holy Spirit while the second addresses the Roman use of *azyma* in the Eucharist.[13] The most interesting of the chapters for our purposes, though, is the third, entitled: 'Of the same [Nektarios], the third chapter about the Latins' fasting on the Sabbath and about why one should not celebrate the Eucharist during Lent, as a demonstration from the holy canons shows. And it is also about the marriage of priests.'[14] These are all topics of anti-Latin polemic that we saw in Italo-Greek texts in Chapters 4, 6, and 9; indeed, they were some of the most common points of controversy between Eastern and Western Christians in the Middle Ages in general.[15] They were all presumably raised in discussions between Cardinal Benedict and the Byzantine clergy in Constantinople in 1205.

Nektarios has a straightforward approach throughout the chapter. Moving through each of his subjects in the order in which they are listed in the title, he cites Greek canons that support the Byzantine church's position in each case and then gives examples of notable Church Fathers who accepted the Byzantine practice. He does understand that contemporary Westerners might not always find his appeals to Greek canon law convincing, however. Early on in the chapter, for example, he remarks that he once came across books belonging to Cardinal Benedict that referred to the Apostolic Canons as apocryphal and that 'you [Latins] have marked [the Apostolic Canons] as apocryphal in your recent decretals', an apparent reference to Gratian's *Decretum*.[16] Not only that, but he even found that someone had written the words 'this is Greek' over a text of the Apostolic Canons in Benedict's possession, which Nektarios found 'laughable and contrary to the truth'.[17]

With this scepticism in mind, Nektarios takes special care to highlight cases of Western Fathers who supposedly accepted the validity of the Byzantine canons.

[12] Cf. Neilos Doxapatres' *Order of the Patriarchal Thrones*, which lifts passages *verbatim* from its source texts; see Chapter 5, 'Monastic Nomocanons I', C5.P45–C5.P51.

[13] First section: BnF suppl. gr. 1232, fols. 15^r–114^r; Pal. gr. 232, fols. 3^r–91^r. Second section: BnF suppl. gr. 1232, fols. 114^v–148^v; Pal. gr. 232, fols. 91^v–120^r.

[14] '*τοῦ αὐτοῦ τρίτον Σύνταγμα περὶ τῆς τῶν Λατίνων ἐν σαββάτῳ νηστείας καὶ περὶ τοῦ ὅτι οὐ δεῖ ἐν Τεσσαρακοστῇ τελείαν γενέσθαι μυσταγωγίαν, ὡς ἐκ τῶν θείων κανόνων ἡ ἀπόδειξις πέφυκεν· ἔτι δὲ καὶ περὶ γάμων ἱερέων*': Muci (2008): 477.

[15] See Chapter 4, 'The Byzantine Background', C4.S3; Chapter 6, 'Monastic Nomocanons II', C6.P7; Chapter 9, 'The Salentine Group', C9.S4.

[16] '*αὐτὸς πολλάκις ἐγκύπτων εὗρον σὺν ἄλλοις ἐκεῖσε τοὺς τῶν θείων Ἀποστόλων καὶ Πατέρων κανόνας, οὕσπερ ὑμεῖς ἐν τοῖς νεωστὶ γεναμένοις δεκρέτοις ἀποκρύφους σημειοῦσθε*': Muci (2008): 478, 479 n. b. See *Decretum Gratiani*, D 15 c. 3.64; D 15 c. 3–4. The Church of Rome had been sceptical of the authenticity of the Apostolic Canons since the fifth century; see Ceccarelli Morolli (2002): 153–154. See also Chapter 4, 'The Byzantine Background', C4.P31.

[17] '*ἐπάνω δὲ τοῦ κειμένου τῶν θείων κανόνων "γραικὸν ἐστὶν" ἐπεγέγραπτο, ὅπερ γελοιῶδες ἦν καὶ κατ᾽ἀλήθειαν, ὅτι δὲ καὶ ἡμῖν καὶ τοῖς λατίνοις ὑμῖν κοινῶς παρεδόθησαν*': Muci (2008): 478.

For example, on the question of fasting on the Sabbath during Lent, he notes that it is forbidden by Apost. c. 66 and observes that both St Jerome and St Augustine accepted the custom that one should not do so. He also cites canon 56 of the Council *in Trullo* (which explicitly condemns the Western practice of fasting on the Sabbath during Lent) and claims (incorrectly) that it was endorsed by the Roman pope Agatho (678–681).[18]

Nektarios uses similar argumentation regarding the other two subjects of the chapter. On the celebration of daily Eucharists during Lent, he asks Latins where they got the custom from, noting that it is forbidden by the Council of Laodicea (c. 49 and 51) and the Sixth Ecumenical Council (*Trullo* c. 52), which, he mistakenly reminds us, was endorsed by Pope Agatho.[19] If the Latins really want to celebrate daily liturgies during Lent, he says, then they should celebrate the presanctified liturgy like the Greeks do. His discussion of clerical marriage is more detailed and gives an insight into his knowledge of more contemporary Latin church writings. Besides references to Byzantine canons on the subject (Apost. c. 5, 18; Gangra c. 4; *Trullo* c. 13—with yet another assertion that Pope Agatho endorsed the Sixth Ecumenical Council) and to 1 Tim. 3:1–4 and Tit. 1:5–6 (which mention bishops and priests with wives), he also quotes from a letter from Pope Urban II to Bishop Pibo of Toul (1074–1107).[20] 'The Roman bishop Urban,' he recounts, 'wrote to Bishop Pibo of Toul and said: "Following the common tradition of the Church, by the authority of our office we prohibit bigamists and the husbands of widows from holy orders."'[21] This is effectively the substance of Apost. c. 18 and *Trullo* c. 3; if even a recent pope like Urban II agreed with the Byzantine canons, then what could the Roman church of the thirteenth century have against them? Of course, Nektarios omits to mention the fact that Urban expressly rejected clerical marriage elsewhere (at the Council of Melfi in 1089, for example, Urban stated that priests' wives should be enslaved if they do not separate from their husbands).[22]

The *Three Chapters* thus seeks to defend the validity of Greek Christian customs by appealing to the authority of Byzantine canon law, arguing that it should also be accepted by the Roman church. Yet Nektarios did not just draw on texts from canon law collections; he also added to them. His letter to the priests of Gioia, for instance, is only known because he inserted it at the end of the Casulan canon law collection BnF gr. 1371. He added another short text on fasting, which

[18] Muci (2008): 486–490. Pope Agatho did indeed endorse the Sixth Ecumenical Council of 681, but the canons associated with the council were not promulgated until the Council *in Trullo* ten years later (after Agatho had died), creating a confusing chronological gap.

[19] Muci (2008): 488–490. Again, Nektarios has confused Agatho's endorsement for the council of 681 with endorsement for the canons of *Trullo*.

[20] Muci (2008): 492–493. As Muci notes, the quote is from Urban II, *Ep*. 24.7 (*PL* 151.307B).

[21] '*Οὐρβανὸς δὲ ὁ τῆς Ῥώμης ἐπίσκοπος, Βίβωνι τῷ Τουλλίας ἐπισκόπῳ γράφων, οὕτω φησί· "διγάμους καὶ χηρῶν ἄνδρας ἀπὸ τῶν ἱερῶν βαθμῶν, κατὰ τὴν κοινὴν τῆς ἐκκλήσιας συνήθειαν, τῇ ἐξουσίᾳ τοῦ ἡμετέρου ὀφφικίου ἀφορίζομεν*"': Muci (2008): 492.

[22] Mansi 20.724. See also Thibodeaux (2015): 47.

he attributes to someone named John Antagonistes, into the nomocanon Barb. gr. 324.[23] Antagonistes, who is otherwise unknown, lays out the position of the Church of Constantinople that one should fast on Wednesdays and Fridays (except on certain feast days), citing as his sources a synod that occurred 'in those times when the renowned Nicholas was guiding the reins of the Church in Constantinople' and 'two canons of the holy Apostles'.[24] These are presumably references to a set of conciliar decrees issued under the patriarchate of Nicholas III Grammatikos (1084–1111) and Apost. c. 53 and 69.[25] Nektarios' addition of this text to Barb. gr. 324 was part of a textual feedback loop (particularly noticeable in the Salentine nomocanons), as Italo-Greek authors drew on canon law collections for source material and the resulting treatises were themselves copied into canon law collections.[26]

Facing Latin Criticism

Byzantine canon law evidently played a role in the defence of Greek rites and customs in medieval southern Italy, but from whom were they being defended? The answer may seem obvious; the controversies were focused on differences between the Roman and Byzantine rites, so naturally the attackers must have been Latin Christians. Nektarios of Otranto's writings imply as much, and it is certainly what previous generations of historians assumed.[27] Yet, more recent studies have pointed out how little evidence there is of inter-community tension.[28] Compared to the situation in Frankish states in Greece and Cyprus, for example, relations between Latin- and Greek-rite Christians in southern Italy were quite good.

There is only one known instance in the thirteenth century of the Roman church condemning an Italo-Greek ritual.[29] This occurred in 1231–1232, when Marinus Filangieri, the Latin archbishop of Bari in Apulia (1226–1251), wrote to

[23] Barb. gr. 324, fol. 10^{v}. Text and discussion in Jacob (2008): 234–236. The text is also preserved in Madrid, Biblioteca nacional de España, MS 4554, fol. 50^{r}, where it is attributed to the twelfth-century Italo-Greek monk Philagathos of Cerami. As Jacob notes, 'the attribution to Philagathos of Cerami is scarcely likely'.

[24] '*καίτοι καὶ πρὸ ἡμῶν σύνοδος ταῦτα διηκριβώσατο καθ' οὓς χρόνους τοὺς οἴακας τῆς ἐν Κωνσταντ(ι)ν(ου)πόλει ἐκκλησίας ἴθυνε Νικόλ(αος) ὁ ἀοίδημος… ὡς οἱ δύοι οὗτοι κανόνες τῶν ἱερῶν ἀπο(στόλων)…*': Jacob (2008): 234.

[25] The text of the decrees can be found in Pitra (1858): 466–476. Antagonistes is probably referring to no. 6 on p. 469.

[26] Another good example of the feedback loop is an *erotapokrisis* added into the beginning of Barocci 86; see section: 'Correcting Greek Mistakes', C10.S3.

[27] See e.g. Morris (1991): 140–142.

[28] See Chapter 2, 'Greek Christianity in Medieval Italy', C2.P54.

[29] There is also the fourteenth-century case of Raymond of Campania, papal vicar in southern Italy, who made a failed attempt in 1334 to force the Italo-Greeks to adopt the Roman rite, but his efforts were short-lived and never repeated. See Chapter 2, 'Greek Christianity in Medieval Italy', C2.P66.

Pope Gregory IX to question the validity of the Greek baptismal rite.[30] Marinus' letter is known only from Gregory's reply of 12th November 1231, in which the pope states that the third-person Greek formula 'N. is baptised in the name of the Father and of the Son and of the Holy Spirit' is invalid, since the priest should say, 'I baptise you in the name of...' in the first person. Not only does Gregory say that everyone in the future should be baptised with that formula, but he adds that, just to be safe, anyone (including clergy) who had previously been baptised with the Greek formula should be re-baptised with the Latin version and then re-ordained.[31] Further to these instructions, Gregory tells Marinus that the Greek practice of allowing priests to perform chrismation (the anointing of a baptised person with holy oil in a ceremony that is roughly equivalent to Western confirmation) should be prevented, since only bishops should be allowed to conduct confirmations. Again, anyone chrismated by a priest should be re-confirmed by a bishop.

Needless to say, Gregory's instructions caused a significant outcry not only among the Italo-Greeks but even abroad, as Avvakumov notes: George Bardanes, the Greek metropolitan of Corfu (d. 1240), composed several letters in the years 1231–1236 in which he described his anguish at Rome's treatment of the Italo-Greeks.[32] Word of objections to the new policy must have reached Rome swiftly, as Gregory sent another letter to Archbishop Marinus on 20th February 1232 in which he said that the Italo-Greeks should send experts to Rome 'with necessary books' so that the Curia could investigate the matter and persuade them to accept the Latin baptismal formula.[33] We learn from George Bardanes that Nektarios of Otranto, abbot of St Nicholas of Casole and author of the *Three Chapters*, was among the delegation to the papal court.[34] Although Gregory was initially unconvinced, Nektarios eventually managed to persuade him of the validity of Greek baptisms. Just a couple of years later, the *Decretals of Gregory IX* (the '*Liber extra*') of 1234 would enshrine the validity of the Greek baptismal rite in Latin canon law.[35]

It is likely that at least two of the 'Against the Latins' marginalia in the Salentine Group nomocanons are related to this specific controversy. As we saw in Chapter 9, the Branch B manuscripts BnF gr. 1370 and Marc. gr. III.2 both have the annotation alongside Carthage c. 6 and 27.[36] These state that chrism may not be made by priests and that a priest who has been deposed cannot be baptised a second time and then re-admitted to the priesthood—both subjects that had

[30] On this subject, see esp. Avvakumov (2011). See also Peters-Custot (2009a): 532–533 and n. 124.

[31] *Fontes III* 3.225–226 (no. 170).

[32] Avvakumov (2011): 71–73; Hoeck and Loenertz (1965): 175–235.

[33] Avvakumov (2011): 72.

[34] Hoeck and Loenertz (1965): 201.

[35] *X* 3.42.6 = *Comp. IV* 3.16 (Lateran IV, c. 4); *Fontes III* 3.229 (no. 173), 234–235 (nos. 178–178a). See also Brundage (1973): 1081. On the treatment of the Greek rite in the *Liber extra* more generally, see Brieskorn (2010).

[36] See Chapter 9, 'The Salentine Group', C9.T3*t*.

arisen in Gregory IX's letter to Marinus of Bari. Canon 6 is admittedly an odd choice, since it does not affirmatively state that a priest can perform chrismation (the issue at stake in Gregory's letter). It may be that the annotators wanted to emphasize that canon law prohibited the *making* of chrism by priests but not its *application*. The relevance of canon 27 is more obvious: Gregory had required that Italo-Greek clergy should be re-baptised and re-ordained, which Carthage c. 27 clearly forbids.[37]

The baptismal controversy also caused a stir elsewhere in southern Italy. It was the implicit subject of an anonymous thirteenth-century tract from Calabria entitled *On Divine Baptism* that attempts to explain why 'one should not say "I baptise you" but "[N.] is baptised,"' an obvious reference to the dispute.[38] Avvakumov has pointed out that the text does not explicitly refer to Gregory IX's intervention and has argued on palaeographical grounds that the text was composed earlier in the thirteenth century, before the events of 1231–1232. 'If so,' he remarks, 'this text bears clear evidence that the conflict concerning the sacrament of baptism in Southern Italy had already begun before the pope's intervention.'[39] It is difficult to date manuscripts so precisely based on their palaeography alone, but the broader point that the baptismal controversy had probably begun simmering before Gregory's correspondence is hard to deny.[40] It also remained a live issue for several decades afterwards: as Avvakumov notes, Thomas Aquinas wrote in the 1250s that the validity of Greek baptisms was still undecided (despite the fact that Gregory IX *had* officially decided the matter).[41]

While scholars such as Peters-Custot are right to stress the Roman church's official tolerance of the Greek rite overall, there was evidently a degree of unofficial intolerance. We see it not only in the baptismal controversy but also in debates over clerical marriage. The Roman church never attempted to prevent Greek clergy from cohabiting with their wives, but it seems to have been very anxious at the thought that they might set a bad example for Latin clergy.[42] Pope Innocent IV (*r.* 1243–1254) wrote that a married Greek priest who lived for an extended period among Latin Christians should have to renounce his wife, though if he only visited Latins for a short time then he could keep her.[43] Not all Westerners agreed; the canonist Hostiensis (Henry of Segusio, *c.* 1200–1271), for instance, felt that

[37] The argumentation is not without flaws: if the Greeks' baptism was found to be invalid, then technically their clergy would never have been baptised or ordained in the first place and hence there would be no re-baptism or re-ordination.

[38] Vatican City, Biblioteca Apostolica Vaticana, MS Vat. gr. 1541, fols. 240^{v}–241^{v}. Text in Giannelli (1944): 166–167. We can infer from notes on fol. 241 that the manuscript belonged to a Greek family of the Val di Tuccio in Calabria named Kandouklas. See also Peters-Custot (2009a): 534 n. 127.

[39] Avvakumov (2011): 75.

[40] As demonstrated by e.g. the *euchologion* of the priest Galaktion; see section: 'Correcting Greek Mistakes', C10.P24.

[41] Thomas Aquinas, *In IV Sententiarum*, d.3 q.1 a.2b ad 1, *Opera ut sunt in Indici thomistico*, quoted in Avvakumov (2011): 80.

[42] Brundage (1973): 1078–1079.

[43] Innocent IV, *App.* to *X* 1.11.9 ad v. *volumus*.

this was too severe and agreed only in cases where a regional custom sanctioned the loss of marital rites.[44] Indeed, Maroula Perisanidi has recently highlighted the cases of the Anglo-Norman Master Honorius (*fl.* 1184/5–1205) and the anonymous author of the *Summa Lipsiensis* (*c.* 1186) who actively supported the Byzantine church's tradition of clerical marriage.[45]

The subject caused heated debate in the Salento peninsula. Not only is it attested in the Salentine Group nomocanons and Nektarios' *Three Chapters*, but it is also mentioned in the letter to the priests of Gioia. Having pronounced his opinion on the matter that the priests raised, Nektarios quotes a section of a Latin text that he refers to as '*Against Married Priests and Those Who Have Concubines*'.[46] He then interrupts himself to clarify that the work is only against married Latin clergy, not Greek ones, '"for their marriage is righteous and the intercourse undefiled." This is legislated in the divine Apostolic Canons and the holy synods, rather than in the Latin canons. But there is no need to write about these things here, since I wrote about them at greater length in the book I composed in Latin and Greek against those who wish to slander our church.'[47] Nektarios evidently anticipated that his correspondents would assume that any Latin text about married clergy would be against Greeks.

The final lines of Nektarios' letter reinforce the impression that the two communities did not enjoy completely harmonious relations. Though he encourages the Greek priests of Gioia to maintain their own traditions, he also exhorts them to try to live peacefully with Latins. 'You see,' he says, 'how much and in what manner the progenitors of the Christian people are suffering, slandered as "heretics" by some ignorant people, with Greeks incited against Latins and Latins against Greeks.'[48] This recalls another letter from the late twelfth century by a Byzantine diplomat named Theorianos 'the Philosopher' to the Greek clergy of his hometown of Oria in the Salento.[49] Addressing a range of familiar topics (the Saturday fast, clerical marriage, and the *azyma*), he states that a certain soldier (presumably from the Salento) 'has explained to me that [these] and many other

[44] Hostiensis, *Comm.* to *X* 1.11.9. [45] Perisanidi (2017): 141–142.

[46] '*κατὰ ἱερέων γεγαμηκότων ἢ καὶ ἑταιρίδας ἐχόντων*': Hoeck and Loenertz (1965): 134 ll. 167–168.

[47] '*Καὶ τοῦτο νόει κατὰ Λατίνων οὐ κατὰ Γραικῶν γεγαμηκότων· "τίμιος γὰρ ὁ γάμος καὶ ἡ κοίτη ἀμίαντος." νενομοθέτηται γὰρ τοῦτο καὶ ἐν τοῖς θείοις τῶν ἀποστόλων κανόσι καὶ ἐν ἱεραῖς συνόδοις, μᾶλλον δὲ κανόσι Λατινικοῖς. ἀλλ' οὐ χρεία τούτων γράφειν τανῦν· ἐγράφη δὲ πλατυτέρως ἐν τῇ συνταχθείσῃ παρ' ἡμῶν βίβλῳ ἑλληνικῶς καὶ ῥωμαϊκῶς κατὰ τῶν τῆς ἐκκλησίας ἡμῶν βουλομένων ληρεῖν*': Hoeck and Loenertz (1965): ll. 168–173.

[48] '*ὁρᾶτε οἷα καὶ πῶς πάσχουσιν οἱ τῆς χριστιανῶν μαρίδος ὑπάρχοντες, αἱρετικοὶ παρὰ τινων ἀμαθῶν δυσφημούμενοι, γραικοὶ κατὰ λατίνων καὶ λατῖνοι κατὰ γραικῶν ἀνθορμώμενοι*': Hoeck and Loenertz (1965): 134–135 ll. 183–186.

[49] See Safran (2014): 213–214. The letter is preserved in Vatican City, Biblioteca Apostolica Vaticana, MS Vat. gr. 1481, fols. 151^{r}–158^{r} and is edited in Loenertz (1948): 326–333. There is some uncertainty about the identification of the letter's recipients; Loenertz originally identified it as Beth Zachariah in the Kingdom of Jerusalem, but later changed his mind to Oria (Loenertz [1970]). I am inclined to support Safran's argument that Theorianos' name was particular to the Salento. See also Magdalino (1993): 387; Magdalino (2003): 53–55.

quarrels have arisen between you and the Latins'.[50] In short, while the Italo-Greeks do not seem to have faced much opposition to their rites from the official church, there were clearly unofficial tensions with Latin-rite Christians at the local level. Nonetheless, this is not the full story.

Correcting Greek Mistakes

'Greeks' and 'Latins' were not monolithic blocs. Though it was convenient for contemporary authors to talk about them as such, the nature of southern Italian society meant that individuals could and often did engage in the cultural practices of more than one group. This was increasingly true for the Italo-Greeks as the twelfth and thirteenth centuries progressed, belonging as they did to a minority community with a social incentive to conform to the customs of their political and ecclesiastical superiors. Furthermore, Greek and Latin Christians often lived alongside one another, intermarried, and even celebrated church services together, especially in the Salento.[51] There was no need for a conscious policy of Latinisation on the part of the Roman church since the Italo-Greeks would gradually adapt on their own.

Scholars have observed several examples of this adaptation in action. There is the *euchologion* (prayer book) of the priest Galaktion, for instance, copied in Otranto in 1177, in which parts of the Roman baptismal rite were translated directly into Greek.[52] Safran has discussed the fascinating image in the thirteenth-century crypt of the cathedral of Taranto depicting St Mary of Egypt receiving communion from the priest Zosimos; while Mary receives the bread and wine together on a spoon in the Byzantine fashion, Zosimos holds a Roman-rite communion bell.[53] Another well-known case is a tract composed by the Salentine monk Theodore of Cursi to denounce Romanising innovations that Archbishop Angelos of Rossano (1266–1287)—a hierarch of the Greek rite—had introduced into the Eucharistic liturgy.[54] Even as he criticises a Greek archbishop for Latinising, Theodore himself uses the Latin term *graecus* to describe the Greeks.[55]

[50] '*διηγεῖτο δ' ἡμῖν καὶ πολλὰς ἄλλας ὁ στρατιώτης φιλονεικίας μεταξὺ τῶν λατίνων καὶ ὑμῶν γενομένας*...': Loenertz (1948): 326 ll. 4–5.

[51] See Safran (2013): 138–142.

[52] Vatican City, Biblioteca Apostolica Vaticana, MS Ottob. gr. 344. See Strittmatter (1946): 55–60; Safran (2014): 125.

[53] Safran (2014): 142. On Byzantine communion spoons, see Taft (1996).

[54] Vatican City, Biblioteca Apostolica Vaticana, MS Vat. gr. 1276, fols. 151^r—165^r. Text partially reproduced in Mercati (1937): 170–171. See Acconcia Longo and Jacob (1980): 220–221; Jacob (1986): 224.

[55] Mercati (1937): 171 l. 138.

Elements of Latinisation (both linguistic and intellectual) appear in the nomocanons as well. In the Sicilian Sin. gr. 432, for example, a fourteenth-century hand added a Latin translation of the Greek text of the Nicene Creed (without the *Filioque*) on fol. 12^{v}. In the Patiron's Vat. gr. 2060, a thirteenth-century hand highlighted Carthage c. 4 (which tells priests and bishops to abstain from their wives) and inaccurately summarised it in Greek as saying 'that clergy should not have wives'.[56] By contrast, a thirteenth-century hand in S. Salv. 59 (belonging to the Holy Saviour of Bordonaro) highlighted Apost. c. 5, which states that priests who renounce their wives on pretence of religion should be excommunicated; he then translated the canon into Latin in the upper margin![57] One reader inscribed the Roman view on clerical marriage in Greek while the other inscribed the Byzantine view in Latin.[58]

Yet there is more to the matter than the simplistic framing of Latinisation would imply. A more interesting phenomenon is the Italo-Greeks' lack of certainty about their *own* rite. The priests of Gioia wrote to Nektarios not just because of Latin criticisms and attacks, but because they could not agree among themselves about the correct Greek practice surrounding the *proskomide*. There is similar evidence of uncertainty about the *proskomide* among the priests of the Salentine town of Nardò, who wrote to the Greek metropolitan George Bardanes of Corfu in *c.* 1235 with a list of queries on the subject.[59]

This uncertainty is reflected in surviving nomocanons. The Rossanese Vat. gr. 2019 provides a perfect example. This manuscript was donated to the Patiron at some point after 1234, as we saw in Chapter 7, and the monks there left a significant number of marginal notes (particularly alongside the supplementary texts included at the end of Aristenos' *Synopsis of Canons*). They are mostly brief marginalia, with the exception of a selection of *erotapokriseis* on fasting, the divine liturgy, and monastic discipline; these include answers by Patriarch Nicholas III Grammatikos, an otherwise unknown Metropolitan Euphemianos of Thessalonica, and the twelfth-century Byzantine *nomophylax* Michael Choumnos.[60] Here a host of hands left traces of their interest in the subject matter. Above an answer of Nicholas III on fasting during the Lenten Holy Week, one reader drew a large asterisk, while another wrote, 'On Great Thursday [of Holy Week] and the fast on that day and communion: a marvellous

[56] 'πε[ρὶ] γυναῖκ[ας] μὴ ἔχ[ειν] ἱερεῖς': Vat. gr. 2060, fol. 67^{r}. He also highlighted Carthage c. 25 on the same subject.

[57] '*ep(iscopu)s aut presbiter aut diacon(us) suam uxore(m) no(n) expellat occasio(n)e religio(n)is. si autem expulserit segregat(ur). mane(n)s aut(em) deponat(ur)*': S. Salv. 59, fol. 76^{v}. The translation from the Greek is extremely literal.

[58] This may suggest that the monks of the Holy Saviour of Bordonaro were beginning to lose their facility with the Greek language.

[59] Hoeck and Loenertz (1965): 207–209.

[60] Euphemianos' text is unedited, but those of Nicholas III and Michael Choumnos can be found in RP 4.417–426, 5.397–398. See Troianos (2003); Cozma (2017).

explanation'.[61] A few folia later, there is an answer of Euphemianos of Thessalonica on Lenten fasting; yet another reader copied out a lengthy *erotapokrisis* on the subject in the margins wrapping around the text and gave citations of other texts that discuss the topic.[62]

Like the priests of the Salento, the monks of Calabria and Sicily could turn to their nomocanons to learn about their customs from textual sources that had the weight of ancient legal authority. They could also turn to canon law to teach *other* Greek people about their customs. We have already seen the example of Nektarios' *Three Chapters*, which was intended for both a Greek and a Latin readership. In addition to this, there is an intriguing text published by Jean Darrouzès that purports to be an *erotapokrisis* of Nicholas III Grammatikos addressed to certain unnamed metropolitans on controversies between Latins and Greeks (specifically clerical marriage, the *Filioque*, Saturday fasting, Lenten fasting, the shaving of beards, and the giving of evidence under oath).[63] Darrouzès found the work in the fourteenth-century Salentine anthology Vat. gr. 1276 and realised that it could not have been a genuine work of the Constantinopolitan patriarch, since the language and form of address do not match the formulas used by the patriarchate. What had happened, he suggested, was that an Italo-Greek redactor had adapted a title from a real *erotapokrisis* of Nicholas III and attached it to a locally produced text to lend authority.[64]

Darrouzès was not aware of the fact, but the same *erotapokrisis* appears in a thirteenth-century hand in a bifolium inserted at the beginning of the nomocanon Barocci 86.[65] This version appears to be older than the one in Vat. gr. 1276 and does not include the attribution to Nicholas III, indicating that Darrouzès was correct to suppose that it was added by a later redactor. The text in Barocci 86 begins:

> You asked us, beloved brother and concelebrant, about the disputes between Greeks [*γραικῶν*] and Latins. And your first question was this: 'What is the reason why Greek priests retain their lawful wives, whom they married in virginity, after their ordination to the priesthood, whereas Latin [priests] do not enjoy their lawful wives but only unlawful women who come from the Devil?' This is what you said.[66]

[61] '*πε(ρὶ) τ(ῆ)ς μεγάλ(ης) πέμπτ(η)ς καὶ τ(ῆ)ς ἐν αὐτῇ νηστεί(ας) καὶ κοινωνί(ας) : λύσις θαυμασία*': Vat. gr. 2019, fol. 124^{v}. The question concerned whether one could take communion on Great Thursday (one could not).

[62] Vat. gr. 2019, fols. 126^{v}–127^{r}. The source of the marginal text is unknown.

[63] Darrouzès (1970b). [64] Darrouzès (1970b): 222. [65] Barocci 86, fols. 1^{v}–2^{r}.

[66] '*ἠρώτησας ἡμᾶς, ἀγαπητὲ ἀδελφὲ καὶ συλλειτουργὲ, περὶ τῶν ἀμφιβαλλομένων παρά τε γραικῶν καὶ λατίνων· ἦν δὲ ἡ πρώτη ὑμῶν ἐρώτησις αὕτη· "τίνος ἕνεκεν οἱ μὲν τῶν γραικῶν ἱερεῖς τὰς νομίμους αὐτῶν καὶ ἐν παρθενίᾳ συνεζευγμένας γαμετὰς καὶ μετὰ τὴν τῆς ἱερωσύνης χειροτονίαν ὡσαύτως ἔχουσιν, οἱ δὲ τῶν λατίνων οὐ χρῶνται γαμεταῖς νομίμοις, ἀλλὰ ἀνόμοις καὶ ἀπὸ διαβόλου γεγενημέναις;" τοῦτο ὑμεῖς*': Barocci 86, fol. 1^{v}. The later version of the text in Vat. gr. 1276 is addressed to 'most holy brothers and concelebrants'.

Not only does the author use the Latin word *graecus*, but his framing of the question (Greek priests have lawful wives, but Latin priests have no wives and therefore fornicate with unlawful women) recalls the scholia on clerical marriage by Bartholomew the Younger of Grottaferrata that we saw in Chapter 5.[67] The biggest clue that the author was not Nicholas Grammatikos is that he sets out to answer the questions on the basis of 'proofs from Holy Scripture or from the holy canons of the divine and ecumenical four councils'.[68] This is a blunder that the patriarch of Constantinople would not have made: the Byzantines recognised *seven* ecumenical councils! However, as we saw in Chapter 4, the most common canon law collection in the medieval Salento was the sixth-century *N50T*, which included only four ecumenical councils. Whether directly or indirectly, the author seems to have drawn his information from an outdated Salentine nomocanon; a later redactor then attempted to pass it off as the work of Nicholas Grammatikos, a Constantinopolitan patriarch who was known to have produced genuine *erotapokriseis*.

It is impossible to know if the addressee of the letter was a real person or simply a literary device. Nonetheless, the format of the letter conforms to a pattern that we have seen several times already: a Greek priest asks an acquaintance to explain his own customs to him and the acquaintance answers by directing him to a combination of Holy Scripture and Byzantine canon law. It is probably not a coincidence that the author of the *erotapokrisis* in Barocci 86 cites Carthage c. 4 and 70 in his explanation of clerical marriage, both of which were highlighted as being 'against the Latins' in the nomocanons Add. 28822, BnF gr. 1370, and Marc. gr. III.2.[69]

One of the most fascinating uses of canon law to educate fellow Greeks comes in a thirteenth-century *prophetologion* from the library of the Holy Saviour of Messina.[70] The opening folia contain a verse text that purports to be a *theotokion* (hymn to the Virgin Mary).[71] While the opening lines begin by praising the *Theotokos*, the 'hymn' quickly transforms into a diatribe about the divergent Greek and Latin practices surrounding fasting and the Eucharist during Lent. The author refutes 'certain people' who claim that the Latins have the same practice as the Greeks in celebrating the presanctified liturgy on Holy Friday during Lent, pointing out (correctly) that this was not true.[72] He goes on to talk

[67] See Chapter 5, 'Monastic Nomocanons I', C5.P40–C5.P44.

[68] '*. . . τὰ ἀποδείξεις ἀπὸ τῆς θείας γραφῆς ἢ ἀπὸ τῶν ἱερῶν κανόνων τῶν θείων καὶ οἰκουμενικῶν τεσσάρων ἁγίων συνόδων*': Barocci 86, fol. 1^{v}.

[69] Barocci 86, fol. 2^{r}. Another text highlighted as 'Against the Latins' that our author mentions is *Apost. Const.* 1.3 (highlighted in Ambros. B 107 sup.).

[70] Messina, Biblioteca Universitaria Regionale, MS S. Salv. 164.

[71] '*τοῦ ἀλφαβήτου τὰ ψαλλόμενα· τὸ θεοτοκίον*': Messina, Biblioteca Universitaria Regionale, MS S. Salvatoris 164, fols. 1^{v}–6^{r}. Text partially transcribed in Mancini (1907): 231–232.

[72] The Orthodox Church celebrates the presanctified liturgy during weekdays in Lent except on the feast of the Annunciation (when it celebrates a normal liturgy) and on Great Thursday and Friday of

at length about why the 'Latins' and the 'Hellenes' (as he calls them) fast in different ways during Lent: 'If anyone ever asks me, "Why are these things so? Why do you not do this [fast] the same [as the Latins] on Saturdays?" I immediately answer truthfully...'[73] After a short theological overview, he explains in more detail that the Greeks' customs are based on Apost. c. 66 and *Trullo* c. 55.[74]

The author of this curious 'hymn' was not attempting to convince a Latin reader of the correct fasting practice; after all, he wrote in Greek. It is instead aimed at Greek-speakers who wrongly believed that their tradition was to celebrate the presanctified liturgy on Holy Friday and could not understand why they fasted differently to their Latin neighbours. Indeed, the use of metric verse and a hymn-like structure may have been a mnemonic device to make the information easier to learn. It gives the strong impression that there were Greek-rite Christians in thirteenth-century Sicily that had grown up with Latin-rite neighbours and were unsure if or why their religious customs were different. Presumably the author of this text was a monk of the Holy Saviour who wanted to edify them on the matter.[75] Like Nektarios of Otranto and others, he directed his reader to Byzantine canon law for instruction.

Nevertheless, the efforts of the anonymous authors above and of Nektarios, Theodore of Cursi, and the anonymous scribes and readers who highlighted texts 'against the Latins' in the Salentine nomocanons were ultimately in vain. In the words of Peters-Custot, the thirteenth century was the time when 'the Italo-Greek religious life began to truly separate itself from the Byzantine model to adhere to Western models'.[76] That is not to say that the Italo-Greeks were transformed wholesale into Latin-rite Christians, but their cultural connection to Byzantine Christianity continued to weaken as the later Middle Ages wore on. Eventually they would cease to see themselves as an outpost of Byzantium in Italy and identify more as a Graecophone subdivision of the Roman church.

A marginal note in the Rossanese nomocanon Vat. gr. 2019 provides one of the most vivid and concise signs of this shift. One of the last items in Aristenos' *Synopsis of Canons*, the central text in the manuscript, is a pro-Constantinopolitan essay of uncertain authorship entitled *To Those Who Say That Rome Is the First*

Holy Week, when no liturgy is performed. The Western church, by contrast, *only* celebrates the presanctified liturgy on Friday of Holy Week.

[73] '*εἰ δὲ τῆς* [*sic*] *εἴπη πρὸς ἱμᾶς· πῶς ταῦτα οὗτος ἔχει; πῶς καὶ τούτῳ σάββατα οὐ ποιήτε ὁμίος;... εὐθὺς ἀποκρινόμεθα ἀληθῶς...*': S. Salv. 164, fol. 3^{v}.

[74] S. Salv. 164, fol. 5$^{r/v}$.

[75] Cf. the argument in Kolbaba (2000): 124–144 that the writers of Byzantine lists of Latin 'errors' were worried less about the fact that the Westerners committed them than that their fellow Byzantines might also commit them.

[76] Peters-Custot (2009a): 532.

Throne.[77] The tract uses a series of historical and canonical examples to argue that Rome does not have primacy over Constantinople. At the beginning of the text, the anonymous author writes that the fourth ecumenical council had placed Constantinople above all the other patriarchates, an inaccurate reference to Chalcedon c. 28 that is highly reminiscent of a similar claim made by Anna Komnene in the twelfth-century *Alexiad*.[78] A fourteenth-century Greek hand has left a simple riposte in the margin: an instruction to the reader to 'flee these lies'.[79] The Italo-Greeks had at last come to accept Roman ecclesiastical primacy.

Conclusion

The period between the late twelfth and the fourteenth centuries was a time of significant cultural change for the Italo-Greeks. The combination of the decline of the Byzantine Empire, the centralisation of papal power, and demographic change in southern Italy unmoored them from the world of Byzantine Christianity around the turn of the thirteenth century. This was a slow process and it did not result in a straightforward Latinisation of the Italo-Greeks; their language, liturgy, and many of their cultural markers survived for centuries to come. With the brief exceptions of the baptismal controversy of 1231–1232 and Raymond of Campania's liturgical intervention of 1334, the Roman church made no active efforts to challenge their use of the Byzantine rite.

Nonetheless, tensions existed at a local level both between Greeks and Latins and among the Greeks themselves. After nearly two centuries of papal efforts to reform the clergy, some Latin-rite Christians in southern Italy must have been scandalised by the presence of priests who looked and dressed differently from them, celebrated the liturgy in another language, and lived openly with their wives and children. At the same time, many Greeks had either begun to adopt aspects of the Latin rite or simply failed to adhere strictly to the customs and traditions of the Church of Constantinople. If Italo-Greek Christians were (according to the views of the time) defined by their adherence to the Byzantine rite, then any deviation from that rite posed a challenge to the community's identity and cohesion.

Largely cut off from the contemporary Byzantine church, tradition-minded Italo-Greeks from the thirteenth century onward needed an alternative resource to help defend their rite against Latin criticism and their own community's ignorance. They found it in their manuscripts of Byzantine canon law, a collection of authoritative legal sources that simultaneously explained and legitimised the

[77] '*πρὸς τοὺς λέγοντας ὡς ἡ Ῥώμη πρῶτος θρόνος*': Vat. gr. 2019, fols. 92^{v}–94^{v}. Text in RP 4.409–415. The text is usually attributed in manuscripts to Photios but is more likely to have been composed in the eleventh or early twelfth century; see Darrouzès (1965): 85–88.

[78] Anna Komnene, *Alexiad* 1.13. See Siciliano (1979): 176–177; Spiteris (1979): 232.

[79] '*ταῦτα ψευδῆ φεῦγε*': Vat. gr. 2019, fol. 93^{v}.

manner in which the Italo-Greeks should practise their faith. Byzantine canon law was also intellectually acceptable to Latins, at least in principle. Although the Roman church's canonical tradition diverged in many ways from that of Byzantium, it did not dispute the basic validity of the Byzantine corpus for Greek Christians (even if it had objections to individual parts).

This context explains the surprisingly long afterlife of the nomocanon in medieval southern Italy. To use Cover's terminology, Byzantine canon law may have ceased to be nomos in an imperial sense, but it was still nomos in a paideic sense, offering a legal narrative for managing and preserving the identity of Greek Christians as a distinct community. At a time when many Italo-Greeks were beginning to adapt to the developing cultural environment of late medieval southern Italy, more conservative monks and clergy could turn to nomocanons like those of the Salentine Group to educate them on the traditions that they were supposed to maintain. The effort was ultimately doomed to failure, but it seems to have lasted well into the fourteenth century.

Conclusion

> It is recounted in earlier histories that the pope of Rome himself and those Christians of the Western region beyond the Ionian Gulf—the Italians, Lombards, the Franks and the Germans, the Amalfitans, Venetians, and the rest—have all been outside the catholic church for many years and are strangers to the traditions of the Gospel and the Apostles. Because of this, it is said, they hold to unlawful and barbarian customs . . . Only the Calabrians are orthodox Christians as they were before.[1]

This sweeping condemnation of Western Christendom forms the concluding paragraph of a polemical essay by Constantine Stilbes, metropolitan bishop of Kyzikos in Asia Minor, written soon after the fall of Constantinople to the crusaders in 1204. The words were not entirely his own; he adapted them from the introduction of an anonymous twelfth-century tract known today as the *Opusculum contra Francos*.[2] Nonetheless, they must have seemed fitting in the aftermath of the Fourth Crusade. To writers like Stilbes, Western Christians were hostile to the Byzantine church and its ancient traditions, instead following 'unlawful and barbarian customs'. The only exceptions were 'the Calabrians', by which Stilbes and the *Opusculum* meant the Italo-Greeks.[3]

To Byzantine observers of the twelfth and thirteenth centuries, the Greeks of southern Italy seemed to be an outpost of Byzantine Christianity in Western Europe, faithfully following the correct and lawful customs of the Church of Constantinople. Italo-Greek writers of the period such as Neilos Doxapatres and Nektarios of Otranto presented a similar impression of themselves as members of a religious community on the threshold, geographically and politically situated in the 'Latin' West but spiritually and legally rooted in Byzantium.

The concept of law played an important role in all these writers' conceptions of religious orthodoxy: the Italo-Greeks were orthodox not just because they held the

[1] '*ἱστόρηται μέντοι τοῖς πρὸ ἡμῶν ὡς καὶ αὐτὸς ὁ πάπας τῆς Ῥώμης καὶ ὅσοι τοῦ δυτικοῦ κλίματος χριστιανοὶ ἔξωθεν κόλπου τοῦ Ἰωνικοῦ, Ἰταλοί, Λογγίβαρδοι, Φράγγοι οἱ καὶ Γερμανοί, Ἀμαλφηνοί, Βενετικοὶ καὶ οἱ λοιποί, πάντες τῆς καθολικῆς ἐκκλησίας ἔξω πρὸ μακρῶν εἰσι χρόνων καὶ τῶν εὐαγγελικῶν ἀλλότριοι καὶ ἀποστολικῶν παραδόσεων, δι' ἅ, φησίν, κρατοῦσι παράνομα καὶ βάρβαρα ἔθη . . . μόνοι δὲ οἱ Καλαβροὶ ἀνέκαθέν εἰσιν ὀρθόδοξοι χριστιανοί*': Darrouzès (1963): 90–91.

[2] Hergenröther (1869): 62–63.

[3] Since Calabria had the highest concentration of Greek-speakers in southern Italy, 'Calabrians' could serve as a simple shorthand for Byzantines who wanted to refer to Italo-Greeks in general.

Byzantine Religious Law in Medieval Italy. James Morton, Oxford University Press (2021). © James Morton.
DOI: 10.1093/oso/9780198861140.003.0012

right beliefs or doctrine, but because they acknowledged the (Byzantine) canons and followed *lawful* customs. Their observance of Byzantine religious law was an important element of their identification as Greek rather than Latin Christians—even if they did come to refer to themselves by the Hellenised Latin term '*graikoi*'.

The surviving nomocanons of southern Italy show that this perception of the southern Italian Greeks as law-abiding orthodox Christians was not simply wishful thinking on the part of Byzantine writers or a faint cultural memory among the Italo-Greeks themselves. As we have seen, the Greeks of southern Italy continued to produce and read manuscripts of Byzantine canon law until the early fourteenth century at least. One must stress the *Byzantine* character of these nomocanons: they do not contain any contemporary Latin canonical texts, nor do they show any noticeable signs of Latin aesthetic or codicological influence. Only one of the texts in the manuscripts, a canonical *erotapokrisis* by Archbishop Leo Grammatikos of Reggio on clerical marriage, was composed in Italy itself, and it dates to the era of Byzantine rule. There are no signs of the hybridity or transculturation observed by scholars in other areas of Italo-Greek life. One must acknowledge, of course, that we can only speak with certainty about the manuscripts that have survived, which are mostly from twelfth-century Calabrian monasteries or from thirteenth-century Salentine parish churches, but it is none-theless striking that these points hold true for all thirty-six codices in this study.

We began this investigation with a simple question: why did the Italo-Greeks continue to produce and read these manuscripts? The practice makes little sense if we approach it from a purely positivistic perspective: the nomocanons had little relevance to the formal legal system of the Roman papacy, which exercised official jurisdiction over southern Italy from the eleventh century on. However, it begins to make good sense when we view it through the lens of legal and cultural pluralism.

The legal order of southern Italy in the Middle Ages was a complex one even by the standards of the time. Medieval historians are well acquainted with the different legal systems that operated alongside one another in most of Europe in this time period: canon and civil law, royal and communal law, or different types of ethnic custom, for example. The mostly tolerated presence of multiple religious and cultural groups within the Kingdom of Sicily (Normans, Lombards, Greeks, Muslims, Jews, etc.), each with their own legal tradition, contributed additional layers of complexity. The Italo-Greek nomocanons give us an insight into how this legal pluralism worked in practice.

Despite southern Italy's well-deserved reputation as a medieval cultural melting pot, the nomocanons are strikingly monocultural. This was a key feature of the legal pluralism of the post-Byzantine period: Byzantine canon law survived the Norman conquest of the eleventh century because it was segregated from the Roman church's legal system. The Norman rulers did not want to concede power to the Roman popes any more than they did to the Byzantine emperors, so they permitted and (in some cases) encouraged the judicial independence of strategically important Greek monasteries and bishops. Rather than answering to the Roman administrative hierarchy to which they were notionally subject, these Greek institutions instead entered a patronage relationship with the Norman kings that resembled the Byzantine Empire's model of church-state relations. Roger II and his successors did not care which canonical tradition they followed.

Consequently, powerful Italo-Greek monasteries such as the Patiron of Rossano and the Holy Saviour of Messina could oversee their own autonomous legal systems based on the canon law that they had inherited from the Byzantine Empire. The evidence for bishops is less clear than that for monasteries, but the survival of manuscripts such as the thirteenth-century Vat. gr. 2019 in Rossano suggests that southern Italy's Greek hierarchs enjoyed a similar degree of autonomy. Indeed, their autonomy was so great that noble families such as the Maleinoi of Rossano could mix civil and canonical authority in ways that contravened *both* Roman *and* Byzantine canon law.

It must be stressed, again, that we can only say this with certainty about the institutions that produced the surviving nomocanons. In many areas of southern Italy, Greek monasteries and clergy were subjected to or replaced by Latins. As scholars such as Peters-Custot and Safran have shown, cultural and religious adaptations *did* occur in many places. However, the production and use of Byzantine nomocanons by many institutions is evidence that there were also Greek Christian communities that maintained their judicial independence throughout the twelfth century. Some monasteries such as Messina and Casole maintained it even into the mid-thirteenth century under the patronage of Frederick II. This created a context in which nomocanons could continue to serve as practical legal reference guides at the local level.

Nonetheless, the legal *status quo* of the Norman era began to change around the turn of the thirteenth century. The demise of the Hauteville dynasty in the 1190s created an opening for the papacy to extend its authority into southern Italy, while the Fourth Lateran Council of 1215 established a blueprint for the integration of non-Latin Christians into the Western church's administrative organisation. Though Frederick II's conflict with the papacy gave respite to some Greek monasteries, the Angevin conquest of 1266 eliminated their legal autonomy for good. With the loss of autonomy came the end of Byzantine canon law as a formal legal system in southern Italy.

Yet this did not mean the end of the nomocanons. As the work of Robert Cover and the legal pluralists has demonstrated, law is more than codified statutes enforced by a state authority. It is better to think of law instead as a field of normative social discourse (Cover's 'nomos') operating at varying degrees of formality; it encompasses not just codified statute law (the 'imperial mode' of law) but also the shared values and narratives of a community (the 'paideic mode'). A legal collection may lose its value as a source of imperial law without ceasing to be a source of paideic law; that is to say, a legal collection could be useless in a judicial setting yet still carry a weight of social and cultural authority.

This is what happened to the Italo-Greek nomocanons in the thirteenth century. As the monks of the Holy Saviour of Messina discovered in their dispute with Archbishop Berardus, a Byzantine nomocanon was of little use when arguing before the papal court. Nonetheless, while the Roman church may not have accepted the contemporary legal validity of the Byzantine canonical corpus, it could not deny its historical value. Moreover, the papacy's *laissez faire* stance towards the Italo-Greeks in the twelfth century had created an unintentional precedent that their 'customs and rites' should be tolerated. The nomocanons were authoritative cultural sources that could explain why the Italo-Greeks' customs and rites differed from those of their Latin neighbours; the antiquity of Byzantine canon law could provide an aura of legitimacy. This was especially important in controversial matters such as the marriage of clergy, the conduct of divine offices during Lent, and divergent fasting practices.

The manuscripts' paideic function was heightened in the context of thirteenth- and fourteenth-century cultural change. As the Italo-Greeks became increasingly cut off from the Church of Constantinople and began to adopt or adapt elements of the Latin rite, conservative factions within the community turned to canon law in an attempt to preserve their distinct religious identity. We see this especially among the secular clergy of the Salento peninsula (where the last Greek-rite dioceses of southern Italy were concentrated) and among the monks of the Holy Saviour of Messina and St Nicholas of Casole. Although this was ultimately a losing battle, the Greek rite itself survived in the Salento and in Calabria until the early modern period.

Finally, it is interesting to consider the historical trajectory of Byzantine canon law in southern Italy in the broader context of medieval law. The traditional narrative of European law in the Middle Ages—dated but not wholly inaccurate—is of a gradual transition from 'primitive' customary law to the codified statute law of modern nation states; in other words, from the paideic to the imperial mode of law. Byzantine canon law in southern Italy, by contrast, went in the opposite direction: what was imperial law under Byzantine rule eventually became paideic law by the later Middle Ages.

Legal pluralism has proved its worth in understanding the law of pre-modern societies from the ancient Roman Empire to China and South East Asia. It is equally useful for understanding the legal and religious culture of the medieval Mediterranean and southern Italy. The symbiotic relationship between law and culture in the Middle Ages merits further attention and additional research in this area will yield great benefits. In terms of medieval Christian religious identity, it promises to help reframe and illuminate long-misunderstood historical problems. Chief among these is the vexed question of the so-called 'Great Schism' between Rome and Constantinople and the emergence of distinct

'Catholic' and 'Orthodox' identities. This book has investigated the relationship between religious law and cultural identity among the Greek Christian minority in southern Italy. There is great scope to take this investigation further and ask how medieval developments in Greek and Latin canon law helped to shape the identities of Eastern and Western Christendom more broadly.

APPENDIX 1

Manuscript Descriptions

1. Florence, Biblioteca Medicea Laurenziana, MS plut. 5.22

Nomocanon, Salentine Group (incomplete)

Date:	12th/13th Century	**Dimensions:**	205 x 145 (150 x 95)
Origin:	Salento	**Material:**	Parchment
Owner:	Unknown	**Folios:**	iv + 177 + iii
Scribe:	Unknown	**Lines:**	32–33
Binding:	Biblioteca	**Ruling:**	X20C1 (System 1)
Hands:	Laurenziana	**Collation:**	$1–9^{8}$, 10^{6}, 11^{10}, 12^{8}, 13^{7}, $14–16^{8}$, 17^{6},
	A: 1–177 b: 60^{v}		18^{10}, 19^{8}, 20^{6}, 21^{10}, $22–23^{4}$, 24^{3}
	a: iv^{r} c: iv^{v}		

Catalogue: *RHBR* 3.102–104 (no. 471); Bandini (1764): 1.45–48. **View Online:** http://www.internetculturale.it/jmms/iccuviewer/iccu.jsp?id=oai%3Ateca.bmlonline.it%3A21%3AXXXX%3APlutei%3AIT%253AFI0100_Plutei_05.22_0036&mode=all&teca=Laurenziana+-+FI

1. ***Nomocanon in 50 Titles***	**1^{r}**
1. **On Forbidden Marriages*	60^{v}
2. Conciliar Canons	**84^{r}**
1. Explanation of the Historical Order of Councils	84^{r}
2. *Trullo*	84^{v}
3. History of the Councils (‘ἰδοὺ καὶ εἰσὶν ἁγίαι σύνοδοι ἃς προειρήκαμεν’)	$111^{r/v}$
4. II Nicaea and *Protodeutera* (Nic. c. 1, 7, 4, 6, 14; *Prot.* c. 11; Nic. c. 16, 8, 13; *Prot.* c. 10; Nic. c. 17, 12; *Prot.* c. 2, 3; Nic. c. 21; *Prot.* c. 4–6; Nic. c. 19, 20, 18, 22; *Prot.* c. 13–15)	112^{r}
3. Symeon Metaphrastes, *Synopsis of Canons*	**119^{r}**
4. Patristic Canons	**139^{v}**
1. Basil of Caesarea c. 1–17, 90, 89, 88	139^{v}
2. Gregory of Nyssa, *Letter to Letoius*	148^{r}
3. Theophilos of Alexandria c. 1, 3–12, 14	154^{r}
4. Peter of Alexandria, *Six Canons from the Sermon on Penitence*	155^{v}
5. Gregory of Neocaesarea, *Canonical Letter*	156^{r}
6. Athanasios of Alexandria c. 1–2, 4.	158^{r}
7. Basil of Caesarea c. 94; *Great Asketikon* 310; *Sermon for the Instruction of Priests* 2	161^{v}
8. Timothy of Alexandria, *Canonical Answers*	$162^{r/v}$
9. Cyril of Alexandria c. 1–5, 8	164^{r}
5. Clerical Discipline and Differences with the Latin Church	**165^{v}**
1. *On the Rights of the Most Holy Throne of Constantinople*	165^{v}
2. History of the Councils (‘πρώτη σύνοδος γέγονεν οἰκουμενική’)	166^{v}

3. I Nicaea, *Decree on Pascha*	$170^{r/v}$
6. Marriage Law	**171^{v}**
1. Sisinnios II of Constantinople, *Tome against the Marriage of Cousins* (excerpt)	171^{v}
2. Short excerpts from Byzantine civil law on marriage	171^{v}
7. Theological Texts	**172^{r}**
1. II Constantinople (553), Actio VIII	$172^{r/v}$
2. Proklos of Constantinople, *Letter to John of Antioch*	172^{v}
3. Victor of Carthage, *Letter to Pope Theodore I*	172^{v}
4. Basil of Caesarea, *Epitimia*	$173^{r/v}$
8. Anti-Latin Texts (des. mut.)	**173^{v}**
1. Photios of Constantinople, *Five Canonical Letters* (des. mut.)	173^{v}

2. Grottaferrata, Badia greca, MS gr. 50 (Z γ VII)

Civil Law Collection (fragmentary)

Date:	14th Century	**Dimensions:**	195 x 145 (145 x 100)
Origin:	Rossano? (Northern Calabria)	**Material:**	Paper ('Western Arabic')
Owner:	Unknown	**Folios:**	i + 199 + i
Scribe:	Unknown	**Lines:**	23
Binding:	Badia greca di Grottaferrata (early modern)	**Ruling:**	Unclear
		Collation:	$1–24^{8}, 25^{7}$
Hands:	A: 1–199		

Catalogue: *RHBR* 1.102 (no. 81); Rocchi (1883): 493–494.

1. *Procheiros Nomos* (inc. mut.)	**1^{r}**
2. Appendix: Civil Law	**121^{r}**
1. *Soldier's Law*	121^{r}
2. *Sailor's Law*	125^{v}
3. *Farmer's Law*	132^{v}
3. Appendix: Canon Law	**141^{v}**
1. Athanasios of Emesa, *Syntagma of Novels* (epitome)	141^{v}
2. Carth. c. 15, 25, 6, 128, 130	145^{r}
3. Canonical collection in 118 chapters	147^{r}
4. *Ecloga privata*	**163^{r}**
5. Back Matter (des. mut.)	**185^{v}**
1. Short excerpts from Byzantine civil law on marriage	185^{v}
2. Pseudo-John Chrysostom, *Dispute Against the Lombards on the Legal and Christian Date of Pascha*	$187^{r/v}$
3. *Alphabetical Acrostic of Bishop Eusebius* (inc. '*Ἀδὰμ κατάρξας του βροτησίου γένους*')	$188^{r/v}$
4. Lexicon of Latin legal terms (des. mut.)	189^{r}

3. Grottaferrata, Badia greca, MS gr. 76 (Z γ III)

Civil Law Collection (fragmentary)

Date:	11th/12th Century	**Dimensions:**	225 x 170 (165 x 115)
Origin:	Rossano? (Northern Calabria)	**Material:**	Parchment
Owner:	Unknown	**Folios:**	i + 175 + i
Scribe:	Unknown	**Lines:**	23–29
Binding:	Badia greca di Grottaferrata (early modern)	**Ruling:**	X22C1, 20C1 (System 1)
Hands:	A: 1–84, 120–175 B: 85–119	**Collation:**	1^4, $2–11^8$, 12^{14}, 13^9, 14^{12}, $15–19^8$

Catalogue: *RHBR* 1.100–101 (no. 79); Rocchi (1883): 488–490.

1. *Procheiros Nomos* (inc. mut.)	**1^r**
2. Appendix: Civil Law	**71^v**
1. *Soldier's Law*	71^v
2. *Sailor's Law*	76^r
3. *Collection of juridical excerpts on various subjects	85^r
4. *Farmer's Law*	120^r
5. *Ekloge* 14.2–9, 11–12	126^v
3. Appendix: Canon Law	**127^v**
1. Laod. c. 18, 20, 24, 28, 32, 36, 38, 44, 49, 51, 53–54	127^v
2. Chalc. c. 6	128^v
3. Neocaes. c. 11, 7	128^v
4. *C87C* 72, 45, 31	128^v
5. *Apost. Const.* 8.42.1–4; 8.44.1–2	129^r
6. Athanasios of Emesa, *Syntagma of Novels* (epitome)	129^r
7. Carth. c. 15, 32, 25, 5–6, 128–131, 80	137^v
8. *Protodeutera*, canons	140^r
9. *C87C* 46–7	147^v
10.Athanasios of Emesa, *Syntagma of Novels*, 10.2.39	148^r
11.Just. *Nov.* 83	148^r
4. *Ecloga privata*	**148^r**
5. Fragments of Marriage Law (des. mut.)	**175^r**

4. Grottaferrata, Badia greca, MS gr. 322 (B δ I)

Nomocanon (fragmentary)

Date:	Before 1135	**Dimensions:**	155 x 120 (100 x 75)
Origin:	Southern Calabria	**Material:**	Parchment
Owner:	Abbot Gerasimos Atoulinos of SS Peter	**Folios:**	i + 129 + i
Scribe:	and Paul of Spanopetro	**Ruling:**	00C1 (System 1)
Binding:	Unknown	**Lines:**	21–2
	Badia greca di Grottaferrata (early modern)	**Collation:**	1^{10}; 2^6; 3^9; $4–13^8$
Hands:	A: 1–129 a: marginalia (*passim*)		

Catalogue: *RHBR* 3.110–111 (no. 474); Rocchi (1883): 183–185.

1. Fragment: Canonical Miscellany (inc. mut.)	**1r**
1. Nikephoros the Confessor c. 51, 43, 44 (inc. mut.)	1r
2. Timothy of Alexandria, *Canonical Answers* 1, 3, 6, 8–7, 12–14, 18	1r
3. History of the Councils (inc. 'χρὴ γινώσκειν, ὅτι ἑπτὰ ἁγίαι καὶ οἰκουμενικαὶ σύνοδοι εἴσιν')	2v
4. John the Faster, *Kanonarion* (excerpt)	15v
5. *Canons of the Holy Apostles*	17r/v
6. *From the First Holy Council, Written to the Pope in Antioch*	17v
7. 'Basil of Caesarea' [Germanos I of Constantinople], *Mystical History of the Catholic Church*	18r
8. Methodios I of Constantinople, *Decree on the Reception of Apostates*	36v
9. *Epitome of Book Eight of the Apostolic Constitutions* 18, 19.1–2, 5–7; *Capitula XXX* 14–30; *Epitome* 22.2–19	38r
10. *Trullo* c. 2, 4, 12, 19–21, 23, 24, 26, 29, 30, 40–44, 46, 48–49, 51–54, 57–59, 61, 66, 72–75, 80, 83–84, 87–88, 90–91, 93, 96, 98, 101	41r
11. II Nicaea c. 1, 4, 7, 14, 16–18, 22	57v
12. *Prot.* c. 9, 14–17	63r
13. Constantinople (879) c. 2, 3	66r
14. Carth. c. 42, 44, 102, 109–112, 116, 126, 128, 130–133	67v
2. *Nomocanon in 50 Titles* (excerpts)	**70v**
3. Appendix: Theology (des. mut.)	**112r**
1. Niketas Stethatos, *Discourse Against the Romans* (with textual variations at the end)	112r
2. John of Damascus, *Exposition of the Orthodox Faith*	126v
3. Gregory of Neocaesarea, *On the Trinity*	127v
4. Athanasios of Alexandria, *On the Catholic Faith* (des. mut.)	128v

5. London, British Library, MS Add. 28822

Nomocanon, Salentine Group (fragmentary)

Date:	12th/13th Century	**Dimensions:**	260 x 170 (195 x 115)
Origin:	Salento	**Material:**	Parchment
Owner:	Unknown	**Folios:**	iii + 49 + iii
Scribe:	Unknown	**Lines:**	32–34
Binding:	British Museum	**Ruling:**	X31D1b (System 1)
Hands:	A: 1–49 a: 6r, 11r, 12r, 43v (in margin)	**Collation:**	1^9, 2^6, 3^{10}, $4–6^8$

Catalogue: *RHBR* 3.135–137 (no. 484); Richard (1952): 51. **View Online:** http://www.bl.uk/manuscripts/Viewer.aspx?ref=add_ms_28822_f001r

1. Patristic Canons (inc. mut.)	**1r**
1. Gennadios I of Constantinople, *Encyclical Letter*	1r
2. Marriage Law	**2v**
1. *Tome of Union* (920)	2v

2. Sisinnios II of Constantinople, *Tome against the Marriage of Cousins*	5^{r}
3. Alexios Stoudites, *Synodal Act on Marriage*	6^{r}
4. *Ekloge* 2.2	$6^{r/v}$
5. Leo of Calabria, *Canonical Answer on Clerical Marriage*	6^{v}
6. Short excerpts from Byzantine civil law on marriage	7^{r}
3. Clerical Discipline and Differences with the Latin Church	**8^{r}**
1. *Apost. Const.* 3.10–11, 6.17, 8.42–44, 1.3.11 (on the rights of the clergy, including marriage)	8^{r}
2. *Rule of the Holy Apostles*	9^{r}
3. I Nicaea, *Decree on Pascha*	$9^{r/v}$
4. Excerpts from Byzantine civil and canon law on marriage, clerical discipline, and feast days	9^{v}
5. John Moschos, *Spiritual Meadow* 149 (excerpt)	12^{r}
6. Nikon of the Black Mountain, *Kanonarion* (excerpts)	12^{r}
7. Council of Carthage, canons	16^{r}
8. Photios of Constantinople, *Encyclical Letter to the Eastern Patriarchs*	37^{v}
4. *Nomocanon in 50 Titles* (des. mut.)	**43^{v}**

6. Messina, Biblioteca Universitaria Regionale, MS S. Salv. 59

Nomocanon, Rossanese Group

Date:	*c.* 1100–1115	**Dimensions:**	325 x 255 (200 x 165)
Origin:	Patiron (Rossano, N. Calabria)	**Material:**	Parchment
Owner:	Holy Saviour of Bordonaro (Sicily)	**Folios:**	ii + 372 + i
Scribe:	Bartholomew and Pachomios (monks)?	**Lines:**	29–32
		Ruling:	44D2 (System 9)
Binding:	Biblioteca Universitaria Regionale	**Collation:**	$1–44^{8}$
Hands:	A: $1–33^{r}$ B: 33^{v}–372		

Catalogue: *RHBR* 3.162–164 (no. 494); Mancini (1907): 107–114.

1. Front Matter	**1^{r}**
1. *Epitome of Book Eight of the Apostolic Constitutions* 22.2–28.1	1^{r}
2. *S50T*, Preface and Table of Canons	3^{v}
2. *Nomocanon in 14 Titles* (Photian recension)	**5^{r}**
3. Conciliar Canons	**76^{v}**
4. Patristic Canons	**306^{r}**
5. Appendix: Civil Law	**251^{r}**
1. Just. *Nov.* 77	251^{r}
2. *C87C*	252^{r}
3. *C25C*	268^{v}
4. *Tripartite Collection* (des. mut.)	300^{r}
5. Heraclius, *Novels* [4,] 1, 3, 2 (inc. mut.)	366^{r}
6. Epilogue: John Moschos, *Spiritual Meadow* 149 (excerpt)	**372^{r}**

7. Milan, Biblioteca Ambrosiana, MS B 107 sup. (gr. 128)

Nomocanon, Salentine Group (incomplete)

Date:	12th/13th Century	**Dimensions:**	240 x 150 (165–185 x 100)
Origin:	Salento	**Material:**	Parchment
Owner:	Unknown	**Folios:**	iv + 159 + ii
Scribe:	Unknown	**Lines:**	22–36
Binding:	Unknown (early modern)	**Ruling:**	X32D1, X52D1, X22D1, U21/1b, 20D1 (system 9)
Hands:	Multiple	**Collation:**	1^{4}, 2^{9}, $3–15^{8}$, 16^{6}, 17^{8}, 18^{9}, 19^{4}, 20^{9}, 21^{8}

Catalogue: *RHBR* 3.147–151 (no. 489); Martini and Bassi (1906): 1.138–144 (no. 128).

1. Conciliar Canons with Historical Introductions (inc. mut.)	**1^{r}**
1. Apostolic Canons	1^{r}
2. *The Ecclesiastical Ranks*	4^{v}
3. I Nicaea	5^{r}
4. Ancyra	9^{r}
5. Neocaesarea	12^{r}
7. Sardica	13^{r}
8. Gangra	19^{r}
9. Antioch	21^{v}
10. Laodicea	26^{v}
11. I Constantinople (381)	30^{r}
12. Ephesus	33^{r}
13. Chalcedon	36^{v}
14. II Constantinople (553)	42^{v}
15. Constantinople (680/1)	$45^{r/v}$
16. *Trullo*	45^{v}
17. II Nicaea (II Nic. c. 1–14; *Prot.* c. 11; II Nic. c. 16–22, 15)	71^{r}
18. *Protodeutera* (*Prot. c.* 1–10; II Nic. c. 17; *Prot.* c. 12–17)	77^{v}
2. Patristic Canons	**83^{r}**
3. Marriage Law	**120^{v}**
1. *Tome of Union* (920)	120^{v}
2. Alexios Stoudites, *Synodal Act on Marriage*	123^{r}
3. *Ekloge* 2.2	$123^{r/v}$
4. Leo of Calabria, *Canonical Answer on Clerical Marriage*	123^{v}
5. Sisinnios II of Constantinople, *Tome against the Marriage of Cousins*	124^{r}
7. Diagrams of acceptable and unacceptable degrees of kinship for marriage	133^{r}
8. Short excerpts from Byzantine civil law on marriage	138^{v}
9. Nicholas III Grammatikos of Constantinople, *Canonical Answers to the Bishop of Zetounion*	143^{r}
10. Methodios I of Constantinople, *Decree on the Reception of Apostates*	144^{v}
11. Short excerpts from Byzantine civil law on marriage	146^{r}
4. Clerical Discipline and Differences with the Latin Church (des. mut.)	**147^{r}**
1. *Apost. Const.* 3.10–11, 6.17, 8.42–44, 1.3.11 (on the rights of the clergy, including marriage)	147^{r}

2.	*Rule of the Holy Apostles*	148^{r}
3.	I Nicaea, *Decree on Pascha*	148$^{r/v}$
4.	Excerpts from Byzantine civil and canon law on marriage, clerical discipline, and feast days	148^{v}
5.	John Moschos, *Spiritual Meadow* 149 (excerpt)	151^{v}
7.	Nikon of the Black Mountain, *Kanonarion* (excerpts)	152^{r}
8.	Socrates, *Ecclesiastical History* 1.11.1–17	158^{v}
9.	Just. *Nov.* 133.1–3 (excerpt; inc. and des. mut.)	159$^{r/v}$

8. Milan, Biblioteca Ambrosiana, MS E 94 sup. (gr. 303)

Nomocanon, Salentine Group (incomplete)

Date:	13th/14th Century	**Dimensions:**	255 x 165 (200 x 125)
Origin:	Soleto? (Salento)	**Material:**	Parchment (1–7 Paper)
Owner:	Unknown	**Folios:**	v + 251 + ii
Scribe:	Unknown	**Lines:**	29–32
Binding:	Biblioteca Ambrosiana	**Ruling:**	P2 X20D1, P2 X4 20D1, V20A1, Xab 20A1, W 20A1, V00A1 (Systems 9, 6, 8, 10, 7)
Hands:	A: 8^{r}–94^{v}, 98^{v}–158^{r}, 167^{v}–181^{v} B: 88^{v} E: 181^{v}–221 C: 94^{v}–98^{v} F: 222–235 D: 158^{v}–167^{r} G: 236–251	**Collation:**	1^{8}, 2^{6}, 3–12^{8}, 13^{7}, 14–28^{8}, 29^{7}, 30–2^{8}

Catalogue: *RHBR* 3.151–155 (no. 490); Martini and Bassi (1906): 1.341–347 (no. 303).

1.	*'Basil of Caesarea' [Germanos I of Constantinople], *Mystical History of the Catholic Church*	1^{r}
1.	**Conciliar Canons with Historical Introductions (inc. mut.)**	**8^{r}**
1.	Apostolic Canons	8^{r}
2.	I Nicaea	14^{r}
3.	Ancyra	21^{r}
4.	Neocaesarea	24^{v}
5.	Sardica	26^{r}
6.	Gangra	33^{v}
7.	Antioch	36^{v}
8.	Laodicea	41^{v}
9.	I Constantinople (381)	44^{r}
10.	Ephesus	47^{v}
11.	Chalcedon	51^{v}
12.	II Constantinople (553)	58^{v}
13.	Constantinople (680)	59^{r}
14.	Sophronios of Jerusalem, *Letter to Sergios* (summary)	60^{r}
15.	Carthage (excerpts)	64^{r}
16.	*Trullo*	82^{r}
17.	II Nicaea (II Nic. c. 1–14; *Prot.* c. 11; II Nic. c. 16–22, 15)	109^{v}

18. *Protodeutera* (*Prot. c.* 1–10; II Nic. c. 17; *Prot.* c. 12–17) 117^{v}

2. Patristic Canons 123^{v}

1. Dionysios of Alexandria, *Letter to Basil* 123^{v}
2. Peter of Alexandria, *Six Canons from the Sermon on Penitence* 125^{v}
3. Gregory of Neocaesarea, *Canonical Letter* 128^{v}
4. Athanasios of Alexandria, *Letters* (excerpts) 130^{v}
5. Basil of Caesarea, *Canonical Letters and Texts* 134^{v}
6. Gregory of Nyssa, *Letter to Letoius* 153^{r}
7. Timothy of Alexandria, *Canonical Answers* 159^{r}
8. Theophilos of Alexandria, *Canonical Texts* 160^{v}
9. Cyril of Alexandria, *Letter to the Bishops of Libya and Pentapolis* 162^{v}
10. Gennadios I of Constantinople, *Encyclical Letter* 163^{r}
11. Sisinnios II of Constantinople, *Tome against the Marriage of Cousins* 165^{r}

3. *Nomocanon in 50 Titles* 166^{r}

4. Marriage Law 199^{r}

1. *Ekloge* 2.2 199^{r}
2. Alexios Stoudites, *Synodal Act on Marriage* 199^{v}

5. Symeon Metaphrastes, *Synopsis of Canons* 200^{r}

6. Theological Texts 218^{v}

1. John Chrysostom, *Homily on Matthew* (excerpt) 218^{v}
2. Note on correct belief 219^{r}
3. II Constantinople (553), *Actio* 8 219^{r}
4. Proklos of Constantinople, *Letter to John of Antioch* (excerpt) 219$^{r/v}$
5. Victor of Carthage, *Letter to Pope Theodore I* 219^{v}

7. Marriage Law and Fasting 219^{v}

1. Sisinnios II of Constantinople, *Tome against the Marriage of Cousins* (summary) 219^{v}
2. Photios of Constantinople, *Canonical Letter* 5 220^{r}
3. Nikephoros the Confessor c. 3, 39, 40 221^{r}
4. Leontios of Constantinople, *Homily* 6 (excerpt) 221^{r}
5. Leo of Calabria, *Canonical Answer on Clerical Marriage* 222^{r}
6. *On False Accusers* 222$^{r/v}$
7. *From the Life of Chrysostom* 222^{v}
8. *Apost. Const.* 3.10–11, 6.17, 8.42–43, 1.3.10 (on the rights of the clergy, including marriage) 222^{v}
9. *Rule of the Holy Apostles* 223^{v}
10. Theodoret of Cyrrhus, *Ecclesiastical History* 2.6 (*PG* 82.1000, ll. 12-24) 223^{v}
11. Basil of Caesarea c. 87 (summary from Sisinnios' *Tome against the Marriage of Cousins*) 224^{r}
12. I Nicaea, *Decree on Pascha* 224^{r}
13. Short excerpts from Byzantine canon and civil law on marriage and adultery 224^{r}
14. John of Jerusalem, *Synodikon Against the Pope of Rome* 230^{r}
15. II Constantinople (553) c. 1–4 235$^{r/v}$

8. Amphilochios of Iconium, *Life of Basil the Great* (excerpts) 236^{r}

9. *Life of Pope Sylvester* (des. mut.) 242^{v}

9. Milan, Biblioteca Ambrosiana, MS F 48 sup. (gr. 341)

Canon Law Collection, Salentine Group (fragmentary)

Date:	Early 12th Century	**Dimensions:**	200 x 140 (140 x 95)
Origin:	Salento	**Material:**	Parchment
Owner:	Church of S. Lorenzo (Mesagne)	**Folios:**	i + 179 + ii
Scribe:	Joacheim (monk)?	**Ruling:**	X20D1 (System 1)
Binding:	Biblioteca Ambrosiana	**Lines:**	25
Hands:	A: 1–179	**Collation:**	1^7, $2–7^8$, 8^6, $9–10^8$, 11^6, 12^8, 13^6, $14–16^8$, 17^6, 18^8, 19^4, 20^6, 21^4, $22–23^8$, 24^3, $25–26^6$

Catalogue: *RHBR* 3.156–157 (no. 491); Martini and Bassi (1906): 1.392–394 (no. 341).

1. Table of Contents	1^r
1. Conciliar Canons with Historical Introductions	2^r
1. Apostolic Canons	2^r
2. I Nicaea	13^v
3. Ancyra	24^r
4. Neocaesarea	29^v
5. Sardica	31^v
6. Gangra	42^v
7. Antioch	47^r
8. Laodicea	55^r
9. I Constantinople (381)	60^v
10. Ephesus	66^r
11. Chalcedon	73^r
12. II Constantinople (553)	84^v
13. Constantinople (680/1)	87^r
14. Carthage (excerpts)	89^r
15. *Trullo*	109^v
16. II Nicaea (II Nic. c. 1–14; *Prot.* c. 11; II Nic. c. 16–22, 15)	155^r
17. *Protodeutera* (*Prot.* c. 1–10; II Nic. *c.* 17; *Prot.* c. 12–17)	169^r
[2. Patristic Canons]	–
[3. Marriage Law]	–
1. [*Tome of Union* (920)]	–
2. [Sisinnios II of Constantinople, *Tome against the Marriage of Cousins*]	–

10. Milan, Biblioteca Ambrosiana, MS G 57 sup. (gr. 400)

Nomocanon (fragmentary)

Date:	11th–12th Century	**Dimensions:**	245 x 180 (180 x 130)
Origin:	Southern Calabria	**Material:**	Parchment
Owner:	St Phantinos of Tauriana, Theotokos of Carrà (14th Century)	**Folios:**	i + 48
		Ruling:	20D1 (System 9)
Scribe:	Unknown	**Lines:**	25–35

Binding:	Biblioteca Ambrosiana	**Collation:**	$1–6^8$
Hands:	A: 1–48		

Catalogue: *RHBR* 2.26–27 (no. 338); Martini and Bassi (1906): 1.476–478 (no. 400).

1. Conciliar Canons (inc. mut.)	$\mathbf{1^r}$
1. *Trullo* (inc. mut.)	1^r
2. II Nicaea	15^v
3. Tarasios of Constantinople, *Letter to Pope Hadrian I of Rome* (des. mut.)	$24^{r/v}$
4. *Protodeutera* (inc. mut.)	25^r
5. Constantinople (879)	26^v
2. Canonical Miscellany	$\mathbf{27^v}$
1. Basil of Caesarea c. 93–94	27^v
2. Anastasios of Antioch, *Holy Narrative on Gregory the Dialogist and Wonderworker, Pope of Rome*	28^v
3. Carth. c. 42, 44, 74, 83, 102, 109, 110, 111–116, 126–133	29^v
4. Basil of Caesarea *c.* 88	$33^{r/v}$
5. History of the Councils (‘*ἑτέρα εἴδησις περὶ τῶν ἁγίων συνόδων οἰκουμενικῶν*’)	33^v
6. *Thirty Chapters of the Apostolic Constitutions* 14, 1–13, 15–30	38^v
7. I Nicaea, *Decree on Pascha*	39^v
8. Methodios I of Constantinople, *Decree on the Reception of Apostates*	$40^{r/v}$
9. Timothy of Alexandria, *Canonical Answers* 18, 1–6, 8, 7, 9–15	40^v
10. *Selection of Penances for All Sins*	41^v
11. Theodore Stoudites, *Epitimia*	43^r
12. John the Faster, *Kanonarion* (excerpts)	43^r

11. Moscow, Gosudarstvennij Istoričeskij Musej, MS Sin. gr. 397 (Vlad. 316)

Nomocanon, Salentine Group (incomplete)

Date:	13th Century	**Dimensions:**	185 x 125 (150 x 190)
Origin:	Salento	**Material:**	Parchment
Owner:	Unknown	**Folios:**	xiii + 185 + i
Scribe:	Unknown	**Lines:**	32–36
Binding:	State Historical Museum	**Ruling:**	X20A1 (System 1)
Hands:	A: 1–185	**Collation:**	$1^7, 2–23^8$

Catalogue: *RHBR* 3.174–178 (no. 498); Fonkič and Poliakov (1993): 107–108 (no. 316).

1. Table of Contents	$1^{r/v}$
2. Photios of Constantinople, *Nomocanon in 14 Titles*, Prologue (excerpt)	1^v
1. Conciliar Canons with Historical Introductions	$\mathbf{2^r}$
1. Apostolic Canons	2^r
2. I Nicaea	7^r

3. *The Ecclesiastical Ranks*	11^{r}
4. Ancyra	11^{r}
5. Neocaesarea	13^{v}
6. Sardica	14^{v}
7. Gangra	20^{r}
8. Antioch	22^{r}
9. Laodicea	26^{r}
10. I Constantinople (381)	29^{r}
11. Ephesus	31^{v}
12. Chalcedon	35^{r}
13. II Constantinople (553)	40^{v}
14. Constantinople (680/1)	41^{v}
15. Carthage (excerpts)	42^{r}
16. *Trullo*	56^{v}
17. II Nicaea (II Nic. c. 1–14; *Prot.* c. 11; II Nic. c. 16–22, 15)	77^{v}
18. *Protodeutera* (*Prot.* c. 1–10; II Nic. c. 17; *Prot.* c. 12–17)	83^{v}
2. Patristic Canons	$\mathbf{88^{v}}$
3. Theological Texts	$\mathbf{124^{v}}$
1. John Chrysostom, *Homily on Matthew* (excerpt)	124^{v}
2. Note on correct belief	124^{v}
3. II Constantinople (553), *Actio* 8	125^{r}
4. Proklos of Constantinople, *Letter to John of Antioch* (excerpt)	125^{r}
5. Victor of Carthage, *Letter to Pope Theodore I*	125^{v}
4. Marriage Law and Fasting	$\mathbf{125^{v}}$
1. Sisinnios II of Constantinople, *Tome against the Marriage of Cousins* (summary)	125^{v}
2. Photios of Constantinople, *Five Canonical Letters*	125^{v}
3. Nikephoros the Confessor, *Canons* 3, 39, 40	126^{v}
4. Leontios of Constantinople, *Homily* 6 (excerpt)	126^{v}
5. *Tome of Union* (920)	127^{v}
6. Sisinnios II of Constantinople, *Tome against the Marriage of Cousins* (excerpts)	$130^{r/v}$
7. Short excerpts from Byzantine civil law on marriage	130^{v}
8. Alexios Stoudites, *Synodal Act on Marriage*	131^{v}
9. Leo of Calabria, *Canonical Answer on Clerical Marriage*	$132^{r/v}$
10. Short excerpts from Byzantine civil law on marriage	132^{v}
5. *Nomocanon in 50 Titles*	$\mathbf{134^{v}}$
6. Symeon Metaphrastes, *Synopsis of Canons*	$\mathbf{162^{r}}$
7. Clerical Discipline and Differences with the Latin Church	$\mathbf{180^{r}}$
1. Nicholas III Grammatikos of Constantinople *c.* 27 (excerpt)	180^{r}
2. *Apost. Const.* 3.10–11, 6.17, 8.42–43	180^{r}
3. Excerpts from Byzantine civil and canon law on marriage, clerical discipline, and feast days	181^{r}
4. I Nicaea, *Decree on Pascha*	182^{r}
5. *Rule of the Holy Apostles*	$182^{r/v}$
6. Short excerpts from Byzantine civil and canon law on marriage and adultery	182^{v}
7. Theological Texts (des. mut.)	$\mathbf{183^{r}}$
1. Theodoret of Cyrrhus, *Ecclesiastical History* 2.6 (*PG* 82.1000, ll. 12-24)	183^{r}
2. John the Faster, *Kanonarion* (excerpt)	$183^{r/v}$

3. *From the Life of Chrysostom*	183^{v}
4. Council of Antioch, Introductory Letter and Signatories	183^{v}
5. Note on the Councils of Constantinople of 553 and 680/1	184^{r}
3. Sophronios of Jerusalem, *Letter to Sergios* (summary)	184^{r}

---

12. Moscow, Gosudarstvennij Istoričeskij Musej, MS Sin. gr. 432 (Vlad. 317)

Nomocanon

Date:	12th Century	**Dimensions:**	230 x 185 (185 x 140)
Origin:	Sicily/Southern	**Material:**	Parchment
Owner:	Calabria	**Folios:**	i + 218 + i
Scribe:	Unknown	**Lines:**	32
Binding:	Unknown	**Ruling:**	20C1 (System 9)
Hands:	Moscow State Historical Museum A: 1–229 b: 12^{v} a: 1^{r}–6^{v} c: $126^{r/v}$, 159	**Collation:**	1^{4}, 2–10^{8}, 11^{4}, 12–16^{8}, 19^{9}, 20–21^{8}, 22^{6}, 23–24^{8}, 25^{11}, 26–30^{8}

Catalogue: *RHBR* 2.44–46 (no. 346); Fonkič and Poliakov (1993): 108 (no. 317).

---

1. Front Matter	**1^{r}**
1. **On the Five Patriarchs and their Regions*	1^{r}
2. *Peter III of Antioch, *Letter to Domenicus of Grado*	1^{v}
3. *Epiphanios of Cyprus, *On the 72 Interpreters of Scripture*	5^{r}
4. Table of contents	6^{r}
5. Prayers for the reception of heretics and Manichaeans	11^{r}
6. *Nicene-Constantinopolitan Creed (Greek text translated into Latin without the *Filioque*)	12^{v}
7. *Epitome of Book Eight of the Apostolic Constitutions*	13^{r}
2. *Synagoge in 50 Titles*	**21^{r}**
3. Conciliar Canons	**63^{r}**
1. Gregory of Nazianzus, *On the Books of the Old and New Testament*	63^{r}
2. Nicene Creed (original text)	64^{r}
3. Gangra, introductory letter	$64^{r/v}$
4. Antioch, introductory letter	64^{v}
5. Laodicea (summary)	65^{r}
6. I Constantinople (381), introductory letter	$65^{r/v}$
7. Ephesus, historical introduction and letter to the synod in Pamphylia	65^{v}
8. *Trullo*	66^{v}
9. II Nicaea	88^{r}
4. Patristic Canons	**93^{v}**
1. Peter of Alexandria, *Six Canons from the Sermon on Penitence*	93^{v}
2. *Diagram of degrees of family kinship	99^{v}
3. Gregory of Neocaesarea, *Canonical Letter*	100^{r}
4. Basil of Caesarea c. 89–92, 87–88, 95, 86	101^{v}
5. Gregory of Nyssa, *Letter to Letoius*	108^{v}

6. Cyril of Alexandria, *Letter to the Bishops of Libya and Pentapolis*	114^r
7. Theophilos of Alexandria c. 1, 6	115^v
8. Timothy of Alexandria *Canonical Answers*	116^r
9. Athanasios of Alexandria c. 1–2	117^r
10. Gennadios I, *Encyclical Letter*	120^v
11. Tarasios of Constantinople, *Letter to Pope Hadrian I of Rome*	122^r
12. Carthage	127^r
13. Carthage (256)	151^r
5. Appendix: Theology	**160^r**
1. John of Damascus, *On Heresies*	160^r
2. Sophronios of Jerusalem, *Synodal Letter to Sergios* (excerpt)	174^v
3. Timothy of Constantinople, *On Those Who Come to the Church*	176^v
4. Anastasios of Antioch, *Demonstration that the Office of Archpriest is Great and Angelic*	182$^{r/v}$
5. Lateran (649) c. 20 (against Monothelitism)	182^v
6. Gregory of Nazianzus, *On Father Gregory* (excerpt)	182^v
7. *Erotapokriseis* on the Creed	183^r
6. Appendix: Canon Law	**183^r**
1. Constantinople (879)	183^r
41. Gennadios I of Constantinople, *Letter to Martyrios*	184$^{r/v}$
42. Dionysios of Alexandria, canons	184^v
43. Gennadios I of Constantinople, *Letter to Martyrios* (repeated)	186^v
44. Athanasios of Alexandria, c. 3	187^r
7. Appendix: Civil Law	**188^r**
1. Just. *Nov.* 77	188$^{r/v}$
2. *C87C*	189^r
3. *C25C*	207^v

13. Naples, Biblioteca nazionale 'Vittorio Emanuele III', MS II C 7

Nomocanon

Date:	16th December 1139	**Dimensions:**	250 x 195 (180 x 145)
Origin:	St John Theristes of Stilo (Southern Calabria)	**Material:**	Parchment
		Folios:	iv + 183 + iv
Owner:	Abbot Pachomios of St John Theristes of Stilo	**Ruling:**	12E2 (System 4)
		Lines:	24–27
Scribe:	Konon (monk)	**Collation:**	1–5^8, 6^6, 7–11^8, 12^6, 13–15^8, 16^6, 17^8, 19^6, 20^7, 21–22^8, 23^7, 24^6, 25^8, 26^4
Binding:	Alessandro Farnese (1520–1589)		
Hands:	A: 1–183		

Catalogue: *RHBR* 2.56–58 (no. 352); Mioni (1981): 1.163–166; Pierleoni (1962): 231.

1. *Nomocanon in 50 Titles*	**1^r**
2. Conciliar Canons	**84^r**
1. *Epitome of Book Eight of the Apostolic Constitutions* 22.2–28.1	84^r

2. Photios of Constantinople, *On the Divine Liturgy* 87^{v}
3. *Trullo* 88^{r}
4. II Nicaea 122^{r}
5. Tarasios of Constantinople, *Letter to Pope Hadrian I of Rome* 131^{r}
6. *Prot.* c. 1–7 (des. mut.), 10–17 (inc. mut.) 134^{r}
7. Constantinople (879) 140^{r}

3. Canonical Miscellany **141^{r}**

1. Basil of Caesarea c. 93–94 141^{r}
2. Anastasios of Antioch, *Holy Narrative on Gregory the Dialogist and Wonderworker, Pope of Rome* 142^{v}
3. Carth. c. 42, 44, 74, 83, 102, 109, 110, 111–16, 126–133 143^{r}
4. Basil of Caesarea c. 88 147^{r}
5. History of the Councils (‘ἑτέρα εἴδησις περὶ τῶν ἁγίων συνόδων οἰκουμενικῶν’) 148^{r}
6. *Thirty Chapters of the Apostolic Constitutions* 14, 1–13, 15–30 156^{r}
7. I Nicaea, *Decree on Pascha* 157^{r}
8. Methodios I of Constantinople, *Decree on the Reception of Apostates* 158^{v}
9. Timothy of Alexandria, *Canonical Answers* 18, 1–6, 8, 7, 9–15 159^{r}
10. *Selection of Penances for All Sins* 161^{r}
11. Theodore Stoudites, *Epitimia* $163^{r/v}$
12. John the Faster, *Kanonarion* (excerpts) 163^{v}
13. ‘Basil of Caesarea’ [Germanos I of Constantinople], *Mystical History of the Catholic Church* 174^{r}

14. Oxford, Bodleian Library, MS Barocci 86

Nomocanon, Salentine Group

Date:	12th Century	**Dimensions:**	220 x 135 (190 x 110)
Origin:	Salento	**Material:**	Parchment (3–12 Paper)
Owner:	Unknown	**Folios:**	173
Scribe:	Kalos (priest)?	**Lines:**	25–30
Binding:	Bodleian Library	**Ruling:**	X20D1 (System 1)
Hands:	A: 13–172 b: 1^{v}–2^{r} c: 2^{v} a: 1^{r} d: 3^{r}–12^{v} e: 172^{v}–173^{v}	**Collation:**	1^{2}, 2^{10}, 3–22^{8}, 23^{1}

Catalogue: Coxe (1858): 147–151; Hutter (1982): 104–105 (no. 69). **View Online:** https://digital.bodleian.ox.ac.uk/inquire/p/69cd1e64-4fd7-4a01-9466-848ab9832fbe

***1. Theological Texts** **1^{r}**

1. Socrates, *Ecclesiastical History* 5.19 (excerpts) 1^{r}
2. Pseudo-Nicholas III Grammatikos, *Answers to Questions on Disputes between Greeks and Latins* 1^{v}
3. Short excerpt on permitted and unpermitted degrees of marriage 2^{v}

***2. Patristic Texts** **3^{r}**

1. Basil of Caesarea, *On the Holy Trinity* (excerpt) 3^{r}
2. Michael the Synkellos, *Treatise on the Orthodox Faith* (excerpt) 4^{v}
3. John Chrysostom, excerpts 6^{r}
4. Basil of Caesarea, excerpt 12^{v}

3. ***Nomocanon in 50 Titles***	**13r**
4. Conciliar Canons with Historical Introductions	**80r**
1. Carthage	80r
2. Summary of the Trullan Canons	93v
3. *Trullo*	95v
4. II Nicaea and *Protodeutera* (Nic. c. 1, 7, 4, 6, 14; *Prot.* c. 11; Nic. c. 16, 8, 13; *Prot.* c. 10; Nic. c. 17, 12; *Prot.* c. 2, 3; Nic. c. 21; *Prot.* c. 4–6; Nic. c. 19, 20, 18, 22; *Prot.* c. 13–15)	114v
5. Patristic Canons	**125r**
1. Dionysios of Alexandria, *Letter to Basil*	125r
2. Peter of Alexandria, *Six Canons from the Sermon on Penitence*	126v
3. Gregory of Neocaesarea, *Canonical Letter*	128v
4. Athanasios of Alexandria, *Letters* (excerpts)	129v
5. Basil of Caesarea, *Canonical Letters and Texts*	133r
6. Timothy of Alexandria, *Canonical Answers*	141v
7. Theophilos of Alexandria, *Canonical Texts*	142v
8. Cyril of Alexandria, *Letter to the Bishops of Libya and Pentapolis*	144r
6. Marriage Law	**144v**
1. Sisinnios II of Constantinople, *Tome against the Marriage of Cousins*	144v
7. Summaries of the Ecumenical Councils	**145v**
8. Symeon Metaphrastes, *Synopsis of Canons*	**156v**
***9. Miscellaneous Notes**	**172v**
1. Note on confession	173r
2. Nicene Creed (original recension)	173r
3. Note on the prohibition of marriage between godparents and godchildren	173r/v

15. Paris, Bibliothèque nationale de France, MS gr. 1370

Nomocanon, Salentine Group (incomplete)

Date:	1296/7	**Dimensions:**	225 x 150 (180 x 100)
Origin:	Salento	**Material:**	Parchment
Owner:	Unknown	**Folios:**	ii + 143 + i
Scribe:	Unknown	**Lines:**	34–9
Binding:	Louis XIII (1610–1643)	**Ruling:**	22C1, 32C1 (Systems 10, 9, 13)
Hands:	A: 1–143	**Collation:**	$1–17^8$, 18^7

Catalogue: Omont (1898a): 2.27–28. **View Online:** https://gallica.bnf.fr/ark:/12148/btv1b107229490

1. Conciliar Canons with Historical Introductions (des. mut.)	**1r**
1. Apostolic Canons	1r
2. I Nicaea	5v
3. Ancyra	9v
4. Neocaesarea	11v
5. Gangra	16v

6. Antioch	18^{v}
7. Laodicea	22^{v}
8. I Constantinople (381)	25^{r}
9. Ephesus	27^{v}
10. Chalcedon (des. mut.)	30^{v}
2. Patristic Canons (inc. mut.)	**33^{r}**
1. Dionysios of Alexandria, *Letter to Basil* (inc. mut.)	33^{r}
2. Peter of Alexandria, *Six Canons from the Sermon on Penitence*	34^{r}
3. Gregory of Neocaesarea, *Canonical Letter*	35^{v}
4. Athanasios of Alexandria, *Letters* (excerpts)	36^{v}
5. Basil of Caesarea, *Canonical Letters and Texts*	37^{v}
6. Gregory of Nyssa, *Letter to Letoius*	51^{r}
7. Timothy of Alexandria, *Canonical Answers*	55^{r}
8. Theophilos of Alexandria, *Canonical Texts*	55^{v}
9. Cyril of Alexandria, *Letter to the Bishops of Libya and Pentapolis*	56^{v}
10. Gennadios I of Constantinople, *Encyclical Letter*	57^{v}
3. Marriage Law	**58^{v}**
1. *Tome of Union* (920)	58^{v}
2. Sisinnios II of Constantinople, *Tome against the Marriage of Cousins*	60^{r}
3. Alexios Stoudites, *Synodal Act on Marriage*	61^{r}
4. *Ekloge* 2.2	61^{r}
5. Leo of Calabria, *Canonical Answer on Clerical Marriage*	61^{v}
6. Short excerpts from Byzantine civil law on marriage	61^{v}
4. Clerical Discipline and Differences with the Latin Church	**62^{v}**
1. *Apost. Const.* 3.10–11, 6.17, 8.42–44, 1.3.11 (on the rights of the clergy, including marriage)	62^{v}
2. *Rule of the Holy Apostles*	63^{v}
3. I Nicaea, *Decree on Pascha*	63^{v}
4. Excerpts from Byzantine civil and canon law on marriage, clerical discipline, and feast days	64^{r}
5. John Moschos, *Spiritual Meadow* 149 (excerpt)	66^{r}
6. Nikon of the Black Mountain, *Kanonarion* (excerpts)	66^{r}
7. Council of Carthage (excerpts)	70^{r}
8. Council of Sardica (excerpts)	83^{r}
9. Photios of Constantinople, *Encyclical Letter to the Eastern Patriarchs*	96^{v}
5. *Nomocanon in 50 Titles* (misattributed to Theodoret of Cyrrhus)	**102^{r}**
6. Miscellaneous Canon Law and Anti-Latin Texts	**123^{v}**
1. History of the Councils (‘πρώτη σύνοδος γέγονεν οἰκουμενική’)	123^{v}
2. Photios of Constantinople, *Five Canonical Letters*	126^{r}
3. Gregory of Neocaesarea, short excerpts	128^{v}
7. Symeon Metaphrastes, *Synopsis of Canons*	**128^{v}**
8. Miscellaneous Canon Law	**140^{r}**
1. Councils of Sardica and Antioch, excerpts	140^{r}
2. *Apostolic Constitutions*, excerpts	140^{v}

16. Paris, Bibliothèque nationale de France, MS gr. 1371

The Casulan Collection

Date:	Late 12th Century	**Dimensions:**	195 x 150 (165 x 115)
Origin:	St Nicholas of Casole (Salento)	**Material:**	Parchment (palimpsest)
Owner:	St Nicholas of Casole (Salento)	**Folios:**	iv + 158 + ii
Scribe:	Unknown	**Ruling:**	Unclear
Binding:	Louis XIII (1610–1643)	**Lines:**	18–21
Hands:	A: 1–149 b: 158 a: 151–157	**Collation:**	$1–16^8$, 17^6, 18^7, $19–20^8$

Catalogue: Omont (1898a): 2.28–29. **View Online:** https://gallica.bnf.fr/ark:/12148/btv1b10721917h

1. Theological Texts **1^r^**
1. *Short and Precise Information on the Lenten Fast* 1^r^
2. Sophronios of Jerusalem, *Synodic Letter to Pope Honorius I* (excerpt) 9^r^
3. Sophronios of Jerusalem, *On the Incarnation of Christ* 15^r^

2. Conciliar Canons **24^v^**
1. History of the Councils ('*χρὴ πάντα Χριστιανὸν γινώσκειν ὅτι ἐξ εἰσὶν . . .*') 24^v^
2. Nicholas III Grammatikos of Constantinople, *Canonical Answers to Certain Monks Outside the Capital* (unattributed and with substantial textual variations) 34^v^
3. Selection of canons and laws on monasticism 44^r^

3. Arsenios of Philotheou, *Synopsis of Canons* **72^r^**

4. Didactic Texts **115^r^**
1. Michael Psellos, *Synopsis of the Nomocanon* 115^r^
2. Michael Psellos, *On the Creed of the Orthodox Faith* 118^v^
3. *Clear and Brief Synopsis of Our Faith in the Holy Trinity* (inc. '*ὀφείλομεν πιστεύειν ὡς ἐβαπτίσθημεν*') 123^r^

5. Alexios I Komnenos, *Edict on the Reform of the Clergy* **125^v^**

***6. Nektarios of Otranto, Assorted Texts** **151^r^**
1. *Letter to the Priests of Gioia* 151^r^
2. *Epigrams on Joseph, Victor, Nicholas, Kallinikos, and Hilarion, Former Abbots of St Nicholas of Casole* 157^v^

17. Rome, Biblioteca Vallicelliana, MS C 11.1

Nomocanon, Rossanese Group

Date:	*c.* 1100–1115	**Dimensions:**	325 x 240 (205 x 175)
Origin:	Patiron (Rossano, N. Calabria)	**Material:**	Parchment
Owner:	Holy Saviour of Messina (Sicily)	**Folios:**	v + 348 + ii
Scribe:	Bartholomew (monk)?	**Lines:**	29
Binding:	Biblioteca Vallicelliana	**Ruling:**	12D2 (System 9)
Hands:	A: $1–347^r$ a: $347^v–348^r$	**Collation:**	1^4, 2^2, $3–7^8$, 8^4, $9–44^8$, 45^6

Catalogue: Martini (1902): 57–59. **View Online:** http://www.internetculturale.it/jmms/iccuviewer/iccu.jsp?id=oai%3Awww.internetculturale.sbn.it%2FTeca%3A20%3ANT0000%3ARM0281_Vall_C_11_I&mode=all&teca=MagTeca+-+ICCU

***1. Episcopal *taktika* (des. mut.)**	**1r/v**
2. Front Matter	**2r**
1. *Epitome of Book Eight of the Apostolic Constitutions* 22.2–28.1	2r
2. *S50T*, Preface and Table of Canons	4r
2. *Nomocanon in 14 Titles* (Photian recension)	**7v**
3. Conciliar Canons	**67v**
4. Patristic Canons	**189v**
5. Appendix: Civil Law	**233r**
1. Just. *Nov.* 77	233r
2. *C87C*	233v
3. *C25C*	250v
4. *Tripartite Collection*	281r
5. Heraclius, *Novels* 4, 1, 3, 2	340r
6. Epilogue: John Moschos, *Spiritual Meadow* 149 (excerpt)	**347r**
***7. Latin bull of Honorius III relating to the Holy Saviour of Messina (1224)**	**347v**

18. Syracuse, Biblioteca Alagoniana, MS gr. 3

Gospel Lectionary

Date:	1st September 1124	**Dimensions:**	265 x 200 (180 x 135)
Origin:	Patiron (Rossano,	**Material:**	Parchment
Owner:	N. Calabria)	**Folios:**	226
Scribe:	Holy Saviour of Messina	**Lines:**	25
Binding:	(Sicily)?	**Ruling:**	20E2, J20E2 (System 9)
Hands:	Basil (monk)	**Collation:**	1–10^8, 11^7, 12–29^8, 29^2
	Unknown (early modern)		
	A: 1–226		

1. Gospel Readings for Moveable Feasts	**1r**
2. Gospel Readings for Fixed Feasts	**181v**
3. Appendix: Canon Law	**215v**
1. Patriarchal *taktika* ('γνῶσις καὶ ἐπίγνωσις τῶν πατριαρχικῶν θρόνων')	215v
2. I Nicaea, *Decree on Pascha*	216v
3. Short excerpts 'from the *Apostolic Constitutions*' and 'from the 318 Fathers [of Nicaea]' on Lenten fasting	217v
4. *On Pascha and Bread*	219r
4. Appendix: Gospel Readings	**219r**
1. *Erotapokriseis* on Gospel Readings	219r
2. Eusebius, *Letter to Carpianus*	224r
3. Index of Gospel Readings for Moveable Feasts	225r

19. Vatican City, Biblioteca Apostolica Vaticana, MS Barb. gr. 323 (III.42/192)

Nomocanon (fragmentary)

Date:	Early 12th Century	**Dimensions:**	165 x 155 (120 x 110)
Origin:	Southern Calabria	**Material:**	Parchment (with paper additions)
Owner:	St Bartholomew of Trigona (Southern Calabria)	**Folios:**	i + 405 + ii
Scribe:	Unknown (later additions by George Basilikos)	**Lines:**	21–3 (parchment), 18–19 (paper)
Binding:	Unknown (early modern)	**Ruling:**	00D1 (Systems 1, 9)
Hands:	A: 49–98, 103–184, 244–306 a: 1–48, 99–102, 185–243, 307–406	**Collation:**	1–30^{8}, 31^{3}, 32–38^{8}, 39^{7}, 40^{3}, 41^{4}, 42^{3}, 43–44^{2}, 45–55^{8}

View Online: https://digi.vatlib.it/view/MSS_Barb.gr.323

***1. George Basilikos' Table of Contents** **1^{r}**

2. Front Matter **49^{r}**

1. History of the Councils ('ἡ ἁγία καὶ οἰκουμενικὴ πρώτη σύνοδος γέγονεν') 49^{r}
2. Niketas Stethatos, *Discourse Against the Romans* (with textual variations at the end) 85^{v}
3. *C87C* (excerpts) 118^{r}

3. Conciliar Canons (des. mut.) **137^{r}**

1. Apostolic Canons 137^{r}
2. *Epitome of Book Eight of the Apostolic Constitutions* 19–21; 18.2–3; 22.2–14, 16, 15, 17–24.7; 25–26 145^{r}
3. I Nicaea 150^{r}
4. Ancyra 154r
5. Neocaesarea 157^{v}
6. Gangra 158^{v}
7. Antioch 162^{r}
8. Laodicea 167^{r}
9. I Constantinople (381) 170^{v}
10. Ephesus 173^{r}
11. Chalcedon 175^{r}
12. Sardica (des. mut.) 178^{v}

***4. Alexios Aristenos, *Synopsis of Canons* (inc. and des. mut.)** **185^{r}**

1. Sardica (inc. mut.) 185^{r}
2. Carthage 185^{v}
3. *Protodeutera* (des. mut.) 240^{v}

5. Conciliar Canons (inc. mut.) **244^{r}**

1. *Protodeutera* (inc. mut.) 244^{r}
2. *Trullo* 249^{r}
3. II Nicaea 285^{v}

6. Patristic Canons (des. mut.) **296^{r}**

1. Dionysios of Alexandria, *Letter to Basil*	296^{r}
2. Basil of Caesarea, *Canonical Letters and Texts* (des. mut.)	296^{v}
***7. Alexios Aristenos, *Synopsis of Canons* (inc. mut.)**	**307^{r}**
1. Basil of Caesarea, *Canonical Letters and Texts* (inc. mut.)	307^{r}
2. Basil of Caesarea, *Epitimia*	315^{r}
3. Basil of Caesarea, *Sermon for the Instruction of Priests*	318^{r}
4. Basil of Caesarea c. 94	319^{r}
5. Basil of Caesarea, *Letter* 288	319^{v}
***8. Appendix: Canon Law**	**320^{r}**
1. John the Faster, *Kanonarion* (excerpt)	320^{r}
2. John the Faster, *Kanonikon*	351^{v}
3. *Trullo* c. 11, 43, 55, 75, 90, 23	354^{r}
4. Basil of Caesarea c. 13	356^{v}
5. Nicholas Grammatikos of Constantinople c. 27 (attributed to I Nicaea)	356^{v}
6. 8 'Canons of Chalcedon'	356^{v}
7. *Trullo* c. 65	356^{v}
8. Dionysios of Alexandria c. 2	358^{r}
9. Basil of Caesarea c. 7, 24–25, 9, 48	358^{v}
10. 1 Corinthians 7:39 with exegesis	359^{v}
11. *From the Letter of Gennadios* [I of Constantinople]	360^{v}
12. Timothy of Alexandria, *Canonical Answers*	360^{v}
13. John the Faster, *Teachings of the Fathers* (excerpts)	364^{r}
14. John Klimakos, *Ladder of Divine Ascent* 4 (excerpt)	368^{r}
15. John the Faster, *Deuterokanonarion* (excerpt)	369^{r}
16. *On the Purity of the Clergy*	369^{v}
17. Diagrams of acceptable and unacceptable degrees of kinship for marriage	370^{v}
18. Short excerpts from Byzantine civil law on marriage	376^{r}
***9. Theological Miscellany**	**378^{r}**
1. *'On Holy Baptism'*	378^{r}
2. *'On How Every Christian Should Prepare for Confession'*	378^{v}
3. *'On Repentance'*	379^{v}
4. *'On Self-Examination'*	380^{v}
5. *'On the Ten Commandments'*	382^{r}
6. Miscellaneous lists on matters relating to spirituality	385^{r}
7. *'New Canons on Remembering the Deadly Sins'*	402^{r}
8. Further lists on matters relating to spirituality	405^{r}

20. Vatican City, Biblioteca Apostolica Vaticana, MS Barb. gr. 324 (III.43/70)

Nomocanon

Date:	Late 12th Century	**Dimensions:**	180 x 135 (140 x 95)
Origin:	St Nicholas of Casole (Salento)	**Material:**	Paper ('Western Arabic')
Owner:	St Nicholas of Casole (Salento)	**Folios:**	i + 165 + i (fols. 1, 70 *bis*)
Scribe:	Unknown	**Ruling:**	Unclear
Binding:	Unknown (early modern)	**Lines:**	22–23

Hands:	A: 1–10^{r}, 12^{r}–13^{r}, 16^{r}–64^{r} B: 64^{v}–165 a: 10^{v}–11^{v}, 13^{v}–15^{v}	**Collation:**	1^{4}, 2^{12}, 3^{6}, 4–17^{8}, 18^{7}, 19^{10}, 20^{6}, 21^{10}

1. Front Matter and Notes of Nektarios of Otranto (inc. mut.) **1^{r}**
1. Table of Contents (inc. mut.) 1^{r}
2. *'John Antagonistes' [Philagathos of Cerami?], *On Wednesdays and Fridays* 10^{v}
3. **On the Death of Infants* 11^{r}
4. Table of canons *How Many and Where* 12^{r}
5. *Brief extracts from Latin and Greek texts on simony and clerical discipline (including clerical marriage) 13^{v}

2. Alexios Aristenos, *Synopsis of Canons* (des. mut.) **16^{r}**

---

21. Vatican City, Biblioteca Apostolica Vaticana, MS Barb. gr. 476 (IV.58/350)

Patristic Collection (incomplete)

Date:	12th Century	**Dimensions:**	245 x 190 (175 x 155)
Origin:	Southern Calabria	**Material:**	Parchment
Owner:	Unknown	**Folios:**	iv + 212 + i
Scribe:	Unknown	**Lines:**	27
Binding:	Unknown (early modern)	**Ruling:**	24E2o (System 1)
Hands:	A: 1–212	**Collation:**	1^{4}, 2–27^{8}

Catalogue: *RHBR* 2.193–194 (no. 406). **View Online:** https://digi.vatlib.it/view/MSS_Barb.gr.476

---

1. Preface: Canon Law (inc. mut.) **1^{r}**
1. *Prot.* c. 2–6 (inc. and des. mut.) 1^{r}
2. Apost. c. 17–18, 20–26, 29, 35, 59, 55–56, 61, 63–72 3^{r}
3. *Thirty Chapters of the Apostolic Constitutions* 28, 30 5^{r}
4. *Epitome of Book Eight of the Apostolic Constitutions* 25 5^{r}
5. I Nicaea c. 3 $5^{r/v}$
6. *Apost. Const.* 1.3.11–12, 8 5^{v}
7. I Nicaea c. 20 5^{v}
8. Neocaes. c. 1, 3–4, 7, 9–10, 12 $6^{r/v}$
9. Gangra c. 4, 18 6^{v}
10. Antioch c. 13 6^{v}
11. Laod. c. 49, 51–53 7^{r}
12. Chalc. c. 16 7^{r}
13. Anastasios of Sinai, *On the Forty-Day Liturgy for the Dead* $7^{r/v}$

2. Basil of Caesarea, Monastic Texts (des. mut.) **8^{r}**
1. *Sermon on the Monastic Life* 8^{r}
2. *Prologue* 34 17^{r}
3. *Letters* 173, 22 23^{v}
4. *Ascetic Constitutions* 28^{r}

5. *Prologue* 5	42^{r}
6. *On Baptism* 1.3	46^{v}
7. *Great Asketikon* ('*recensio Italica*'; des. mut.)	90^{v}

22. Vatican City, Biblioteca Apostolica Vaticana, MS Ottob. gr. 186

Nomocanon, Salentine Group (fragmentary)

Date:	12th/13th Century	**Dimensions:**	185 x 130 (150 x 90)
Origin:	Salento	**Material:**	Parchment (palimpsest)
Owner:	Unknown	**Folios:**	ii + 69 + i
Scribe:	Unknown	**Lines:**	27–29
Binding:	Leo XIII (1878–1903)	**Ruling:**	Unclear
Hands:	A: 1–8 C: 23–61 B: 9–22 D: 62–69	**Collation:**	1^{8}, $2–3^{7}$, 4^{6}, 5^{8}, 6^{7}, $7–9^{8}$

Catalogue: *RHBR* 1.286 (no. 255); Feron and Battaglini (1893): 106. **View Online:** https://digi.vatlib.it/view/MSS_Ott.gr.186

***1. Fragment: Civil Law**	**1^{r}**
1. *Ekloge* 1–2	1^{r}
2. Fragment: Nomocanon (inc. and des. mut.)	**9^{r}**
1. II Nicaea, canons (with historical introduction)	9^{r}
2. Short excerpts from Byzantine civil law on marriage (including clerical marriage)	16^{r}, 18^{v}
3. Alexios Stoudites, *Synodal Act on Marriage*	17^{r}
4. Leo of Calabria, *Canonical Answer on Clerical Marriage*	17$^{r/v}$
5. *Tome of Union* (920), excerpt	17^{v}, 20^{r}
6. Sisinnios II of Constantinople, *Tome against the Marriage of Cousins*	19^{r}
***3. Fragment: Grammatical Text**	**23^{r}**
***4. Fragment: Theodoret of Cyrrhus, *Commentary on the Letters of St Paul* (excerpts)**	**62^{r}**

23. Vatican City, Biblioteca Apostolica Vaticana, MS Vat. gr. 1168

Civil Law Collection (incomplete)

Date:	11th–12th Century	**Dimensions:**	255 x 190 (185 x 125)
Origin:	Rossano? (Northern Calabria)	**Material:**	Parchment
Owner:	Unknown	**Folios:**	vii + 160 + iii
Scribe:	Unknown	**Lines:**	27
Binding:	Colonna family (16th century)	**Ruling:**	20D1 (System 1)
Hands:	A: 1–160 a: 1^{r}, 10^{r} (repetition of main text)	**Collation:**	$1–19^{8}$, 20^{7}

Catalogue: *RHBR* 1.270–271 (no. 242).

---

1. *Procheiros Nomos*, Table of Contents **2r**
2. *Ecloga privata* **10r**
3. *Procheiros Nomos* (derivative) **28v**
4. Appendix: Civil Law **107r**
1. *Soldier's Law* 107r
2. *Sailor's Law* 109v
3. *Farmer's Law* 115v
4. *Ekloge* 14.2–6, 8–9, 11–12 122r
5. *Procheiros Nomos* 39.35–39 123r/v
5. Appendix: Canon Law **123v**
1. Athanasios of Emesa, *Syntagma of Novels* (epitome) 123v
2. Carth. c. 15, 32, 25, 5–6, 128–131, 80 134v
3. *Prot.* c. 1–6, 8–13, 15–17 138r
4. Apost. c. 1–9, 11–12, 10, 13–17, 22–25, 27, 29–30, 32–33, 35, 38, 40–41, 44, 50 48, 51–56, 58, 60, 63–64, 68, 72, 76–79, 83, 31, 70–71, 82, 84 147v
5. *Mosaic Law* (des. mut.) 153r

---

24. Vatican City, Biblioteca Apostolica Vaticana, MS Vat. gr. 1287

Nomocanon, Salentine Group (fragmentary)

Date:	12th Century	**Dimensions:**	300 x 190 (230 x 130)
Origin:	Salento (Lecce?)	**Material:**	Parchment
Owner:	Unknown	**Folios:**	i + 65 + i
Scribe:	Unknown	**Lines:**	38–41
Binding:	Antonio Carafa (1538–1591)	**Ruling:**	X11D1bm, Xb12D1, Xb32D1, X20D1 (System 5)
Hands:	A: 1–65	**Collation:**	$1–2^4$, 3^2, $4–9^8$, 10^7, 11^6

Catalogue: *RHBR* 2.184–185 (no. 402).

---

1. Conciliar Canons with Historical Introductions (inc. mut.) **1r**
1. *Trullo* 1r
2. II Nicaea (II Nic. c. 1–14; *Prot. c.* 11; II Nic. c. 16–22) 10r
3. *Protodeutera* (*Prot.* c. 1–10; II Nic. c. 17; *Prot.* c. 12–17) 14v
2. Patristic Canons **18v**
3. Marriage Law **45r/v**
1. Sisinnios II of Constantinople, *Tome against the Marriage of Cousins* 45r/v
4. *Nomocanon in 50 Titles* (des. mut.) **45v**

---

25. The Messinese Collection (via Vat. gr. 1426)

Theological Compendium (incomplete)

Date:	17th August 1213	**Dimensions:**	Unknown
Origin:	Holy Saviour of Messina (Sicily)	**Material:**	Parchment?
Owner:	Holy Saviour of Messina	**Folios:**	665
Scribe:	Symeon *tou Boulkaramou*	**Lines:**	Unknown
Binding:	Unknown	**Ruling:**	Unknown
Hands:	Unknown	**Collation:**	Unknown

1. Ps.-Dionysios the Areopagite, Theological Writings	**1^r**
1. *On the Celestial Hierarchy*	$1^{r/v}$
2. *On the Divine Names*	3^r
3. *On the Ecclesiastical Hierarchy*	67^r
4. Christopher of Mytilene, *Epigram on Mystical Theology*	103^v
5. *On Mystical Theology*	103^r
6. *Letters* 1–10	109^r
2. Symeon *tou Boulkaramou*, Manuscript Colophon in Dodecasyllabic Meter	**130^r**
3. Oecumenius, *Commentary on the Apocalypse*	**131^r**
4. Conciliar and Canonical Miscellany	**161^r**
1. History of the Councils ('χρὴ μὲν γινώσκειν πάντα χριστιανὸν ὅτι ἑπτὰ εἰσὶν αἱ ἁγίαι οἰκουμενικαὶ σύνοδοι . . .')	161^r
2. *Trullo* c. 2	163^v
3. Photios of Constantinople, *To His Brother Tarasios on the Writings of Athanasius of Alexandria*	164^v
4. *Letter of Liberius to Athanasius*	164^v
5. Marcellus of Ancyra, *Against the Theopaschites*	$165^{r/v}$
6. Athanasius of Alexandria, *On the Faith* (excerpts)	165^v
7. Conciliar and patristic excerpts on Christian belief	174^r
8. *Synodikon* of the Sunday of Orthodoxy	175^v
9. Decree of 843 on the Restoration of Icons	178^v
10. Athanasius of Alexandria, *On the Common Essence of the Father, Son, and Holy Spirit*	180^r
11. Cyril of Alexandria, *Anathema against Nestorius*	190^v
12. Athanasius of Alexandria, *Disputation against Arius*	191^v
13. Maximus the Confessor, *Disputation with Pyrrhus*	205^r
14. Anastasius Apocrisiarius, *Dialogue of Maximus with Bishop Theodosius of Caesarea in Bithynia*	216^v
15. Conciliar and patristic excerpts	224^r
16. Athanasius of Alexandria, *Oration Against the Heathens*	235^r
17. Athanasius of Alexandria, *Oration on the Incarnation of the Word*	255^v
18. Anonymous, *On the Incarnation of the Word*	279^r
19. Marcellus of Ancyra, *On the Incarnation and Against the Arians*	280^r
5. Neilos Doxapatres, *De oeconomia Dei* (Book 1, Book 2 des. mut.)	**296^v**

26. Vatican City, Biblioteca Apostolica Vaticana, MS Vat. gr. 1506

Apostolic Compilation (fragmentary)

Date:	25th March 1024	**Dimensions:**	290 x 225 (205 x 155)
Origin:	Rossano? (Northern Calabria)	**Material:**	Parchment
Owner:	Cathedral of Rossano?	**Folios:**	ii + 80 + i
Scribe:	Athanasios (priest)	**Lines:**	34
Binding:	Leo XIII (1878–1903) and Jean-Baptiste Pitra (1869–1889)	**Ruling:**	34C2 (System unclear)
		Collation:	$1^9, 2^6, 3^{10}, 4–7^8, 8^9, 9^6, 10^9$
Hands:	A: 1–80 a: 59^v (in margin)		

Catalogue: Giannelli (1950): 41–43. **View Online:** https://digi.vatlib.it/view/MSS_Vat.gr.1506

1. *Apostolic Constitutions* (inc. mut.)	**1^r**
1. *Apost. Const.* 3.7–8.11 (inc. mut.)	1^r
2. *Gregory of Nazianzus, *Oration* 30.14	59^v
3. *Apost. Const.* 8.12–39	59^v
2. Apostolic Canons	**69^r**
1. Apost. c. 1–4	69^r
2. *Apost. Const.* 8.40–46	69^r
3. Apost. c. 5–9, 14, 17–63, 66, 64–65, 67–84	72^v
3. Appendix: Historical Information	**78^r**
1. *On the Twelve Apostles—Where They Preached and Where They Died*	$78^{r/v}$
2. Note on the Gospels (‘*δεῖ γινώσκειν τὸ πῶς συνεγράφησα τὰ Δ′ εὐαγγέλια*’)	78^v

27. Vatican City, Biblioteca Apostolica Vaticana, MS Vat. gr. 1980 (Basil. 19)

The Carbone Nomocanon (1st Half)

Date:	Late 11th Century	**Dimensions:**	190 x 145 (145 x 105)
Origin:	Lucania	**Material:**	Parchment
Owner:	SS Elias and Anastasios of Carbone	**Folios:**	ii + 195 + i
Scribe:	Unknown	**Lines:**	22
Binding:	Pius IX (1846–1878) and Angelo Mai (1853–1854)	**Ruling:**	20A1 (System 9)
		Collation:	$1^4, 2–5^8, 6^9, 7^6, 8^7, 9–20^8, 21^9, 22^8, 23^7, 24–25^8$
Hands:	A: 1–195 b: 1^v, 4^v a: 1^v c: 4^r		

Catalogue: *RHBR* 3.247–249 (no. 525).

1. Front Matter	**1^v**
1. *Short excerpts from Byzantine civil and canon law on marriage and judicial process	1^v
2. Table of Contents	2^r
3. *Salad recipe	4^r

4. *Short excerpts from Byzantine civil law on judicial process and debt 4v
2. Conciliar Canons **5r**
1. *Epitome of Book Eight of the Apostolic Constitutions* 1–2, 22.2–28.13, 19–21 5r
2. *Thirty Chapters of the Apostolic Constitutions* 1–5, 8, 11–13, 17–20, 26–30 17v
3. Apost. c. 1–5, 7, 6, 8–50, 51–65, 67–85 18v
4. I Nicaea (with historical introduction 28r
5. I Constantinople (381; with historical introduction) 34v
6. Ephesus (with historical introduction) 39v
7. Chalcedon (with historical introduction) 45v
8. Flavian of Constantinople, *Letter to Pope Leo the Great* 55v
9. Pope Leo the Great, *Letter to Flavian of Constantinople* 58r
10. Constantinople (394) 69r
11. *Trullo* (with historical introduction) 70v
12. II Nicaea (with historical introduction) 117r
13. History of the Councils ('ἑτέρα εἴδησις περὶ τῶν ἁγίων συνόδων οἰκουμενικῶν') 130r
14. Ancyra 134v
15. Neocaesarea 139r
16. Gangra 140v
17. Antioch 145r
18. Laodicea 152v
19. Sardica 157v
20. Carthage 167v

---

28. Vatican City, Biblioteca Apostolica Vaticana, MS Vat. gr. 1981 (Basil. 20)

The Carbone Nomocanon (2nd Half)

Date:	Late 11th Century	**Dimensions:**	190 x 145 (145 x 105)
Origin:	Lucania	**Material:**	Parchment
Owner:	SS Elias and Anastasios of	**Folios:**	ii + 200 + i
Scribe:	Carbone	**Lines:**	22
Binding:	Unknown	**Ruling:**	20A1 (System 9)
Hands:	Pius IX (1846–1878) and Angelo Mai (1853–1854) A: 1–200 b: 200v a: 200r/v c: 200v	**Collation:**	$1–2^8, 3^6, 4^9, 5–8^8, 9^6, 10^7, 11–23^8, 24^{10}$

Catalogue: *RHBR* 3.249–251 (no. 526). **View Online:** https://digi.vatlib.it/view/MSS_Vat.gr.1981

---

1. Conciliar Canons (cont.) **1r**
1. Carthage (cont.) 1r
2. Carthage (256) 13r
2. Patristic Canons **14v**
1. Dionysios of Alexandria, *Letter to Basil* 14v
2. Peter of Alexandria, *Six Canons from the Sermon on Penitence* 18v

3. Gregory of Neocaesarea, *Canonical Letter*	29^{r}
4. *On False Accusers*	$32^{r/v}$
5. Athanasios of Alexandria c. 1	32^{v}
6. Anastasios of Sinai, *Erotapokriseis* 95	$36^{r/v}$
7. John Moschos, *Spiritual Meadow* 198	36^{v}
8. Athanasios of Alexandria c. 5	37^{r}
9. Timothy of Alexandria c. 1–11, 20, 12–15, 19, 16	38^{r}
10. Basil of Caesarea, *Canonical Letters and Texts*	41^{v}
11. Gregory of Nyssa, *Letter to Letoius*	76^{r}
12. Theophilos of Alexandria, *Canonical Texts* (des. mut.)	86^{r}
13. Cyril of Alexandria, *Letter to the Bishops of Libya and Pentapolis* (inc. mut.)	89^{r}
14. Basil of Caesarea, *Epitimia*	$91^{r/v}$
3. *Nomocanon in 14 Titles* (original recension)	**92^{r}**
4. Appendix: Church History (with later additions)	**181^{v}**
1. Nikephoros the Confessor, *Brief Chronicle*	181^{v}
2. *Life of Constantine* (excerpt)	189^{v}
3. Dorotheos of Tyre, *On the 70 Disciples of Christ*	190^{r}
4. List of Patriarchs of Constantinople to the year 931	197^{v}
5. Episcopal *taktika* (Darrouzès 6)	199^{r}
6. Apost. c. 85	200^{r}
7. *Photios of Constantinople, *On the Divine Liturgy*	$200^{r/v}$
8. **Reckoning of the Ages of Man*	200^{v}
9. **On the Children of Debtors*	200^{v}

29. Vatican City, Biblioteca Apostolica Vaticana, MS Vat. gr. 2019 (Basil. 99)

The 'Nomocanon of Doxapatres'

Date:	Before 1234	**Dimensions:**	210 x 170 (180 x 135)
Origin:	Rossano (Northern Calabria)	**Material:**	Parchment (palimpsest)
Owner:	Sinator of Kritene (1234/5); Raudas (monk?); Patiron (Rossano)	**Folios:**	i + 166 + i
		Lines:	24–28
Scribe:	Unknown	**Ruling:**	20A1 (System unclear)
Binding:	Pius IX (1846–1876) and Angelo Mai (1853–1854)	**Collation:**	$1–2^{8}$, 3^{2}, 4^{6}, $5–7^{8}$, 8^{10}, $9–20^{8}$, 21^{3}, 22^{14}
Hands:	A: $1–155^{r}$ e: $160a^{r/v}$, $164^{r}–165^{r/v}$ a: 155^{v} f: $161r–164^{v}$ b: $156^{r}–158^{v}$ g: $165^{r/v}$ c: $159^{r}–160^{r}$ h: 166^{r} d: 160^{v} i: 166^{v}		

Catalogue: *RHBR* 3.252–256 (no. 527); Turyn (1964): 28–34. **View Online:** https://digi.vatlib.it/view/MSS_Vat.gr.2019

1. Table of Contents	1^{r}
1. Alexios Aristenos, *Synopsis of Canons*	**9^{v}**

2. Appendix: Canon Law	**95^{v}**
1. John the Faster, *Kanonarion* (excerpt)	95^{v}
2. John the Faster, *Kanonikon*	105^{r}
3. *Trullo* c. 11, 43, 55, 75, 90, 23	105^{r}
4. Basil of Caesarea c. 13	107^{v}
5. 8 'Canons of Chalcedon'	107^{v}
6. *Trullo* c. 65	107^{v}
7. Dionysios of Alexandria c. 2	108^{r}
8. Basil of Caesarea c. 7, 24–25, 9, 48	$108^{r/v}$
9. 1 Corinthians 7:39 with exegesis	108^{v}
10. *From the Letter of Gennadios* [I of Constantinople]	108^{v}
11. John the Faster, *Teachings of the Fathers* (excerpts)	108^{v}
12. John Klimakos, *Ladder of Divine Ascent* 4 (excerpt)	110^{r}
13. John the Faster, *Deuterokanonarion* (excerpt)	110^{r}
14. '*On the Purity of the Clergy*'	110^{v}
15. History of the Councils ('*ἡ πρώτη ἁγία καὶ οἰκουμενικὴ σύνοδος γέγονεν*')	110^{v}
16. Diagrams of acceptable and unacceptable degrees of kinship for marriage	112^{r}
17. Short excerpts from Byzantine civil law on marriage	113^{r}
18. Alexios Stoudites, *Synodal Act on Marriage*	114^{v}
19. *Tome of Union* (920)	$115^{r/v}$
20. Sisinnios II of Constantinople, *Ekthesis*	115^{v}
21. *Epitome of Book Eight of the Apostolic Constitutions* 3–21, 1–2	117^{v}
22. Nicholas III Grammatikos of Constantinople, *Canonical Answers*	122^{r}
23. Nikephoros the *Chartophylax*, *Letters* 5, 1	124^{v}
24. Euphemianos of Thessalonica, *Canonical Answers to Gerasimos*	126^{v}
25. Michael Choumnos, *Canonical Answers to Neophytos*	135^{v}
26. *From the Constitution of the* Typikon *of the Lord Paul, Founder of the Monastery of the Theotokos Evergetis*	139^{r}
27. Just. *Nov.* 3, 5–7, 12, 14–15	141^{v}
***3. Miscellaneous Fragments**	**156^{r}**
1. *Theodore Stoudites, *In Praise of John the Theologian*	156^{r}
2. *Verses on the Apostle John	158^{v}
3. *Basil of Caesarea, *Sermon for the Instruction of Priests*	159^{v}
4. *Fragment of a deed of sale between the brothers Philip and Pankalos and the bishop Nicholas relating to property in Rossano	160^{v}
5. *Homily of John [Chrysostom?] (des. mut.)	$160a^{r/v}$
6. *Hippolytos of Thebes, *Chronicle* (excerpt)	161^{r}
7. *On the Family of Christ	162^{r}
8. *Hippolytos of Thebes, *Chronicle* (excerpt)	164^{v}
9. *Anonymous homily (inc. mut.)	$165^{r/v}$
10. *Fragment of a schedographic text	$165a^{r/v}$
11. *Note on fasting	166^{r}
12. *Astronomical diagram	166^{v}

30. Vatican City, Biblioteca Apostolica Vaticana, MS Vat. gr. 2060 (Basil. 99)

Nomocanon, Rossanese Group (fragmentary)

Date:	*c.* 1100–1115	**Dimensions:**	305 x 240 (235 x 160)
Origin:	Patiron (Rossano,	**Material:**	Parchment
Owner:	N. Calabria)	**Folios:**	v + 263
Scribe:	Patiron	**Lines:**	37
Binding:	Bartholomew (monk)?	**Ruling:**	22E2s, 22D2s (Systems 9, 1, 10)
	Pius IX (1846–1876) and	**Collation:**	$1–2^8$, $3–4^7$, $5–8^8$, 9^6, 10^8, 11^6,
	Angelo Mai (1853–1854)		$12–22^8$, 23^5
Hands:	A: 1–263		

View Online: https://digi.vatlib.it/view/MSS_Vat.gr.2060

[1. Front Matter]	–
1. [*Epitome of Book Eight of the Apostolic Constitutions* 22.2–28.1]	–
2. [*S50T*, Preface and Table of Canons]	–
2. *Nomocanon in 14 Titles* (Photian recension; inc. mut.)	**1^r**
3. Conciliar Canons	**36^r**
4. Patristic Canons	**131^r**
3. Appendix: Civil Law (des. mut.)	**168^v**
1. Just. *Nov.* 77	168^v
2. *C87C*	169^v
3. *C25C*	183^r
4. *Tripartite Collection*	208^r
5. Heraclius, *Novels* 4, 1, 3, [2] (des. mut.)	258^v
[4. Epilogue: John Moschos, *Spiritual Meadow* 149 (excerpt)]	–

31. Vatican City, Biblioteca Apostolica Vaticana, MS Vat. gr. 2075 (Basil. 114)

Civil Law Collection (incomplete)

Date:	Late 10th Century	**Dimensions:**	220 x 155 (175 x 120)
Origin:	Calabria	**Material:**	Parchment
Owner:	Unknown	**Folios:**	ii + 263 + ii
Scribe:	Unknown	**Lines:**	27–31
Binding:	Pius IX (1846–1876) and	**Ruling:**	20C1 (Systems 9, 10)
	Angelo Mai (1853–1854)	**Collation:**	$1–20^8$, 21^{10}, 22^8 (wants 1 after
Hands:	A: 1^r–110^v		fol. 169), 23^8, 24^8 wants 1 after
	B: 110^v–120^v, 140^r, 145^r–		fol. 188, $25–32^8$, 33^8 (wants 1
	146^r, 153^v–156^v, 159^r–161^r,		after fol. 263)
	162r–251^r, 252^v–261^v, $263^{r/v}$		
	C: 121^r–140^r, 140^v,		
	141^r–144^v, 157^r–158^v, 161^v		

D: 146^{v}–153^{r}
E: 140^{v}, 251^{r}, $262^{r/v}$
F: 251^{v}–252^{v}

Catalogue: *RHBR* 1.270–271 (no. 242). **View Online:** https://digi.vatlib.it/view/MSS_Vat.gr.2075

---

1. Front Matter	**1^{r}**
1. *Protodeutera*, canons	1^{r}
2. Just. *Nov.* 5	8^{r}
3. *Appendix Eclogae* 1; 2.4, 6–9	13^{v}
4. Apost. c. 1–9, 11–12, 10, 13–17, 22–25, 27, 29–30, 32–33, 35, 38, 40–41, 50, 44, 48–49, 51–61, 63–64, 68, 72–74, 76–79, 83, 31, 65–67, 69, 71, 75, 80–82, 84, 70	13^{v}
5. *Basil of Caesarea c. 50, 80	17^{v}
6. **Trullo* c. 67	18^{r}
7. *Procheiros Nomos* 34.17	19^{v}
8. Lexicon of Latin legal terms	20^{r}
9. Chronology of ecumenical councils	24^{r}
10. Aphorism on fair judgment in court cases	24^{r}
2. *Epitome Vaticana*	**24^{v}**
1. *Sailor's Law*	25^{v}
2. *Farmer's Law*	35^{v}
3. Appendix: Civil Law	**251^{r}**
1. *Basilika* (excerpts from books 50 and 51)	251^{r}
2. *Soldier's Law*	254^{r}
3. Maurice, *Strategikon* 8.2 (excerpts; des. mut.)	$257^{r/v}$
4. Just. *Nov.* 1	258^{r}
5. *Basilika* (excerpts from books 50 and 28)	259^{v}

---

32. Vatican City, Biblioteca Apostolica Vaticana, MS Vat. gr. 2115 (Basil. 154), fols. 78–96

Civil Law Collection (fragmentary)

Date:	11th/12th Century	**Dimensions:**	185 x 130 (150 x 100)
Origin:	Rossano (Northern	**Material:**	Parchment
Owner:	Calabria)	**Folios:**	i + 185 + i
Scribe:	Unknown	**Lines:**	27–29
Binding:	Unknown	**Ruling:**	X00D1 (System 9)
	Pius IX (1846–1878) and Angelo Mai (1853–1854)	**Collation:**	$1-3^{4}$, 4^{6}, $5-7^{8}$, 8^{6}, 9^{7}, 10^{8}, 11^{2}, 12^{4}, 13^{8}, 14^{7}, 15^{8}, 16^{4}, 17^{2}, 18^{8}, 19^{2}, 20^{4}, 21^{6}, 22^{4}, $23-25^{8}$, 26^{4}, 27^{8}, $28-29^{6}$, 30^{8}, 31^{6}
Hands:	A: 78–96		

View Online: https://digi.vatlib.it/view/MSS_Vat.gr.2115

***1. Biblical and Patristic Fragments**	**1^{r}**
1. New Testament commentary (inc. and des. mut.)	1^{r}
2. John Chrysostom, *Comparison between Kings and Monks* (inc. and des. mut.)	5^{r}
3. Antiochos the Monk, *Pandecta Scripturae Sacrae*, *Homily* 27.50–35, 63 (inc. and des. mut.)	13^{r}
4. Fragments from 2 Samuel and 2 Kings (inc. and des. mut.)	27^{r}
5. Basil of Caesarea, *Great Asketikon*, preface (inc. and des. mut.)	70^{r}
6. Evagrius Ponticus, *Practicus* 6–14 (inc. and des. mut.)	73^{v}
2. Nomocanonical Fragment	**78^{r}**
1. Carth. c. 15, 32, 25, 5–6, 128–131, 80	78^{r}
2. *Prot.* c. 1–6, 8–13, 15–17	80^{r}
3. Apost. c. 1–9, 11–12, 10, 13–17, 22–25, 27, 29–30, 32–33, 35, 38, 40–41, 44, 50 48, 51–56, 58, 60, 63–64, 68, 72, 76–79, 83, 31, 70–71, 82, 84	86^{v}
4. *Ekloge*, preface (des. mut.)	91^{r}
5. *Ekloge* 6–10.1 (des. mut.)	93^{r}
***3. Civil Law Fragments**	**97^{r}**
1. *Procheiros Nomos* 21.1–10	97^{r}
2. *Epitome of the Laws* (excerpts)	98^{r}
***4. Miscellaneous Fragments**	**99^{r}**
1. John Chrysostom, *Homily on Matthew* 6.4–6 (continued in Vat. gr. 2089, fols. 73–150)	99^{r}
2. Fragmentary parainetic text (inc. 'ὡσαύτως δὲ καὶ οἱ τὸν πλοῦτον ἀγαπόντες')	107^{r}
3. Fragmentary *Life* of Abba Apollo (inc. '... μετάστρεψον τὸν πόλεμον τοῦ ἀδελφοῦ ...')	119^{r}
4. *Barlaam and Ioasaph* (fragment)	123^{r}
5. Fragmentary text on tax law	147^{r}
6. Liturgy of St John Chrysostom, communion prayers (fragment)	151^{r}
7. Gregory of Nazianzus, *Apologetica*, *Oration* 2	160^{r}
8. Luke 5:11–16:14	116^{r}
9. *Barlaam and Ioasaph* (fragment)	180^{r}

33. Venice, Biblioteca Nazionale Marciana, MS gr. 169 (coll. 475)

Nomocanon

Date:	11th/12th Century	**Dimensions:**	340 x 250 (230 x 155)
Origin:	Constantinople?	**Material:**	Parchment
Owner:	Holy Saviour of Messina	**Folios:**	ii + 311 + ii
Scribe:	(Sicily)	**Lines:**	33
Binding:	Unknown	**Ruling:**	54C1, 84C4 (System 1)
Hands:	Biblioteca Marciana A: 1–311 b: 311b a: 311^{v}	**Collation:**	$1–4^{8}$, 5^{6}, $6–14^{8}$, 15^{6}, $16–24^{8}$, 25^{3}, $26–38^{8}$, 39^{7}

Catalogue: *RHBR* 2.214–217 (no. 417); Mioni (1981): 1.249–253.

1. Front Matter	**1^{r}**
1. *Epitome of Book Eight of the Apostolic Constitutions*, 22.2–28.17	1^{r}
2. *S50T*, Preface and Table of Canons	4^{r}
2. *Nomocanon in 14 Titles* (Photian recension with scholia)	**5^{r}**
1. *A Simple Outline of What is Contained in Each Part of the Present Volume*	56^{v}
3. Conciliar Canons (with scholia)	**58^{r}**
4. Patristic Canons (with scholia)	**161^{v}**
5. Appendix: Civil Law	**197^{r}**
1. Just. *Nov.* 77	$197^{r/v}$
2. *C87C*	197^{v}
3. *C25C*	212^{r}
4. *Tripartite Collection*	241^{v}
5. Heraclius, *Novels* 4, 1, 3, 2	296^{r}
6. Back Matter	
1. Photios of Constantinople, *Canonical Letters* 292–296	302^{v}
2. Nicholas I Mystikos of Constantinople, *On the Free Display of Patriarchal Letters*	$306^{r/v}$
3. Episcopal *taktika* (Darrouzès 8, 5, 7)	307^{r}
4. Plutarch, *Life of Caesar*, 69.10–11 (summary)	311^{r}
5. Stephanos of Byzantium, *Ethnika* (excerpts)	$311^{r/v}$
6. Sisinnios II of Constantinople, *Tome against the Marriage of Cousins* (summary)	311^{v}
7. *On Marcian the Ascetic*	311^{v}
8. *Michael Psellos, *On the Bath* (‘πολλῶν τὸ λουτρὸν αἴτιον δωρημάτων’), ll. 1–3, 10, 5, 7–8, 11, 13–16 (with notable differences)	311^{v}
9. *Latin document of 1288 recording a debt owed by the Holy Saviour of Messina to the nobleman Pandolfo Falcone	311b

34. Venice, Biblioteca Nazionale Marciana, MS gr. 171 (coll. 741)

Nomocanon (incomplete)

Date:	*c.* 1220–1230	**Dimensions:**	265 x 170 (195 x 120)
Origin:	Grottaferrata (Lazio)	**Material:**	Paper (Italian non-watermarked)
Owner:	Theotokos of Grottaferrata	**Folios:**	ii + 129 + ii
Scribe:	Unknown	**Lines:**	28–30
Binding:	Biblioteca Marciana	**Ruling:**	20D1 (System 13)
Hands:	A: 1^{v}–129 a: 1^{r} b: 2^{r}	**Collation:**	1^{10}, $2–14^{8}$, 15^{6}, 16^{9}

Catalogue: *RHBR* 2.217–218 (no. 418); Mioni (1981): 1.256–257.

1. Front Matter	**1^{r}**
1. *Summary of an agreement between Pankratios the *praepositus* of Grottaferrata and the lords John and Jacob Frangipane	1^{r}

2. Table of contents	1^{v}
3. *Miscellaneous quotes from Scripture and Classical literature	2^{r}
4. *N14T*, 1st and 2nd Preface	3^{r}
5. History of the Councils ('ἑτέρα εἴδησις περὶ τῶν ἁγίων συνόδων οἰκουμενικῶν')	6^{r}
2. Conciliar Canons	**15^{r}**
1. Apostolic Canons	15^{r}
2. *Epitome of Book Eight of the Apostolic Constitutions* 19–21; 18.2–3; 22.2–14, 16, 15, 17–24.7; 25–26	22^{v}
3. I Nicaea	27^{r}
4. Ancyra	30^{v}
5. Neocaesarea	34^{v}
6. Gangra	35^{v}
7. Laodicea	45^{v}
8. I Constantinople (381)	49^{v}
9. Ephesus	53^{r}
10. Chalcedon	57^{v}
11. *Trullo*	64^{v}
12. II Nicaea	95^{v}
3. Patristic Canons (des. mut.)	**105^{v}**
1. Gregory of Nyssa, *Letter to Letoius*	105^{v}
2. Athanasios of Alexandria c. 5	114^{r}
3. Theophilos of Alexandria c. 1	114^{v}
4. Basil of Caesarea (des. mut.)	115^{r}

35. Venice, Biblioteca Nazionale Marciana, MS gr. 172 (coll. 574)

Civil Law Collection (the 'Epitome Marciana')

Date:	July 1175	**Dimensions:**	365 x 260 (240–250 x 170)
Origin:	Calabria	**Material:**	Parchment
Owner:	Philip Malegras (notary)	**Folios:**	258
Scribe:	John (notary)	**Lines:**	31–34
Binding:	Biblioteca Marciana	**Ruling:**	K44A2 (System unclear)
Hands:	A: 1–256 a: 257–258	**Collation:**	1–3^{8}, 4^{3}, 5–13^{8}, 14^{7}, 15–23^{8}, 24^{7}, 25–9^{8}, 30^{7}, 31–3^{8}, 34^{1}

Catalogue: *RHBR* 1.330–331 (no. 289); Mioni (1981): 1.261–265.

1. *Epitome Marciana*	**1^{r}**
1. Table of contents	1^{r}
2. Lexicon of Latin legal terms	23^{r}
3. Miniatures of Justinian I, Leo III, and Constantine V; diagram of degrees of family kinship	
4. *Sailor's Law*	30^{v}
5. *Farmer's Law*	37^{r}
6. *Epitome of the Laws*	43^{r}

7. Lexicon of Latin legal terms	167^r
8. *Soldier's Law*	227^v
9. *Sailor's Law* (excerpts)	230^r
10. Leo VI, *Nov.* 5 (excerpt)	231^r
11. Irene, Novels on oaths and marriage	231^r
12. Just. *Nov.* 1	$243^{r/v}$
2. Appendix: Canon Law	**243^v**
1. Apostolic Canons	243^v
2. *On the Patriarchs and their Regions*	248^v
3. Assorted canons on ecclesiastical discipline: Laod. c. 41–42, 44; Neocaes. c. 11, 7; Laod. c. 49–52; Apost. c. 61; Gangra, *c.* 18; Laod. c. 36; Gangra, c. 15–16; Apost. c. 47–51	249^r
3. Appendix: Civil Law	**250v**
1. *Mosaic Law* (excerpts)	250^v
2. Oath for Jews to swear to Christians	$256^{r/v}$
3. Aphorisms on fair judgment	256^v
***4. Roger II, Novel on Inheritance (a. 1150)**	**257^r**

36. Venice, Biblioteca Nazionale Marciana, MS gr. III.2 (coll. 1131)

Nomocanon, Salentine Group (incomplete)

Date:	12th/13th Century	**Dimensions:**	230 x 165 (185 x 120)
Origin:	Salento	**Material:**	Parchment
Owner:	Unknown	**Folios:**	i + 222 + iii
Scribe:	Unknown	**Lines:**	31
Binding:	Biblioteca Marciana	**Ruling:**	X21D1b (System 1)
Hands:	A: 1–222	**Collation:**	$1–4^8, 5^9, 6^6, 7–26^8, 27^7, 28^8$

Catalogue: Mioni (1981): 2.138–141.

1. Conciliar Canons with Historical Introductions	**1^r**
1. Apostolic Canons	1^r
2. *The Ecclesiastical Ranks*	6^v
3. I Nicaea	6^v
4. Ancyra	11^r
5. Neocaesarea	14^r
6. Sardica	15^r
7. Gangra	20^v
8. Antioch	23^r
9. Laodicea	27^r
10. I Constantinople (381)	30^v
11. Ephesus	33^r
12. Chalcedon	37^r
13. II Constantinople (553)	43^r
14. *Trullo*	45^r

15. II Nicaea (II Nic. c. 1–14; *Prot.* c. 11; II Nic. c. 16–22, 15)	68^{r}
16. *Protodeutera* (*Prot.* c. 1–10; II Nic. c. 17; *Prot.* c. 12–17)	74^{v}
2. Patristic Canons	**79^{r}**
3. Marriage Law	**114^{r}**
1. *Tome of Union* (920)	114^{r}
2. Sisinnios II of Constantinople, *Tome against the Marriage of Cousins*	116^{v}
3. Alexios Stoudites, *Synodal Act on Marriage*	117^{v}
4. *Ekloge* 2.2	118^{r}
5. Leo of Calabria, *Canonical Answer on Clerical Marriage*	$118^{r/v}$
4. Clerical Discipline and Differences with the Latin Church	**118^{v}**
1. *Apost. Const.* 3.10–11, 6.17, 8.42–44, 1.3.11 (on the rights of the clergy, including marriage)	118^{v}
2. *Rule of the Holy Apostles*	120^{v}
3. I Nicaea, *Decree on Pascha*	120^{v}
4. Excerpts from Byzantine civil and canon law on marriage, clerical discipline, and feast days	121^{r}
5. John Moschos, *Spiritual Meadow* 149 (excerpt)	123^{v}
6. Nikon of the Black Mountain, *Kanonarion* (excerpts)	124^{r}
7. Socrates, *Ecclesiastical History* 1.11.1–17	
8. Council of Carthage, canons	129^{r}
9. Photios of Constantinople, *Encyclical Letter to the Eastern Patriarchs*	163^{v}
5. *Nomocanon in 50 Titles* (misattributed to Theodoret of Cyrrhus)	**170^{r}**
6. Anti-Latin Texts	**198^{v}**
1. History of the Councils (‘*πρώτη σύνοδος γέγονεν οἰκουμενική*’)	198^{v}
2. Photios of Constantinople, *Canonical Letters*	202^{r}
7. Symeon Metaphrastes, *Synopsis of Canons*	**203^{r}**
8. Texts on Fasting (des. mut.)	**221^{r}**
1. John the Faster, fragment on Lent (des. mut.)	221^{r}

APPENDIX 2

Statistical Overview

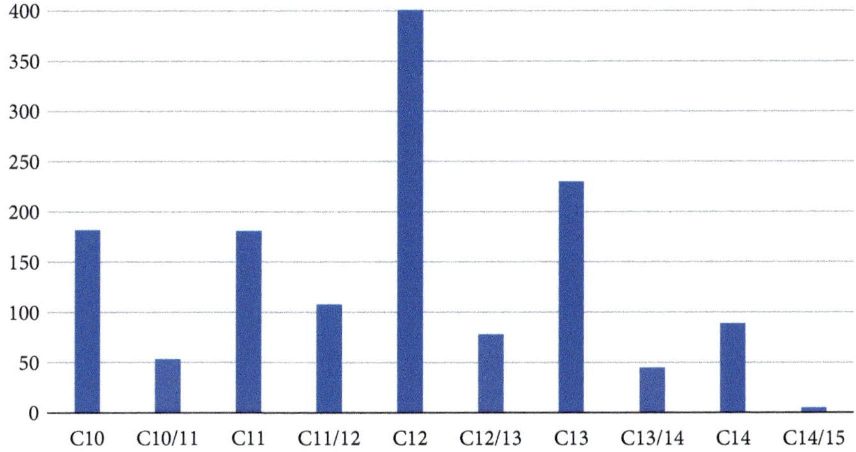

Figure App. 2.1. Overall Italo-Greek Manuscript Production by Century[1]

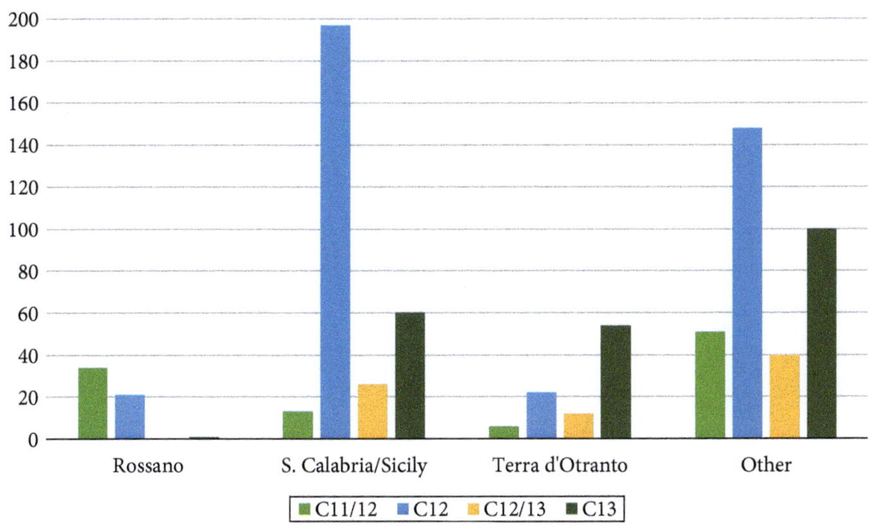

Figure App. 2.2. Overall Italo-Greek Manuscript Production by Region and Century[2]

[1] Based on figures in Canart (1982): 121.

[2] Canart (1982): 122–123.

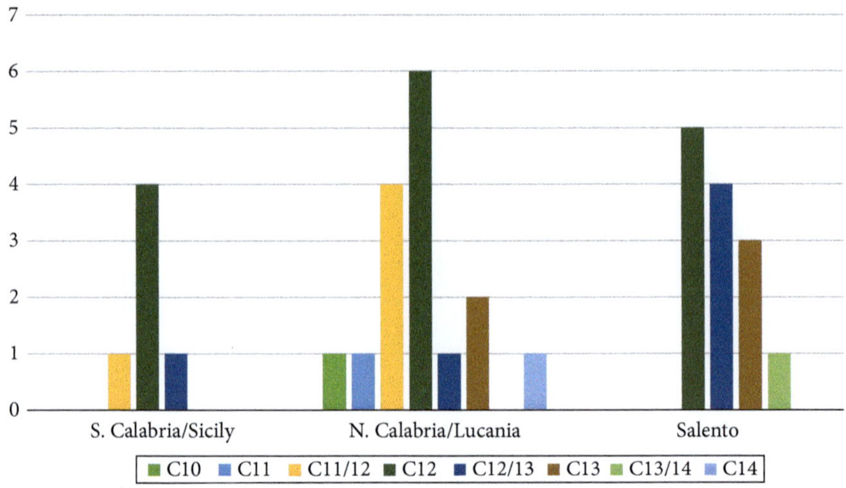

Figure App. 2.3. Nomocanonical Manuscript Production by Region and Century

Table App. 2.1. Manuscript Dimensions (Smallest to Largest)

	Shelfmark	Date	Origin	Dimensions	Written Space	Written Lines	Cols.
1.	Crypt. gr. 322	Pre-1135	S. Calabria	155 x 120	100 x 75	222	1
2.	Barb. gr. 323	Early C12	S. Calabria	165 x 155	120 x 110	23	1
3.	Barb. gr. 324	Late C12	St Nicholas of Casole	180 x 135	140 x 195	223	1
4.	Sin. gr. 397	C13	Salento	185 x 125	150 x 90	336	1
5.	Ottob. gr. 186 (fols. 22)	C12/13	Salento	185 x 130	150 x 105	229	1
6.	Vat. gr. 2115 (fols. 796)	C11/12	Rossano?	185 x 130	150 x 100	27–29	1
7.	Vat. gr. 1980–1981	C11/12	Carbone	190 x 145	145 x 105	22	1
8.	Crypt. gr. 50	C14	N. Calabria	195 x 145	145 x 100	23	1
9.	BnF gr. 1371	C12/13	St Nicholas of Casole	195 x 150	165 x 115	18–21	1
10.	Ambros. F 48 sup.	*c.* 1110– 1120	Salento	200 x 140	140 x 95	25	1
11.	Laur. plut. 5.22	C12/13	Salento	205 x 145	150 x 95	32–33	1
12.	Vat. gr. 2019	Pre-1234	Rossano	210 x 170	180 x 135	24–28	1
13.	Barocci 86	C12	Salento	220 x 135	190 x 110	25–30	1
14.	Vat. gr. 2075	Late C10	Calabria	220 x 155	175 x 120	27–31	1
15.	BnF gr. 1370	*c.* 1296/7	Salento	225 x 150	180 x 100	34–39	1
16.	Crypt. gr. 76	C12/13	Rossano?	225 x 170	165 x 115	23–29	1
17.	Marc. gr. III.2	C12/13	Salento	230 x 165	185 x 120	31	1
18.	Sin. gr. 432	C12	Sicily/S. Calabria?	230 x 185	185 x 140	32	1
19.	Ambros. B 107 sup.	C12/13	Salento	240 x 150	165–185 x 100	22–36	1
20.	Ambros. G 57 sup.	Early C12	S. Calabria	245 x 180	180 x 130	25–35	1
21.	Barb. gr. 476	C12	S. Calabria	245 x 190	175 x 155	27	2
22.	BN II C 7	1139	St John Theristes of Stilo	250 x 195	180 x 145	24–27	2
23.	Ambros. E 94 sup.	C13/14	Salento	255 x 165	200 x 125	29–32	1
24.	Vat. gr. 1168	C11/12	Rossano?	255 x 190	185 x 125	27	1
25.	Add. 28822	C12/13	Salento	260 x 170	195 x 115	32–34	1
26.	Marc. gr. 171	*c.* 1220–1230	Grottaferrata	265 x 170	195 x 120	28–30	1

Continued

Table App. 2.1. *Continued*

	Shelfmark	Date	Origin	Dimensions	Written Space	Written Lines	Cols.
27.	Alag. gr. 3	1124	Patiron of Rossano	265 x 200	180 x 135	25	2
28.	Vat. gr. 1506	1024	Rossano?	290 x 225	205 x 155	34	2
29.	Vat. gr. 1287	C12	Salento (Lecce?)	300 x 190	230 x 130	38–41	1
30.	Vat. gr. 2060	*c.* 1100–1115	Patiron of Rossano	305 x 240	235 x 160	37	2
31.	Vall. C 11.1	*c.* 1100–1115	Patiron of Rossano	325 x 240	205 x 175	29	2
32.	S. Salv. 59	*c.* 1100–1115	Patiron of Rossano	325 x 255	200 x 165	29–32	2
33.[a]	Marc. gr. 172	1175	Calabria	365 x 260	240–250 x 170	31–34	2

[a] Though the total number of manuscripts in this study is 36, only 33 are listed here. Vat. gr. 1980–1981 are counted as one manuscript. Vat. gr. 1426 is a sixteenth-century copy of a thirteenth century manuscript; since it likely does not represent that original manuscript's dimensions, it has not been included here. Finally, Marc. gr. 169 was produced on the Byzantine mainland and later brought to southern Italy, so it has also been omitted.

Table App. 2.2. Ruling Types and Systems (Smallest to Largest by Region)

Shelfmark	Date	Origin	Ruling Type(s)	Ruling System(s)	Written Lines
Northern Calabria and Lucania					
1. Vat. gr. 2115 (fols. 78–96)	C11/12	Rossano?	X00D1	9	27–29
2. Vat. gr. 1980–1981	C11/12	Carbone	20A1	9	22
3. Crypt. gr. 50	C14	Rossano?	Unclear	Unclear	23
4. Vat. gr. 2019	Pre-1234	Rossano	20A1	Unclear	24–28
5. Vat. gr. 2075	Late C10	Calabria	20C1	9, 10	27–31
6. Crypt. gr. 76	C12/13	N. Calabria	X22C1, 20C1	1	23–29
7. Vat. gr. 1168	C11/12	Rossano?	20D1	1	27
8. Alag. gr. 3	1124	Patiron of Rossano	20E2, J20E2	9	25
9. Vat. gr. 1506	1024	Rossano?	34C2	Unclear	34
10. Vat. gr. 2060	*c.* 1100–1115	Patiron of Rossano	22E2s, 22D2s	9, 1, 10	37
11. Vall. C 11.1	*c.* 1100–1115	Patiron of Rossano	12D2	9	29
12. S. Salv. 59	*c.* 1100–1115	Patiron of Rossano	44D2	9	29–32
13. Marc. gr. 172	1175	Calabria	K44A2	Unclear	31–34
Southern Calabria and Sicily					
14. Crypt. gr. 322	Pre-1135	S. Calabria	00C1	1	21–22
15. Barb. gr. 323	C12	S. Calabria	00D1	1, 9	23
16. Ambros. G 57 sup.	Early C12	S. Calabria	20D1	9	25–35
17. Barb. gr. 476	C12	S. Calabria	24E2o	1	27
18. BN II C 7	1139	St John Theristes of Stilo	12E2	4	24–27
19. Sin. gr. 432	C12	Sicily/S. Calabria?	20C1	9	32
Grottaferrata					
20. Marc. gr. 171	*c.* 1220–1230	Grottaferrata	20D1	13	28–30
Salento					
21. Barb. gr. 324	Late C12	St Nicholas of Casole	Unclear	Unclear	22–23
22. Sin. gr. 397	C13	Salento	X20A1	Unclear	32–36

Continued

Table App. 2.2. *Continued*

	Shelfmark	Date	Origin	Ruling Type(s)	Ruling System(s)	Written Lines
23.	Ottob. gr. 186 (fols. 9–22)	C12/13	Salento	Unclear	Unclear	27–29
24.	BnF gr. 1371	C12/13	St Nicholas of Casole	Unclear	Unclear	
25.	Ambros. F 48 sup.	C12	Salento	X20D1	1	25
26.	Barocci 86	C12	Salento	X20D1	1	25–30
27.	Laur. plut. 5.22	C12/13	Salento	X20C1	1	32–33
28.	BnF gr. 1370	*c.* 1296/7	Salento	22C1, 32C1	10, 9, 13	34–39
29.	Marc. gr. III.2	C12	Salento	X21D1b	1	31
30.	Ambros. B 107 sup.	C12–13	Salento	X32D1, X52D1, X22D1, U21/1b, 20D1	9	22–36
31.	Ambros. E 94 sup.	C13/14	Salento	P2 X20D1, P2 X4 20D1, V20A1, Xab 20A1, W20A1, V00A1	9, 6, 8, 10, 7	29–32
32.	Add. 28822	C12–13	Salento	X31D1b	1	32–34
33.	Vat. gr. 1287	C12	Lecce?	X11D1bm, Xb12D1, Xb32D1, X20D1	5	38–41

Table App. 2.3. Manuscripts with Visible Quire Numbers

	Shelfmark	Date	Origin	Location of Quire Numbers
1.	Vat. gr. 1168	C11/12	Rossano?	Upper right corner of first recto of quire
2.	S. Salv. 59	*c.* 1100–1115	Patiron of Rossano	Lower right corner of first recto
3.	Vall. C 11.1	*c.* 1100–1115	Patiron of Rossano	Upper right corner of first recto
4.	Vat. gr. 2060	*c.* 1100–1115	Patiron of Rossano	Lower left corner of first recto
5.	Crypt. gr. 322	Pre-1135	S. Calabria	Centre of lower margin of first recto and last verso
6.	BN II C 7	1139	St John Theristes of Stilo	Lower right corner of last verso
7.	Barb. gr. 323	Early C12	S. Calabria	Lower right corner of first recto
8.	Sin. gr. 432	C12	Sicily/S. Calabria?	Upper right corner of first recto
9.	Marc. gr. 172	1175	Calabria	Lower right corner of first recto
10.	Barb. gr. 324	Mid–Late C12	St Nicholas of Casole	Upper right corner of first recto
11.	Ambros. E 94 sup.	C13/14	Salento	Lower right corner of first recto

APPENDIX 3
Uncertain and Disputed Manuscripts

My practice in this study has been to draw conclusions only from those manuscripts of whose provenance and dating I am reasonably certain. However, there are several other nomocanonical manuscripts that may potentially derive from medieval southern Italy. There are also codices that were once thought to be southern Italian that have since been shown to originate in other areas of the Mediterranean world. I include brief discussions of each of these manuscripts below for the sake of completeness.

Nomocanons of Possible Southern Italian Provenance

Naples, Biblioteca nazionale 'Vittorio Emanuele III', MS II C 4

This nomocanon once belonged to the library of Cardinal Alessandro Farnese (1520–1589), as we can see from distinctive markings on the binding.[1] Mioni states that it was executed by 'an Italo-Greek scribe, quite experienced in Greek', who 'added Greek letters mixed in with Latin in some inscriptions and a few lemmata'.[2] Fol. 271^{v} bears the name 'Dionysios the monk', which Mioni takes to be the scribe's name, while two pen trials in a fourteenth-century hand on fol. 153^{r} read 'Theodosios the hieromonk'. Besides the style of script, there is no evidence in the manuscript to explicitly tie it to southern Italy.

The presence of Latin letters mixed in among the Greek is not in itself a sign of a southern Italian provenance. On the contrary, it is a very common phenomenon in Byzantine legal manuscripts; after all, Byzantine law was based on original Latin texts and many technical terms were left untranslated. Byzantine scribes developed their own version of the Latin alphabet that was based on Greek letter forms, not on scripts that were in use in the contemporary Latin West. It is this Hellenised Latin script that we find in BN II C 4, most notably in an opening glossary of Latin legal terms on fol. $1^{r/v}$. If anything, this shows that the scribe was *unfamiliar* with Latin, since he was clearly just copying from a model.

Contra Mioni, Mühlenberg associates the manuscript with Sinai 1111, an eleventh-century Constantinopolitan nomocanon with very similar contents.[3] While a southern Italian provenance cannot be ruled out, I suspect that an origin in mainland Byzantium is more likely.

Paris, Bibliothèque nationale de France, MS gr. 1324

A colophon on fol. 387^{v} of BnF gr. 1324 states that it was copied on Saturday 3rd December 1104 by a priest named John at the request of a certain Nicholas. Unfortunately, the surviving section of the colophon does not state *where* the codex was made. Nonetheless,

[1] On the contents of BN II C 4, see Chapter 1, 'Introducing the Byzantine Nomocanon', C1.P23–C1.P27.
[2] Mioni (1992): 157. [3] Mühlenberg (2008): lxvi.

Johannes Konidaris noticed in a study of manuscripts of Heraclius' *Novels* that BnF gr. 1324 has a clear relationship with the Rossanese nomocanons S. Salv. 59, Vall. C 11.1, and Vat. gr. 2060.[4] The contents of the four manuscripts are essentially identical (with the exception of a copy of a text by Gennadios Scholarios added at the end of BnF gr. 1324).[5] Moreover, all four manuscripts were written at approximately the same time and John's hand appears similar to the Style of Rossano.

Konidaris postulates that BnF gr. 1324 (which he calls M), S. Salv. 59 (P), Vall. C 11.1 (N), and Vat. gr. 2060 (*Λ*) formed a discrete family of manuscripts split into two branches: M and N, and P and *Λ*. He further states that 'M and N form Group n within this family. M was definitely not the prototype of N, but the opposite cannot be known for sure. *Λ* and P on the other hand form Group r. Here, the independence of P from *Λ* is certain, while one cannot rule out that P was the prototype of *Λ*.'[6] That is to say, Vall. C 11.1 may be a copy of BnF gr. 1324, while Vat. gr. 2060 may be a copy of S. Salv. 59; the two pairs would form separate branches of one family (see Figure App. 3.1).

However, Konidaris was unaware of the fact that P, N, and *Λ* were all copied at the Patiron of Rossano. The work of Foti and Lucà has shown that Vat. gr. 2060 and S. Salv. 59 are unlikely to form a separate branch from Vall. C 11.1, since the same scribe Bartholomew appears to have worked on all three.

One possibility is that BnF gr. 1324 (or another manuscript like it) was the ultimate source for the three Rossanese nomocanons. It was copied in 1104, around the time that St Bartholomew of Simeri visited Constantinople to acquire books and liturgical items for the Patiron in Rossano.[7] Perhaps BnF gr. 1324 was one of the manuscripts that Alexios Komnenos gave to Bartholomew and served as the model for the Rossanese Group? Alternatively, it may have been closely related to the manuscript that Bartholomew received. This latter option may be more convincing; the presence in BnF gr. 1324 of a text by the fifteenth-century patriarch Gennadios Scholarios suggests that the manuscript remained in Constantinople or Greece in the Late Middle Ages.

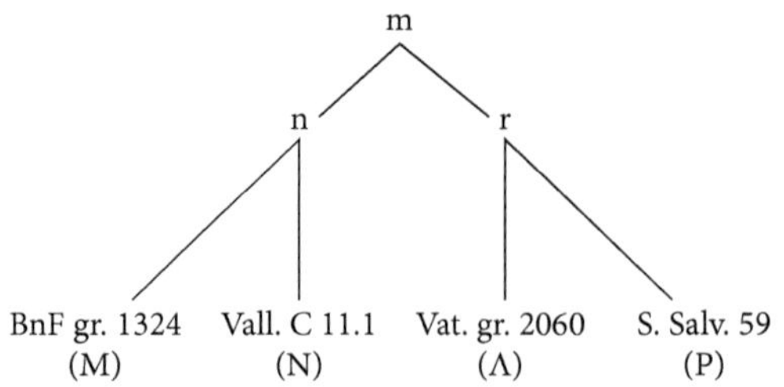

Figure App. 3.1. Relationship of BnF gr. 1324 to the Rossanese Group according to Konidaris (1982)

[4] Konidaris (1982): 48.

[5] 'Treatise Against the Latins Concerning the Correct Belief Regarding the Holy Spirit' ('ἔκθεσις περὶ τῆς ὀρθῆς πίστεως κατὰ Λατίνων περὶ τοῦ ἁγίου πνεύματος'): BnF gr. 1324, fols. 388^{r}–389^{v}. Text in Turner (1965): 338–342.

[6] Konidaris (1982): 48.

[7] See Chapter 6, 'Monastic Nomocanons II', C2.P38.

Florence, Biblioteca Laurenziana, MS plut. 9.8

The twelfth-century nomocanon Laur. plut. 9.8 entered the Medici collection in Florence before 1510, when it appears in Fabio Vigili's inventory.[8] Cavallo proposed (with a degree of doubt) that it may be an Italo-Greek manuscript.[9] The editors of the *RHBR* suggest (again with some uncertainty) that it may have originated in Palestine or Cyprus.[10] In the absence of any clear evidence, scholars have had to fall back on palaeographical analysis. Unfortunately, minuscule Greek hands from peripheral areas of the Byzantine world (especially southern Italy and Cyprus) can be difficult to distinguish.[11]

One factor that casts doubt on a southern Italian provenance is a note in a thirteenth- or fourteenth-century Greek hand on fol. i^{v}.[12] It wrongly states that the manuscript contains Theodore Balsamon's commentary on the *N14T*; in reality, it is the much older *S50T*. I have not discovered any evidence that Balsamon's work ever circulated in southern Italy, but it was known in Cyprus and Palestine. Whoever wrote the note evidently did not read the manuscript carefully but simply assumed that it must have been Balsamon's work; I would argue that a person in the eastern Mediterranean would have been much more likely to make this assumption than a person from southern Italy.

Moscow, Gosudarstvennij Istoričeskij Musej, MS Sin. gr. 398 (Vlad. 315)

The late tenth-century nomocanon Sin. gr. 398 was acquired by Arsenii Sukhanov in 1654 from the Athonite monastery of Iviron.[13] In their catalogue of the Moscow State Historical Museum's Greek manuscripts of the Patriarchal Synod collection, Fonkič and Poliakov stated that it originated in southern Italy, noting that the script was '*en as de pique*', a style that palaeographers used to associate with southern Italian scribes.[14] It has since been shown that the style is present in manuscripts from other parts of the Byzantine world as well, not just southern Italy.[15]

Kurysheva more recently produced a study of the manuscript that concluded that it was produced in northern Calabria or southern Campania.[16] She bases her argument on three main points: the script *en as de pique*, the manuscript's unusual ruling system, and the presence of Latin notes in the text. The first and third of these points are unconvincing: the *as de pique* style was not exclusive to southern Italy and the Latin script in Sin. gr. 398 is the same faux Latin that is common in Byzantine legal manuscripts. Kurysheva is right to note that the ruling system is unusual, but so few Byzantine manuscripts survive from the tenth century that it is difficult to know if this system was unique to Calabria/Campania or was more widespread. In my view, there is not enough evidence to determine the provenance of Sin. gr. 398 with any confidence.

[8] Rao (2012): no. 164. See also Fryde (1996): 2.770–771. [9] Cavallo (1985a): 93.

[10] *RHBR* 1.80 (no. 61). [11] Canart (1981): 20.

[12] See Chapter 3, 'Patterns of Source Survival', C3.P25 n.33.

[13] On Sukhanov's mission to gather manuscripts from Mount Athos, see Chapter 3, 'Patterns of Source Survival', C3.P51.

[14] Fonkič and Poliakov (1993): 107. The '*as de pique*', or 'ace of spades', refers to a distinctive ligature of the letters ερ in the shape of the eponymous card suit (♠), so-named by Devreesse (1955): 34–35.

[15] E.g. the Gospel manuscript Paris, Bibliothèque nationale de France, MS suppl. gr. 911, copied in Jerusalem in 1043; see Canart (1969): 61.

[16] Kurysheva (2008): 374–378.

Munich, Bayerische Staatsbibliothek, MS gr. 309, fols. 250–257

The last quire of Staatsbibl. gr. 309 is a fragment of the twelfth or thirteenth century containing a selection of monastic penances and canons from the Council *in Trullo* that was bound into a fourteenth-century collection of civil law and theological writings. The first volume of the *RHBR* assigns this quire (but not the rest of the manuscript) to southern Italy, likely on palaeographical grounds.[17] It is not clear when the quire was bound into the manuscript. The codex was purchased in Constantinople in 1578 by the Protestant scholar Stephan Gerlach (1546–1612), a theology professor in Tübingen, as we read in a note on fol. 1ʳ. There is nothing remarkable about the contents of the quire. With only eight folia available, it seems difficult to assign a provenance with any certainty on palaeographical grounds alone.

Rome, Biblioteca Vallicelliana, MS F 47

The editors of the *RHBR* also tentatively suggested a possible southern Italian origin for Vall. F 47, a canon law collection of *c.* 1000 with additions of the fourteenth and fifteenth centuries.[18] The manuscript once belonged to Aquiles Estaço ('Achilles Statius'; 1524–1581), a Portuguese humanist from Pernambuco in Brazil who moved to Rome in the early 1560s.[19] On his death, his manuscript collection was bequeathed to the Congregazione dei Oratoriani and became the core of the Biblioteca Vallicelliana in Rome.[20] Unfortunately, I have been unable to find any evidence as to where Estaço acquired the codex.

The script appears similar to the School of Neilos, a distinctive style of northern Calabria in the tenth- and early-eleventh centuries; indeed, Lucà, the scholar who first described the style, stated that the manuscript was copied in southern Italy in the tenth century.[21] If true, this would make it one of the oldest surviving Italo-Greek nomocanons. However, there is no corroborating evidence beyond the style of script (e.g. colophons, ownership history, unusual contents, ruling patterns, etc.), so it is not possible to assign provenance with confidence.

Vatican City, Biblioteca Apostolica Vaticana, MS Vat. gr. 847

Vat. gr. 847 is a fourteenth-century civil law miscellany that entered the Vatican's *fondo antico* by 1455.[22] The collection includes two novels of Emperor Andronikos II (*r.* 1282–1328) and Patriarch Athanasios I (*r.* 1289–1293, 1303–1309), as well as two synodal acts of Patriarch Nephon I (*r.* 1310–1314) on ecclesiastical administration.

Cavallo claimed a southern Italian provenance for this manuscript but did not give a reason.[23] Although this is possible, I am not aware of any clear evidence to support the assertion. The presence of fourteenth-century Byzantine imperial novels would be surprising in a southern Italian manuscript, so I am inclined to scepticism.

[17] *RHBR* 1.166 (no. 141). [18] *RHBR* 1.308 (no. 274).

[19] On Estaço's career, see Almagro (2012): 354–361. [20] See Russo (1978).

[21] Lucà (1985): 155 n. 305. See also Chapter 4, 'The Byzantine Background', C4.P26 n.23.

[22] The manuscript appears as number 256 in an inventory of the *fondo antico* drawn up by the papal librarian Cosimo di Montserrat in 1455. Text in Devreesse (1965): 11–42.

[23] Cavallo (1985a): 94.

Mount Athos, *Μονή Βατοπεδίου*, MS 555

Vatop. 555 is a canon law collection of the early to mid-twelfth century that the *RHBR* identifies as being from 'southern Italy/Epirus'.[24] Several texts in the collection (especially those on fasting and feast days) are reminiscent of ones found in southern Italian manuscripts, though none are exclusive to southern Italy.[25] In addition, the archaic-looking minuscule script and the use of a yellow wash to highlight lemmata in the text have often been seen as characteristic of southern Italy.[26]

However, in the same article in which he showed that the yellow wash could also be found in manuscripts from Epirus, Reinsch pointed out a marginal note alongside a historical overview of the seven ecumenical councils on fols. 220^{r}–222^{r}.[27] Alongside the entry on the seventh ecumenical council (787), a hand has written: 'From the seventh synod until the year of the reign of Manuel Komnenos [i.e. 1143–1180] and the rebellion and raid of the king of Sicily, 357 years'.[28] This is an apparent reference to King Roger II's attack on Byzantine Greece in 1147 (the calculation is slightly off: 787 + 357 = 1144). Reinsch suggested that the description of Roger's attack as a 'rebellion' suggests that the person who left the note had a Byzantine, not southern Italian, perspective.[29] This is certainly persuasive, though it is also possible that the manuscript was copied in Italy and later brought to Epirus; alternatively, the note may have been inserted by an Italo-Greek who still felt more loyalty to the Byzantine emperor than to the king of Sicily.

Nomocanons of Non-Southern Italian Provenance

Paris, Bibliothèque nationale de France, MS suppl. gr. 482

Sofia, National Centre for Slavo-Byzantine Studies 'Ivan Dujčev, MSS gr. 397+371

In 1864, the Bibliothèque nationale de France acquired the manuscript collection of the recently deceased Greek book collector Minoides Mynas.[30] Among these was BnF suppl. gr. 482, a fragmentary manuscript of the *Procheiros Nomos* with several supplementary texts on canon law, fasting, and the conversion of heretics. A colophon written in cryptogram reads: 'Christ, grant Nicholas the archdeacon remission of his sins. This was written under Alexios Komnenos in the year 6613 [1104/5], indiction 13.'[31] The editors of the *RHBR*

[24] *RHBR* 1.27 (no. 21).

[25] E.g. '*τῆς ἐν Νικαίᾳ συνόδου τῶν τιη' ἁγίων πατέρων διάταξις περὶ ἑορτῶν καὶ νηστειῶν καὶ περὶ τῆς τεσσαρακοστής τοῦ πάσχα*' (fols. 15^{r}–16^{v}) and '*ἐκ τῶν ἀποστολικῶν διατάξεων καὶ συνόδων περὶ τῆς ἁγίας μ' καὶπερὶ νηστείας*' (fols. 66^{v}–68^{v}); cf. the Rossanese MS Alag. gr. 3 (a. 1124), fols. 216^{v}–217^{v}: '*ἐκ τ[ῆς] ἐν Νικαίᾳ συνόδ[ου] τιη' π[ατ]ρῶν καὶ τ[ῶν] διατάξε[ων] τῶν ἁγίων ἀπ[οστόλων] περὶ ἑορτ[ῶν] καὶ νηστειῶν καὶ τ[ῆ]ς τεσσαρακοστ[ῆ]ς καὶ τοῦ πάσχ[α]*'.

[26] On the use of yellow wash, see Chapter 6, 'Monastic Nomocanons II', C6.P14.

[27] Reinsch (1991): 93.

[28] '*ἀπὸ τῆς ζ συνόδου ἕως τοῦ ἔτους τῆς βασιλείας Μανουὴλ τοῦ Κομνηνοῦ καὶ τῆς ἀνταρσίας καὶ κούρσου τοῦ ῥηγὸς Σικελλῶν ἔτη τνζ*': Vatop. 555, fol. 222^{r}.

[29] Cataldi Palau (2006): 575 shares the view that Vatop. 555 originates in Epirus.

[30] On the life of Minoides Mynas, see Omont (1916). On the bequest of manuscripts, see Omont (1883): xii–xiii.

[31] '*Νικολάῳ ἀρχηδιακόνῳ* [*sic*], *Χριστὲ, παράσχου λύσιν τῶν ὀφλημάτων. ἐγράφη ἐπὶ Ἀλεξίου τοῦ Κομνηνοῦ ἔτους ,ςχιγ', ἰνδ. ιγ'*': BnF suppl. gr. 482, p. 104 (the manuscript has page numbers, not folio

noted a similarity between the contents of BnF suppl. gr. 482 and Vatop. 555 and gave the provenance of the former as southern Italy.[32] Jaçob was more precise, localising it specifically to the Salento on the basis of the 'crushed rectangular style' of the script.[33]

Nonetheless, Schminck later discovered that BnF suppl. gr. 482 is actually the second half of another manuscript fragment in the National Centre of Slavo-Byzantine Studies 'Ivan Dujčev' in Sofia.[34] The codex originally belonged to the monastery of St John the Forerunner near Serres in northern Greece under the shelfmark *Γ* 29. Its contents strongly resemble fols. 16^{v}–74^{v} of Vatop. 555 (except for the inclusion of the *Procheiros Nomos*, which the latter manuscript does not have). Clearly the Parisian and Sofian manuscripts have a relationship with Vatop. 555.

Mynas acquired BnF suppl. gr. 482 on a mission to northern Greece in the years 1841–1843 on behalf of the French Minister of Public Education.[35] While I have been unable to discover where he found the Parisian fragment, his notes describe a manuscript in the monastery of John the Forerunner near Serres that is undoubtedly NCID gr. 397+371.[36] It is a fair assumption that he acquired BnF suppl. gr. 482 in northern Greece as well.

In principle, it is possible that the original manuscript was copied in southern Italy and later brought to northern Greece, where it was divided into the two sections BnF suppl. gr. 482 and NCID gr. 397+371. Note, however, that the colophon in the Parisian fragment states that it was copied 'under [the rule of] Alexios Komnenos', which implies that it originated within the Byzantine Empire. I suspect that it was produced in an area such as Epirus that shared similar scripts to those of southern Italy, rather than in southern Italy itself.

Oxford, Bodleian Library, MS Laud gr. 39

Laud gr. 39 is a manuscript of the *N14T* with a fascinating history, as we learn from a sixteenth-century description written on fol. vii^{v}. After the fall of Constantinople in 1453, the codex found its way to Egypt, where a Jewish convert to Christianity acquired it and brought it to Malta. There he sold it to a Rhodian knight of the Order of St John, who sold it again to Lorenz Schrader (*c.* 1530–1606), a German Protestant book collector who served as an adviser to the Catholic bishops of Osnabrück, in 1580. In 1634, it was obtained by the English ambassador Samson Johnson in Frankfurt and, in the following year, it entered the collection of Archbishop William Laud, whence it ended up in the Bodleian Library in Oxford.

Cavallo proposed a southern Italian origin for Laud gr. 39 on palaeographical grounds.[37] This seems implausible, however. On the lower half of fol. 13^{r}, a person (presumably an owner) wrote a narrative in a fifteenth-century Greek hand of a series of unspecified trials and tribulations that he suffered at the hands of 'enemies' in Mystras and Corinth in southern Greece.[38] Given that the manuscript's known history points to Greece and

numbers). The original text and key to the cryptogram can be found in Omont (1898b): 354. See also Wessely (1905): 185–189; Gardthausen (1905): 616.

[32] *RHBR* 1.233 (no. 207). [33] Jacob (1995): 105; Jacob (2001): 42.

[34] Schminck (2001): 719. The last four folia of MS 397 were originally at the beginning of 371.

[35] Omont (1916): 55.

[36] Mynas' notes are scattered across various manuscripts in the BnF supplement grec. For NCID gr. 397+371, see Paris, Bibliothèque nationale de France, MS suppl. gr. 755, fols. 89^{r}–91^{v}, at 91^{r}.

[37] Cavallo (1985a): 93. [38] Hutter (1982): 1–2 (no. 1).

Constantinople, and that it does not contain any texts that would suggest a southern Italian origin, it seems reasonable to conclude that it was not copied in southern Italy.

Mount Athos, *Μονὴ Μεγίστης Λαύρας*, MS B 93

Lavra B 93 is an eleventh-century canon law collection that Cavallo identified as southern Italian (specifically Apulian); the *RHBR* follows him in this.[39] In response, Jacob categorically stated that it 'has nothing Italo-Greek about it'.[40] Jacob is probably correct—there do not seem to be any uniquely Italo-Greek or Apulian/Salentine stylistic features or textual contents.

Vatican City, Biblioteca Apostolica Vaticana, MS Vat. gr. 1167

Vat. gr. 1167 is a copy of Alexios Aristenos' *Synopsis of Canons* with a miscellany of other texts on canon law and church administration that entered the Vatican Library in 1587 as part of the group Vat. gr. 1167–1217.[41] Paper flyleaves at the beginning and end contain a series of notes from the early sixteenth century: fol. i^r has three birth notices from 1517, 1521, and 1523 (written according to the *anno domini* system in Arabic numerals), while fol. 140^r has two notes from 1523 and 1524 (in the Byzantine *anno mundi* system and Greek numerals) that record bequests from Stamatios Angelopoulos and Basil Gounaropoulos 'to the monastery of the Saviour'.[42] Could this be the Holy Saviour of Messina? The *anno domini* dating system did not become common in the Orthodox Church until the seventeenth century, so the author of the first three notes was clearly a Greek writer familiar with Western dating styles, perhaps someone who lived in Venetian territories (like Cyprus and Crete) or someone from southern Italy.

The 1563 inventory of the Holy Saviour of Messina by Francesco Antonio Napoli contains the following entry: 'Ecclesiastical history, without the name of the author and without beginning, starting from the birth of the Saviour and going up to the emperorship of Theophilos the son of Michael; perhaps [written] by a certain George. Also a disputation of a certain Orthodox [Christian] against the Latins, incomplete at the end.'[43] More or less the same description appeared as item seven in Antonio Carissimo's late fifteenth-century inventory.[44]

This appears to be an accurate summary of the first and last contents of the manuscript: the opening folia contain a list of historical rulers from the Israelites to the Byzantines, a list of Roman popes and Constantinopolitan patriarchs up to the year 843 (a later hand continued it to 858), and extracts from George of Cyprus' *Description of the Roman World*; George of Cyprus is the first authorial name to appear in the codex. At the end, fol. $137^{r/v}$ contains a series of short texts (without attribution) entitled: 'Of the Theologian [i.e. Gregory of Nazianzus] on the Holy Spirit'; 'Explanation of the Orthodox Faith'; 'On the Word of God and of the Father'; and, finally, 'On the Holy Spirit'. Carissimo and Napoli

[39] Cavallo (1985a): 96; *RHBR* 1.39 (no. 29). [40] Jacob (1993): 128. [41] Janz (2014): 512.

[42] '*εἰς τὸν Σωτῆρα εἰς τὸ ἀσκητηρίω* [*sic*]': Vat. gr. 1167, fol. 140^r.

[43] '*Historia ecclesiastica, absque nomine authoris et sine principio, incipiens a nativitate Salvatoris usque ad imperium Theophili filij Michaelis; fortasse cuiusdam Georgij. Item Orthodoxi cuiusdam disputatio adversus Latinos, imperfecta in fine*': Mercati (1935): 241. On Francesco Antonio Napoli's inventory, see Chapter 3, 'Patterns of Source Survival', C3.P48.

[44] Mercati (1935): 270. See also Chapter 3, 'Patterns of Source Survival', C3.P49 n.81.

omitted to mention the manuscript's main content, Alexios Aristenos' commentary on the *Synopsis*, but this is not unusual; their inventories frequently mention only the first and last contents of a manuscript.

The modern *fondo* S. Salvatore in Messina does not contain a manuscript that matches Napoli's description, but Vat. gr. 1167 does. I suspect that it is the same codex and that it was present in Sicily in the fifteenth and sixteenth centuries. Nonetheless, it was almost certainly not produced there. The leaves are made from paper of the 'Eastern Arabic' type that is highly unusual in southern Italy and the manuscript contains extracts from Theodore Balsamon, a writer whose works are not securely attested in any southern Italian manuscript.[45]

The late fifteenth century saw an influx of educated Greeks fleeing to Italy from the Ottoman Empire. Many settled in northern cities such as Venice and Florence, but some were drawn to areas in the south where Greek was still spoken. A good example was Constantine Laskaris, a Byzantine intellectual who settled in Messina in 1466 and became a famous local scholar and teacher.[46] Vat. gr. 1167 probably came to Messina in the mid- to late fifteenth century in the possession of a Byzantine such as Laskaris who was fleeing from the Ottoman conquest. It therefore serves as a good reminder of the remarkable mobility of Greek manuscripts in the early modern period.

[45] On 'Eastern Arabic' paper, see Canart et al. (1993): 1.327. Cf. Messina, Biblioteca Universitaria Regionale, MS S. Salv. 40, another manuscript of the eastern Mediterranean on the same type of paper that was brought to Messina: Rodriquez (2003): 140–143.

[46] On Constantine Laskaris' life and career, see Manzano (1994).

Bibliography

Manuscript Catalogues and Inventories

Arnesano, Daniele (2005). 'Il repertorio dei codici greci salentini di Oronzo Mazotta. Aggiornamenti e integrazioni.' In *Tracce di storia. Studi in onore di mons. Oronzo Mazzotta*, edited by Mario Spedicato, 25–80. Quaderni de L'Idomeneo 1. Galatina: Edizioni Panico.

Arnesano, Daniele (2010). 'Manoscritti greci di Terra d'Otranto—Recenti scoperti e attribuzione (2005–2008).' In *Toxotes*. Studies for Stefano Parenti, edited by Daniel Galadza, Nina Glibetić, and Gabriel I. Radle, 63–101. *Αναλέκτα Κρυπτοφέρρης* 9. Grottaferrata: Monastero Esarchico.

Bandini, Angelo M. (1764). *Catalogus codicum graecorum Bibliothecae Laurentianae*. 3 vols. Florence: Typis Regiis.

Batiffol, Pierre (1889a). 'Vier Bibliotheken von alten Basilianischen Klöstern in Unteritalien.' *Römische Quartalsschrift* 3: 31–41.

Coxe, Henry O. (1858). *Catalogi codicum manuscriptorum Bibliothecae Bodleianae partis secundae fasciculus primus*. Oxford: Oxford University Press.

Feron, Ernest, and Fabiano Battaglini (1893). *Codices manuscripti Graeci Ottoboniani Bibliothecae Vaticanae*. Bibliothecae Vaticanae Codices manu scripti recensiti. Rome: Biblioteca Apostolica Vaticana.

Fonkič, Boris L., and Fedor B. Poliakov (1993). *Grečeskie rukopisi Moskovskoj sinodal'noj biblioteki: paleografičeskie, kodikologičeskie i bibliografičeskie dopolnenija k katalogu arhimandrita Vladimira (Filantropova)*. Moscow: Sinadol'naja Biblioteka.

Fryde, Edmund B. (1996). *Greek Manuscripts in the Private Library of the Medici 1469–1510*. 2 vols. Aberystwyth: National Library of Wales.

Giannelli, Ciro (1950). *Codices vaticani graeci 1485–1683*. Bibliothecae Vaticanae Codices manu scripti recensiti. Vatican City: Biblioteca Apostolica Vaticana.

Hutter, Irmgard (1982). *Corpus der byzantinischen Miniaturenhandschriften. 3.1. Oxford Bodleian Library III, Textband*. Denkmäler der Buchkunst 5. Stuttgart: Hiersemann.

Mancini, Augusto (1907). *Codices graeci monasterii messanensis S. Salvatoris*. Messina: Typis d'Amico.

Martini, Emidio (1902). *Catalogus codicum graecorum qui in Bibliotheca vallicellana Romæ adservantur*. Catalogo di manoscritti greci esistenti nelle biblioteche italiane 2. Milan: Hoepli.

Martini, Emidio, and Domenico Bassi (1906). *Catalogus codicum graecorum Bibliothecae Ambrosianae*. 2 vols. Milan: Hoepli.

Mingarelli, Giovanni L. (1784). *Graeci codices manu scripti apud Nanios patricios Venetos asservati*. Bologna: Laelii a Vulpe.

Mioni, Elpidio (1981). *Bibliothecae Divi Marci Venetiarum Codices Graeci manuscripti. 1. Thesaurus antiquus*. Indici e cataloghi. Nuova serie 6. Rome: Istituto Poligrafico dello Stato.

Mioni, Elpidio (1992). *Catalogus codicum Graecorum Bibliothecae Nationalis Neapolitanae I.I*. Indici e cataloghi. Nuova serie 8. Rome: Istituto Poligrafico dello Stato.

Omont, Henri (1883). *Inventaire sommaire des manuscrits du supplément grec de la Bibliothèque nationale*. Paris: Picard.

Omont, Henri (1898a). *Inventaire sommaire des manuscrits grecs de la Bibliothèque nationale et des autres bibliothèques de Paris et des Départements. Introduction et table alphabétique*. 2 vols. Paris: Leroux.

Omont, Henri (1898b). 'Manuscrits grecs datés récemment acquis par la Bibliothèque nationale.' *Revue des bibliothèques* 8: 353–360.

Pierleoni, Gino (1962). *Catalogus codicum Graecorum Bibliothecae Nationalis Neapolitanae*. Rome: Istituto Poligrafico dello Stato.

Rao, Ida G. (2012). *L'inventario di Fabio Vigili della Medicea Privata (Vat. lat. 7134)*. Studi e testi 473. Vatican City: Biblioteca Apostolica Vaticana.

Richard, Marcel (1952). *Inventaire des manuscrits grecs du British Museum I. Fonds Sloane, Additional, Egerton, Cottonian et Stowe*. Paris: Centre nationale de la recherche scientifique.

Rocchi, Antonio (1883). *Codices Cryptenses seu Abbatiae Cryptae Ferratae in Tusculano digesti et illustrati*. Tusculum: Typis Abbatiae Cryptae Ferratae.

Repertorium der Handschriften des byzantinischen Rechts (1995–2017). Frankfurt am Main: Löwenklau.

1. Burgmann, Ludwig, Marie-Theres Fögen, and Andreas Schminck, eds. (1995). *Die Handschriften des weltlichen Rechts (Nr. 1–327)*. Forschungen zur byzantinischen Rechtsgeschichte 20.
2. Schminck, Andreas, and Dorotei Getov, eds. (2010). *Die Handschriften des kirchlichen Rechts I (Nr. 328–427)*. Forschungen zur byzantinischen Rechtsgeschichte 28.
3. Schminck, Andreas, and Dorotei Getov, eds. (2017). *Die Handschriften des kirchlichen Rechts II (Nr. 428–527)*. Forschungen zur byzantinischen Rechtsgeschichte 34.

Serrai, Alfredo (2008). *La Biblioteca Altempsiana, ovvero le raccolte librarie di Marco Sittico III e del nipote Giovanni Angelo Altemps*. Bibliotecario 22. Rome: Bulzoni.

Turco, Gianluca (2004). 'Un antico elenco di manoscritti greci ambrosiani. L'Ambr. X 289 inf., ff. 110–141.' In *Nuove ricerche sui manoscritti greci dell'Ambrosiana*, edited by Carlo M. Mazzucchi and Cesare Pasini, 79–143. Bibliotheca erudita 24. Milan: Vita e Pensiero.

Turyn, Alexander (1964). *Codices Vaticani graeci saeculis XIII et XIV scripti annorumque notis instructi*. Codices e Vaticanis selecti phototypice expressi 28. Vatican City: Biblioteca Apostolica Vaticana.

Edited Texts and Documents

Allen, Pauline, and Cornelis Datema, eds. (1987). *Leontii presbyteri Constantinopolitani homiliae*. Corpus Christianorum, Series Graeca 17. Turnhout: Brepols.

Amatus of Montecassino (2011). *Ystoire de li Normant*. Edited by Michèle Guéret-Laferté. Classiques français du Moyen Âge 166. Paris: Champion.

Apostolidis, Apostolos, ed. (1983). *Il typikon di S. Nicola di Casole secondo il codice Taur.* gr. C III 17 (Introduzione, Testo critico, Indici). Doctoral Thesis, Rome: Pontificia Università San Tommaso D'Aquino.

Bekker, Immanuel, ed. (1838). *Theophanes Continuatus, Ioannes Cameniata, Symeon Magister, Georgius Monachus*. Corpus scriptorium historiae Byzantinae 33. Bonn: Weber.

Bees-Seferli, Eleni, ed. (1971). 'Unedierte Schriftstücke aus der Kanzlei des Johannes Apokaukos des Metropoliten von Naupaktos (in Aetolien).' *Byzantinisch-neugriechische Jahrbücher* 21: 57–243.

Beneševič, Vladimir N., ed. (1937). *Ioannis Scholastici Synagoga L titulorum ceterumque eiusdem opera iuridica*. Abhandlungen. Philosophisch-historische Klasse 14. Munich: Verlag der Bayerischen Akademie der Wissenschaften.

Burgmann, Ludwig, ed. (1983). *Ecloga. Das Gesetzbuch Leons III. und Konstantinos' V*. Forschungen zur byzantinischen Rechtsgeschichte 10. Frankfurt am Main: Löwenklau-Gesellschaft.

Constantinides, Angela H., John P. Thomas, and Giles Constable, eds. (2000). *Byzantine Monastic Foundation Documents: A Complete Translation of the Surviving Founders' Typika and Testaments*. 5 vols. Dumbarton Oaks Studies 37. Washington, DC: Dumbarton Oaks.

Corpus iuris civilis (1872–1895). Berlin: Weidmann.

1. Krueger, Paul, and Theodor Mommsen, eds. (1872) *Institutiones et Digesta*.
2. Krueger, Paul, ed. (1877). *Codex Iustinianus*.
3. Schöll, Rudolf, and Wilhelm Kroll, eds. (1895). *Novellae*.

Cozza-Luzi, Giuseppe, ed. (1905). *Novum patrum bibliotheca X*. Vatican City: Biblioteca Apostolica Vaticana.

Darrouzès, Jean, ed. (1981). *Notitiae episcopatuum ecclesiae constantinopolitanae. Texte critique, introduction et notes*. Géographie ecclésiastique de l'Empire Byzantin 1. Paris: Centre nationale de la recherche scientifique.

Delatte, Armand, ed. (1927). *Anecdota Atheniensia et alia. 1. Textes grecs inédits relatifs à l'histoire des religions*. Bibliothèque de la Faculté de philosophie et lettres de l'Université de Liège 36. Liége: Vaillant-Carmanne.

Douramani, Katherine, ed. (2003). *Il typikon del monastero di S. Bartolomeo di Trigona*. Orientalia Christiana Analecta 269. Rome: Pontificio Istituto Orientale.

Eadmer (1962). *The Life of St Anselm, Archbishop of Canterbury*. Edited by R.W. Southern. Nelson's Medieval Texts. London: Nelson.

Falco of Benevento. *Chronicon Beneventanum. Città e feudi nell'Italia dei normanni*. Edited by Edoardo D'Angelo. Per verba 9. Florence: SISMEL-Edizioni del Galluzzo, 1998.

Friedberg, Emil, ed. (1881). *Liber extravagantium decretalium*. Corpus Iuris Canonici 2. Leipzig: Tauchnitz.

Gautier, Paul, ed. (1973). 'L'édit d'Alexis Ier Comnène sur la réforme du clergé.' *Revue des études byzantines* 31: 165–201.

Gigante, Marcello, ed. (1979). *Poeti bizantini di Terra d'Otranto nel secolo XIII*. Byzantina et neo-hellenica neapolitana 7. Naples: Università di Napoli.

Giovanelli, Germano, ed. (1972). *Βίος καὶ πολιτεία τοῦ ὁσίου πατρὸς ἡμῶν Νείλου τοῦ Νέου*. Grottaferrata: Badia di Grottaferrata.

Glaber, Rodulf (1989). *Historiarum libri quinque*. Edited by John France. Oxford Medieval Texts. Oxford: Oxford University Press.

Gratian (1879). *Decretum magistri Gratiani*. Edited by Aemilius L. Richter and Emil Friedberg. Corpus Iuris Canonici 1. Leipzig: Tauchnitz.

Gregory of Nazianzus (1963). *Die fünf Theologischen reden*. Edited by Joseph Barbel. Testimonia 3. Düsseldorf: Patmos.

Guillou, André, ed. (1963). *Les actes grecs de S. Maria di Messina. Enquête sur les populations grecques d'Italie du sud et de Sicile, XIe–XIVe siècle*. 2 vols. Testi e monumenti. Testi 8. Palermo: Istituto Siciliano di Studi Bizantini e Neoellenici.

Guillou, André, ed. (1974a). *Le brébion de la métropole byzantine de Règion (vers 1050)*. Corpus des actes grecs d'Italie du sud et de Sicile 4. Vatican City: Biblioteca Apostolica Vaticana.

Guillou, André, ed. (1980). *Saint-Jean-Théristès (1054–1264)*. Corpus des actes grecs d'Italie du sud et de Sicile 5. Vatican City: Biblioteca Apostolica Vaticana.

Heimbach, Gustav E., ed. (1840). *Ἀνεκδότα II*. Leipzig: Barth.

Hergenröther, Joseph, ed. (1869). *Monumenta graeca ad Photium eiusque historiam pertinentia*. Regensburg: Manz.

Hunger, Herbert, Otto Kresten, and Cupane Carolina, eds. (1981). *Das Register des Patriarchats von Konstantinopel*. Corpus fontium historiae Byzantinae 19. Vienna: Verlag der Österreichischen Akademie der Wissenschaften.

Ideler, Julius-Ludwig, ed. (1842). *Physici et medici Graeci minores*. Berlin: Reimer.

John of Damascus (1963). *De Schriften des Johannes von Damaskos*, vol. 2. Edited by Bonifatius Kotter. Patristische Texte und Studien 12. Berlin: De Gruyter.

Kehr, Karl A., ed. (1902). *Die Urkunden der normannisch-sicillischen Könige*. Innsbruck: Wagner.

Komnene, Anna (2001). *Alexias*. Edited by Diether Reinsch. Corpus fontium historiae Byzantinae 40. Berlin: De Gruyter.

Konidaris, Johannes, ed. (1982). 'Die Novellen des Kaisers Herakleios.' *Fontes Minores* 5: 33–106.

Kravari, Vassiliki, Mirjana Živojinović, and Christophe Giros, eds. (1998). *Actes de Chilandar*. Archives de l'Athos 20. Paris: Lethielleux.

Laourdas, Basileios, Bernard Outtier, and Leendert G. Westerink, eds. (1985). *Photii patriarchae Constantinopolitani Epistulae et Amphilochia. III. Epistularum pars tertia*. Bibliotheca scriptorum Graecorum et Romanorum Teubneriana. Leipzig: Teubner.

Laurent, Marie-Hyacinthe, and André Guillou, eds. (1960). *Le 'Liber Visitationis' d'Athanase Chalkéopoulos (1457–1458). Contribution à l'histoire du monachisme grec en Italie méridionale*. Studi e testi 206. Vatican City: Biblioteca Apostolica Vaticana.

Liudprand of Cremona (2010). *Relatio de legatione Constantinopolitana*. MGH SS 41. Turnhout: Brepols.

Malaterra, Geoffrey (1927–1928). *De rebus gestis Rogerii Calabriae et Siciliae Comitis et Roberti Guiscardi Ducis fratris eius*. Edited by Ernesto Pontieri. Rerum Italicarum Scriptores 5.1. Bologna: Zanichelli.

Mansi, Giovanni D., ed. (1901–1927). *Sacrorum conciliorum nova et amplissima collectio*. 2nd ed. 54 vols. Paris: Welter.

Metzger, Marcel, ed. (1985). *Les constitutions apostoliques. I. Livres I et II*. Sources chrétiennes 320. Paris: Éditions du Cerf.

Migne, Jacques-Paul, ed. (1844–1891). *Patrologiae cursus completus. Series Latina*. 220 vols. Paris: Migne.

Migne, Jacques-Paul, ed. (1857–1866). *Patrologiae cursus completus. Series graeca*. 161 vols. Paris: Migne.

Millet, Gabriel, Germaine Rouillard, and Collomp, eds. (1937). *Actes de Lavra. 1. 897–1178*. Archives de l'Athos 1. Paris: Lethielleux.

Minieri-Riccio, Camillo, ed. (1882). *Saggio di Codice diplomatico formato sulle antiche scritture dell'Archivio di Stato di Napoli*. Naples: Rinaldi e Sellitto.

Minuto, Domenico, ed. (2003). *La vita e miracoli del santo e glorioso servo di Cristo, Fantino*. Reggio Calabria: Pontari.

Muci, Maria M., ed. (2008). 'Il terzo Syntagma di Nicola Nettario di Otranto.' *Rivista di Storia della Chiesa in Italia* 62.2: 449–505.

Mühlenberg, Ekkehard, ed. (2008). *Gregorii Nysseni Epistula canonica*. Gregorii Nysseni Opera 3.5. Leiden: Brill.

Odo of Deuil (1948). *De profectione Ludovici VII in orientem: The Journey of Louis VII to the East.* Edited by Virginia G. Berry. Records of Civilization: Sources and Studies 42. New York: Norton.

Oikonomides, Nicholas, ed. (1990). *Actes d'Iviron. 2. Du milieu du 11. siècle à 1204.* Archives de l'Athos 16. Paris: Lethielleux.

Oikonomides, Nicholas, Dionysia Papachryssanthou, and Jacques Lefort, eds. (1985). *Actes d'Iviron. 1. Des origines au milieu du 11. siècle.* Archives de l'Athos 14. Paris: Lethielleux.

Parthey, Gustav, ed. (1967). *Hieroclis Synecdemus et notitiae graecae episcopatuum. Accedunt Nili Doxapatri Notitia Patriarchatum et locorum nomina immutata.* 2nd ed. Amsterdam: Hakkert.

Pirro, Roccho (1733). *Sicilia sacra disquisitionibus et notitis illustrata.* 2 vols. Palermo: Coppula.

Pitra, Jean-Baptiste, ed. (1858). *Spicilegium solesmense IV. In quo monumenta tam africanae quam byzantinae Ecclesiae proferuntur et illustrantur.* Paris: Didot.

Pitra, Jean-Baptiste, ed. (1868). *Iuris ecclesiastici graecorum historia et monumenta. II. A VI ad IX saeculum.* Rome: Collegium Urbani.

Pitra, Jean-Baptiste, ed. (1891). *Juris ecclesiastici graecorum selecta paralipomena.* Analecta sacra et classica Spicilegio solesmensi parata 6. Paris: Roger et Chernowitz.

Pontificia commissio ad redigendum Codicem Iuris Canonici orientalis. Fontes, Series III (1943–1990). Vatican City: Typis Polyglottis Vaticanis.

1. Tăutu, Aloysius L., ed. (1943). *Acta Romanorum Pontificum a S. Clemente I (an. c. 90) ad Coelestinum III († 1198).*

2. Halŭšcynskyj, Theodosius, ed. (1944). *Acta Innocentii P.P. III (1198–1216).*

3. Tăutu, Aloysius L., ed. (1950). *Acta Honorii III (1216–1227) et Gregorii IX (1227–1241).*

4.1. Halŭšcynskyj, Theodosius, ed. (1962). Acta Innocentii P.P. IV (1243–1254).

4.2. Halŭšcynskyj, Theodosius, ed. (1966). *Acta Alexandri P.P. IV (1254–1261).*

5.1. Tăutu, Aloysius L., ed. (1953). *Acta Urbani IV, Clementis IV, Gregorii X (1261–1276).*

5.2. Delorme, Ferdinand Marie, ed. (1954). *Acta Romanorum pontificum ab Innocentio V ad Benedictum XI (1276–1304).*

Prinzing, Günter (2002). *Demetrii Chomateni Ponemata Diaphora.* Corpus fontium historiae Byzantinae 38. Berlin: De Gruyter.

Ralles, Georgios A., and Michael Potles, eds. (1852–1859). *Σύνταγμα τῶν θείων καὶ ἱερῶν κανόνων.* Athens: Chartophylax.

1. *Φωτίου πατριάρχου Κωνσταντινουπόλεως Νομοκάνων μετὰ τῶν σχολίων Θεοδώρου τοῦ Βαλσαμῶνος* (1852).

2. *Κανόνες ἁγίων καὶ πανευφήμων Ἀποστόλων καὶ τῶν οἰκουμενικῶν συνόδων (1852).*

3. *Κανόνες τῶν τοπικῶν συνόδων* (1853).

4. *Κανόνες τῶν κατὰ μέρος ἁγίων πατέρων* (1854).

5. *Ἀπόφασεις συνοδικαί καὶ διατάξεις τῶν Κωνσταντινουπόλεως ἀρχιεπισκόπων καὶ πατριάρχων ἔτι δὲ νεαραί διατάξεις τῶν βυζαντινῶν αὐτοκράτορων* (1855).

Robinson, Gertrude, ed. (1929). *History and Cartulary of the Greek Monastery of St Elias and St Anastasius of Carbone. 2.1. Cartulary.* Orientalia Christiana 53. Rome: Pontificium Institutum Orientalium Studiorum.

Robinson, Gertrude, ed. (1930). *History and Cartulary of the Greek Monastery of St Elias and St Anastasius of Carbone. 2.2. Cartulary.* Orientalia christiana 62. Rome: Pontificium Institutum Orientalium Studiorum.

Rognoni, Cristina, ed. (2004). *Les actes privés grecs de l'Archivo Ducal de Medinaceli (Tolède). 1. Les monastères de Saint-Pancrace de Briatico, de Saint-Philippe-de-Bojôannès et de Saint-Nicolas-des Drosi (Calabre, XIe–XII sècles).* Textes, documents, études sur le monde byzantin, néohellénique et balkanique 7. Paris: Association Pierre Belon.

Rognoni, Cristina, ed. (2011). *Les actes privés grecs de l'Archivo Ducal de Medinaceli (Tolède). 2. La Vallée du Tuccio (Calabre, XIIe–XIIIe siècle).* Textes, documents, études sur le monde byzantin, néohellénique et balkanique 12. Paris: Association Pierre Belon.

Rossi Taibbi, Giuseppe, ed. (1962). *Vita di sant'Elia il Giovane.* Vite dei sancti siciliani 3. Palermo: Istituto Siciliano di Studi Bizantini e Neoellenici.

Scarfò, Giovanni-Grisostomo (1737). *Poesie varie.* Venice.

Scheltema, Herman J., and Nicolaas van der Wal, eds. (1955–1974). *Basilicorum libri LX.* 17 vols. Groningen.

Schirò, Giuseppe, ed. (1954). *Vita di S. Luca, vescovo di Isola Capo Rizzuto.* Vite dei santi siciliani 1. Palermos: Istituto Siciliano di Studi Bizantini e Neogreci.

Schwartz, Eduard, ed. (1914–1984). *Acta conciliorum oecumenicorum.* 7 vols. Berlin: De Gruyter.

Simon, Dieter, and Spyridon N. Troianos, eds. (1979). 'Die Epitome des Novellensyntagma von Athanasios.' *Fontes Minores* 3: 280–315.

Simon, Dieter, and Spyridon N. Troianos, eds. (1989). *Das Novellensyntagma des Athanasios von Emesa.* Forschungen zur byzantinischen Rechtsgeschichte 16. Frankfurt am Main: Löwenklau-Gesellschaft.

Švecov, Arsenij, ed. (1896). *Nikolaja Gidruntskago (Otrantskago), igumena grečeskago monastyrja v Kazulach, tri zapisi o sobesědovanijach Grekov s Latinjanami po povodu raznostej v věrě i obyčajach cerkovnych.* Novgorod: Ignatovskij.

Swainson, Charles A., ed. (1884). *The Greek Liturgies, Chiefly from Original Authorities.* Cambridge: Cambridge University Press.

Van der Wal, Nicolaas, and Bernard H. Stolte, eds. (1994). *Collectio Tripartita: Justinian on Religious and Ecclesiastical Affairs.* Groningen: Forsten.

Theiner, Augustin, ed. (1856). *Annales eccleisastici.* 3 vols. Rome: Typographia Tiberina.

Trinchera, Francesco, ed. (1865). *Syllabus Graecarum membranarum quae partim Neapoli in maiori tabulario et primaria bibliotheca partim in Casinensi Coenobio ac Cavensi et in episcopali tabulario Neritino iamdiu delitescentes et a doctis frustra expetitae.* Naples: Cataneo.

Turner, Christopher J.G. (1965). 'Another Anti-Latin Work Attributed to Gennadius Scholarius.' *Byzantinische Zeitschrift* 58: 337–347.

Voell, Guillaume, and Christophe F. Justel, eds. (1661). *Bibliotheca iuris canonici veteris in duos tomos distributa.* 2 vols. Paris: Billaine.

William of Apulia (1961). *La geste de Robert Guiscard.* Edited by Marguerite Mathieu. Testi e monumenti 4. Palermo: Istituto siciliano di studi bizantini e neoellenici.

Zaccagni, Gaia, ed. (1996). 'Il Bios di San Bartolomeo da Simeri (BHG 235).' *Rivista di studi bizantini e neoellenici* 33: 205–274.

Zachariä von Lingenthal, Karl-Eduard, ed. (1837). *Ὁ Πρόχειρος Νόμος.* Heidelberg: Mohr.

Zachariä von Lingenthal, ed. (1881). *Imp. Iustiniani pp.a. Novellae quae vocantur sive Constitutiones quae extra Codicem supersunt, ordine chronologico digestae.* Leipzig: Teubner.

Academic Studies and Secondary Literature

Abulafia, David (1997). *The Western Mediterranean Kingdoms 1200–1500: The Struggle for Dominion.* Medieval World. London: Longman.

Acconcia Longo, Augusta, and André Jacob (1980). 'Une anthologie salentine du XIVe siècle: le Vaticanus gr. 1276.' *Rivista di studi bizantini e neoellenici* 17–19: 149–228.

Ackerman-Liberman, Phillip I. (2014). 'Legal Pluralism among the Court Records of Medieval Egypt.' *Bulletin d'études orientales* 63: 79–112.

Aletta, Alessia A. (2009). 'I luoghi del diritto nel Paris. suppl. gr. 1085 (II).' *Rivista di studi bizantini e neoellenici* 46: 33–71.

Aletta, Alessia A. (2013). 'Testo e ornamentazione nei corpora canonum bizantini del IX–X secolo.' *Rivista di storia della miniatura*: 17–28.

Allison, Robert W. (1996). 'The Libraries of Mt Athos: The Case of Philotheou.' In *Mount Athos and Byzantine Monasticism: Papers from the Twenty-Eighth Spring Symposium of Byzantine Studies, Birmingham, March 1994*, edited by Anthony Bryer and Mary Cunningham, 135–154. Publications (Society for the Promotion of Byzantine Studies) 4. Aldershot: Variorum.

Almagro, Alejandra G. (2012). 'A Portuguese Contribution to 16th-Century Roman Antiquarianism: The Case of Aquiles Estaço (1524-1581).' In *Portuguese Humanism and the Republic of Letters*, edited by Maria L. Berbera and Karl A.E. Enenkal, 353–376. Leiden: Brill.

Anastos, Milton V. (1957). 'The Transfer of Illyricum, Calabria, and Sicily to the Jurisdiction of the Patriarchate of Constantinople in 732–33.' *Studi bizantini e neoellenici* 9: 14–31.

Andrea, Alfred J. (2005). 'Innocent III and the Byzantine Rite, 1198–1216.' In *Urbs Capta: The Fourth Crusade and Its Consequences*, edited by Angeliki E. Laiou, 111–122. Paris: Lethielleux.

Andreano, Manuela (2000). 'Tempietto di San Lorenzo a Mesagne. Nuovo studio.' *Brundisii Res* 23: 131–163.

Angold, Michael (1995). *Church and Society in Byzantium under the Comneni 1081–1261.* Cambridge: Cambridge University Press.

Angold, Michael (2003). *The Fourth Crusade: Event and Context.* Medieval World. Harlow: Longman.

Arnesano, Daniele (2007). 'Copisti salentini del cinquecento.' In *'Colligite fragmenta'. Studi in memoria di Mons. Carmine Maci*, edited by Dino Levante, 83–94. Campi Salentini: Centro Studi 'Mons. Carmine Maci'.

Arnesano, Daniele (2008a). *La minuscola 'barocca'. Scritture e libri in Terra d'Otranto nei secoli XIII e XIV.* Fonti medievali e moderne 12. Galatina: Congedo.

Arnesano, Daniele (2008b). 'San Nicola di Casole e la cultura greca in Terra d'Otranto nel Quattrocento.' In *La conquista turca di Otranto (1480) tra storia e mito. Atti del convegno internazionale di studio, Otranto-Muro Leccese, 28–31 marzo 2007*, edited by Hubert Houben and Francisco de Araujo, 107–140. Università degli Studi (Lecce), Dipartimento dei Beni delle Arti e della Storia 41. Galatina: Congedo.

Arnesano, Daniele (2014). 'La penitenza dei monaci a S. Maria del Patir e a S. Nicola di Casole.' *Revue des études byzantines* 72: 249–273.

Arnesano, Daniele, and Elisabetta Sciarra (2010). 'Libri e testi di scuola in Terra d'Otranto.' In *Libri di scuola e pratiche didattiche dall'Antichità al Rinascimento. Atti del Convegno Internazionale di Studi, Cassino, 7–10 maggio 2008*, edited by Oronzo Pecere and Lucio Del Corso, 425–473. Collana scientifica 26. Cassino: Università di Cassino.

Astruc, Charles (1988). 'Une collection canonique d'Italie du Sud de la fin du XIIIe siècle (le Parisinus graecus 1370).' *Revue d'histoire des textes* 16: 37–62.

Avrin, Leila (1991). *Scribes, Script, and Books: The Book Arts from Antiquity to the Renaissance.* Chicago: American Library Association.

Avvakumov, Yury P. (2011). 'The Controversy over the Baptismal Formula under Pope Gregory IX.' In *Greeks, Latins, and Intellectual History 1204–1500*, edited by Martin

Hinterberger and Chris Schabel, 69–84. Recherches de théologie et philosophie médiévales. Bibliotheca 11. Leuven: Peeters.

Baldi, Davide (2010). 'Il Codex Florentinus del Digesto e il "Fondo Pandette" della Biblioteca Laurenziana (con un'appendice di documenti inediti).' *Segno e testo* 8: 88–186.

Batiffol, Pierre (1889b). 'La Vaticane depuis Paul III.' *Revue des questions historiques* 45: 177–218.

Batiffol, Pierre (1890). *La Vaticane de Paul III à Paul V d'après des documents nouveaux*. Petite bibliothèque d'art et d'archéologie. Paris: Leroux.

Batiffol, Pierre (1891). *L'abbaye de Rossano. Contribution à l'histoire de la Vaticane*. Paris: Picard.

Bayer, Axel (2004). *Spaltung der Christenheit: Das sogenannte Morgenländische Schisma von 1054*. Beihefte zum Archiv für Kulturgeschichte 53. Cologne: Böhlau.

Beck, Hans-Georg (1981). *Nomos, Kanon und Staatsraison in Byzanz*. Sitzungsberichte (Österreichische Akademie der Wissenschaften. Philosophisch-Historische Klasse) 384. Vienna: Österreichischen Akademie der Wissenschaften.

Beneševič, Vladimir N. (1905). *Kanoničeskij sbornik. XIV titulov so vtoroj četverti VII věka do 883 g. K drevnějšej istorii istočnikov prava grekovostočnoj cerkvi*. St Petersburg: Vajsberg & Geršunin.

Beneševič, Vladimir N. (1906). *Drevneslavjanskaja Kormčaja XIV titulov bez tolkovanij*. St Petersburg.

Beneševič, Vladimir N. (1914). *Sinagogá v 50 titulov i drugie juridičeskie sborniki Joanna Scholastika: K drevějšej istorii istočnikov prava greko-voskočnoj cerkvi*. St Petersburg.

Benoît, Fernand (1879). 'Farnesiana.' *Atti e mem. della Deput. di storia patria per le provincie dell'Emilia* 4.2: 37–106.

Bénou, Lisa (2011). *Pour une nouvelle histoire du droit byzantin: Théorie et pratique juridiques au XIVe siècle*. Textes, documents, études sur le monde byzantin, néohellénique, et balkanique 11. Paris: Association Pierre Belon.

Berman, Paul S. (2009). 'The New Legal Pluralism.' *Annual Review of Law and Social Science* 5: 225–242.

Bernard, Floris (2014). *Writing and Reading Byzantine Secular Poetry, 1025–1081*. Oxford Studies in Byzantium. Oxford: Oxford University Press.

Bloch, Herbert (1946). 'Monte Cassino, Byzantium, and the West in the Earlier Middle Ages.' *Dumbarton Oaks Papers* 3: 146–224.

Boeck, Elena N. (2015). *Imagining the Byzantine Past: The Perception of History in the Illustrated Manuscripts of Skylitzes and Manasses*. Cambridge: Cambridge University Press.

Brandileone, Francesco (1886). 'Il diritto greco-romano nell'Italia meridionale sotto la dominazione normanna.' *Archivio Giuridico* 36: 63–101, 238–291.

Breccia, Gastone (1991). 'Archivum basilianum. Pietro Menniti e il destino degli archivi monastici italo-greci.' *Quellen und Forschungen aus italienischen Archiven und Bibliotheken* 17: 14–105.

Breccia, Gastone (1997). 'Dalla "Regina delle città". I manoscritti della donazione di Alessio Comneno a Bartolomeo da Simeri.' *Bollettino della Badia greca di Grottaferrata* 51: 209–224.

Breccia, Gastone (1998). 'Alle origini del Patir. Ancora sul viaggio di Bartolomeo da Simeri a Costantinopoli.' *Rivista di studi bizantini e neoellenici* 35: 37–43.

Breccia, Gastone (2002). 'Bullarium Cryptense. I documenti pontifici per il monastero di Grottaferrata.' In *La storia e la memoria. In onore di Arnold Esch*, edited by Roberto Delle Donne and Andrea Zorzi, 3–31. Reti medievali 1. Florence: Firenze University Press.

Bresc, Henri, and Isabelle Heullant-Donat (2007). 'Pour une réévaluation de la "Révolution du papier" dans l'Occident médieval.' *Scriptorium* 61: 354–383.

Brieskorn, Norbert (2010). '"Licet graecos..." Wie der Liber Extra die Beziehungen zur griechisch-orthodoxen Kirche regelt.' In *Proceedings of the Thirteenth International Congress of Medieval Canon Law, Esztergom, 3–8 August 2008*, edited by Peter Erdö and Sz. Anzelm Suromi, 609–620. Monumenta iuris canonici, Series C, Subsidia 14. Vatican City: Biblioteca Apostolica Vaticana.

Brittain Bouchard, Constance (1987). *Sword, Miter, and Cloister: Nobility and the Church in Burgundy, 980–1198*. Ithaca, NY: Cornell University Press.

Broia, Daniele, and Chiara Faraggiana di Sarzana (1999). 'Per una rilettura del palinsesto Vat. gr. 2061A: saggio di ripristino digitale e di edizione diplomatica del Nomocanone alla luce del sistema RE.CO.RD©.' *Bollettino della Badia greca di Grottaferrata* 53: 67–78.

Brooks, Thom (2006). 'Let a Thousand Nomoi Bloom? Four Problems with Robert Cover's Nomos and Narrative.' *Issues in Legal Scholarship* 6.1.

Brown, Peter (1982). *Society and the Holy in Late Antiquity*. Berkeley: University of California Press.

Brown, Thomas S. (1992). 'The Political Use of the Past in Norman Sicily.' In *The Perception of the Past in Twelfth-Century Europe*, edited by Paul Magdalino, 191–210. London: Hambledon.

Brubaker, Leslie, and John F. Haldon (2011). *Byzantium In the Iconoclast Era (c. 680–850): A History*. Cambridge: Cambridge University Press.

Brundage, James A. (1973). 'The Decretalists and the Greek Church of South Italy.' In *La Chiesa greca in Italia dall'VIII al XVI secolo. Atti del convegno storico interecclesiale (Bari, 30 Apr.—4 Magg. 1969)*, 3.1075–1081. Italia sacra 22. Padua: Antenore.

Brundage, James A. (1987). *Law, Sex, and Christian Society in Medieval Europe*. Chicago: University of Chicago Press.

Brunella, Bruno (2004). 'Il Triconco di San Lorenzo a Mesagne.' In *Puglia preromanica*, edited by Gioia Bertelli and Marina F. Castelfranchi, 248–250. Milan: Jaca.

Bryen, Ari Z. (2014). 'Law in Many Pieces.' *Classical Philology* 109.4: 346–365.

Buchthal, H. (1955). 'A School of Miniature Painting in Norman Sicily.' In *Late Classical and Mediaeval Studies in Honor of A.M. Friend Jr*, 312–339. Princeton: Princeton University Press.

Burgmann, Ludwig (2009). 'Die Nomoi stratiotikos, georgikos und nautikos.' *Zbornik radova Vizantološkog Instituta* 46: 53–64.

Canart, Paul (1969). 'Le problème du style d'écriture dit 'en as de pique' dans les manuscrits Italo-Grecs.' In *Atti del 4. Congresso storico calabrese*, 53–70. Naples: Fiorentino.

Canart, Paul (1978). 'Le livre grec en Italie méridionale sous les règnes normands et souabe: aspects matériels et sociaux.' *Scrittura e civiltà* 2: 103–162.

Canart, Paul (1979). *Les vaticani graeci 1487–1962. Notes et documents pour l'histoire d'un fonds de manuscrits de la Bibliothèque Vaticane*. Studi e testi 284. Vatican City: Biblioteca Apostolica Vaticana.

Canart, Paul (1981). 'Les écritures livresques chypriotes du milieu du XIe siècle au milieu du XIIIe et le style palestino-chypriote "epsilon".' *Scrittura e civiltà* 5: 17–76.

Canart, Paul (1982). 'Aspetti materiali e sociali della produzione libraria italo-greca tra Normanni e Svevi.' In *Libri e lettori nel mondo bizantino. Guida storica e critica*, edited by Guglielmo Cavallo, 103–153. Universale Laterza 612. Rome-Bari: Laterza.

Canart, Paul (1983). 'Gli scriptoria calabresi dalla conquista normanna alla fine del secolo XIV.' In *Calabria bizantina. Tradizione di pietà e tradizione scrittoria nella Calabria greca medievale*, 143–160. Mezzogiorno e democrazia 11. Reggio Calabria: Casa del Libro.

Canart, Paul, and Julien Leroy (1977). 'Les manuscrits en style de Reggio. Étude paléographique et codicologique.' In *La Paléographie grecque et byzantine. Paris, 21–25 octobre 1974*, edited by Jean Glénisson, Jacques Bompaire, and Jean Irigoin, 241–261. Colloques internationaux du Centre national de la recherche scientifique 559. Paris: Centre nationale de la recherche scientifique.

Canart, Paul, and Lidia Perria (1991). 'Les écritures livresques des XIe et XIIe siècles.' In *Paleografia e codicologia greca. Atti del II Colloquio internazionale (Berlino-Wolfenbüttel, 17–21 ottobre 1983)*, edited by Dieter Harlfinger and Giancarlo Prato, 1.67–116. Biblioteca di scrittura e civiltà 3. Alessandria: Edizione dell'Orso.

Canart, Paul, Simona di Zio, Lucina Polistena, and Daniela Scialanga (1993). 'Un enquête sur le papier de type "arabe occidental" ou "espagnol non filigrané".' In *Ancient and Medieval Book Materials and Techniques*, edited by Marilena Maniaci and Paola F. Munafò, 1.323–394. Studi e testi 357. Vatican City: Biblioteca Apostolica Vaticana.

Cantarella, Glauco Maria (2014). 'I Normanni e la chiesa di Roma. Aspetti e momenti.' In *Chiese locali e chiese regionali nell'alto medioevo. Spoleto, 4–9 aprile 2013*, 377–406. Settimane di studio del Centro italiano di studi sull'alto Medioevo 61. Spoleto: Centro Italiano di Studi sull'Alto Medioevo.

Capialbi, Vito (1940). 'Sopra alcune biblioteche di Calabria.' *Archivio storico per la Calabria e la Lucania* 10: 250–266.

Capialbi, Vito (1941). *Le memorie delle tipografie calabresi*. Edited by Carlo F. Crispo. 2nd ed. Collezione di studi meridionali 23. Tivoli: Arte Grafiche Aldo Ciccha.

Capizzi, Carmelo (1999). 'Il Concilio di Bari (1098): riflessi e silenzi nella tradizione bizantina e nella storiografia orientale.' In *Il Concilio di Bari del 1098. Atti del Convegno Storico Internazionale e celebrazioni del IX Centenario del Concilio*, edited by Salvatore Palese and Giancarlo Locatelli, 69–90. Per la storia della chiesa di Bari 17. Bari: Edipuglia.

Castiglione, Ruggiero di (2011). *La massoneria nelle Due Sicilie e i fratelli meridionali del '700. Saggio di prosopografia latomica. 5. Sicilia*. Rome: Gangemi.

Cataldi Palau, Annaclara (1992). 'Manoscritti greci originari dell'Italia meridionale nel fondo "Additional" della "British Library" a Londra.' *Bollettino della Badia greca di Grottaferrata* 46: 199–261.

Cataldi Palau, (2006). 'The Burdett-Coutts Collection of Greek Manuscripts: Manuscripts from Epirus.' *Codices manuscripti* 54–55: 31–64.

Cavallo, Guglielmo (1985a). 'La circolazione di testi giuridici in lingua greca nel Mezzogiorno medievale.' In *Scuole, diritto e società nel Mezzogiorno medievale d'Italia*, edited by Manlio Bellomo, 2.87–136. Studi e ricerche dei Quaderni catanesi 8. Catania: Tringale.

Cavallo, Guglielmo (1985b). 'The Purple Codex of Rossano: Book, Object, Symbol.' In *Codex Purpureus Rossanensis*, edited by Guglielmo Cavallo and William C. Loerke, translated by Salvatore Lilla, 27–32. Rome: Salerno Editrice.

Ceccarelli Morolli, Danilo (2002). 'Alcune riflessioni intorno ad una importante collezione canonica delle origini: Gli 85 Canoni degli Apostoli.' *Studi sull'oriente cristiano* 6.1: 151–175.

Charanis, Peter (1946). 'On the Question of the Hellenization of Sicily and Southern Italy During the Middle Ages.' *American Historical Review* 52.1: 74–86.

Charanis, Peter (1949). 'Byzantium, the West, and the Origin of the First Crusade.' *Dumbarton Oaks Papers* 19: 17–36.

Charanis, Peter (1961a). 'The Armenians in the Byzantine Empire.' *Byzantinoslavica* 22: 196–240.

Charanis, Peter (1961b). 'The Transfer of Population as a Policy in the Byzantine Empire.' *Comparative Studies in Society and History* 3.2: 140–154.

Cheynet, Jean-Claude (2007). 'Le schisme de 1054: un non-événement?' In *Faire l'événement au Moyen Âge*, edited by Claude Carozzi and Huguette Taviani-Carozzi, 299–312. Le temps de l'histoire. Aix-en-Provence: Publications de l'Université de Provence.

Chiriatti, Mattia Cosimo (2017). 'Lo Scriptorium di San Nicola di Casole (Otranto, Lecce) e il suo typikon (Codex Taurinensis Graecus 216): Un'analisi storico-letteraria.' *Hortus Artium Medievalium* 23.1: 428–438.

Chitwood, Zachary (2017). *Byzantine Legal Culture and the Roman Legal Tradition, 867–1056*. Cambridge: Cambridge University Press.

Christophilopoulos, Anastasios (1949). '*Ἡ κανονικὴ σύνοψις καὶ ὁ Συμεὼν ὁ Μεταφραστής*.' *Ἐπετερίς ἑταιρείας βυζαντινῶν σπουδῶν* 19: 155–157.

Ciggaar, Krijna Nelly (1996). *Western Travellers to Constantinople: The West and Byzantium, 962–1204*. Medieval Mediterranean 10. Leiden: Brill.

Coureas, Nicholas (2014). 'The Latin and Greek Churches in former Byzantine Lands under Latin Rule.' In *A Companion to Latin Greece*, edited by Nickiphoros I. Tsougarakis and Peter Lock, 145–184. Brill's Companions to European History 6. Leiden: Brill.

Cover, Robert M. (1983). 'The Supreme Court, 1982 Term – Foreword: Nomos and Narrative.' *Harvard Law Review* 97.4: 4–68.

Cozma, Ioa (2017). 'A Historical and Canonical Analysis of the Answers of Patriarch Nicholas III Grammatikos to the Athonite Monks.' *Orientalia Christiana Periodica* 83.2: 253–276.

Croce, Giuseppe M. (1990). *La Badia greca di Grottaferrata e la rivista 'Rome e l'Oriente.' Cattolicesimo e ortodossia fra unionismo ed ecumenismo (1799–1923)*. Storia e attualità 12. Vatican City: Libreria Editrice Vaticana.

Dagron, Gilbert (2003). *Emperor and Priest: The Imperial Office in Byzantium*. Translated by Jean Birrell. Past and Present. Cambridge: Cambridge University Press.

D'Aiuto, Francesco, and Paolo Vian (2011). *Guida ai fondi manoscritti, numismatici, a stampa della Biblioteca Vaticana. I. Dipartimento Manoscritti*. Studi e testi 466. Vatican City: Biblioteca Apostolica Vaticana.

Danella, Patrizia (1989). 'Le Glossae nomicae del Vat. gr. 2075, del Vat. gr. 845, del Cas. T 550 e del Vind. Phil. gr. 124.' *Bollettino della Badia greca di Grottaferrata* 43: 111–130.

Darrouzès, Jean (1963). 'Le mémoire de Constantin Stilbès contre les Latins.' *Revue des études byzantines* 21: 50–100.

Darrouzès, Jean (1965). 'Les documents byzantins du XIIe siècle sur la primauté romaine.' *Revue des études byzantines* 23: 42–88.

Darrouzès, Jean (1967). 'Bulletin critique.' *Revue des études byzantines* 25: 239–293.

Darrouzès, Jean (1970a). 'Listes synodales et notitiae.' *Revue des études byzantines* 28: 57–96.

Darrouzès, Jean ed. (1970b). 'Un faux acte attribué au patriarch Nicholas (III).' *Revue des études byzantines* 28: 221–237.

Davis, John A. (2006). *Naples and Napoleon: Southern Italy and the European Revolutions, 1780–1860*. Oxford: Oxford University Press.

De Groote, Marc (1995). 'Die handschriftliche Überlieferung des Oecumenius-Kommentars zur Apokalypse.' *Sacris Erudiri* 35: 5–29.

De Vos, Ilse (2011). 'East or West, Home Is Best. Where to Situate the Cradle of the *De Oeconomia Dei*?' In *Encyclopedic Trends in Byzantium? Proceedings of the International*

Conference Held in Leuven, 6–8 May 2009, edited by Peter Van Deun and Caroline Macé, 245–255. Orientalia Lovaniensia analecta 212. Leuven: Uitgeverij Peeters.

Delle Donne, Saulo (2014). 'Il codice Greco Corpus Christi College 486 di Cambridge: contenuto, organizzazione testuale e legami con l'Italia meridionale.' *Revue d'histoire des textes* 9: 375–393.

Delle Donne, Saulo (2015). 'Un nuovo testimone e una nuova redazione dell'Epistola a Paolo vescovo di Gallipoli: il cod. greco Corpus Christi College nr. 486.' In *Circolazione di testi e scambi culturali in Terra d'Otranto tra Tardoantico e Medioevo*, edited by Alessandro Capone. Studi e testi 489. Vatican City: Biblioteca Apostolica Vaticana.

Delouis, Olivier (2009). 'L'higoumène comme père sprirituel dans la tradition stoudite.' *Irénikon* 82: 5–32.

Demacopoulos, George E. (2019). *Colonizing Christianity: Greek and Latin Religious Identity in the Era of the Fourth Crusade*. Orthodox Christianity and Contemporary Thought. New York: Fordham University Press.

Devreesse, Robert (1955). *Les manuscrits grecs de l'Italie méridionale (histoire, classement, paléographie)*. Studi e testi 183. Vatican City: Biblioteca Apostolica Vaticana.

Devreesse, Robert (1965). *Le fonds grec de la Bibliothèque Vaticane des origines à Paul V*. Studi e testi 244. Vatican City: Biblioteca Apostolica Vaticana.

Dölger, Franz, and Peter Wirth (1995). *Regesten der Kaiserurkunden des oströmischen Reiches von 565–1453. 2. Teil: Regesten von 1025–1204*. Corpus der griechischen Urkunden des Mittelalters und der Neueren Zeit. Reihe A, Regesten 2. Munich: Beck.

Donahue, Charles (2008). *Law, Marriage, and Society in the Later Middle Ages: Arguments about Marriage in Five Courts*. Cambridge: Cambridge University Press.

Dronke, Peter (1998). 'La poesia.' In *Federico II e la Sicilia*, edited by Pierre Toubert and Agostino P. Bagliani, 218–241. Isola. Palermo: Sellerio.

Easterling, Pat (2001). 'Byzantium and the Revival of Learning.' In *Greek Scripts: An Illustrated Introduction*, 51–63. London: Society for the Promotion of Hellenic Studies.

Ekonomou, Andrew J. (2007). *Byzantine Rome and the Greek Popes: Eastern Influences on Rome and the Papacy from Gregory the Great to Zacharias, A.D. 590–752*. Lanham, MD: Lexington.

Enzensberger, Horst (1973). 'Der Ordo Sancti Basilii, eine monastische Gliederung der römischen Kirche (12.–16. Jahrhundert).' In *La Chiesa greca in Italia dall'VIII al XVI secolo. Atti del convegno storico interecclesiale (Bari, 30 Apr.—4 Magg. 1969)*, 3.1139–1151. Italia sacra 22. Padua: Antenore.

Enzensberger, Horst (2000). 'Der Archimandrit zwischen Papst und Erzbischof: Der Fall Messina.' *Bollettino della Badia greca di Grottaferrata* 53: 209–225.

Enzensberger, Horst (2002). 'Chanceries, Charters and Administration in Norman Italy.' In *The Society of Norman Italy*, 117–150. Medieval Mediterranean 38. Leiden: Brill.

Falkenhausen, Vera von (1968). 'Taranto in epoca bizantina.' *Studi medievali* 9: 133–166.

Enzensberger, Horst (1978). *La dominazione bizantina nell'Italia meridionale dal IX all'XI* secolo. Translated by Franco di Clemente and Livia Fasola. Bari: Ecumenica Editrice.

Enzensberger, Horst (1998). 'I diplomi dei re normanni in lingua greca.' In *Documenti medievali greci e latini. Studi comparativi (Atti del seminario di Erice, 23–29 ottobre 1995)*, edited by Giuseppe de Gregorio and Otto Kresten, 253–308. Incontri di studio 1. Spoleto: Centro Italiano di Studi sull'Alto Medioevo.

Enzensberger, Horst (1999). 'S. Bartolomeo di Trigona: storia di un monastero greco nella Calabria normanno-sveva.' *Rivista di studi bizantini e neoellenici* 36: 93–116.

Enzensberger, Horst (2009). 'I funzionari greci nel regno normanno.' In *Byzantino-Sicula V: Giorgio di Antiochia—L'arte della politica in Sicilia nel XII secolo tra Bisanzio e l'Islam*, edited by Mario Re and Cristina Rognoni, 165–202. Quaderni 17. Palermo: Istituto Siciliano di Studi Bizantini e Neoellenici 'Bruno Lavagnini'.

Enzensberger, Horst (2013). 'The Graeco-Byzantine Heritage in the Norman Kingdom of Sicily.' In *Norman Tradition and Transcultural Heritage: Exchange of Cultures in the 'Norman' Peripheries of Medieval Europe*, edited by Stefan Burkhardt and Thomas Foerster, 57–77. Aldershot: Ashgate.

Enzensberger, Horst (2014). 'Il monachesimo greco nel Lazio medievale.' In *L'Officina dello sguardo. Scritti in onore di Maria Andaloro. 1. I luoghi dell'arte*, edited by Giulia Bordi, Maria L. Fobelli, Maria R. Menna, and Paola Pogliani, 305–314. Rome: Gangemi.

Enzensberger, Horst (2015). 'Roma greca. Greci e civiltà greca a Roma nel medioevo.' In *Roma e il suo territorio nel medioevo. Le fonti scritte fra tradizione e innovazione. Atti del Convegno internazionale di studio dell'Associazione italiana dei Paleografi e Diplomatisti (Roma, 25–29 ottobre 2012)*, edited by Cristina Carbonetti, Santo Lucà, and Maddalena Signorini, 39–72. Studi e ricerche 6. Spoleto: Centro Italiano di Studi sull'Alto Medioevo.

Enzensberger, Horst (2016). 'Die Capitanata in byzantinischer Zeit.' *Quellen und Forschungen aus italienischen Archiven und Bibliotheken* 96: 35–65.

Enzensberger, Horst (2017). 'Onouphrios, Archimandrit von S. Salvatore de Lingua Phari, und die Erzbischöfe von Messina.' In *Prosopon Rhomaikon. Ergänzende Studien zur Prosopographie der mittelbyzantinischen Zeit*, edited by Alexander Beihammer, Bettina Krönung, and Claudia Ludwig, 241–263. Millennium-Studien zu Kultur und Geschichte des ersten Jahrtausends n. Chr. 68. Berlin: De Gruyter.

Fedele, Pietro (1905). 'Il leopardo e l'agnello di Casa Frangipane.' *Archivio della Società romana di storia patria* 28: 207–220.

Follieri, Enrica (1988). 'Il crisobollo di Ruggero II per la badia di Grottaferrata (aprile 1131).' *Bollettino della Badia greca di Grottaferrata* 42: 49–81.

Fonkič, Boris L. (1977). *Grečesko-russkie kul'turnye svjazi v XV–XVII vv.: Greč. Rukopisi v Rossii*. Moscow: Nauka.

Foti, Maria B. (1985). 'Antonius de Messana ed alcuni manoscritti del SS. Salvatore di Messina.' *Archivio Storico Messinese* 36: 1–14.

Foti, Maria B. (1993). 'Copisti greci di Calabria.' In *Mestieri, lavoro e professioni nella Calabria medievale. Tecniche, organizzazioni, linguaggi. Atti dell'VII Congresso storico calabrese, Palmi (RC), 19–22 novembre 1987*, 267–282. Soveria Mannelli: Rubbettino.

Foti, Maria B. (1995). 'Note su due nomocanoni.' In *Hestiasis. Studi di tarda antichità offerti a Salvatore Calderone 5*, 331–352. Studi tardoantichi 5. Messina: Sicania.

Freeman, James (2016). 'Paper in Byzantium.' *Greek Manuscripts*. Available at <https://www.bl.uk/greek-manuscripts/articles/paper-in-byzantium>. Accessed 5 June 2019.

Gardthausen, Victor (1905). 'Zur byzantinischen Kryptographie.' *Byzantinische Zeitschrift* 14: 616–619.

Garitte, Gérard (1946). 'Deux manuscrits italo-grecs (Vat. gr. 1238 et Barber. gr. 475).' In *Miscellanea Giovanni Mercati. III. Letteratura e storia bizantina*, 16–40. Studi e testi 123. Vatican City: Biblioteca Apostolica Vaticana.

Gaul, Niels (2014). 'Rising Elites and Institutionalization – Ēthos/Mores – "Debts" and Drafts: Three Concluding Steps towards Comparing Networks of Learning in Byzantium and the "Latin" West, *c.* 1000–1200.' In *Networks of Learning: Perspectives on Scholars in Byzantine East and Latin West, c. 1000–1200*, edited by Sita Steckel, Niels Gaul, and Michael Grünbart, 235–280. Byzantinistische Studien und Texte 6. Berlin: LIT Verlag.

Geanakoplos, Deno J. (1966). *Byzantine East and Latin West: Two Worlds of Christendom in the Middle Ages and Renaissance*. Studies in Ecclesiastical and Cultural History. Oxford: Blackwell.

Giannelli, Ciro (1944). 'Un documento sconosciuto della polemica tra greci e latini intorno alla formula battesimale.' *Orientalia Christiana Periodica* 10: 150–167.

Giannelli, Ciro (1953). 'Reliquie dell'attività letteraria di uno scrittore italo-greco del sec. XI med. (Nicola Arcivescovo di Reggio Calabria?).' *Studi bizantini e neoellenici* 7: 93–119.

Girgensohn, Dieter (1973). 'Dall'episcopato greco all'episcopato latino nell'Italia meridionale.' In *La Chiesa greca in Italia dall'VIII al XVI secolo. Atti del convegno storico interecclesiale (Bari, 30 Apr.—4 Magg. 1969)*, 1.25–43. Italia sacra 20. Padua: Antenore.

Griffiths, John (1986). 'What Is Legal Pluralism?' *Journal of Legal Pluralism* 1: 1–55.

Guest, Montague J. (1911). *Lady Charlotte Schreiber's Journals: Confidences of a Collector of Ceramics and Antiques Throughout Britain, France, Holland, Belgium, Spain, Portugal, Turkey, Austria & Germany, From the Year 1869 to 1885*. London: Lane.

Guillou, André (1970). 'La classe dei monaci-proprietari nell'Italia bizantina (sec. X–XI).' *Bullettino dell'Istituto Storico Italiano per il Medio Evo* 82: 159–172.

Guillou, André (1974b). 'Production and Profits in the Byzantine Province of Italy (Tenth to Eleventh Centuries).' *Dumbarton Oaks Papers* 28: 91–109.

Hamilton, Bernard (1965). 'The Monastery of S. Alessio and the Religious and Intellectual Renaissance of Tenth-Century Rome.' *Studies in Medieval and Renaissance History* 2: 265–310.

Harris, Jonathan (2003). *Byzantium and the Crusades*. Crusader Worlds. London: Hambledon.

Hart, H.L.A. (1961). *The Concept of Law*. 1st ed. Oxford: Oxford University Press.

Haskins, Charles Homer (1927). *The Renaissance of the Twelfth Century*. Cambridge, MA: Harvard University Press.

Hawkes-Teeples, Steven (2014). 'The Prothesis of the Byzantine Divine Liturgy: What Has Been Done and What Remains.' In *Rites and Rituals of the Christian East: Proceedings of the Fourth International Congress of the Society of Oriental Liturgy, Lebanon, 10–15 July 2012*, edited by Bert Groen, Daniel Galadza, Nina Glibetić, and Gabriel I. Radle, 317–327. Eastern Christian Studies 22. Leuven: Peeters.

Herde, Peter (1967). 'Die Legation des Kardinalbischofs Gerhard von Sabina während des Krieges der sizilischen Vesper und die Synode von Melfi (28. März 1284).' *Rivista di Storia della Chiesa in Italia* 21: 1–53.

Herde, Peter (2002). 'The Papacy and the Greek Church in Southern Italy between the Eleventh and the Thirteenth Century.' In *The Society of Norman Italy*, edited by Graham A. Loud and Alex Metcalfe, 213–251. Medieval Mediterranean 38. Leiden: Brill.

Herklotz, Ingo (2007). 'The Academia Basiliana. Greek Philology, Ecclesiastical History and the Union of the Churches in Barberini Rome.' In *I Barberini e la cultura Europea del seicento. Atti del convego internazionale Palazzo Barberini alle Quattro Fontane, 7–11 dicembre 2004*, edited by Lorenza Mochi Onori, 147–154. Rome: De Luca.

Herklotz, Ingo (2008). *Die Academia Basiliana. Griechische Philologie, Kirchengeschichte und Unionsbemühungen im Rom der Barberini*. Römische Quartalschrift für christliche Altertumskunde und Kirchengeschichte. Supplementheft 60. Rome: Herder.

Heygate, Catherine (2013). 'Marriage Strategies among the Normans of Southern Italy in the Eleventh Century.' In *Norman Expansion: Connections, Continuities and Contrasts*, edited by Keith J. Stringer and Andrew Jotischky, 165–187. Farnham: Ashgate.

Hoeck, Johannes M., and Raimund J. Loenertz (1965). *Nikolaos-Nektarios von Otranto, Abt von Casole. Beiträge zur Geschichte der ost-westlichen Beziehungen unter Innozenz III. und Friedrich II*. Studia patristica et Byzantina 11. Ettal: Buch-Kunstverlag.

Hoffmann, Philippe (1984). 'La décoration du Parisinus graecus 2572, schédographie otrantaise de la fin du XIIIe siècle (a.1295–1296).' *Mélanges de l'École française de Rome, Moyen Âge* 96.2: 617–645.

Hoffmann, Philippe (1989). 'Aspetti della cultura bizantina in Aradeo dal XIII al XVII secolo.' In *Paesi e figure del vecchio Salento. 3*, edited by Aldo De Bernart, 65–88. Documentari 11. Galatina: Congedo.

Høgel, Christian (2002). *Symeon Metaphrastes: Rewriting and Canonization*. Copenhagen: Museum Tusculanum Press.

Holtzmann, Walther (1928). 'Die Unionsverhandlungen zwischen Kaiser Alexios I. und Papst Urban II. im Jahre 1089.' *Byzantinische Zeitschrift* 28: 38–67.

Houben, Hubert (1996). *Mezzogiorno normanno-svevo: monasteri e castelli, ebrei e musulmani*. Nuovo Medioevo 52. Naples: Liguori.

Houben, Hubert (2002). *Roger II of Sicily: A Ruler between East and West*. Translated by Graham A. Loud and Diane Milburn. Cambridge Medieval Textbooks. Cambridge: Cambridge University Press.

Houben, Hubert (2013). 'Between Occidental and Oriental Cultures: Norman Sicily as a "Third Space"?' In *Norman Tradition and Transcultural Heritage: Exchange of Cultures in the 'Norman' Peripheries of Medieval Europe*, edited by Stefan Burkhardt and Thomas Foerster, 19–33. Aldershot: Ashgate.

Humphreys, Michael T.G. (2015). *Law, Power and Imperial Ideology in the Iconoclast Era, c.680–850*. Oxford Studies in Byzantium. Oxford: Oxford University Press.

Hunger, Herbert (1954). 'Die Perlschrift, eine Stilrichtung der griechischen Buchschrift des 11. Jahrhunderts.' In *Studien zur griechischen Paläographie*, 22–32. Biblos-Schriften 5. Vienna: Hollinek.

Hunger, Herbert (1972). 'Die Sogennante Fettaugen-Mode in griechischen Handschriften des 13. und 14. Jahrhunderts.' *Byzantinische Forschungen* 4: 105–113.

Hussey, Joan M. (1986). *The Orthodox Church in the Byzantine Empire*. Oxford History of the Christian Church. Oxford: Oxford University Press.

Hutter, Irmgard (1996). 'Decorative Systems in Byzantine Manuscripts, and the Scribe as Artist: Evidence from Manuscripts in Oxford.' *Word and Image* 12.1: 4–22.

Hutter, Irmgard (2006). 'La décoration et la mise en page des manuscrits grecs de l'Italie méridionale. Quelques observations.' In *Histoire et culture dans l'Italie byzantine. Acquis et nouvelles recherches*, edited by André Jacob, Jean-Marie Martin, and Ghislain Noyé, 69–93. Collection de l'École française de Rome 363. Rome: École française de Rome.

Irigoin, Jean (1953). 'Les débuts de l'emploi du papier à Byzance.' *Byzantinische Zeitschrift* 46: 314–319.

Irigoin, Jean (1963). 'Les origines de la fabrication du papier en Italie.' *Papiergeschichte* 13: 62–67.

Irigoin, Jean (1966). 'Structure et évolution des écritures livresques de l'époque byzantine.' In *Polychronion. Festschrift Franz Dölger zum 75. Geburtstag*, edited by Peter Wirth, 253–265. Forschungen zur griechischen Diplomatik und Geschichte 1. Heidelberg: C. Winter Universitätsverlag.

Irigoin, Jean (1977). 'Papiers orientaux et papiers occidentaux.' In *La Paléographie grecque et byzantine. Paris, 21–25 octobre 1974*, edited by Jean Glénisson, Jacques Bompaire, and Jean Irigoin, 45–54. Colloques internationaux du Centre national de la recherche scientifique 559. Paris: Centre nationale de la recherche scientifique.

Izbicki, Thomas M. (1981a). 'Notes on the Manuscript Library of Cardinal Johannes de Turrecremata.' *Scriptorium* 35.2: 306–311.

Izbicki, Thomas M. (1981b). *Protector of the Faith: Cardinal Johannes de Turrecremata and the Defense of the Institutional Church.* Washington, DC: Catholic University of America Press.

Jacob, André (1977). 'Les écritures de Terre d'Otrante.' In *La Paléographie grecque et byzantine. Paris, 21–25 octobre 1974*, edited by Jean Glénisson, Jacques Bompaire, and Jean Irigoin, 269–281. Colloques internationaux du Centre national de la recherche scientifique 559. Paris: Centre nationale de la recherche scientifique.

Jacob, André (1980). 'Culture grecque et manuscrits en Terre d'Otrante.' In *Atti del III. congresso internazionale di studi salentini e del I. congresso storico di Terra d'Otranto (Lecce, 22–25 ottobre 1976)*, edited by Pier F. Palumbo, 51–77. Congressi (Centro di Studi Salentini) 4. Lecce: Centro Studi Salentini.

Jacob, André (1985a). 'Nicolas d'Oria—Un copiste de Pouille au Saint-Sauveur de Messine.' *Quellen und Forschungen aus italienischen Archiven und Bibliotheken* 65: 133–158.

Jacob, André (1985b). 'Une bibliothèque mediévale de Terre d'Otrante.' *Rivista di studi bizantini e neoellenici* 22–23: 285–315.

Jacob, André (1986). 'La formazione del clero Greco nel Salento medievale.' *Ricerche e Studi in Terra d'Otranto* 2: 223–236.

Jacob, André (1987). 'La lettre patriarcale du typikon de Casole et l'évêque Paul de Gallipoli.' *Rivista di studi bizantini e neoellenici* 24: 143–163.

Jacob, André (1993). 'Les annales du monastère de San Vito del Pizzo, près de Tarente, d'après les notes marginales du Parisinus gr. 1624.' *Rivista di studi bizantini e neoellenici* 30: 123–153.

Jacob, André (1995). 'Une date précise pour l'Euchologe de Carbone: 1194–1195.' *Archivio storico per la Calabria e la Lucania* 63: 97–114.

Jacob, André (2001). 'Tra Basilicata e Salento. Precisazioni necessarie sui menei del monastero di Carbone.' *Archivio storico per la Calabria e la Lucania* 68: 21–52.

Jacob, André (2008). 'Autour de Nicolas-Nectaire de Casole.' In *Vaticana et medievalia. Études en l'honneur de Louis Duval-Arnould*, edited by Jean-Marie Martin, Bernadette Martin-Hisard, and Agostino P. Bagliani, 231–251. Millenio medievale 71. Florence: SISMEL-Edizioni del Galluzzo.

Jansen, Nils (2010). *The Making of Authority: Non-Legislative Codifications in Historical and Comparative Perspective.* Oxford: Oxford University Press.

Jansen, Nils (2012). 'Legal Pluralism in Europe: National Laws, European Legislation, and Non-Legislative Codifications.' *Legal Pluralism.* Available at <http://ssrn.com/abstract=1,840,356>.

Janz, Timothy (2014). 'Lo sviluppo dei Vaticani greci tra fondo antico e accessioni seicentesche.' In *La Vaticana nel seicento (1590–1700): una biblioteca di biblioteche*, edited by Claudia Montuschi, 503–542. Storia della Biblioteca Apostolica Vaticana 3. Vatican City: Biblioteca Apostolica Vaticana.

Johns, Jeremy (1995). 'The Greek Church and the Conversion of Muslims in Norman Sicily?' *Byzantinische Forschungen* 21: 133–157.

Johns, Jeremy (2002). *Arabic Administration in Norman Sicily: The Royal Dīwān.* Cambridge Studies in Islamic Civilization. Cambridge: Cambridge University Press.

Jotischky, Andrew (2003). 'Ethnographic Attitudes in the Crusader States: The Franks and the Indigenous Orthodox People.' In *East and West in the Crusader States: Context, Contacts, Confrontations. III*, edited by Krijna Nelly Ciggaar, Herman G.B. Teule, and A.A. Brediusstichting, 1–19. Orientalia Lovaniensia analecta 125. Leuven: Uitgeverij Peeters.

Kalavrezou, Ioli, and Courtney Tomaselli (2017). 'The Study of Byzantine Illustrated Manuscripts Since Kurt Weitzmann: Art Historical Methods and Approaches.' In *A Companion to Byzantine Illustrated Manuscripts*, edited by Vasiliki Tsamakda, 23–34. Brill's Companions to the Byzantine World 2. Leiden: Brill.

Kaldellis, Anthony (2007). *Hellenism in Byzantium: The Transformations of Greek Identity and the Reception of the Classical Tradition.* Greek Culture in the Roman World. Cambridge: Cambridge University Press.

Kaldellis, Anthony (2017). 'The Social Scope of Roman Identity in Byzantium: An Evidence-Based Approach.' *Byzantina Symmeikta* 27: 173–210.

Kamp, Norbert (1973). *Kirche und Monarchie im staufischen Königreich Sizilien.* Münstersche Mittelalter-Schriften 10. München: Fink.

Kamp, Norbert (1977). 'Vescovi e diocesi nell'Italia meridionale nel passaggio dalla dominazione bizantina allo Stato normanno.' In *Forme di potere e struttura sociale in Italia nel Medioevo*, edited by Gabriella Rossetti, 379–397. Istituzioni e società nella storia d'Italia 1. Bologna: Il mulino.

Kamp, Norbert (1982). 'Die sizilischen Verwaltungsreformen Kaiser Friedrichs II. als Problem der Sozialgeschichte.' *Quellen und Forschungen aus italienischen Archiven und Bibliotheken* 62: 119–142.

Kamp, Norbert (1985). 'Monarchia ed episcopato nel Regno svevo di Sicilia.' In *Potere, società e popolo nell'età sveva (1210–1266). Atti delle seste giornate normanno-sveve, Bari-Castel del Monte-Melfi, 17–20 ottobre 1983*, 123–149. Atti (Università di Bari. Centro di studi normanno-svevi) 6. Bari: Dedalo.

Kamp, Norbert (1995). 'I vescovi siciliani nel periodo normanno: origine sociale e formazione spirituale.' In *Chiesa e società in Sicilia. L'età normanna. Atti del I Convegno internazionale organizzato dall'arcidiocesi di Catania, 25–27 novembre 1992*, edited by Gaetano Zito, 63–89. Storia. Turin: Società Editrice Internazionale.

Kaplan, Michel (1995). 'Le "schisme" de 1054. Quelques éléments de chronologie.' *Byzantinoslavica* 56: 147–157.

Kazhdan, Alexander P. (1989). 'Do We Need a New History of Byzantine Law?' *Jahrbuch der Österreichischen Byzantinistik* 39: 1–28.

Kedar, Benjamin Z. (1999). 'On the Origins of the Earliest Laws of Frankish Jerusalem: The Canons of the Council of Nablus, 1120.' *Speculum* 74.2: 310–335.

Kehr, Paul F. (1903). 'Papsturkunden in Rom. Die römische Bibliotheken.' *Nachrichten von der Gesellschaft der Wissenschaften zu Göttingen. Philologisch-Historische Klasse* 5.1: 1–161.

Kolbaba, Tia M. (2000). *The Byzantine Lists: Errors of the Latins.* Illinois Medieval Studies. Urbana: University of Illinois Press.

Kolbaba, Tia M. (2005). 'On the Closing of the Churches and the Rebaptism of Latins: Greek Perfidy or Latin Slander?' *Byzantine and Modern Greek Studies* 29.1: 39–51.

Kolbaba, Tia M. (2013). 'Byzantines, Armenians, and Latins: Unleavened Bread and Heresy in the Tenth Century.' In *Orthodox Constructions of the West*, edited by George E. Demacopoulos and Aristotle Papanikolaou, 45–57. Orthodox Christianity and Contemporary Thought. New York: Fordham University Press.

Kölzer, Theo (1985). 'Zur Geschichte des Klosters S. Nicola di Casole.' *Quellen und Forschungen aus italienischen Archiven und Bibliotheken* 65: 418–426.

Kölzer, Theo (1996). 'Die Verwaltungsreformen Friedrichs II.' In *Friedrich II. Tagung des Deutschen Historischen Instituts in Rom im Gedenkjahr 1994*, edited by Arnold Esch and Norbert Kamp, 299–315. Bibliothek des Deutschen Historischen Instituts in Rom 85. Tübingen: Niemeyer.

Kotzabassi, Sofia (2017). 'Codicology and Palaeography.' In *A Companion to Byzantine Illustrated Manuscripts*, edited by Vasiliki Tsamakda, 35–52. Brill's Companions to the Byzantine World 2. Leiden: Brill.

Kreutz, Barbara (1991). *Before the Normans. Southern Italy in the Ninth and Tenth Centuries*. Middle Ages. Philadelphia: University of Pennsylvania Press.

Kurysheva, Marina A. (2008). 'Some Paleographic Observations on Two Greek Nomocanons from Southern Italy in the State Historical Museum (Moscow).' In *Puer Apuliae: Mélanges offerts à Jean-Marie Martin*, edited by Errico Cuozzo, Vincent Déroche, and Annick Peters-Custot, 373–381. Monographies (Centre de recherche d'histoire et civilisation de Byzance) 30. Paris: ACHCByz.

Kyriacou, Chrysovalantis (2018). *Orthodox Cyprus under the Latins, 1191–1571: Society, Spirituality, and Identities*. Byzantium. Lanham, MD: Lexington.

Labowsky, Lotte (1979). *Bessarion's Library and the Biblioteca Marciana: Six Early Inventories*. Sussidi eruditi 31. Rome: Edizioni di storia e letteratura.

Leonardi, Claudio (1964). 'Per la storia dell'edizione romana dei concili ecumenici (1608–1612). Da Antonio Agustín a Francesco Aduarte.' In *Mélanges Eugène Tisserant. VI. Bibliothèque Vaticane. Première partie*. Studi e testi 236. Vatican City: Biblioteca Apostolica Vaticana.

Leroy, Julien (1977). 'La description codicologique des manuscrits grecs de parchemin.' In *La Paléographie grecque et byzantine. Paris, 21–25 octobre 1974*, edited by Jean Glénisson, Jacques Bompaire, and Jean Irigoin, 27–44. Colloques internationaux du Centre national de la recherche scientifique 559. Paris: Centre nationale de la recherche scientifique.

Leroy, Julien (1978). 'Les manuscrits grecs d'Italie.' In *Codicologica 2. Éléments pour une codicologie comparée*, edited by Albert Gruys and Johan Peter Gumbert, 52–71. Litterae textuales 6. Leiden: Brill.

Leroy, Julien (1983). 'Caratteristiche codicologiche dei codici greci di Calabria.' In *Calabria bizantina. Tradizione di pietà e tradizione scrittoria nella Calabria greca medievale*, 103–132. Mezzogiorno e democrazia 11. Reggio Calabria: Casa del Libro.

Lilla, Salvatore (2004). *I manoscritti vaticani greci. Lineamenti di una storia del fondo*. Studi e testi 415. Vatican City: Biblioteca Apostolica Vaticana.

Lo Parco, Francesco (1910). 'Scolario-Saba bibliofilo italiota, vissuta tra l'XI e il XII secolo e la Biblioteca del Monastero basiliano del SS. Salvatore di Bordonaro presso Messina.' *Società Reale di Napoli. Atti della Reale Accademia di Archeologia, Lettere e Belle Arti* 1.2: 207–286.

Locchi, Maria Chiara (2014). 'Brief Reflections on Legal Pluralism as a Key Paradigm of Contemporary Law in Highly Differentiated Western Societies.' *Revista Brasileira de Direito* 10.2: 74–84.

Loenertz, Raimund J. (1948). 'L'épître de Theorien le Philosophe aux prêtres d'Oreiné.' In *Memorial Louis Petit. Mélanges d'histoire et d'archéologie byzantines*, 317–335. Archives de l'Orient latin 1. Bucharest: Institut français d'études byzantines.

Loenertz, Raimund J. (1970). *Byzantina et Franco-Graeca I*. Storia e letteratura 118. Rome: Edizioni di storia e letteratura.

Lokin, J.H.A. (1994). 'The Significance of Law and Legislation in the Law Books of the Ninth to Eleventh Centuries.' In *Law and Society in Byzantium: Ninth–Twelfth Centuries*, edited by Angeliki E. Laiou and Dieter Simon, 71–91. Washington, DC: Dumbarton Oaks.

Loud, Graham A. (1982). 'Royal Control of the Church in the Twelfth-Century Kingdom of Sicily.' *Studies in Church History* 18: 147–159.

Loud, Graham A. (2007). *The Latin Church in Norman Italy*. Cambridge: Cambridge University Press.

Loud, Graham A. (2016). 'Communities, Cultures and Conflict in Southern Italy, from the Byzantines to the Angevins.' *Al-Masāq* 28.2: 132–152.

Lucà, Santo (1985). 'Rossano, il Patir e lo stile rossanese.' *Rivista di studi bizantini e neoellenici* 22–23: 93–170.

Lucà, Santo (1986). 'Antonio di Messina (alias Antonio Carissimo).' *Bollettino della Badia greca di Grottaferrata* 40: 151–164.

Lucà, Santo (1991a). 'Scrittura e produzione libraria a Rossano tra la fine del sec. XI e l'inizio del sec. XII.' In *Paleografia e codicologia greca. Atti del II Colloquio internazionale (Berlino-Wolfenbüttel, 17–21 ottobre 1983)*, edited by Dieter Harlfinger and Giancarlo Prato, 1.117–130. Biblioteca di scrittura e civiltà 3. Alessandria: Edizione dell'Orso.

Lucà, Santo (1991b). 'Scritture e libri della scuola niliana.' In *Scritture, libri e testi nelle aree provinciali di Bisanzio. Atti del Seminario di Erice (18–25 settembre 1988)*, edited by Guglielmo Cavallo, Giuseppe de Gregorio, and Marilena Maniaci, 1.319–387. Biblioteca del Centro per il collegamento degli studi medievali e umanistici nell'Università di Perugia 5. Spoleto: Centro Italiano di Studi sull'Alto Medioevo.

Lucà, Santo (1993). 'I Normanni e la "rinascita" del sec. XII.' *Archivio storico per la Calabria e la Lucania* 60: 1–91.

Lucà, Santo (2001). 'Teodoro sacerdote, copista del Reg. gr. Pii II 35. Appunti su scribi e committenti di manoscritti greci.' *Bollettino della Badia greca di Grottaferrata* 55: 127–165.

Lucà, Santo (2002). 'Un codice greco del 1124 a Siracusa.' *Rivista di studi bizantini e neoellenici* 38: 69–94.

Lucà, Santo (2004a). 'Graeco-Latina di Bartolomeo Iuniore, Egumeno di Grottaferrata († 1055 ca.)?' *Νέα Ῥώμη* 1: 143–184.

Lucà, Santo (2004b). 'L'apporto dell'Italia meridionale alla costituzione del fondo greco dell'Ambrosiana.' In *Nuove ricerche sui manoscritti greci dell'Ambrosiana. Atti del convegno, Milano, 5–6 giugno 2003*, edited by Carlo M. Mazzucchi and Cesare Pasini, 191–232. Bibliotheca erudita 24. Milan: Vita e Pensiero.

Lucà, Santo (2010). 'Frustuli di manoscritti greci a Troina in Sicilia.' *Erytheia* 31: 75–132.

Lucà, Santo (2011). 'Doroteo di Gaza e Niceta Stetato. A proposito del Neap. Gr. 7.' In *Bisanzio e le periferie dell'impero. Atti del Convegno Internazionale nell'ambito delle Celebrazioni del Millenario della fondazione dell'Abbazia di San Nilo a Grottaferrata (Catania, 26–28 novembre 2007)*, edited by Renata G. Messina, 145–180. Catania: Bonanno.

Lucà, Santo (2012). 'Scritture e libri in terra d'Otranto fra XI e XII secolo.' In *Bizantini, Longobardi e Arabi in Puglia nell'alto medioevo. Atti del XX Congresso internazionale di studio sull'alto medioevo. Savelletri di Fasano (BR), 3–6 novembre 2011*, 487–548. Spoleto: Centro Italiano di Studi sull'Alto Medioevo.

Macrides, Ruth J. (1990). 'Nomos and Kanon on Paper and in Court.' In *Church and People in Byzantium*, edited by Rosemary Morris, 61–86. Birmingham: Centre for Byzantine, Ottoman and Modern Greek Studies.

Madden, Thomas F. (2018). 'Oaths Broken, Yet Fulfilled: Venice, Innocent III, and the Patriarchate of Constantinople.' In *The Fourth Lateran Council and the Crusade Movement*, 59–74. Outremer: Studies in the Crusades and the Latin East 7. Turnhout: Brepols.

Madigan, Susan P. (1987). 'Three Manuscripts by the "Chrysostom Initialer": The Scribe as Artist in Tenth-Century Constantinople.' *Scriptorium* 41–42: 205–220.

Magdalino, Paul (1993). *The Empire of Manuel I Komnenos, 1143–1180*. Cambridge: Cambridge University Press.

Magdalino, Paul (1996). 'The Reform Edict of 1107.' In *Alexios I Komnenos*, edited by Margaret Mullett and Dion Smythe, 199–218. Belfast Byzantine Texts and Translations 4. Belfast: Belfast Byzantine Enterprises.

Magdalino, Paul (2003). 'Prosopography and Byzantine Identity.' In *Fifty Years of Prosopography: The Later Roman Empire, Byzantium and Beyond*, edited by Averil Cameron, 41–56. Proceedings of the British Academy 118. Oxford: Oxford University Press.

Malatesta Zilembo, Giuseppina Maria (1965). 'Gli ammanuensi di Grottaferrata.' *Bollettino della Badia greca di Grottaferrata* 19: 39–56.

Manzano, Teresa M. (1994). *Konstantinos Laskaris. Humanist, Philologe, Lehrer, Kopist*. Meletemata 4. Hamburg: Universität Hamburg.

Martin, Jean-Marie (1985). 'Une origine calabraise pour la Grecía salentine?' *Rivista di studi bizantini e neoellenici* 22–23: 51–63.

Martin, Jean-Marie (1993). *La Pouille du VI au XII siècle*. Collection de l'École française de Rome de Rome 179. Rome: École française de Rome.

Martin, Jean-Marie (1998). 'Léon, archevêque de Calabre, l'Église de Reggio et la lettre de Photius (Grumel-Darrouzès no 562).' In *ΕΥΨΥΧΙΑ. Mélanges offerts à Hélène Ahrweiler*, edited by Michel Balard, 481–491. Paris: Publications de la Sorbonne.

Martin, Jean-Marie (2016). 'Évêchés et monastères "grecs" en Italie méridionale au Moyen Âge (VIIe–XIIIe siècle).' *Revue Mabillon* 27: 5–22.

Mayr-Harting, Henry (2001). 'Liudprand of Cremona's Account of His Legation to Constantinople (968) and Ottonian Imperial Strategy.' *English Historical Review* 116.467: 539–556.

Mazzotta, Oronzo (1989). *Monaci e libri greci nel Salento medievale*. Scriptorium 2. Novoli: Bibliotheca Minima.

McNulty, Patricia M., and Bernard Hamilton (1963). 'Orientale lumen et magistra latinitas: Greek Influences on Western Monasticism (900–1100).' In *Le Millénaire du Mont Athos, 963–1963. Études et mélanges*, 1.181–216. Chevetogne: Éditions de Chevetogne.

Melissaris, Emmanuel (2009). *Ubiquitous Law: Legal Theory and the Space for Legal Pluralism*. Law, Justice, and Power. Farnham: Ashgate.

Ménager, Léon-Robert (1958). 'Notes sur les codifications byzantines et l'Occident.' In *Varia. Études de droit romain. III*, edited by Jules Roussier, Henri-Jacques Legier, and Léon-Robert Ménager, 239–303. Publications de l'Institut de droit romain de L'Université de Paris 16. Paris: Sirey.

Ménager, Léon-Robert (1959). 'Points de vue sur l'étude des institutions byzantines en Italite méridionale.' *Archivio storico pugliese* 12: 47–52.

Menevisoglou, Pavlos (1990). *Ιστορική εισαγωγή εις τους κανόνας της ορθοδόξου εκκλησίας*. Stockholm: Iera Mitropolis Souidias kai Pasis Skandinavias.

Mercati, Giovanni (1935). *Per la storia dei manoscritti greci di Genova, di varie badie basiliane d'Italia e di Patmo*. Studi e testi 68. Vatican City: Biblioteca Apostolica Vaticana.

Mercati, Giovanni (1937). 'Non Russia, ma Rossano nell'Antirretico di Teodoro Cursiota.' In *Opere Minori*, 4.169–171. Studi e testi 79. Vatican City: Biblioteca Apostolica Vaticana.

Mercati, Giovanni (1938). *Codici latini Pico Grimani Pio e di altra biblioteca ignota del secolo XVI esistenti nell'Otoboniana e i codici greci Pio di Modena con una digressione per la storia dei codici di S. Pietro in Vaticano*. Studi e testi 75. Vatican City: Biblioteca Apostolica Vaticana.

Merry, Sally E. (1988). 'Legal Pluralism.' *Law & Society Review* 22.5: 869–896.

Metastasio, Giorgio, and Fulvio Calabrese (2008). 'San Giovanni il Nuovo di Stilo e la biblioteca dei padri basiliani.' *Annali di studi religiosi* 9: 67–110.

Metcalfe, Alex (2003). *Muslims and Christians in Norman Sicily: Arabic-Speakers and the End of Islam*. Culture and Civilisation in the Middle East. London: Routledge.

Metcalfe, Alex (2009). *The Muslims of Medieval Italy*. New Edinburgh Islamic Surveys. Edinburgh: Edinburgh University Press.

Metcalfe, Alex (2019). 'Before the Normans: Identity and Societal Formation in Muslim Sicily.' In *Sicily: Heritage of the World*, edited by Dirk Booms and Peter J. Higgs, 102–119. British Museum Research Publications 222. London: British Museum, 2019.

Michel, Anton (1925). *Humbert und Kerullarios. Quellen und Studien zum Schisma des 11. Jahrhunderts. I. Teil*. Quellen und Forschungen aus dem Gebiet der Geschichte 21. Paderborn: Schöningh.

Michel, Anton (1930). *Humbert und Kerullarios. Quellen und Studien zum Schisma des 11. Jahrhunderts. II. Teil*. Quellen und Forschungen aus dem Gebiet der Geschichte 23. Paderborn: Schöningh.

Milaš, Nikodim (1905). *Das Kirchenrecht der morgenländischen Kirche. Nach den allgemeinen Kirchenrechtsquellen und nach den in den autokephalen Kirchen geltenden Spezial-Gesetzen*. Mostar: Pacher & Kisić.

Mioni, Elpidio (1968). 'Bessarione bibliofilo e filologo.' *Rivista di studi bizantini e neoellenici* 5: 61–83.

Mioni, Elpidio (1973). *Introduzione alla paleografia greca*. Studi bizantini e neogreci 5. Padua: Liviana.

Montfaucon, Bernard de (1702). *Diarium Italicum. Sive monumentorum veterum, bibliothecarum, museorum, etc. Notitiae singulares in itinerario Italico collectae*. Paris: Anisson.

Mioni, Elpidio (1708). *Palaeographia graeca, sive, De ortu et progressu literarum Graecarum*. Paris: Guerin.

Mor, Carlo G. (1951). 'La lotta fra la Chiesa greca e la Chiesa latina in Puglia nel sec. X.' *Archivio storico pugliese* 4: 58–64.

Morini, Enrico (2017). 'Monastic Interactions between Calabria and Mount Athos in the Middle Ages.' In *Greek Monasticism in Southern Italy: The Life of Neilos in Context*, edited by Barbara Crostini and Ines Angeli Murzaku, 191–206. New York: Routledge.

Morris, Colin (1991). *The Papal Monarchy: The Western Church from 1050 to 1250*. Oxford History of the Christian Church. Oxford: Oxford University Press.

Morris, Rosemary (1995). *Monks and Laymen in Byzantium, 843–1118*. Cambridge: Cambridge University Press.

Morton, James (2013). 'Latin Patrons, Greek Fathers: St Bartholomew of Simeri and Byzantine Monastic Reform in Norman Italy, 11th–12th Centuries.' *Allegorica* 29: 20–35.

Morton, James (2017). 'A Byzantine Canon Law Scholar in Norman Sicily: Revisiting Neilos Doxapatres' Order of the Patriarchal Thrones.' *Speculum* 92.3: 724–754.

Moulet, Benjamin (2011). *Évêques, pouvoir et société à Byzance (VIIIe–XIe siècle). Territoires, communautés et individus dans la société provinciale byzantine*. Byzantina Sorbonensia 25. Paris: Éditions de la Sorbonne.

Muci, Maria M. (2005). 'Il terzo Syntagma di Nicola Nettario e la difesa delle tradizioni liturgiche bizantine dei greci della Terra d'Otranto.' *Itinerari di ricerca storica* 19: 25–47.

Muratore, Davide (2009). *La biblioteca del cardinale Niccolò Ridolfi*. Hellenica 32. Alessandria: Edizioni dell'Orso.

Negro, Piero del (1971). 'Giacomo Nani. Appunti biografici.' *Bollettino de Museo Civico di Padova* 60: 115–147.

Neirynck, Stefaan (2010). 'The *De oeconomia Dei* by Nilus Doxapatres: Some Introductory Remarks to the Work and its Edition.' *Byzantion* 80: 265–306.

Neocleous, Savvas (2019). *Heretics, Schismatics, or Catholics? Latin Attitudes to the Greeks in the Long Twelfth Century*. Studies and Texts 216. Toronto: Pontifical Institute of Medieval Studies.

Nichols, Stephen (1990). 'The New Philology. Introduction: Philology in a Manuscript Culture.' *Speculum* 65.1: 1–10.

Ohme, Heinz (1995). 'Die sogenannten "antirömischen Kanones" des Concilium Quinisextum (692). Vereinheitlichung als Gefahr für die Einheit der Kirche.' In *The Council in Trullo Revisited*, edited by George Nedungatt and Michael Featherstone, 307–321. Kanonika 6. Rome: Pontificio Istituto Orientale.

Ohme, Heinz (2012). 'Sources of the Greek Canon Law to the Quinisext Council (691/2): Councils and Church Fathers.' In *The History of Byzantine and Eastern Canon Law to 1500*, edited by Wilfred Hartmann and Kenneth Pennington, 24–114. History of Medieval Canon Law. Washington, DC: Catholic University of America Press.

Oldfield, Paul (2005). 'Rural Settlement and Economic Development in Southern Italy: Troia and its contado, c.1020–c.1230.' *Journal of Medieval History* 31: 327–145.

Omont, Henri (1890). 'Le Typicon de Saint-Nicolas di Casole près d'Otrante. Notice du ms. C. III, 17 de Turin.' *Revue des études grecques* 3: 389–390.

Omont, Henri (1916). *Minoïde Mynas et ses missions en orient (1840–1855)*. Paris: Imprimerie Nationale.

Pacaut, Marcel (1981). 'Papauté, Royauté et épiscopat dans le Royaume de Sicile.' In *Potere, società e popolo nell'età dei due Guglielmi. Atti delle quarte giornate normanno-sveve, Bari, Gioia del Colle, 8–10 ottobre 1979*, 31–62. Atti (Università di Bari. Centro di studi normanno-svevi) 4. Bari: Dedalo.

Page, Gill (2008). *Being Byzantine: Greek Identity Before the Ottomans*. Cambridge: Cambridge University Press.

Papadoyannakis, Yannis (2006). 'Instruction by Question and Answer: The Case of Late Antique and Byzantine *Erotapokriseis*.' In *Greek Literature in Late Antiquity: Dynamism, Didacticism, Classicism*, edited by Scott F. Johnson, 91–105. Aldershot: Ashgate.

Paredi, Angelo (1981). *Storia dell'Ambrosiana*. Fontes ambrosiani 68. Vicenza: Pozza.

Parenti, Stefano (2005). *Il monastero di Grottaferrata nel Medioevo (1004–1462). Segni e percorsi di una identità*. Orientalia Christiana Analecta 274. Rome: Pontificio Istituto Orientale.

Pargoire, Jules (1907). 'Archimandrite.' In *Dictionnaire d'archéologie chrétienne et de liturgie*, edited by Fernand Cabrol, 1.2.2739–2761. Paris: Letouzey.

Parlangèli, Ada, and Oronzo Parlangèli (1951). 'Il monastero di San Nicola di Casole. Centro di cultura bizantina in Terra d'Otranto.' *Bollettino della Badia greca di Grottaferrata* 5: 30–45.

Parrish, Helen (2010). *Clerical Celibacy in the West: c.1100–1700*. Catholic Christendom, 1300–1700. London: Routledge.

Pasini, Cesare (2005). 'Il progetto biblioteconomico di Federico.' *Studia Borromaica* 19: 247–279.

Patlagean, Evelyne (1966). 'Une représentation byzantine de la parenté et ses origines occidentales.' *Homme. Revue française d'anthropologie* 6.4: 59–81.

Pennington, Kenneth (2006). 'The Birth of the Ius commune: King Roger II's Legislation.' *Rivista internazionale del diritto comune* 17: 1–40.

Peri, Vittorio (1967). 'La Congregazione dei Greci (1566–1596) e i suoi primi documenti.' *Studia Gratiana* 13: 129–256.

Perisanidi, Maroula (2017). 'Anglo-Norman Canonical Views on Clerical Marriage and the Eastern Church.' *Bulletin of Medieval Canon Law* 34: 113–142.

Perisanidi, Maroula (2019). *Clerical Continence in Twelfth-Century England and Byzantium: Property, Family, and Purity*. London: Routledge.

Perria, Lidia (1999). 'Libri e scritture del monachesimo italo-greco nei secoli XIII e XV.' In *Libro, scrittura, documento della civiltà monastica e conventuale nel Basso Medioevo (secoli XIII–XV). Atti del Covegno di studio, Fermo (17–19 settembre 1997)*, edited by Giuseppe Avarucci, Rosa Marisa Verducci, and Giammario Borri, 99–132. Studi e ricerche 1. Spoleto: Centro Italiano di Studi sull'Alto Medioevo.

Pertusi, Agostino (1964). 'Monasteri e monaci italiani all'Athos nell'alto medioevo.' In *Le Millénaire du Mont Athos, 963–1963. Études et mélanges*, 2.217–251. Chevetogne: Éditions de Chevetogne.

Peters-Custot, Annick (2006). 'Les communautés grecques de Basilicate à l'époque byzantine.' In *Histoire et culture dans l'Italie byzantine. Acquis et nouvelles recherches*, edited by André Jacob, Jean-Marie Martin, and Ghislain Noyé, 559–587. Collection de l'École française de Rome 363. Rome: École française de Rome.

Peters-Custot, Annick (2009a). *Les grecs de l'Italie méridionale post-byzantine (IXe–XIVe siècle). Une acculturation en douceur*. Collection de l'École française de Rome 420. Rome: École française de Rome.

Peters-Custot, Annick (2009b). 'L'identité d'une communauté minoritaire au Moyen Âge. La population grecque de la principauté lombarde de Salerne (IXe–XIIe siècles).' *Mélanges de l'École française de Rome* 121.1: 83–97.

Peters-Custot, Annick (2011). 'La mention du sénatus-consulte velléien dans les actes grecs d'Italie du Sud et de Sicile.' In *L'héritage byzantin en Italie (VIIIe–XIIe siècle). II. Les cadres juridiques et sociaux et les institutions publiques*, edited by Jean-Marie Martin, Annick Peters-Custot, and Vivien Prigent, 51–72. Collection de l'École française de Rome de Rome 461. Rome: École française de Rome.

Peters-Custot, Annick (2013). 'Convivencia between Christians: The Greek and Latin Communities of Byzantine South Italy (9th–11th Centuries).' In *Negotiating Co-Existence: Communities, Cultures and 'Convivencia' in Byzantine Society*, edited by Barbara Crostini and Sergio La Porta, 203–220. Bochumer altertumswissenschaftliches Colloquium 96. Trier: Wissenschaftlicher Verlag.

Peters-Custot, Annick (2017). 'Bessarion et le monachisme italo-grec: l'Orient en Italie du Sud?' *Cahiers d'études italiennes* 25.

Petit, Louis (1924). 'Jean de Jérusalem.' In *Dictionnaire de théologie catholique. T. 8, Pt. 1. Isaac—Jeûne*, edited by Alfred Vacant, 766–767. Paris: Letouzey.

Petrovič, Miodrag M. (1970). *Ὁ Νομοκάνων εἰς ΙΔ' τίτλους καὶ οἱ βυζαντινοί σχολιασταί. Συμβολὴ εἰς τὴν ἔρευναν τῶν θεμάτων περὶ σχέσεων Ἐκκλησίας καὶ Πολιτείας καὶ τῶν ἐπισκόπων Παλαιᾶς καὶ Νέας Ῥώμης*. Athens: Papoulias.

Petrovič Rimljanin, Venedikt (2005). 'Meminisse iuvabit: Uno sguardo a dieci secoli di storia.' In *San Nilo. Il monastero italo-bizantino di Grottaferrata. 1004–2004. Mille anni di storia, spiritualità e cultura*, edited by Emiliano Fabbricatore, 13–30. Rome: De Luca.

Petta, Marco (1972a). 'Codici del Monastero di S. Elia di Carbone conservati nella biblioteca dell'Abbazia di Grottaferrata.' *Vetera christianorum* 9: 151–171.

Petta, Marco (1972b). 'Codici greci della Puglia trasferiti in biblioteche italiane ed estere.' *Bollettino della Badia greca di Grottaferrata* 26: 83–129.

Philip, Ian G. (1983). *The Bodleian Library in the Seventeenth and Eighteenth Centuries*. Lyell Lectures. Oxford: Oxford University Press.

Polidori, Valerio (2012). 'La lettera patriarcale a Paolo di Gallipoli.' *Bollettino della Badia greca di Grottaferrata* 9: 191–220.

Pott, Thomas (2010). *Byzantine Liturgical Reform: A Study of Liturgical Change in the Byzantine Tradition*. Translated by Paul Meyendorff. Orthodox Liturgy Series 2. Crestwood, NY: St Vladimir's Seminary Press.

Prinzing, Günter (1986). 'Das Bild Justinians I. in der Überlieferung der Byzantiner vom 7.–15. Jhdt.' *Fontes Minores* 7: 1–99.

Quaranta, Francesco (2001). 'In difesa dei matrimoni greci e del mattutino pasquale: un testo pugliese inedito del XIII secolo.' *Studi sull'oriente cristiano* 5.2: 91–117.

Quaranta, Francesco (2009). 'Pagine e scoli attribuibili a Bartolomeo di Grottaferrata.' In *Il monachesimo d'Oriente e d'Occidente nel passaggio dal primo al secondo millennio. Atti del Convegno internazionale, Grottaferrata, 23–25 settembre 2004*, 181–212. Analekta Kriptoferres 6. Grottaferrata: Monastero Esarchico.

Radle, Gabriel I. (2012). 'The Byzantine Marriage Tradition in Calabria: Vatican Reginensis gr. 75 (a. 982/3).' *Bollettino della Badia greca di Grottaferrata* 9: 221–245.

Ramseyer, Valerie (2006). *The Transformation of a Religious Landscape: Medieval Southern Italy, 850–1150*. Conjunctions of Religion & Power in the Medieval Past. Ithaca, NY: Cornell University Press.

Rapp, Claudia (2005). *Holy Bishops in Late Antiquity: The Nature of Christian Leadership in an Age of Transition*. Transformation of the Classical Heritage 37. Berkeley: University of California Press.

Rapp, Claudia (2016). *Brother-Making in Late Antiquity and Byzantium: Monks, Laymen, and Christian Ritual*. Onassis Series in Hellenic Culture. New York: Oxford University Press.

Re, Mario (1997). 'Sul viaggio di Bartolomeo da Simeri a Costantinopoli.' *Rivista di studi bizantini e neoellenici* 34: 71–76.

Re, Mario (2001). 'I manoscritti in stile di Reggio vent'anni dopo.' In *Ο Ιταλιώτης Ελληνισμός από τον Ζ' στον ΙΒ' αιώνα. Μνήμη Νίκου Παναγιωτάκη*, edited by Nicholas Oikonomides, 99–124. International Symposia 8. Athens: Ethniko Idryma Erevnon.

Re, Mario (2004). 'Copisti Salentini in Calabria e in Sicilia.' *Rivista di studi bizantini e neoellenici* 41: 95–112.

Reinsch, Diether R. (1991). 'Bemerkungen zu epirotischen Handschriften.' In *Scritture, libri e testi nelle aree provinciali di Bisanzio. Atti del Seminario di Erice (18–25 settembre 1988)*, edited by Guglielmo Cavallo, Giuseppe de Gregorio, and Marilena Maniaci, 1.79–97. Biblioteca del Centro per il collegamento degli studi medievali e umanistici nell'Università di Perugia 5. Spoleto: Centro Italiano di Studi sull'Alto Medioevo.

Rennie, Kriston R., and Jason Taliadoros (2014). 'Why Study Medieval Canon Law?' *History Compass* 12.2: 133–149.

Rey, André-Louis (2004). 'Les Erotapokriseis dans le monde byzantin. Tradition manuscrite des textes anciens et production de nouveaux textes.' In *Erotapokriseis: Early Christian Question-and-Answer Literature in Context*, 165–180. Contributions to Biblical Exegesis and Theology 37. Leuven: Peeters.

Reynolds, Roger E. (1987). 'South-Italian Liturgica and Canonistica in Catalonia (New York, Hispanic Society of America MS HC 380/819).' *Mediaeval Studies* 49: 480–495.

Reynolds, Roger E. (1990). 'The South-Italian Canon Law Collection in Five Books and its Derivatives: New Evidence on its Origins, Diffusion, and Use.' *Mediaeval Studies* 52: 278–295.

Reynolds, Roger E. (1997). 'Canonistica Beneventana.' In *Proceedings of the Ninth International Congress of Medieval Canon Law, Munich, 13–18 July 1992*, edited by Peter Landau and Jörg Müller, 21–40. Monumenta iuris canonici. Series C, Subsidia 10. Vatican City: Biblioteca Apostolica Vaticana.

Rietbergen, Peter J.A. (2006). *Power and Religion in Baroque Rome: Barberini Cultural Policies*. Brill's Studies in Intellectual History 135. Leiden: Brill.

Rocchi, Antonio (1893). *De coenobio Cryptoferratensi eiusque bibliotheca et codicibus praesertim graecis commentarii*. Tusculum: Typographia Tusculana.

Rocchi, Antonio (1904). *La badia di Grottaferrata*. 2nd ed. Rome: Cuggiani.

Rodriquez, Maria T. (2003). 'Due manoscritti di carta orientale nel fondo del SS. Salvatore di Messina.' In *Tra Oriente e Occidente. Scritture e libri greci fra le regioni orientali di Bisanzio e l'Italia*, edited by Lidia Perria, 135–143. Testi e studi bizantino-neoellenici 14. Rome: Università di Roma La Sapienza.

Rodriquez, Maria T. (2013). 'Riflessioni sui palinsesti giuridici dell'area dello Stretto.' In *Vie per Bisanzio. VIIo Congresso Nazionale dell'Associazione Italiana di Studi Bizantini*, edited by Antonio Rigo, Andrea Babuin, and Michele Trizio, 2.625–645. Due punti 25. Bari: Pagina.

Rodriquez, Maria T. (2017). 'Note sulla storia della biblioteca del S. Salvatore di Messina.' *Medieval Sophia* 19: 121–136.

Rohlfs, Gerhard (1933). *Scavi linguistici nella Magna Grecia*. Translated by Bruno Tomasini. Collezione di studi meridionali. Rome: Collezione meridionale editrice.

Rosis, Luca de (1838). *Cenno storico della città di Rossano e delle sue nobili famiglie*. Naples: Mosca.

Rousseau, Olivier (1973). 'La visite de Nil de Rossano au Mont-Cassin.' In *La Chiesa greca in Italia dall'VIII al XVI secolo. Atti del convegno storico interecclesiale (Bari, 30 Apr.—4 Magg. 1969)*, 3.1111–1137. Italia sacra 22. Padua: Antenore.

Russo, Francesco (1969). 'Tradizione calligrafica Calabro-Greca.' In *Atti del 4. Congresso storico calabrese*, 37–52. Naples: Fiorentino.

Russo, Francesco (1973). 'La partecipazione dei vescovi calabro-greci ai concili (sec. VI–XIV).' In *La Chiesa greca in Italia dall'VIII al XVI secolo. Atti del convegno storico interecclesiale (Bari, 30 Apr.—4 Magg. 1969)*, 2.781–792. Italia sacra 22. Padua: Antenore.

Russo, Francesco (1982). *Storia della Chiesa in Calabria dalle origini al Concilio di Trento*. 2 vols. Quaderni di scienze umane 5. Soveria Mannelli: Rubbettino.

Russo, Teresa B. (1978). 'Origine e vicende della Biblioteca Vallicelliana.' *Studi Romani* 26.1: 121–128.

Safran, Linda (2013). 'Betwixt or Beyond? The Salento in the Fourteenth and Fifteenth Centuries.' In *Renaissance Encounters: Greek East and Latin West*, edited by Marina S. Brownlee and Dimitri H. Gondicas, 115–144. Medieval and Renaissance Authors and Texts 8. Leiden: Brill.

Safran, Linda (2014). *The Medieval Salento: Art and Identity in Southern Italy*. Middle Ages. Philadelphia: University of Pennsylvania Press.

Sambin, Paolo (1954). *Il vescovo cotronese Niccolò da Durazzo e un inventario di suoi codici latini e greci (1276)*. Note e discussioni erudite. Rome: Edizioni di storia e letteratura.

Sansterre, Jean-Marie (1983). *Les moines grecs et orientaux à Rome aux époques byzantine et carolingienne (milieu du VIe s.—fin du IXe s.)*. 2 vols. Mémoires de la Classe des lettres 66. Brussels: Palais des académies.

Sautel, Jacques-Hubert, and Julien Leroy (1995). *Répertoire de réglures dans les manuscrits grecs sur parchemin*. Bibliologia 13. Turnhout: Brepols.

Scaduto, Mario (1947). *Il monachismo basiliano nella Sicilia medievale. Rinascità e decadenza (sec. XI–XIV)*. Storia e letteratura 18. Rome: Edizioni di storia e letteratura.

Schabel, Chris, and Nickiphoros I. Tsougarakis (2016). 'Pope Innocent III, the Fourth Lateran Council, and Frankish Greece and Cyprus.' *Journal of Ecclesiastical History* 67.4: 741–789.

Schiano, Claudio (2017). 'Nicholas-Nektarios of Otranto: A Greek Monk under Roman Obedience.' In *Greek Monasticism in Southern Italy: The Life of Neilos in Context*, edited by Barbara Crostini and Ines Angeli Murzaku, 208–224. New York: Routledge.

Schminck, Andreas (1986). *Studien zu mittelbyzantinischen Rechtsbüchern*. Forschungen zur byzantinischen Rechtsgeschichte 13. Frankfurt am Main: Löwenklau-Gesellschaft.

Schminck, Andreas (1989). '"Frömmigkeit ziere das Werk." Zur Datierung der 60 Bücher Leons VI.' *Subseciva Groningana* 3: 79–114.

Schminck, Andreas (1998). 'Das Prooimion der Bearbeitung des Nomokanons in 14 Titeln durch Michael und Theodoros.' *Fontes Minores* 10: 357–386.

Schminck, Andreas (2001). Review of Dorotei Getov, Vassilis Katsaros and Charalambos Papastathis, *Καταλόγος των ελληνικών νομικών χειρογραφών των αποκειμένων στο Κέντρο Σλαβο-βυζαντινών Σουδών 'Ivan Dujčev' του Πανεπιστημίου 'S.V. Kliment Ohridski' της Σοφίας* (Thessaloniki: Aristoteleio Panepistimio Thessalonikis, 1994). *Byzantinische Zeitschrift* 94.2: 719–722.

Schweinburg, Kurt (1934). 'Die Textgeschichte des Gesprächs mit den Franken von Niketas Stethatos.' *Byzantinische Zeitschrift* 34: 313–347.

Scirocco, Elisabetta, and Gerhard Wolf, eds. (2018). *The Italian South: Transcultural Perspectives*. Convivium 5.1. Brno: Masarykova Universita.

Siciliano, Joseph J.A.S. (1979). 'The Theory of the Pentarchy and Views on Papal Supremacy in the Ecclesiology of Neilos Doxapatrius and His Contemporaries.' *Byzantine Studies* 6: 167–177.

Siecienski, A. Edward (2017). *The Papacy and the Orthodox: Sources and History of a Debate*. Oxford Studies in Historical Theology. Oxford: Oxford University Press.

Simon, Dieter (1986). 'Byzantinische Provinzialjustiz.' *Byzantinische Zeitschrift* 79: 310–343.

Simon, Dieter (1994). 'Legislation as Both a World Order and a Legal Order.' In *Law and Society in Byzantium: Ninth–Twelfth Centuries*, edited by Angeliki E. Laiou and Dieter Simon, 1–25. Washington, DC: Dumbarton Oaks.

Simon, Dieter (2005). 'Wozu?' *Fontes Minores* 11: 1–4.

Sommar, Mary E. (2009). *The Correctores Romani: Gratian's Decretum and the Counter-Reformation Humanists*. Pluralisierung & Autorität 19. Munster: LIT Verlag.

Spiteris, Yannis (1979). *La Critica bizantina del Primato romano nel secolo XII*. Orientalia Christiana Analecta 208. Rome: Pontificium Institutum Orientalium Studiorum.

Stephanides, Vasileios K. (1947). '*Νέα ἑρμηνεία τοῦ ὀνόματος τῆς Πρωτοδευτέρας συνόδου.*' *Ἐκκλησία* 24: 132–134.

Stiernon, Daniel (1964). 'Basile de Reggio, le dernier métropolite grec de Calabre.' *Rivista di Storia della Chiesa in Italia* 18: 189–208.

Stolte, Bernard H. (1997). 'A Note on the un-Photian Revision of the Nomocanon XIV Titulorum.' In *Analecta atheniensia ad ius byzantinum spectantia. I.*, edited by Spyridon N. Troianos, 115–130. Forschungen zur byzantinischen Rechtsgeschichte 10. Athens: Sakkoulas.

Stolte, Bernard H. (2008). 'The Decline and Fall of Legal Manuscripts: Reflexions on Some Legal Palimpsests.' In *Κατευόδιον: In Memoriam Nikos Oikonomides*, edited by Spyridon N. Troianos, 173–189. Forschungen zur byzantinischen Rechtsgeschichte 15. Athens: Sakkoulas.

Stolte, Bernard H. (2010). 'The Organization of Information: Observations on the Manuscripts of the Nomocanon XIV Titulorum.' In *The Legacy of Bernard de Montfaucon: Three Hundred Years of Studies on Greek Handwriting. Proceedings of the Seventh International Colloquium of Greek Palaeography (Madrid-Salamanca, 15–20 September 2008)*, edited by Antonio Bravo García, Inmaculada Pérez Martín, and Juan Signes Codoñer, 521–532. Bibliologia 31. Turnhout: Brepols.

Strittmatter, Anselm (1946). 'Liturgical Latinisms in a Twelfth-Century Greek Euchology (Ottob. gr. 344).' In *Miscellanea Giovanni Mercati. III. Letteratura e storia bizantina*, 41–64. Studi e testi 123. Vatican City: Biblioteca Apostolica Vaticana.

Szabó-Bechstein, Brigitte (1991). 'Libertas ecclesiae vom 12. bis zur Mitte des 13. Jahrhunderts. Verbreitung und Wandel des Begriffs seit seiner Prägung durch Gregor VII.' In *Die Abendländlische Freiheit vom 10. bis zum 14. Jahrhundert. Der Wirkungszusammenhang von Idee und Wirklichkeit im europäischen Vergleich*, edited by Johannes Fried, 147–175. Vorträge und Forschungen 39. Sigmaringen: Thorbecke.

Taft, Robert F. (1996). 'Byzantine Communion Spoons: A Review of the Evidence.' *Dumbarton Oaks Papers* 50: 209–238.

Tamanaha, Brian Z. (1993). 'The Folly of the "Social Scientific" Concept of Legal Pluralism.' *Journal of Law and Society* 20.2: 192–217.

Tamanaha, Brian Z. (2000). 'A Non-Essentialist Version of Legal Pluralism.' *Journal of Law and Society* 27.2: 296–321.

Tamanaha, Brian Z. (2008). 'Understanding Legal Pluralism: Past to Present, Local to Global.' *Sydney Law Review* 30: 375–411.

Tamanaha, Brian Z. (2017). *A Realistic Theory of Law*. Cambridge: Cambridge University Press.

Thibodeaux, Jennifer D. (2015). *The Manly Priest: Clerical Celibacy, Masculinity, and Reform in England and Normandy, 1066–1300*. Philadelphia: University of Pennsylvania Press.

Thomas, John P. (2007). 'Your Sword, Our Shield: The Imperial Monastery in Byzantine Civilization.' In *Church and Society: Orthodox Christian Perspectives, Past Experiences, and Modern Challenges. Studies in Honor of Rev. Dr Demetrios J. Constantelos*, edited by George P. Liacopulos, 27–44. Boston: Somerset Hall.

Thompson, Daniel V. (1956). *The Materials and Techniques of Medieval Painting*. New York: Dover Publications.

Tiftixoglu, Viktor (1969). 'Gruppenbildungen innerhalb des Konstantinopolitanischen Klerus während der Komnenenzeit.' *Byzantinische Zeitschrift* 62: 25–72.

Torre, Cristina (2017). 'Italo-Greek Monastic Typika.' In *Greek Monasticism in Southern Italy: The Life of Neilos in Context*, edited by Barbara Crostini and Ines Angeli Murzaku, 44–76. New York: Routledge.

Troianos, Spyridon N. (2003). 'Kanonistische Antworten und Abhandlungen in der Ostkirche (9.–15. Jh.). Eine Übersicht.' In *Ius Canonicum in Oriente et Occidente: Festschrift für Carl Gerold Fürst zum 70. Geburtstag*, edited by Hartmut Zapp, Andreas Weiß, and Stefan Korta, 403–419. Adnotationes in Ius Canonicum 25. Frankfurt am Main: Peter Lang.

Troianos, Spyridon N. (2011). *Οι πηγές του βυζαντινού δικαίου. Εισαγωγικό βοήθημα*. 3rd ed. Athens: Sakkoulas.

Troianos, Spyridon N. (2012a). 'Byzantine Canon Law from the Twelfth to the Fifteenth Centuries.' In *The History of Byzantine and Eastern Canon Law to 1500*, edited by Wilfred Hartmann and Kenneth Pennington, 170–214. History of Medieval Canon Law. Washington, DC: Catholic University of America Press.

Troianos, Spyridon N. (2012b). 'Byzantine Canon Law to 1100.' In *The History of Byzantine and Eastern Canon Law to 1500*, edited by Wilfred Hartmann and Kenneth Pennington, 115–169. History of Medieval Canon Law. Washington, DC: Catholic University of America Press.

Tsougarakis, Demetrios (1988). *Byzantine Crete: From the 5th Century to the Venetian Conquest*. Istorikes Monographies 4. Athens: Basilopoulos.

Turner, Jack (2016). 'Was Photios an Anti-Latin? Heresy and Liturgical Variation in the Encyclical to the Eastern Patriarchs.' *Journal of Religious History* 40.4: 475–489.

Van der Wal, Nicolaas, and J.H.A. Lokin (1985). *Historiae iuris graeco-romani delineatio. Les sources du droit byzantin de 300 à 1453*. Groningen: Forsten.

Van Tricht, Filip (2011). *The Latin Renovatio of Byzantium: The Empire of Constantinople (1204–1228)*. Medieval Mediterranean 90. Leiden: Brill.

Vitolo, Giovanni (1996). 'Les monastères grecs de l'Italie méridionale.' In *Moines et monastères dans les sociétés de rite grec et latin*, 99–113. Hautes études médiévales et modernes 76. Geneva: Droz.

Wagschal, David (2015). *Law and Legality in the Greek East: The Byzantine Canonical Tradition, 381–883*. Oxford Early Christian Studies. Oxford: Oxford University Press.

Wagschal, David (2019). 'The Byzantine Canonical Scholia: A Case Study in Reading Byzantine Manuscript Marginalia.' *Byzantine and Modern Greek Studies* 43.1: 24–41.

Watt, John A. (1999). 'The Papacy.' In *The New Cambridge Medieval History. Volume 5: c.1198–1300*, 105–163. Cambridge: Cambridge University Press.

Weiss, Roberto (1951). 'The Greek Culture of South Italy in the Later Middle Ages.' *Proceedings of the British Academy* 37: 23–50.

Weitzmann, Kurt (1935). *Die byzantinische Buchmalerei des 9. und 10. Jahrhunderts*. 2 vols. Denkschriften 243–244. Berlin: Mann.

Wellas, Michael B. (1983). *Griechisches aus dem Umkreis Kaiser Friedrichs II*. Münchener Beiträge zur Mediävistik und Renaissance-Forschung 33. Munich: Arbeo.

Wessely, Carl (1905). 'Ein neues System griechischer Geheimschrift.' *Wiener Studien* 26: 185–189.

Westerink, Leendert G., ed. (1992). *Michaelis Pselli Poemata*. Bibliotheca scriptorum Graecorum et Romanorum Teubneriana. Stuttgart: Teubner.

Westra, Haijo J. (2014). 'What's in a Name: Old, New, and Material Philology, Textual Scholarship, and Ideology.' In *Neo-Latin Philology: Old Tradition, New Approaches. Proceedings of a Conference Held at the Radboud University, Nijmegen, 26–27 October 2010*, 13–24. Supplementa humanistica Lovaniensia 35. Leuven: Leuven University Press.

Whalen, Brett (2007). 'Rethinking the Schism of 1054: Authority, Heresy, and the Latin Rite.' *Traditio* 62: 1–24.

White, Lynn T. (1938). *Latin Monasticism in Norman Sicily*. Publications (Medieval Academy of America) 31. Cambridge, MA: Medieval Academy of America.

Wilson, Nigel G. (2017). *From Byzantium to Italy: Greek Studies in the Italian Renaissance*. 2nd ed. Classical Studies and Archaeology. London: Bloomsbury.

Zachariä von Lingenthal, Karl-Eduard (1887). 'Die Synopsis canonum. Ein Beitrag zur Geschichte der Quellen des kanonischen Rechts der griechischen Kirche.' *Sitzungsberichte der Preußischen Akademie der Wissenschaften*: 1147–1163.

Zerbi, Pietro (1983). 'Papato e regno meridionale dal 1189 al 1198.' In *Potere, società e popolo tra età normanna ed età sveva (1189–1198). Atti delle quinte giornate normanno-sveve. Bari-Conversano, 26–28 ottobre 1981*, 49–73. Atti (Università di Bari. Centro di studi normanno-svevi) 5. Bari: Dedalo.

Zerdoun Bat-Yehouda, Monique (1983). *Les encres noires au moyen âge (jusqu'à 1600)*. Documents, études et répertoires. Paris: Centre nationale de la recherche scientifique.

Zorzi, Marino (1987). *La Libreria di San Marco. Libri, lettori, società nella Venezia dei Dogi*. Collana di studi 1. Milan: Mondadori.

Index of Manuscripts

Note: Tables and figures are indicated by an italic '*t*' and '*f*' respectively, following the page number.

For the benefit of digital users, indexed terms that span two pages (e.g., 52–53) may, on occasion, appear on only one of those pages.

General Index

Note: Tables and figures are indicated by an italic '*t*' and '*f*', respectively, following the page number.

For the benefit of digital users, indexed terms that span two pages (e.g., 52–53) may, on occasion, appear on only one of those pages.